Theory and Methods in Political Science

Fourth edition

Edited by
Vivien Lowndes, David Marsh
and
Gerry Stoker

BLOOMSBURY
NEW DELHI • LONDON • OXFORD • NEW YORK • SYDNEY

BLOOMSBURY INDIA
Bloomsbury Publishing India Pvt. Ltd
Second Floor, LSC Building No. 4, DDA Complex,
Pocket C – 6 & 7, Vasant Kunj,
New Delhi 110070

BLOOMSBURY, BLOOMSBURY ACADEMIC INDIA and the Diana logo are trademarks of Bloomsbury Publishing Plc

First edition published 1995
Second edition published 2002
Third edition published 2010
Fourth edition published 2018 by PALGRAVE
First published in India 2022

This edition published with permission from Bloomsbury Publishing Plc,
50 Bedford Square, London, WC1B3DP, UK

ISBN:PB: 978-93-54354-37-3
2 4 6 8 10 9 7 5 3 1

Printed in India
For sale in the Indian subcontinent only

Exclusively Distributed in Indian Subcontinent:
Atlantic Publishers & Distributors Pvt. Ltd.
7/22, Ansari Road, Darya Ganj, New Delhi - 110002, India
Tel.: 91-11-40775252, 23273880
E-mail: orders@atlanticbooks.com
Website: www.atlanticbooks.com

Political Analysis

Series Editors: B. Guy Peters, Jon Pierre and Gerry Stoker

Political science today is a dynamic discipline. Its substance, theory and methods have all changed radically in recent decades. It is much expanded in range and scope and in the variety of new perspectives – and new variants of old ones – that it encompasses. The sheer volume of work being published, and the increasing degree of its specialization, however, make it difficult for political scientists to maintain a clear grasp of the state of debate beyond their own particular subdisciplines.

The *Political Analysis* series is intended to provide a channel for different parts of the discipline to talk to one another and to new generations of students. Our aim is to publish books that provide introductions to, and exemplars of, the best work in various areas of the discipline. Written in an accessible style, they provide a 'launching-pad' for students and others seeking a clear grasp of the key methodological, theoretical and empirical issues, and the main areas of debate, in the complex and fragmented world of political science.

A particular priority is to facilitate intellectual exchange between academic communities in different parts of the world. Although frequently addressing the same intellectual issues, research agendas and literatures in North America, Europe and elsewhere have often tended to develop in relative isolation from one another. This series is designed to provide a framework for dialogue and debate which, rather than advocacy of one regional approach or another, is the key to progress.

The series reflects our view that the core values of political science should be coherent and logically constructed theory, matched by carefully constructed and exhaustive empirical investigation. The key challenge is to ensure quality and integrity in what is produced rather than to constrain diversity in methods and approaches. The series is intended as a showcase for the best of political science in all its variety, and demonstrates how nurturing that variety can further improve the discipline.

Political Analysis

Series Editors: B. Guy Peters, Jon Pierre and Gerry Stoker

Published

David Beetham
The Legitimation of Power (2nd edition)

Peter Burnham, Karin Gilland Lutz, Wyn Grant and Zig Layton-Henry
Research Methods in Politics (2nd edition)

Lina Eriksson
Rational Choice Theory: Potential and Limits

Jean Grugel and Matthew Louis Bishop
Democratization: A Critical Introduction (2nd edition)

Colin Hay
Political Analysis

Colin Hay, Michael Lister and David Marsh (eds)
The State: Theories and Issues

Andrew Hindmoor and Brad Taylor
Rational Choice (2nd edition)

Johanna Kantola and Emanuela Lombardo
Gender and Political Analysis

Vivien Lowndes and Mark Roberts
Why Institutions Matter

Vivien Lowndes, David Marsh and Gerry Stoker (eds)
Theory and Methods in Political Science (4th edition)

Ioannis Papadopoulos
Democracy in Crisis? Politics, Governance and Policy

B. Guy Peters
Strategies for Comparative Research in Political Science

Jon Pierre and B. Guy Peters
Governance, Politics and the State

Heather Savigny and Lee Marsden
Doing Political Science and International Relations

Rudra Sil and Peter J. Katzenstein
Beyond Paradigms: Analytic Eclecticism in the Study of World Politics

Martin J. Smith
Power and the State

Gerry Stoker, B. Guy Peters and Jon Pierre (eds)
The Relevance of Political Science

Cees van der Eijk and Mark Franklin
Elections and Voters

Keith Dowding
The Philosophy and Methods of Political Science

Dimiter Toshkov
Research Design in Political Science

Contents

List of Figures, Tables and Boxes

Figures

Tables

Boxes

Preface to the Fourth Edition

The first discussions about the idea of *Theories and Methods* took place about a quarter of a century ago and the first edition of the book emerged in 1995. So, it is with a combination of surprise and pleasure that we can welcome the fourth edition in 2017. For this edition, the original editors David Marsh and Gerry Stoker have been joined by one of the chapter contributors from the second edition onwards, Vivien Lowndes. The new energy and ideas for the project provided by Vivien have been gratefully received by her fellow editors.

We would like to thank all our authors who have responded to our demands for copy and changes with good grace. In this fourth edition, we have again added some new authors and some new topics to reflect developments in the discipline. All the chapters have been extensively updated and, in our view, improved. The framing and development of the fourth edition was also helped a great deal by Andy Hindmoor and Liam Stanley, who organised a workshop for contributors in Sheffield, UK in 2015. We thank them and the Politics Department of Sheffield University for the funding.

The referee comments we received on the first draft of the book were very helpful and speedily provided. The input from Palgrave editor Lloyd Langman was invaluable. We thank Maximilian Lemprière and Abena Dadze-Arthur of the University of Birmingham, UK, for their assistance in preparing the manuscript. We also thank our families for their forbearance through the production stages of the book. Most of all we acknowledge the help and support of all those teachers and students who use the book. We constantly learn from your comments and feedback. We hope that you will continue to find the book what we intend it to be: an accessible introduction to the way that political scientists carry out their work in today's world.

Vivien Lowndes
David Marsh
Gerry Stoker

Notes on Contributors

The editors

Vivien Lowndes is Professor of Public Policy at the University of Birmingham, UK. She is the author (with Mark Roberts) of *Why Institutions Matter* (Palgrave, 2013). Her research focuses on institutional design and change in subnational governance, focusing on the sources and dynamics of local variation. She also works on gender and institutions, including recent research on police governance.

David Marsh is a Fellow at the Institute for Governance and Policy Analysis, University of Canberra, Australia.

Gerry Stoker is Professor of Governance at the Institute for Governance and Policy Analysis, University of Canberra, Australia, and the University of Southampton, UK.

The contributors

Chris Armstrong is Professor of Political Theory at the University of Southampton, UK. He works in normative political theory, and especially global justice, climate justice, and territorial rights.

Selen A. Ercan is Senior Research Fellow in Political Science at the Institute for Governance and Policy Analysis, University of Canberra, Australia. She works in the area of deliberative democracy focusing particularly on the capacity of this approach to address intractable policy controversies in contemporary democracies. Her recent publications appeared in *International Political Science Review, Policy and Politics, Critical Policy Studies* and *Policy Studies* among others.

Paul Furlong is Emeritus Professor of European Studies at Cardiff University, UK. He has written widely on European politics and on political theory. His next book is entitled *The new politics of Italy: In search of the Second Republic* and will be published by MUP in Spring 2018.

Paul 't Hart is Professor of Public Administration at the Utrecht School of Governance, The Netherlands. He currently leads an ERC Advanced Grant program on Successful Public Governance, supplanting his prior research focus on public leadership, crisis management and political psychology.

Andrew Hindmoor is Professor of Politics at the University of Sheffield, UK. He is engaged in work on British politics and banking and finance as well as public choice theory. *What's Left Now? The History and Future of Social Democracy* was published by Oxford University Press in 2017. His earlier book on the 2008/9 financial crisis, *Masters of the Universe but Slaves of the Market*, was published by Harvard University Press in 2015.

Michael J. Jensen is Senior Research Fellow at the Institute for Governance and Policy Analysis, University of Canberra, Australia. He is a political communication scholar studying political parties, campaigns, and social movements using predominantly digital methods. His research has appeared in the *International Journal of Press/Politics, Information, Communication and Society,* and the *Journal of Information Technology and Politics.*

Peter John is Professor of Public Policy, King's College London, UK. Peter uses field experiments in his research on nudges and political participation. His book, *Field Experiments in Political Science and Public Policy*, was published by Routledge in 2017.

Meryl Kenny is Lecturer in Gender and Politics at the University of Edinburgh, UK. She is Co-Director of the Feminism and Institutionalism International Network (FIIN) and has published widely on aspects of gender and political institutions, political parties and representation, including *Gender and Political Recruitment* (Palgrave, 2013).

Ray Kiely is Professor of Politics at Queen Mary University of London. His publications include *The BRICS, US 'Decline' and Global Transformations* (2015) and *The Neoliberal Paradox* (2018).

Fiona Mackay is Professor of Politics at the University of Edinburgh, UK. Her research interests include gender and politics, political representation, and gender and institutional theory. Her most recent co-edited collection is *Gender Politics and Institutions: Towards a Feminist Institutionalism* (2011/2015).

Helen Margetts is Professor of Society and the Internet and Director of the Oxford Internet Institute at the University of Oxford, UK. Her research focuses on government and politics in a digital world. Her most recent book is *Political Turbulence: How Social Media Shape Collective Action* (Princeton University Press, 2016), with Peter John, Scott Hale and Taha Yasseri.

Frank Mols is Lecturer in Political Science at the University of Queensland, Australia. His political psychology research has been published in leading international journals, such as the *European Journal of Political Research, Political Psychology, West European Politics, Journal of Common Market Studies, Public Administration, Evidence and Policy*, and the *Australian Journal of Public Administration.*

Craig Parsons is Head of Department and Professor of Political Science at the University of Oregon, USA. He is a specialist of the European Union, political economy, and comparative federalism.

B. Guy Peters is Maurice Falk Professor of Governance at the University of Pittsburgh, USA. His research is primarily in comparative public policy and public administration. His recent books include *Governance and Comparative Politics* (with Jon Pierre) and *Pursuing Horizontal Management.*

Jon Pierre is Professor of Political Science at the University of Gothenburg, Sweden and Professor of Public Governance at the University of Melbourne, Australia. He is also Adjunct Professor at the University of Pittsburgh, USA. His research interests are theories and empirical research on governance, public administration and urban politics.

Matt Ryan is Lecturer in Governance and Public Policy at the University of Southampton, UK. His research in comparative politics and public policy focuses in particular on changing relationships between citizens and institutions of governance. His most recent publications appear in *European Journal of Political Research, PS: Political Science and Politics,* and *Political Studies Review.*

David Sanders is Regius Professor of Government at the University of Essex, UK. He is currently working on the character, sources and consequences of authoritarian populism in Europe.

Brad Taylor is Lecturer in Economics and Political Economy at the University of Southern Queensland, Australia. His main research interests are in political rationality, competitive governance, and analytic political philosophy.

Dimiter Toshkov is Associate Professor at the Institute of Public Administration, Leiden University, The Netherlands. He studies comparative public policy, European integration and research methodology. His book *Research Design in Political Science* was published by Palgrave in 2016.

Ariadne Vromen is Professor of Political Sociology at the University of Sydney, Australia. She has long-term research interests in political participation and digital politics, and her latest book *Digital Citizenship and Political Engagement* was published in early 2017.

Mark Wenman is Senior Lecturer in Political Theory at the University of Birmingham, UK. He has published numerous articles on pluralism, poststructuralism, and contemporary democratic theory, and is author of *Agonistic Democracy: constituent power in the era of globalisation* published in 2013 by Cambridge University Press.

Chapter 1

Introduction

VIVIEN LOWNDES, DAVID MARSH AND GERRY STOKER

This book introduces the theories and methods that political scientists use, which we think tells us a great deal about the nature of political science. To us, political science is best defined in terms of what political scientists do. Of course, there are thousands of political scientists around the world and we have tried to capture and clarify the variety of ways they seek to understand, explore and analyse the complex processes of politics in the modern era. We are interested in how they differ in their approach, but also in what they share. Our book identifies nine approaches used by political scientists and then explores some of the specific research methods, which are used in different combinations by scholars from these different approaches.

All disciplines tend to be chaotic, to some extent, in their development (Abbott, 2001) and political science is certainly no exception. However, we would argue that the variety of approaches and debates explored in this book are a reflection of its richness and growing maturity. When trying to understand something as complex, contingent and chaotic as politics, it is not surprising that academics have developed a great variety of approaches. For those studying the discipline for the first time, it may be disconcerting that there is no agreed approach or method of study. Indeed, as we shall see, there is not even agreement about the nature of politics itself. But, we argue that political scientists should celebrate diversity, rather than see it as a problem. The Nobel Prize winner Herbert Simon makes a powerful case for a plurality of approaches, which he sees as underpinning the scientist's commitment to constant questioning and searching for understanding:

> I am a great believer in pluralism in science. Any direction you proceed in has a very high *a priori* probability of being wrong; so it is good if other people are exploring in other directions – perhaps one of them will be on the right track. (Simon, 1992: 21)

Studying politics involves making an active selection among a variety of approaches and methods; this book provides students and researchers with the capacity to make informed choices. However, whatever your choice, we hope to encourage you to keep an open mind and consider whether some other route might yet yield better results.

The study of politics can trace its origins at least as far back as Plato (Almond, 1996); as such, it has a rich heritage and a substantial base on which to grow and develop. More specifically, it has been an academic discipline for just over a century; the American Political Science Association was formed in 1903 and other national associations followed. As Goodin and Klingemann (1996) argue, in the last few decades the discipline has become a genuinely international enterprise. Excellent and challenging political science is produced in many countries and this book reflects the internationalisation of the discipline in two senses. First, we have authors who are based in the UK, elsewhere in Europe, the USA and Australia. Second, many of the illustrations and examples provided by authors offer up experiences from a range of countries, or provide a global perspective. Our authors draw on experiences from around the world and relate domestic political science concerns to those of international relations. This makes sense in an ever more globalised world.

The increasing influence of global forces in our everyday lives makes globalisation a central feature of the modern era. Debates about collective decisions which we observe at the international, national and local levels take place through a dynamic of governance (Chhotray and Stoker, 2009). In the world of governance, outcomes are not determined by cohesive, unified nation states or formal institutional arrangements. Rather, they involve individual and collective actors both inside and beyond the state, who operate via complex and varied networks. In addition, the gap between domestic politics and international relations has narrowed, with domestic politics increasingly influenced by transnational forces. Migration, human rights, issues of global warming, pandemics of ill-health and the challenges of energy provision cannot, for example, be contained or addressed within national boundaries alone.

A new *world politics* (different from 'international relations') is emerging, in which non-state actors play a vital role, alongside nation states (Cerny, 2010). The study of world politics is not a separate enterprise, focused on the study of the diplomatic, military and strategic activities of nation states. Non-state and international institutions, at the very least, provide a check to the battle between nation states. At the same time, the role of cities and sub-national regions has expanded, as they make links across national borders in pursuit of economic investment in a global marketplace, while seeking also to collaborate in tackling complex governance challenges (such as migration and global warming), which do not themselves respect national boundaries. Indeed, some analysts go as far as to suggest that cities may become the 'new sovereign' in international orders in which both nation states and multilateral bodies are challenged (Barber, 2013; Katz and Bradley, 2013).

Moreover, the breadth of the issues to be addressed at the international level has extended into a range of previously domestic concerns, with a focus on financial, employment, health, human rights and poverty reduction issues. At the same time, the nature of politics at the international level has become more politically driven, through bargaining, hegemonic influence and soft power – rather than driven solely by military prowess and economic strength, although the latter remain important. However, the questions to be asked about politics at local, national and global levels are fundamentally the same. How is power exercised to determine outcomes? What are the roles of competing interests and identities? How is coordination and cooperation achieved to achieve shared purposes? How are issues of justice and fairness of outcome to be identified and understood? Consequently, the examples and illustrations of the academic study of politics in this book reflect the growing interlinkage of domestic politics and international relations.

This book focuses upon the ways of thinking or theorising offered by political scientists and the methods they are using to discover more about the subject at the beginning of the twenty-first century. It is inevitable that the book will neither be fully comprehensive in its coverage of political science, nor able to provide sufficient depth in approaching all of the issues that are considered. Rather, our intention is to provide an introduction to the main approaches to political science and a balanced assessment of some of the debates and disagreements that have characterised a discipline with several thousand years of history behind it, and many thousands of practitioners in the modern world.

The book is divided into two broad parts. The chapters in the first part map the broad ways of approaching political science that have had, and are likely to have, a major effect on the development of political science: behaviouralism, rational choice theory, institutionalism, constuctivism, feminism, Marxism, poststructuralism and political psychology (see Table 1.1). Each of the approaches focuses upon a set of issues, understandings and practices that define a particular way of doing political science. We asked each of our authors not simply to advocate their approach, but also to explore criticisms of that approach. In this respect, we hope that each author offers a robust, but self-aware and critical, understanding of his or her way of doing political science. We have also asked authors to provide 'worked examples' of their approach in action within political science. As such, our understanding of theory is neither abstract, nor abstruse. In our experience, students often regard theory as a burden, something that gets in the way of studying real-life politics. We want to show how theory facilitates, rather than obstructs. The approaches discussed in this book show how theory frames new questions and provides important leverage for understanding political puzzles. Theory allows us to see things we wouldn't otherwise see. Each of our approaches could be seen as a different pair of spectacles; when we put them on our focus changes, and different aspects of a phenomenon come into view. Beyond the academy, political science not only influences the world of politics and governance by providing evidence from research, but also has the potential to shape the way in which political actors themselves regard their opportunities and develop their strategies (as reflected, for example, in the influence of rational choice theory on

Table 1.1 *Approaches to political science*

	Scope of Political Studies	*Understanding of the Scientific Claim*	*Attitude to Normative Political Theory*	*Relationship to the Practice of Politics*
Behaviouralism	Concentrates on processes of politics associated with mainstream politics and government	The generation of general laws and at a minimum the development of theoretical statements that can be falsified. Keen to subject claims to empirical test through direct observation	In early phase keen to emphasise difference between the new science and old armchair theorising. Now gives due recognition to the value of political theory	Claims to be value free, neutral and detached
Rational Choice Theory	Concerned with conditions for collective action in mainstream political world	The generation of general laws and in particular laws with predictive power	Gives recognition to the value of political theory but focus is less on what could be and more on what is feasible	Claims to be able to offer value-free expert advice about how to organise politics
Institutionalism	Focus is on the rules, norms and values that govern political exchanges, tends to look at institutional arrangements in mainstream political world	Science is the production of organised knowledge. The best political science is empirically grounded, theoretically informed and reflective	Keen to make connections between empirical analysis and normative theory	Keen to make connections, sees itself as working alongside the practitioners of politics
Constructivism	Politics is driven by the meanings that actors attach to their actions and their context. Politics can be broad in scope, reflecting people's diverse world views about what it involves	Understanding of human activity is inherently different to that of the physical world	Tends towards the view that there is fusion between all types of theorising. Political analysis is essentially contested and has a necessarily normative content	A mixed range of responses but tendency is towards wry commentary on the narrative battles of the political world

Psychological approaches	Views politics through the lens of the personality and cognition of the individuals who engage in its practice, primarily within the mainstream political world	How individuals identify and frame the political challenges they face can be studied in a way that allows for theoretical generalisations to be tested by empirical investigation	Tends to view assumptions made about human nature in much political theory as inadequate. Generally not oriented towards normative theory	Often seeks to offer insights into how politics works and how it could be made to work better
Feminism and gendered approaches	A broad process definition that recognises that the personal can be political	A mixed range of responses to this issue but with strong tendencies towards anti-foundational and critical realist perspectives	Normative theory, like all aspects of political studies, needs to take gender issues seriously	Political engagement is strongly part of the feminist impulse
Marxism	Politics is a struggle between social groups, in particular social classes	Critical realist: the discovery of below-the-surface forces that guide but do not determine historical events	Normative theory is at its most useful when it provides a guide to action: the point is to change the world	Committed to engagement in struggles of suppressed social groups or classes
Poststructuralism	Politics takes place and achieves impact across a range of social institutions and environments and in a variety of ways	There can be no scientific claim as our experience of 'reality' is intrinsically mediated by language or discourse	Some criticise it for ethical relativism. But the approach does sustain a normative critique of power and domination and promotes agonistic theories of democracy	Arguably a major impact through popular culture and a strong capacity to develop a critique of others' truth claims

many right-wing governments, or of institutional approaches like governance on transnational bodies and development agencies).

The final chapter in this first part of the book explores the issue of normative theory, although it is important to recognise that there are normative elements in all approaches. This is one of the most traditional approaches to political science, but it remains relevant today. Political science should be (and is) interested in understanding both 'what is', usually seen as the empirical dimension, and also 'what should be', the normative dimension. Further, we agree with Baubock (2008: 40) that 'empirical research can be guided by normative theory; and normative theory can be improved by empirical research'. The distinctiveness of normative theory is clear, but the dialogue between normative theory and the other approaches is crucial. Empirical theorists can benefit from the specification and clarification of arguments provided by normative theory and, in our view, normative theorists need to look to empirical research, as well as hypothetical arguments, to help support their case. Moreover, the emergence of new empirically driven theoretical insights, for example those associated with the governance school (Chhotray and Stoker, 2009), may open up new issues and challenges for normative theory.

The second half of the book moves to issues of methodology and research design. We begin, in Chapter 11, by introducing debates about the ontological and epistemological positions which shape our answers to the crucial questions of what we study, how we study it and, most significantly, what we can claim on the basis of our research. These ontological and epistemological positions also underpin what in Chapter 12 we term meta-theoretical issues, specifically, the relationships between structure and agency, the material and the ideational and continuity and change, which cut across all the different approaches.

Subsequently, in Chapter 13, we turn to the important question of how we design our research project or programme. Finally, in the last five substantive chapters we examine different research methods. We examine the range of both qualitative and quantitative techniques that are available and how these techniques can be combined in meeting the challenge of research design, before moving on to consider the potential and limitations of the comparative (often cross-national) method for understanding political phenomena. We then turn to two methods which have come to prominence in political science more recently, experimental methods and 'big data'. In an increasingly digital age enormous volumes of data are generated outside the academy and can be used to reveal patterns of human behaviour and interaction that have political significance. The final chapter in the book assesses the utility of political science not in terms of its methods, but by examining whether it has anything relevant to say to policymakers, public servants and, most importantly, citizens.

In the remainder of this introductory chapter we aim to provide an analysis of the term 'political' and some reflections on justifications of the term 'scientific' to describe its academic study. We close by returning to the issue of variety within political science by arguing that diversity should be a cause of celebration rather than concern.

What is politics? What is it that political scientists study?

When people say they 'study politics' they are making an ontological statement because, within that statement, there is an implicit understanding of what the polity is made up of, and its general nature. They are also making a statement that requires some clarification. In any introduction to a subject it is important to address the focus of its analytical attention. So, simply put, we should be able to answer the question: what is the nature of the political that political scientists claim to study? A discipline, you might think, would have a clear sense of its terrain of enquiry. Interestingly, that is not the case in respect of political science. Just as there are differences of approach to the subject, so there are differences about the terrain of study.

As Hay (2002: chapter 2) argues, ontological questions are about what is and what exists. Ontology asks: what's there to know about? Although a great variety of ontological questions can be posed (discussed in Chapters 11 and 12), a key concern for political scientists relates to the nature of the political. There are two broad approaches to defining the political, seeing politics in terms of an arena or a process (Leftwich, 1984; Hay, 2002). An arena definition regards politics as occurring within certain limited 'arenas', initially involving a focus upon Parliament, the executive, the public service, political parties, interest groups and elections, although this was later expanded to include the judiciary, army and police. Here, political scientists, especially behaviouralists but also rational choice theorists and some institutionalists, focus upon the formal operation of politics in the world of government and those who seek to influence it. This approach to the political makes a lot of sense and obviously relates to some everyday understandings. For example, when people say they are fed up or bored with politics, they usually mean that they have been turned off by the behaviour or performance of those politicians most directly involved in the traditional political arena.

The other definition of 'politics', a process definition, is much looser than the arena one (Leftwich, 2004: 3) and reflects the idea that power is inscribed in all social processes (for example, in the family and the schoolroom). This broader definition of the political is particularly associated with feminism, constructivism, poststructuralism and Marxism. For feminists in particular there has been much emphasis on the idea that the 'personal is political' (Hanisch, 1969). This mantra partly originated in debates about violence against women in the home, which had traditionally been seen as 'non-political', because they occurred in the private rather than the public realm. Indeed, in the UK at least, the police, historically, referred to such violence as 'a domestic', and therefore not their concern. The feminist argument, in contrast, was that such violence reflected a power relationship and was inherently 'political'.

Marxists have also generally preferred a definition of politics that sees it as a reflection of a wider struggle between social classes in society. Politics in capitalist systems involves a struggle to assert the interest of the proletariat (the disadvantaged) in a system in which the state forwards the interests of the ruling class. Constructivists tend to see politics as a process conducted in a range of arenas, with the main struggles around political identity (hence the focus on identity politics). Poststructuralists take this position further, arguing that politics is not 'contained' within a single structure of domination; rather, power is diffused throughout social institutions and processes, and even inscribed in people's bodies.

Process definitions are usually criticised by those who adopt arena definitions, because of what is termed 'conceptual stretching' or the 'boundary problem' (see Ekman and Amnå, 2012; Hooghe, 2014). If politics occurs in all social interactions between individuals, then we are in danger of seeing everything as political, so that there is no separation between the 'political' and the 'social'. The alarm bells might be ringing here since it appears that political scientists cannot even agree about the subject matter of their discipline. Yet our view is that both 'arena' and 'process' definitions have their value; indeed, the relationship between process and arena definitions may be best seen as a duality, that is interactive and iterative, rather than a dualism, or an either/or (Rowe et al., 2017). Moreover, all of the different approaches to political science we identify would at least recognise that politics is about power and that we need to widen significantly an arena definition of politics.

Goodin and Klingemann (1996: 7) suggest that a broad consensus could be built around a definition of politics along the lines: 'the constrained use of social power.' The political process is about collective choice, without simple resort to force or violence, although it does not exclude at least the threat of those options. It is about what shapes and constrains those choices and the use of power and its consequences. It would cover unintended as well as intended acts, and passive as well as active practices. Politics enables individuals or groups to do some things that they would not otherwise be able to do, while it also constrains individuals or groups from doing what they might otherwise do. Although the different approaches to political science may have their own take on a definition of politics, contesting how exactly power is exercised or practised, they might accept Goodin and Klingemann's broad definition.

It is clear that politics is much broader than what governments do, but there is still something especially significant about political processes that are, or could be, considered to be part of the public domain. In a pragmatic sense, it is probably true to say that most political scientists tend to concentrate their efforts in terms of analysis and research on the more collective and public elements of power struggles. But, it is important that we develop a sense of the collective or public arena that takes us beyond the narrow machinations of the political elite.

What is a scientific approach to politics?

As Goodin and Klingemann (1996: 9) comment, 'much ink has been spilt over the question of whether, or in what sense, the study of politics is or is not truly a science. The answer largely depends upon how much one tries to load into the term "science".' If you adopt what they call a minimalist approach the question can be answered fairly straightforwardly, namely that political science is science in the sense that it offers ordered knowledge based on systematic enquiry. There is no reason to doubt that political science in all its forms has achieved, or could achieve, that level of knowledge. But, beyond such a basic agreement, the approaches that we consider in this book take diverse views on the issue of 'science'.

What is at stake here is the various ontological and epistemological positions taken by the different approaches. As Marsh, Ercan and Furlong argue in Chapter 11, ontology is concerned with what we can know about the world, and epistemology with how we can know it. There is a fundamental ontological difference between realists (or foundationalists) and constructivists (or anti-foundationalists). The former argue that a real world exists independently of our knowledge of it and can be discovered as such if we use the right methods in the right way. Constructivists, on the other hand, view the world as socially constructed and capable of being interpreted in different ways. Crucial for a constructivist is the idea that there is a double hermeneutic (Giddens, 1987), that is, two levels of 'understanding'. From this perspective, the world is interpreted by the actors (one hermeneutic level), and their interpretation is interpreted by the observer (a second hermeneutic level). For researchers, the aim becomes to explore their own interpretation of the interpretations made by actors about their behaviour.

If ontological realists are epistemological positivists rather than critical realists (see Chapter 11), they are concerned to identify causal relationships, developing explanatory, and, most often, predictive models (following natural scientists). Critical realists, in contrast, do not privilege direct observation; rather, they posit the existence of deep structures, which cannot be directly observed but shape the actions of agents. Constructivists can draw upon a long tradition within social and political studies, but it is fair to say that this is an approach of growing importance in the discipline which has seen a growth in research within the interpretivist school (see Chapter 5), alongside broader intellectual currents associated with poststructuralism (see Chapter 8).

It is by no means straightforward to divide the various approaches considered in this volume on the basis of their epistemological position.

The behavioural and rational choice approaches are those that most obviously claim the positivist position. The former aims to identify general laws about political action/life, while the latter places more of an emphasis on the predictive capabilities of its models. At the same time, the epistemological positions underpinning the different approaches reviewed in this book have been subject to change and development.

As Sanders points out in Chapter 2, behaviouralists have increasingly acknowledged the first level of the hermeneutic, acknowledging that an individual's action may reflect the way in which s/he thinks about the world, as much as any external 'reality'. So, in explaining voting behaviour, they would recognise that a voter's subjective perception of his/her class position is as important as his/her objective class position. Nevertheless, a positivist, whether a behaviouralist or a rational choice theorist, does seek to establish causal relationships between political phenomena, which are reproducible and generalisable – a position which would be questioned by any constructivist. At the same time, as Marsh, Ercan and Furlong argue in Chapter 11, a positivist has great difficulty in accepting the second level of the hermeneutic, which emphasises that the researcher's interpretation of what s/he discovers is partial, in both senses of the word. Most positivists would defend the idea that a researcher can be objective, with their conclusions unaffected by those partialities.

A similarly nuanced stance on epistemological positions is taken by Parsons in relation to constructivist approaches. There are, as Parsons points out in Chapter 5, several different positions within the broad school of constructivism. One view argues that our concern should be with understanding, not explanation, thus challenging the scientific pretensions of positivists. In this view, there is no 'real world', independent of the social construction of it, for political scientists to study. As such, social science involves an interpretive search to *understand* the meanings attached to actions, rather than a scientific search for *explanation*, establishing causal relations between social phenomena. However, other constructivists do not break so sharply with science and causality, allowing for greater dialogue and exchange. Such constructivists would argue that, although action depends on meaning, this does not necessarily imply that there can be no explanation of why certain people do certain things. If we can show that people's action is shaped by meaningful social constructs, then a careful observer can show this to be the case, thus offering an explanation of that action (while being circumspect about the possibility of generalising from the case).

Of the other approaches that we cover in the first part of the book it is clear that institutional, psychological and feminist approaches all include scholars who take different ontological and epistemological positions. The psychologists lean towards positivism, but many would be comfortable with the modern behaviouralist position outlined by Sanders (Chapter 2). In contrast, institutionalism and feminism are marked by ontological and epistemological debates, as Lowndes shows in relation to institutionalism in Chapter 4. As for feminism, many contemporary scholars adopt a constructivist position, while other feminist researchers consider how gender explains political action in a way that would fit with a positivist perspective (see Chapter 6). Poststructuralists, however, see epistemology as prior to ontology, and argue that our experience of 'reality' is intrinsically mediated by language and discourse; as such, we can never get beyond appearances to underlying essences (Chapter 8). We certainly cannot assume that (political) 'reality' takes the form of law-like relationships, nor are there any criteria (following Parsons) to establish the veracity of certain modes of interpretation or interpretations; hence, this is a radical form of constructivism. The critical realist position dominates the Marxist camp (Chapter 7), although it is also evident among historical institutionalists; indeed, both approaches have given some ground to constructivist arguments.

We finish this section by emphasising again that the different approaches reviewed in this book have been, and are, subject to change and development. Different parts of the discipline have listened to, and learnt from, each other. We strongly support the idea of further dialogue. The contributions in this book suggest that there may be more common ground than we usually acknowledge. In particular, we would emphasise the need to be sensitive to the importance of meaning in explaining human action, and a willingness to explore arguments in a rigorous empirical manner, where appropriate.

The discipline of political science: a celebration of diversity?

Read many of the reviews of political science and they agree that political science has become more diverse and more cosmopolitan in character (see, for example, Almond, 1990; Goodin and Klingemann, 1996; and on the social sciences in general, see Della Porta and Keating, 2008). Some of those who pioneered what they called the scientific treatment of the subject expected that the scientific revolution would lead to a unity in the understanding of political science (Weisberg, 1986: 4). There can be little doubt that those ambitions have not been realised; indeed, constructivists would say they can't be realised. There is a basis for some common agreement about what constitutes 'minimal professional competence', but as Goodin and Klingemann (1996: 6) note, when it comes to judging the value of work beyond some agreed baseline of coherence and craftsmanship 'the higher aspirations are many and varied'. Consequently, there is a de facto plurality of views about the nature of political science endeavour.

So, has peace broken out in the political sciences? There is a grudging public acceptance of plurality, but in private there is a quiet war going on. Some positivists are very dismissive of the 'storytelling' approaches of others. Some constructivists imply that philosophical ignorance and naivety about human behaviour are associated with the ambitions of positivist, big data-driven and experimental political science. As James Mahoney and Gary Goertz (2006: 227–228) suggest, when it comes to the cultures of quantitative and qualitative methods each 'is sometimes privately suspicious or skeptical of the other though usually more publicly polite. Communication across traditions tends to be difficult and marked by misunderstanding. When members of one tradition offer their insights to members of the other community, the advice is likely to be viewed (rightly or wrongly) as unhelpful and even belittling.'

Our hope is that political science can move from at best grudging acceptance to something closer to a celebration of diversity. We started the chapter with Herbert Simon's argument that, if you are not sure of what the answer is, then there is inherent value in having the option of several paths being travelled at the same time. Beyond this, we can think of three factors to support the case for a plurality of approaches. First, there is evidence of epistemological gain through the richness of approaches. Broadly, as Sanders shows in Chapter 2, behaviouralists have had to rethink and improve their approach under challenge from constructivist perspectives. Equally, as Parsons notes in Chapter 5, constructivists have been encouraged to be more explicit about data collection and methods of analysis under pressure from those coming from a more positivist tradition.

Second, although there is a danger of too much plurality – in the sense that there could be so many varieties of political science that fragmentation makes effective dialogue impossible – such a point has not yet been reached. There is the opportunity to learn from different approaches at present, although this is certainly challenging, given the enormous range and variety of journals, research outputs and books. Of course, part of the aim behind this book is to enable political scientists with different approaches to understand one another better. Perhaps we need more effective rules of engagement. There are implicit shared standards in most work – whatever tradition within which we are working – but we need to make these more explicit. Good work, whatever its approach, should be clear about its conceptual framing and also transparent, and reflective, about its methods of data collection and analysis. It should frame its arguments in the context of work that has gone before and, where relevant, it should aim to address (or at least engage with) concerns held by stakeholders and actors within society.

Our third argument for a plurality of approaches concerns the relevance of political science to the wider world, which is the focus of the final chapter of the book. There are, as noted in Chapter 19, several ways for political scientists to address relevance; but what cannot be avoided is a commitment to addressing it. Political science exists in a society where politics plays a vital role and as such its findings should be made accessible (and of value) to our fellow citizens. At times, it has been argued that political scientists suffer from economist-envy. Because that discipline has a promoted a strong one-size-fits-all approach to understanding policy problems, it has often been more successful in gaining the ear of policymakers (Bowles, 2016). Yet that strength has also proved to be a significant weakness, as the limits to the role of incentives and self-interested behaviour in steering good public policy have been increasingly exposed (Thaler and Sunstein, 2008; Bowles, 2016). Economists' perceived capacity to make effective predictions has been challenged, notably in relation to the global financial crisis of 2008 (Wilson, 2015). As political science steps up its commitment to relevance, having a plurality of approaches could be an advantage. Reaching out to a pluralistic world, where there is no one prince, principal or governor – as economists tend to imagine – seems likely to require a diversity of approaches.

We believe that, at this stage in its development, it is important for political science not to depict itself as a small club of like-minded people. Rather, it is a broad church with different starting points and concerns, which also shares a commitment to developing a better understanding of politics. The key challenge is not to launch a campaign for unity, but to argue in favour of diversity, combined with dialogue. Almond (1990, 1996) warns that the discipline should avoid constructing itself into an uneasy collection of separate sects. There is a plurality of methods and approaches out there that should not be denied but, at the same time, there should be interaction between the approaches rather than isolation within an approach. Political science should be eclectic and synergistic; this is why we think it is important to celebrate diversity. We argue that political science is enriched by the variety of approaches that are adopted within the discipline. Each has something of considerable value to offer, but each can benefit from its interaction with other approaches. In giving space to a variety of ways of doing political science, our book aims to provide the essential ingredients for an ongoing exchange that can enable different approaches to gain a baseline understanding of one another.

In this introduction we have briefly addressed two questions. What is the scope of political studies? And can it claim the label of science? We conclude that, while political scientists are divided on these issues, there is scope for identifying some common ground. We argue that diversity within the field should be embraced at the present time. Utilising a plurality of approaches is the best way to face up to the challenging task of understanding a core human activity such as politics.

Part 1

Theory and Approaches

Introduction to Part 1

VIVIEN LOWNDES, DAVID MARSH AND GERRY STOKER

Part 1 begins with the behavioural approach to political science in Chapter 2, written by David Sanders. It is appropriate to start with this approach since the behavioural revolution constitutes the key development in the establishment of modern political science against which all other approaches must situate themselves. Above all the behavioural movement confirmed the call to shift decisively attention away from the formal, legalistic study of political institutions and constitutions. That shift remains an accepted part of the terrain for all political scientists. All empirically oriented political science shares with the behaviouralists a concern with the way in which politics operates in practice. Sanders offers a subtle account of how the behaviouralist approach has evolved and provides a convincing and powerful account of where modern behaviouralism stands now.

The second approach to be considered is rational choice theory (Chapter 3). It too claimed to bring a revolutionary new approach to the discipline. There can be little doubt about the impact of this approach. Some of its advocates argue that it constitutes the key approach for delivering a political science that is cumulative in its knowledge production and a powerful member of a wider social science community, unified through the adoption of axioms and methods initially derived from economics. While some emphasise the overweening virtues of an approach that favours formal theory and mathematical rigour, others now see rational choice approaches as one among a variety of paths that can be taken. That second option is certainly the position taken by Andy Hindmoor and Brad Taylor in their chapter, and one that is shared by the editors. The way of thinking and the challenge posed by rational choice analysis has something to offer all in the discipline but its claim to be a high priest is rightly regarded with scepticism.

The third style of political science examined in the book is institutional analysis. As Vivien Lowndes points out in Chapter 4, those interested in institutional studies may have found themselves out of favour as first behaviouralists and then rational choice theorists blazed a trail for a new political science unencumbered by the old interest in institutions and constitutions. However, a new intuitionalism has emerged, as a check to the undersocialised accounts of political action offered by behaviouralism and rational choice, which shares a core view that institutions shape political relationships in important ways. There are many ways in which that interest in institutionalism has been expressed, including through a focus on institutional rules, norms and narratives. Indeed, the new interest in institutions has provided a basis for a rapprochement within the discipline, as both behaviouralists and rational choice students have come to grant increasing recognition to the importance of institutions.

In Chapter 5 Craig Parsons gives full coverage to constructivist approach and interpretive theory and in so doing challenges the approaches outlined in the previous chapters, although, as he notes, many institutionalists also make constructivist arguments. What is distinctive about this approach is the claim that political action is related to the presence of certain 'social constructs' – ideas, beliefs, norms, identities. These interpretive filters work through affecting the way people see the world; human action is in turn structured by the meanings that people attach to themselves and their circumstances. While these filters are downplayed in most versions of rational choice theory, they can be a focus of attention in many of the other approaches discussed in this book. Constructivism therefore offers a distinctive, plausible means of understanding why people act the way they do. Constructivists need to think about and engage with non-constructivist alternatives to their claims, but non-constructivists should also routinely consider constructivist competitors in their own research.

Political science remains in need of challenge from all quarters. As Meryl Kenny and Fiona Mackay show in Chapter 6, feminist and gendered approaches share an understanding that politics needs to be defined in a broad sense, in that the personal can be political and that engagement with progressive change is part of the mission of research. The chapter reminds us that gender approaches are not only about women, discussing the role of men and masculinities in explaining unequal political outcomes. Intersectional identities are also highlighted, with the authors showing how 'race-gendered institutions' distribute political power. Using a variety of different theoretical and methodological starting points, feminist and gendered scholarship enriches our understanding of major political issues – particularly around power and difference – and their implications for the ways in which we conduct research.

In Chapter 7, Ray Kiely considers the question of the continued relevance of Marxism for understanding contemporary globalisation. By framing the understanding of politics within a broader political economy, the chapter shows how it is possible – both historically and in the context of the contemporary world – to trace the way in which politics works, not in a vacuum, but within the context of a wider economic and social system. These dynamics shape both the challenges faced by politics and the solutions it can provide. Our understanding of the globalised world we live in – and its persistent and rising inequalities – would be the poorer if it lacked the insights from both traditional and present-day Marxism. Sharing with feminist approaches a commitment to progressive social change, Marxist analyses throw light on the rise of anti-globalisation and social justice movements (like Occupy) and the emergence of influential new political parties such as Podemos in Spain and Syriza in Greece.

Marxist analyses are often used in dialogue with poststructuralist approaches, which are the subject of Chapter 8, a new contribution for this fourth edition of the *Theories and Methods*. The inclusion of a chapter on poststructuralism reflects the growing volume and significance of work within this approach. Mark Wenman traces the origins of the approach and offers a clear commentary on its core claims, which challenge many of the mainstream political science approaches covered in the book. The crucial argument is that there can be no scientific claim as our experience of 'reality' is intrinsically mediated by language or discourse; the core strength of approach is a critique of others' truth claims. The chapter provides readers with a robust defence against poststructuralism's critics – notably by showing how the approach can be used in empirical as well as philosophical work, for example in research on the rise of populism. The chapter mounts a set of arguments that need to be addressed by all political scientists, and are taken up again in David Marsh's discussion of meta-theoretical issues in Part 2 of the book.

In Chapter 9, we remind readers of the importance of political psychology approaches which have also gained prominence in recent decades. As Frank Mols and Paul 't Hart argue, political psychologists tap into a reservoir of concepts, propositions and paradigms about human and social behaviour that all mainstream political science should be willing to consider. Furthermore, its methodological sophistication and commitment to careful research design provide lessons for all political scientists.

We should also not forget that normative political theory continues to play a key role in political studies. Chris Armstrong, in Chapter 10, provides an overview of key themes from normative political theory, focusing on both the feasibility and the achievability of political ideals. The discussion shows how core issues of justice and liberty remain at the heart of politics – notably in discussions around human rights and the future of democracy – and are therefore of continuing relevance to political science.

Chapter 2

Behavioural Analysis

DAVID SANDERS

The behavioural approach to social and political analysis concentrates on a single, deceptively simple question: Why do people behave in the way they do? What differentiates behaviouralists from other social scientists is their insistence that (1) *observable* behaviour, whether it is at the level of the individual or the social aggregate, should be the focus of analysis; and (2) any explanation of that behaviour should be susceptible to empirical testing. Behavioural scholars take the view that, whatever theoretical categories any analysis uses, social enquiry is fundamentally about trying to understand what it is that (some) people do, think or say.

Scholars working in the behavioural tradition have investigated a wide range of substantive problems. Behaviouralists have extensively analysed the reasons that underlie the main form of mass political participation in democratic countries: voting (for example, Heath et al., 1994; Clarke et al., 2009). They have also examined the origins of participation in other, more unconventional, forms of political activity such as demonstrations, strikes and even riots (for example, Barnes and Kaase, 1979; Parry et al., 1992; Anderson and Mendes, 2006). At the elite level, behaviouralists have analysed leadership behaviour, placing particular emphasis on the connections between the way in which leaders view the world (their attitudes and values) and the particular actions that they take (for example, Allison, 1971; King, 1985; Sanders, 1990; Dunleavy and Jones, 1993; King, 2002). In terms of social aggregates, behavioural analysis has examined the actions of interest groups (for example, Grant and Marsh, 1977; Wilson, 1990; Nownes and Lipinski, 2005) and political parties (for example, Budge and Fairlie, 1983; Budge and Laver, 1992; Dalton, 2002; Ezrow, 2008). At the international level, behavioural analysis has also focused on the actions of nation states (for example, Rosenau, 1969; Lebovic, 2004), as well as on the behaviour of non-state actors such as multinational corporations, international terrorist groups and supranational organisations such as the European Union (for example, Keohane, 1984; Baldwin, 1993; Cederman et al., 2013). In all these diverse contexts, the central questions that behaviouralists seek to answer are simple: what do the actors involved actually do? How can we best explain why they do it? These are obviously not the only questions that can be asked about individual and social actors. Behaviouralists simply believe that they are the most important ones.

This chapter is divided into four sections. The first provides a brief outline of the origins of behaviouralism and summarises the core analytic assertions that underpin it. The second section reviews the main criticisms that, with varying degrees of justification, have been levelled at the behavioural approach. The third part describes one major study – Cederman, Gleditsch and Buhaug's analysis (2013) of the effects of inequality on the occurrence of civil war – which illustrates some of the more positive features of behavioural analysis. The final section considers the influence that behaviouralism continues to exert on contemporary political researchers.

The rise of the behavioural movement and its core characteristics

The behavioural movement assumed an important position in the social sciences in the 1950s and 1960s. Its philosophical origins were in the writings of Auguste Comte (Comte, 1974) in the nineteenth century and in the logical positivism of the 'Vienna Circle' in the 1920s. Positivism, which was popularised in Britain by Alfred Ayer and in Germany by Carl Hempel, asserted that analytic statements made about the physical or social world fell into one of three categories. First, such statements could be useful tautologies; they could be purely definitional statements that assigned a specific meaning to a particular phenomenon or concept. For example, we might define families living on less than one-third of the average weekly wage as 'living below the poverty line'. Second, statements could be empirical, that is to say, they could be tested against observation in order to see if they were true or false. Third, statements that fell into neither of the first two categories were devoid of analytic meaning. For the positivists, in short, meaningful analysis could proceed only on the basis of useful tautologies and empirical statements; metaphysics, theology, aesthetics and even ethics merely introduced meaningless obfuscation into the process of enquiry.

It would not be correct, of course, to assume that behaviouralism accepted all the philosophical precepts of positivism. Even as behaviouralism was gaining increasingly wide acceptance among social scientists in the 1950s, positivism itself was being subjected to ferocious philosophical criticism – not least on the grounds that it was unclear whether positivism's assertion that there were only three types of statement was itself tautological, empirical or meaningless. This said, behaviouralism's view of the nature of empirical theory and of explanation was strongly influenced by the positivist tradition. Although there are many definitions of these two critical terms, most behaviouralists would probably accept something along the lines of the following:

- An *empirical theory* is a set of interconnected abstract statements, consisting of assumptions, definitions and empirically testable hypotheses, which purports to describe and explain the occurrence of a given phenomenon or set of phenomena.
- An *explanation* is a causal account of the occurrence of some phenomenon or set of phenomena. An explanation of a particular (class of) event(s) consists in the specification of the minimum non-tautological set of antecedent necessary and sufficient conditions required for its (their) occurrence.

The importance of these definitions of theory and explanation lies in the implications that they have for theory evaluation. For positivists, the crucial question that should always be asked about any purportedly explanatory theory is: *How would we know if this theory were incorrect?* Behaviouralism's endorsement of the central importance of this question is precisely what demonstrates its intellectual debt to positivism. For both positivists and behaviouralists there are three main ways in which explanatory theories can be evaluated:

1. A 'good' theory must be internally consistent; it must not make statements such that both the presence and the absence of a given set of antecedent conditions are deemed to 'cause' the occurrence of the phenomenon that is purportedly being explained.
2. A 'good' theory relating to a specific class of phenomena should, as far as possible, be consistent with other theories that seek to explain related phenomena.
3. And, crucially, genuinely explanatory theories must be capable of generating empirical predictions that can be tested against observation. The only meaningful way of deciding between competing theories (which might appear to be equally plausible in other respects) is by empirical testing. This testing can be conducted either at the level of the individual s†ocial actor or at the level of the social aggregate – whichever is appropriate given the nature of the theory that is being tested.

It is this emphasis on empirical observation and testing that produces the two characteristic features of the behavioural approach to social enquiry:

The first – and least contentious – of these is behaviouralism's commitment to the systematic use of all the relevant empirical evidence rather than a limited set of illustrative supporting examples. This commitment simply means that when a particular theoretical statement is being investigated, the researcher must not limit her/himself to a consideration of only those observed cases that provide 'anecdotal' support for the theoretical claims that are being made. Rather, the researcher must consider all the cases – or at least a representative sample of them – that are encompassed by the theoretical statement that is being evaluated.

It is in this context that the use and development of statistical techniques is justified by behaviouralists – as a vehicle for analysing large amounts of 'relevant empirical evidence'. It should be emphasised in the strongest possible terms, however, that behaviouralism is not synonymous either with quantification or with the downgrading of qualitative research. Certainly, behavioural researchers have frequently used quantitative techniques as heuristic devices for handling evidence. There is nothing intrinsic in behaviouralism's epistemological position, however, that requires quantification. On the contrary, quantitative and qualitative forms of empirical analysis are equally acceptable to behavioural researchers. What matters for them is not whether evidence is qualitative or quantitative but (1) that it is used to evaluate theoretical propositions; and (2) that it is employed systematically rather than illustratively.

The second characteristic feature of behavioural analysis is slightly subtler in its implications – but no less important. It is simply that scientific theories and/or explanations must, in principle, be capable of being falsified. Note here that the reference is to 'scientific' rather than simply to 'empirical' or 'explanatory' theories. This usage reflects behaviouralism's commitment to Karl Popper's revision of traditional positivism in which he (1) substituted the principle of falsifiability for that of verification; and (2) simultaneously identified the falsifiability criterion as the line of demarcation between 'scientific' and 'pseudo-scientific' enquiry (Popper, 1959).

In order fully to appreciate the import of this statement, a brief digression is necessary. We need to consider precisely what is meant by a theory or an explanation being 'falsifiable'. Consider the familiar statement that Popper himself used as an example: 'All swans are white.' Suppose that we observe a black swan. What does this tell us about the statement? One interpretation is that observing the black swan shows the statement to be empirically false; the statement was in principle *capable* of being falsified and it has been falsified. But there is another way of interpreting the statement in the light of a black swan being observed. The statement says that all swans are white. It follows that the black swan that we have observed cannot be a swan because it is not white; the statement, therefore, is not false.

Can both of these interpretations be correct? The answer is that they can. Each interpretation makes a different set of assumptions about the definition of a swan. The first assumes that a swan is a large bird with a long neck that looks very pretty when it paddles through water; it says nothing of the bird's colour. In these circumstances, the definitions of 'swan' and 'colour' are *independent*; there is no overlap between them. In other words, it *is possible* to observe something that has all the characteristics of a swan regardless of its colour. We have observed a black swan and, therefore, the initial statement must have been false. The second interpretation assumes that a swan is a large bird with a long neck that looks very pretty when it paddles through water *and that it is also white*. In other words, this second interpretation assumes that whiteness is part of the *definition* of being a swan. In these circumstances, when a black 'swan' is observed it cannot be a swan, because part of the definition of it being a swan is that it is white.

What is clear from this discussion is that the status of the statement depends upon whether or not its constituent terms are independently defined. With the first interpretation, the terms 'swan' and 'white' *are* independently defined. As a result, the statement is an empirical or falsifiable one; it is possible to test it against the world of observation. With the second interpretation, however, the terms 'swan' and 'white' are not independently defined. As a result, the statement is (partially) tautological; it is simply an untestable assertion that one of the defining features of a swan is that it is white.

This problem of interpretation is common in the social sciences. Consider the following statement: 'In general elections people vote against the incumbent government if they are dissatisfied with its performance.' Without further information, we cannot tell whether this is a testable empirical statement or merely a definitional tautology. The statement can, in fact, be interpreted in two completely different ways. First, we can interpret the statement in purely tautological terms. Looking at a particular election, we could say: (1) that every voter who voted for the government must have been satisfied with its performance (otherwise s/he would not have voted for it); and (2) that every voter who did not vote for the government could not have been satisfied with its performance (otherwise s/he would have voted for it). With this interpretation, we can always 'believe' in the statement but we have not *demonstrated* that it is empirically correct; we have treated it purely as a tautology. The second interpretation is to regard the statement as an empirical one – but this is possible only if we provide a definition of dissatisfaction with the government that is independent of the act of voting. If we were to devise some independent way of measuring dissatisfaction, then we would obviously be able to test our initial statement against any available empirical evidence. We might find that all those who voted for the government were satisfied with its performance and that all those who voted against it were dissatisfied – in which case we would have corroborated the statement. Crucially, however, by providing independent definitions of 'voting' and of 'dissatisfaction' we create the possibility that the 'statement' might be empirically incorrect; we render the statement *falsifiable* – even though we might hope that it will not be falsified.

Having distinguished between falsifiable and non-falsifiable statements, Popper goes on to suggest that theories can only be regarded as 'scientific' if they generate empirical predictions that are capable of being falsified. Theories that do not generate such predictions are merely sophisticated tautologies that explain nothing – no matter how elegant and elaborate they might appear. Many behaviouralists are unconcerned as to whether or not their research should be described as 'scientific'. Crucially, however, they are unequivocally committed to the principle of falsifiability. Behaviouralists do not deny that there are other ways of evaluating the adequacy of a particular theory. They nonetheless insist that a genuinely explanatory theory must engender falsifiable propositions of the form 'If A, then B; if not A, then not B'; and it must specify causal antecedents that are defined independently of the phenomenon that is supposedly being explained.

All this is not to suggest, however, that behaviouralists believe that all aspects of their theories must be capable of being falsified. As Lakatos (1971) has argued, most theories in the physical and social sciences contain a non-falsifiable set of 'core' propositions. These core propositions often take the form of highly abstract assumptions that are not susceptible to empirical testing. The non-falsifiability of the 'core' propositions, however, does not necessarily mean that the theory itself is non-falsifiable. Provided that a series of testable predictions, which can be examined in the light of empirical observation, can be derived logically from the 'core', then the theory as a whole can be regarded as falsifiable. It does represent something more than sophisticated tautology; it does provide the analyst with an opportunity to specify the conditions under which s/he would know that the theory was 'incorrect'.

Behaviouralists, then, emphasise the twin notions that theories should: (1) seek to explain something; and (2) be capable, in principle, of being tested against the world of observation. For behaviouralists, non-falsifiable theories are not really theories at all. They are merely elaborate fantasies – of varying degrees of complexity – that scholars can choose to believe or disbelieve as they wish. For behaviouralists, theory evaluation must proceed beyond merely examining a theory in order to assess its internal consistency and the nature of the 'puzzles' that it seems to resolve; theory evaluation must also involve subjecting theoretical propositions to empirical test.

Criticisms of the behavioural approach

As with any other general approach in the social sciences, behaviouralism has been the target of a number of important criticisms. These criticisms can be grouped under three broad headings and each will be examined in turn below.

Objections to the positivist claim that statements which are neither definitions (useful tautologies) nor empirical are meaningless

It was noted earlier that behaviouralism has its philosophical roots in positivism. It would appear to follow that any weaknesses inherent in positivism must also therefore be inherent in behaviouralism. Among the many criticisms that have been levelled at positivism, perhaps the most important is the simple proposition that the large class of statements that positivism labels as 'meaningless' in fact contains many ideas that can add very significantly to our understanding of social behaviour and the human condition. In strict positivist terms, there can be no role for normative theory for the investigation of what ought to be – because normative discourses are not restricted to definitional and empirical statements. Similarly, there can be no role for aesthetic or moral arguments, for the same reason. And there can be no role for the sort of hermeneutic analysis that seeks to understand social behaviour through deep reflection about the nature of human perceptions, thought processes and motivations. If positivism seeks to exclude these forms of reflection, the argument runs, it must be in error.

The extent to which positivists genuinely ever did deny the value of non-empirical analysis need not concern us here. It is important to point out, however, that most contemporary researchers who continue to work in the behaviouralist tradition would almost certainly reject the notion that there can be no role for normative theory, aesthetics or hermeneutics in political and social analysis. They would argue, instead, that these approaches yield a different form of knowledge or understanding – not that they are 'meaningless'. In essence, modern behaviouralists acknowledge freely this particular criticism of positivism. They deflect it from themselves by recognising that other, potentially useful, forms of knowledge can be acquired by scholars working in other intellectual traditions. Modern behaviouralists – 'post-behaviouralists' – simply prefer to subject their own theoretical claims to empirical test. They also suspect that scholars working in non-empirical traditions are never able to provide a satisfactory answer to the crucial question: *How would you know if you were wrong?*

The tendency towards mindless empiricism

One of the claims of the early positivists was that theoretical understanding could be obtained only through a process of enquiry that began with theory-free observation of 'all the facts up to now' and which then derived law-like generalisations inductively from the empirical regularities that were observed. Later positivists, notably Hempel and Popper, strongly rejected this 'narrow inductivist' view of the nature of scientific enquiry, arguing that enquiry could only proceed if the researcher's efforts to observe 'relevant facts' were guided either by clear theoretical expectations or, at a minimum, by some kind of explanatory 'hunch'. Hempel (1966: 11–12) is worth quoting at length in this context:

> [A narrow inductivist investigation] ... could never get off the ground. Even its first [fact gathering] phase could never be carried out, for a collection of all the facts would have to await the end of the world, so to speak; and even all the facts up to now cannot be collected since there

> are an infinite number and variety of them. Are we to examine for example, all the grains of sand in all the deserts and on all the beaches, and are we to record their shapes, their weights, their chemical composition, their distances from each other, their constantly changing temperature, and their equally changing distance from the centre of the moon? Are we to record the floating thoughts that cross our minds in the tedious process? The shapes of the clouds overhead, the changing color of the sky? The construction and the trade name of our writing equipment? Our own life histories and those of our fellow investigators? All these, and untold other things, are, after all, among 'all the facts up to now'.

In spite of positivism's moves away from inductivism, there can be no doubt that, between the early 1950s and the mid-1970s, a number of scholars working within the behavioural tradition did still appear to be committed to an inductivist approach to research. It would be unnecessarily invidious to isolate particular examples of this tendency. It is nonetheless fair to say that, during this period, many behaviouralists acted as if law-like scientific generalisations could be constructed purely by identifying the statistical regularities evident in large quantities of empirical data. This emphasis on data and the concomitant downgrading of a priori theoretical reasoning in turn produced three undesirable tendencies in behavioural research.

The first of these was a tendency to emphasise what can be easily measured rather than what might be theoretically important. This sort of criticism is always easy to make, in the sense that one person's triviality may be another's profundity. Nonetheless, the tendency to play down the potential importance of phenomena that are intrinsically difficult to measure has always been a matter of concern to both critics and advocates of behavioural research. This has been especially true in relation to the analysis of electoral behaviour. Since the explosion of behavioural research in the 1950s, voting studies have concentrated primarily on electors' social profiles, partisan identifications, ideological positions, policy preferences and economic perceptions. Complex models have been devised – and tested empirically – which show the relative importance, and causal ordering, of different aspect of these various phenomena in the determination of the vote (see, for example, Sarlvik and Crewe, 1983; Heath, 1991; Heath et al., 1985).

Yet, despite the considerable contribution that behavioural analysis has made to our understanding of a voter's decision calculus, it has often been argued that, somehow, an important part of what it means to vote – as well as part of the calculus itself – may have been omitted from behavioural analyses. There has perhaps been insufficient attention paid to inconsistencies and contradictions in voters' political perceptions and to the possibility not only that many voters change their political preferences frequently, but also that their preferences vary, quite genuinely, with the social context in which they are expressed. There are other areas – relating to the way in which individuals reflect, to a greater or lesser degree, upon themselves – where behavioural electoral research has simply not dared to tread. What sort of person do I think I am? What aspirations and expectations do I have about my future life? What sort of life do I think I am capable of leading or should lead? How do I relate my notions of personal morality to the moral stances of the major political parties? The answers to questions such as these may have no bearing on the way in which political preferences are formed and transformed. Within the behavioural frame of reference, however, it is very hard to envisage how the responses to such questions – given the difficulty of measuring those responses systematically – could ever be incorporated into formal analysis. As a result, they are largely excluded from the analytic frame.

A second, and related, undesirable feature of behavioural research that arises from its overly empirical focus has been a tendency to concentrate on readily observed phenomena – such as voting – rather than the subtler, and perhaps deeper, structural forces that promote stability and change in social and political systems. One obvious concept that has been neglected by behavioural research in this context is that of *interests*. The notion of interests has played an important part in a wide variety of social and political theories ranging from Marx, Max Weber and Vilfredo Pareto in the domestic field to Hans Morgenthau and E. H. Carr in the field of international relations. In all these contexts, social actors – whether they are individuals, groups of individuals or even nation states – are seen as pursuing strategies that are aimed at maximising their 'interests'. Yet, as scholars working in the behavioural tradition have found repeatedly, it is extraordinarily difficult to observe the 'interests' of a particular individual, group or state directly. In consequence, behavioural research has tended to shy away from the theoretical and empirical analysis of interests – preferring to leave the field clear for scholars working in other, non-empirical, traditions.

The third undesirable feature of behavioural research, which is increasingly prominent, has been a tendency towards what can best be described as 'statistical correctness'. This has involved an increasing focus on the precision of statistical estimates and their standard errors (the confidence bands around estimates of statistical effect magnitudes) at the expense of providing and assessing *explanations* of the behaviours of interest. Current behavioural analyses typically focus on the proper estimation of small statistical effects (to three and even four decimal points in some publications) and ignore the fact that most of the variation in the dependent variable in question remains (statistically) unexplained. They also fail to acknowledge the clunky and imprecise nature of much of the data that are actually analysed in behavioural research, a failure that frequently turns precise statistical estimation into an almost meaningless exercise.

The assumed independence of theory and observation

The early behaviouralists proclaimed their approach to social enquiry as being both 'scientific' and 'value-free'. They claimed not to be seeking to justify any particular ethical or political stance. Rather, they sought simply to uncover 'the facts' through impartial observation and to offer politically neutral theories that would explain them in the most parsimonious way. As the passage from Hempel quoted earlier shows, the degree of inductivism thus implied – in which 'explanatory theory' emerges only after all the relevant facts have been surveyed impartially – was always impossible. Some sort of initial theoretical understanding is necessary before the researcher can decide what it is that should be observed.

Modern behaviouralists, along with researchers working in other intellectual traditions, roundly reject the notion that theory and observation are independent. On the contrary, most post-behaviouralists would now accept the relativist view that what is observed is in part a consequence of the theoretical position that the analyst adopts in the first place. Modern behaviouralists, however, are distinguishable from most relativists. It is one thing to allow that observations are coloured by theory; it is quite another to conclude that this means that one set of theories and observations is as good as another. For modern behaviouralists, the ultimate test of a good theory is still whether or not it is consistent with observation – with the available empirical evidence. Modern behaviouralists are perfectly prepared to accept that different theoretical positions are likely to elicit different descriptions of 'reality' – that they are likely to produce different 'observations'. They insist, however, that whatever 'observations' are implied by a particular theoretical perspective, those observations must be used in order to conduct a systematic empirical test of the theory that is being posited.

Finally, it is worth noting that behaviouralists are sometimes criticised – with some justification – for failing to comprehend the 'big picture' of social and political transformation. That is to say, by emphasising the description and explanation of observable individual and group behaviour, behaviouralists underestimate the importance of 'more profound' social and political changes that might be taking place. For example, theorists who debate the ways in which 'the state' evolves under conditions of advanced capitalism (for example, Adorno, 1976; Habermas, 1976; Jessop, 1990) tend to deride behavioural analysis as being concerned merely with superficialities and with failing to offer a theory (or explanation) of significant social or political change. Behaviouralists respond by pointing out that broad-ranging social theories which purport to analyse significant social change must be based on some sort of empirical observation. If a writer wishes to argue, for example, that 'the capitalist state' is in 'crisis', then s/he must be able to specify what the observable referents of the crisis actually are. If there is a 'crisis' (some), people must be taking certain sorts of action or must be thinking certain things that enable the analyst to 'know' that a 'crisis' exists. Similarly, if some new form of social relationship is emerging (perhaps as a result of new patterns of economic production) then that new form of relationship must have some empirical referent or referents, otherwise, how can the analyst 'know' that the new form is indeed occurring?

Behaviouralists are entirely prepared to recognise that broad-ranging social and political theories are both possible and desirable. They merely insist that, if such theories are to be credible, they cannot be couched indefinitely at so high a level of abstraction as to render them incapable of being tested empirically. For behaviouralists, social and political theories are supposed to describe and explain that which can be observed – whether it involves stasis or change. Theories of social change only start to be interesting to behaviouralists when they: (1) specify the empirical referents that are used in order to make the judgement that profound change is indeed taking place; and (2) provide the empirical evidence which shows that these referents are indeed changing in the specified direction. Behaviouralism is entirely neutral as to what the 'referents' in any theory should be – this is the domain of the social theorist her/himself. To behaviouralists, however, a social 'theory' without clear empirical referents is nothing more than mere assertion.

The strengths of the behavioural approach: an example

While it is clear from the foregoing discussion that the behavioural approach can be subjected to serious criticism, it would be very wrong to infer that all examples of behavioural research are flawed. On the contrary, behavioural research at its best can make a considerable theoretical and empirical contribution to the understanding and explanation of social behaviour.

The strengths of the behavioural approach derive primarily from its advocates' determination to pursue forms of analysis that are *capable of replication.* Scholars working in the behavioural tradition are always concerned to establish that other researchers who make similar sets of assumptions as them and examine the same evidence would draw broadly similar conclusions. This need to ensure that research findings are capable of replication necessarily means that behaviouralists are obliged to be very clear in their specification of: (1) what it is that they are trying to explain; (2) the precise theoretical explanation that is being advanced; and (3) the way in which they are using empirical evidence in order to evaluate that theoretical explanation. The need for clarity of exposition in turn means that behaviouralists rarely enter into that most sterile area of academic debate: *What did writer X mean when s/he argued Y?* For behaviouralists, unless X makes it clear what s/he means in the first place, then X's work is clearly not capable of being replicated and argument Y is therefore likely to be treated with suspicion in any case.

The strengths of 'good' behavioural analysis can be illustrated by reference to Lars-Erik Cederman, Kristian Skrede Gleditsch and Halvard Buhaug's study of the effects of inequality and grievances on civil war (Cederman et al., 2013). Their analysis involves a combination of rigorous theorising, careful model specification and systematic empirical testing. It offers both a methodological advance in the way that the sources of civil war can be assessed and a substantive account of the way in which economic and political inequalities across different groups facilitates civil conflict between 1945 and 2009.

Cederman, Gleditsch and Buhaug (CGB) focus on a question that has concerned scholars, international relations analysts and human rights activists for many years: to what extent is inequality responsible for generating the sort of grievances that lead to conflict and civil war? It has long been recognised that anger (or grievance) about political exclusion and relative economic deprivation can lead to violence and that these effects can be particularly intense when they are aligned with ethnic cleavages. Paradoxically, quantitative studies of political violence have generally found very limited support for grievance-based explanations of political violence and civil war (Lichbach, 1989; Fearon and Laitin, 2003; Collier and Hoeffler, 2004). CGB argue that this is because previous studies have focused either on country-level data, which fail properly to measure ethnonationalism among the different groups within a given country, or on individual-level data, which fail to take proper account of group-level inequalities. CGB follow Stewart (2008b) in distinguishing between 'vertical' inequalities, which exist among different individuals and households, and 'horizontal' inequalities among established (typically ethnic) groups. The book develops improved measures of group-level, horizontal inequalities – which focus on the access that different ethnic groups have to (economic and political) state power. Using these measures, the research establishes the superiority of grievance-based explanations of civil war. Such explanations provide a better fit with the data and offer a powerful and convincing account of the occurrence and duration of civil war over the period between 1945 and 2009.

CGB begin their study with a theoretical analysis of the sequential linkages between horizontal inequalities and civil war. They summarise the stages in their theory as: **Horizontal Inequality**→Group Identification→Intergroup comparison→Evaluation of Injustice→Framing and Blaming→**Grievances**→Mobilisation→Rebel Claims and State Repression→**Civil War**.

In this schema, Horizontal Inequality between groups is an objective condition that, although directly observable, does not necessarily lead to Grievance and Civil War. Group inequalities matter only when there is a corresponding *Group Identification* that derives from classificatory schemes (such as in the census or in the country's major administrative units) and/or laws and/or 'cultural innovations' developed by scholars, writers and activists. These identifications in turn lead to *Intergroup Comparisons*, which can be constructed or even misperceived, but which activists articulate as observable economic and political inequalities between/among groups. The next stage is the *Evaluation or Identification of Injustice,* the process whereby the leadership of deprived groups specifies what is unfair about the status quo. This is followed by *Framing and*

Blaming, in which activists succeed in getting group members to blame the state for the perceived inequalities. In the *Mobilisation* phase, elites use pre-existing social networks to stimulate protest and opposition; mobilisation is considered by CGB to be generally other-regarding – an important counterweight to individual-level rational choice explanations of violence. The final stage of the grievance process is characterised as *Rebel Claims and State Repression*. Here, rebels typically present collective demands for a reduction in Horizontal Inequality and then seek to characterise any state reaction as the repression of legitimate grievances and protest.

CGB's core aim is to estimate as precisely as possible the effects of horizontal (group) inequalities on the onset of civil war. They are not able to test all of the stages of their theoretical model directly because the necessary data across a wide range of countries and years are not available. What they are able to do, however, is to specify what sort of statistical relationships should exist between or among the variables that they *can* observe and measure if their theory is correct. They are then able to analyse the data to establish whether or not these statistical relationships exist. They are able, in short, to test whether or not the empirical evidence is consistent with their theoretical claims.

Note that in all of this statistical exercise, CGB are dealing with what is a comparatively rare phenomenon (most countries most of the time do not experience civil war) and that their key purpose is to establish the *general* relationship between inequality and conflict onset (any given instance of civil war will always be the result both of general factors like inequality and of specific factors related to the particular historical context and the pivotal actors involved). This means that, in considering the effects of inequality, CGB are engaged in an enterprise similar to that conducted in epidemiological medical research. They are looking for relatively small statistical effects that significantly change the probability that the phenomenon of interest (in this case, civil war) will occur. This in turn places a considerable premium on the accurate estimation of statistical effects using models that are very carefully specified. For this reason, CGB develop a series of statistical models that allows them to apply 'controls' for a range of other factors (such as GDP/capita, population size, prior experience of conflict and degree of democracy) that could also affect the likelihood of civil war. This idea of applying controls is crucial to CGB's case. They need to take account of other potentially relevant factors in order to show that any observed correlation between inequality and violent conflict is not simply a 'coincidence' – that it represents a real causal effect.

CGB's first task is to assemble an evidence base that allows them to explore these various relationships, both across countries and over time. They use a variety of data sources, including their own collection of Ethnic Power Relations data through an expert survey; spatially disaggregated data on GDP (G-Econ), population (GRUMP) and ethnic settlement (Geo-EPR); and the frequently-used Uppsala Conflict Data

Program/Peace Research Institute Oslo Armed Conflict dataset. These are combined to construct a dataset in which 'conflict onset measures are mapped on the corresponding... ethnic group, provided that the rebel organisation expresses an aim to support the ethnic group and members of the group participate in combat' (CGB, p. 69). Each case in the dataset is a group-year. The main *dependent variable* – the phenomenon that CGB are trying to explain – is a dummy variable that reflects whether or not a group experienced an outbreak of conflict in a given year (=1) or not (=0). Cases where a single group is so dominant that there is no challenge from other groups (the dominant group cannot rebel against itself) or where a conflict has already begun are dropped from the analysis. This yields a dataset, in the first instance, with 29,533 group-year cases over the period 1945–2009.

The two principal independent or explanatory variables in CGB's analysis are (1) whether or not an ethnic group is excluded from political power and (2) whether it is economically excluded (that is relatively poor) or included (that is, relatively rich), comparing the per capita income in the settlement area of a group to the national average. By way of illustration, Table 2.1 shows the simple bivariate relationship between political inclusion/exclusion and the dependent variable, the onset of civil war. The figures confirm that civil war onset is a very rare phenomenon, with onsets occurring in only 0.7 per cent of cases. Crucially, where an ethnic group is excluded from political power in a country, civil war onset is more than twice as likely (it occurs in 0.86 per cent of cases) than in situations where a group is included in the country's power structure (here, civil war onset occurs in only 0.32 per cent of cases). The critical question is whether this simple association is still evident when statistical controls are applied for other relevant variables and, if it is, how far group political exclusion *changes the probability* that civil war will occur.

The empirical analysis that CGB pursue is developed in two broad parts. This is because their data on political exclusion cover the full period between 1945 and 2009 whereas their data on economic exclusion are available only since 1990. This means that while they can develop political exclusion models from 1945 onwards (with an N of over 29,000 cases), the effects of economic exclusion can be estimated only from 1990 (with an N of 5,377).

Table 2.1 *Relationship between conflict onset and group political inclusion/exclusion*

	Group Years	*Onsets*
Group Included	8,951	29 (0.32%)
Group Excluded	20,582	178 (0.86%)
Total	29,533	207 (0.70%)

Sig $p < .0001$
Source: CGB, p. 71.

Table 2.2 shows the core results of CGB's attempts to model the effects of group-level political exclusion ('Political Horizontal Inequality') on the onset of civil war. The table distinguishes between effects at two different levels – the *group level* (which refers to the characteristics of the groups analysed) and the *country level* (which refers to the characteristics of the countries in which each group is located). The key explanatory variable in the table is Group Excluded. All the other variables can be regarded as statistical controls that need to be included because previous research has indicated that they have important effects on the onset of civil war. At the group level, the controls comprise Group Downgraded (which measures whether or not the group has suffered a recent loss of political power), Relative Group Size (excluded large groups are more likely to be associated with conflict than excluded small ones) and Number of Previous Conflicts (groups with a record of past conflict are more likely to encounter conflicts today and in the future). The country-level controls are whether or not there is ongoing violent conflict in the country concerned, the country's relative wealth (measured by the log of GDP/capita), its relative size (measured by the log of population) and the level of democracy (as measured by the Scalar Index of Polities produced by Gates et al., 2006).

Table 2.2 *Political horizontal inequality and group-level onset of civil war*

	Core Model
Group-level variables	
Group Politically Excluded	1.22 (0.25)**
Group Politically Downgraded	1.43 (0.34)**
Relative Group Size	1.31 (0.39)**
Number of Previous Conflicts	0.72 (0.09)**
Country-level variables	
Ongoing conflict (lagged)	0.67 (0.30)*
GDP/capita (logged and lagged)	–0.23 (0.09)*
Population (logged and lagged)	0.01 (0.09)
Level of Democracy	0.60 (0.44)
Constant	–4.53 (1.05)**
Observations	26,306

Estimation by logistic regression; coefficients reported indicate the effect on the log odds of conflict occurring given a unit change in the independent variable.
* $p < .05$. Robust standard errors in parentheses
** $p < .01$

The key to understanding results of the sort shown in Table 2.2 is to look at the *significance* levels, the *signs* (positive or negative) and *relative magnitudes* of the various coefficients in the model. The significance levels indicate with what degree of certainty we can be sure that a particular statistical effect operates (or not). For example, the coefficients that have two asterisks (**) next to them are highly significant statistically: we can be 99 per cent certain that the independent variable indicated has an effect on the dependent variable that we are trying to explain. One asterisk means we can be 95 per cent certain that there is an effect. No asterisk means that a variable is not significant at conventionally accepted levels – in essence that the variable has no statistical effect on the dependent variable in question, in this case the onset of civil war. The signs on the coefficients indicate whether the independent variable concerned serves to increase (a positive sign) or decrease the dependent variable. Given the nature of the dependent variable here, a positive sign means that the chances of civil war increase; whereas a negative sign means that it falls – that the chances of civil war are reduced. Finally, the relative magnitudes of the different coefficients indicate which variables have the largest (and smallest) effects on the probability of civil war; though these effects are conditioned by the metrics in which the independent variables are measured.

Viewed in this light, it is clear that all but two of the predictor variables in Table 2.2 (Population and Level of Democracy) have significant effects on civil war onset. Country-level average income reduces the chances of civil war occurring (see the negative sign on the GDP/capita coefficient), but all the other variables have positive effects, that is, they all increase the probability that civil war will occur. This is particularly important, of course, in relation to political exclusion. Taking account of all the other variables specified in the model, politically excluded ethnic groups are significantly more likely than non-excluded groups to engage in civil war. CGB estimate that in fact, although the absolute magnitudes of the changes in probability are quite small, politically excluded groups are roughly four times more likely to engage in civil war (p = .008) than their non-excluded counterparts (p = .002).

One final point is worth making about CGB's empirical analyses. As noted above, the data they analyse cover the period 1945–2009. The final chapter of their book presents what is in effect an out-of-sample set of forecasts as to where, on the basis of their findings, civil war is most likely to occur in the period after 2009. Table 2.3 identifies the top-ten countries, in 2009, with the highest shares of politically excluded populations. Other things being equal, these are also, by implication, the countries most likely to experience the onset of civil war. The number-one position of Syria, which was plunged into civil war in 2011, speaks for itself; the remainder suggest a list of countries where pre-emptive action might be concentrated in future.

CGB's findings are important because they show that ethnic group-level inequality is an important underlying cause of civil conflict. This

Table 2.3 *Top-ten countries in 2009 with the highest shares of excluded populations*

Country	*Share of Excluded Population*
Syria	87.6%
Rwanda	84.8%
Democratic Republic of Congo	80.2%
Sudan	75.4%
Bhutan	75.0%
Congo	74.2%
Angola	70.5%
Bahrain	70.0%
Jordan	59.2%
Guatemala	52.0%

contrasts with the findings of a previous generation of quantitative studies (such as those conducted by Collier and Hoeffler, and by Fearon and Laitin) that concluded that inequality was much less important than the relative military capabilities of rebels versus the state. The findings in turn have important policy implications. Explanations rooted in relative military capabilities imply policy solutions focused on repression, deterrence and 'peace through military strength'. Explanations rooted in the grievances that derive from political and/or economic exclusion argue for policy solutions that address the exclusion in the first place.

CGB do not claim to have developed a definitive model of civil war onset across time and space. The implication of their empirical analysis is that further theoretical work is required – theorising which will in turn require further rounds of empirical evaluation. In all this they are engaging in a process of *retroduction* (Hanson, 1958). That is to say, their research involves a continuous interplay between theory and empirical testing, in which theory acts as a guide to empirical observation, operationalisation and testing, and in which empirical findings are subsequently used to modify, revise and refine theory.

Crucially, however, because CGB's research follows behaviouralist precepts, it is always possible for the dispassionate observer to know exactly what it is that they are arguing and to know exactly what evidence they are using to substantiate their theoretical claims. In the often vague and confused world of social science theorising and research – in which some writers seem almost deliberately to deploy obfuscation as a means of prideational realm these are qualities to be cherished and nurtured. CGB's work analysis can obviously be criticised – on the grounds, for example, that its empirical analysis does not fully operationalise all of the stages of the theoretical argument that underpins it. But, like all good behaviouralists, CGB at least present a clearly expressed target for would-be critics. For behaviouralists, it is better to be clear and (possibly) wrong than to be so impenetrable that other writers are obliged to debate the 'meaning' of what has been written.

Conclusion: the behavioural legacy in the twenty-first century

Among contemporary behaviouralists, it is widely accepted that theoretical analysis must almost always be the starting point for serious empirical enquiry. This is not to say that theories cannot be modified, enhanced or rejected on the basis of empirical observation. Rather, theory acts as a vehicle for distancing the analyst from the potentially overwhelming detail of what can be directly observed, so that abstract deductions can be made about the connections between different phenomena. In addition, theory not only generates testable hypotheses but also provides guidelines and signposts as to the sort of empirical evidence that should be gathered in the first place. In short, theory plays an indispensable role in post-behavioural empirical analysis. Many post-behaviouralists would go even further than this in the direction of epistemological relativism. It often used to be argued that there was an objective social reality 'out there' in the world of observation waiting to be discovered by 'scientific' analysis. This view is by no means so widely held in contemporary post-behavioural circles. Not only do post-behaviouralists accept that theory must play a central role in social analysis, they also recognise the possibility that different theoretical perspectives might generate different observations. Obviously, this possibility renders the task of subjecting rival theories to empirical testing rather more complicated. According to post-behaviouralists, however, it does not render the task any less necessary. Whatever observations a theory may engender, if it is to be considered a truly explanatory theory it must generate falsifiable predictions that are not contradicted by the available empirical evidence. All social enquiry is by definition about what people do, think or say. There is, ultimately, nothing else other than people doing, thinking and saying things – whatever fancy concepts analysts might use in order to characterise 'reality'. Post-behaviouralism allows all theories to make whatever characterisation of 'reality' they like. However, if they are to be considered explanatory, they must make statements about what people will do, think or say given certain conditions. There is no reason why each theory should not be evaluated on its own observational terms. But unless a theory can be evaluated – that is, tested empirically – on its own observational terms, post-behaviouralists are not prepared to grant it the status of explanatory theory in the first place.

For behaviouralists and their modern post-behavioural counterparts, the main purpose of social scientific enquiry is to explain behaviour at individual and aggregate levels. The central questions that behaviouralists ask are: *Why do individuals, institutional actors and nation states behave the way they do?* And what are the consequences of their actions? Embedded in the behaviouralist notion of explanation is the idea of causality. Although behaviouralists are aware that causality may be as much a reflection of the way we think about the world as it is of 'reality', they nonetheless insist that, unless a theory makes some sort of causal statement, it cannot be deemed to explain anything. They also insist that, if an explanation is to be believed, it must make empirically falsifiable predictions that can be tested against observation. While it is never possible definitively to establish that a particular causal relationship exists, it is possible to determine how far a particular set of empirical observations is consistent with a specific proposition that links different phenomena together. For behaviouralists, in short, believable explanatory theories must be capable of receiving, and must receive, empirical support. Post-behaviouralists argue, with considerable justification, that nearly all social researchers who work with empirical materials subscribe broadly to this view. In this sense, the legacy of behaviouralism among empirical researchers is enormous. In many respects, we are all post-behaviouralists now.

Further reading

The list that follows provides an outline of texts that both employ and offer critiques of the behavioural approach to social explanation.

- The best introduction to the philosophy of science in general, and to behaviouralism's place within it, is Chalmers (1986).
- For various critiques and related ideas, see Winch (1958), Rudner (1966) and Thomas (1979).
- On positivism and 'scientific' approaches to social explanation more generally, see Kuhn (1970), Hempel (1965, 1966), Hanson (1958), Halfpenny (1982) and Chalmers (1990).
- On the philosophical origins of behaviouralism, see Carnap (1936, 1950), Schlick (1974) and Ayer (1971).
- For a useful explanation of some of the terms used in these studies, see Lacey (1976).
- For justifications of quantitative approaches to the analysis of empirical evidence in the social sciences, see Blalock (1964, 1969, 1970, 1972) and King (1989).
- For a summary of the ways in which qualitative data can be employed within the 'behavioural-scientific' approach, see King et al. (1994).

Chapter 3

Rational Choice

ANDREW HINDMOOR AND BRAD TAYLOR

Introduction

The rational choice approach to the study of politics involves the application of the methods of economics to the study of politics. We say more about this in the following section, but two key assumptions which are of absolutely central importance to rational choice can be immediately highlighted: rationality and self-interest. No matter what aspect of politics they are looking at and no matter whose behaviour they are seeking to account for, rational choice theorists, with some exceptions discussed below, start by assuming that people can be relied upon to act in ways which best secure their goals and that these goals reflect their self-interest.

The plausibility of these assumptions can be challenged. But their utility cannot be doubted because *if* people are rational and self-interested it is possible to construct simple but potentially powerful explanations about political events. Rational choice theorists often assemble dizzyingly complex models of political behaviour replete with equations and mathematical appendices. But the explanatory work being done by the assumptions of self interest and rationality is nevertheless easy to grasp. Why did government ministers cut taxes shortly before an election? The rational choice theorist will be at one with the cynical voter in suggesting that the government cut taxes in order to boost its own chances of re-election and did so in the belief that voters reward governments who can deliver the appearance of prosperity.

Rational choice theorists were not the first to employ the assumptions of rationality and self-interest. A 'realist' tradition within international relations tracing its origins back to ancient Greece and Thucydides' *History of the Peloponnesian War* suggests (at its simplest) that states' actions are explicable in terms of a self-interested drive for power and that their leaders' commitments to justice, peaceful co-existence and international norms of behaviour are 'cheap talk'. Since the 1980s it is, however, rational choice theorists who have most zealously applied the assumptions of rationality and self-interest to the broadest range of political activities.

Rational choice theory was developed by a small number of economists and political scientists working in a handful of American universities in the 1960s. Having initially been confined to the pages of economics journals, rational choice entered the political science mainstream in the early 1980s and, for a time, looked like it might dominate the study of politics. Indeed, during this period rational choice grew in popularity to such an extent that it acquired a number of different names: rational choice theory; rational action theory; public choice theory (which its proponents regarded as a more specialised version of rational choice theory dealing specifically with the behaviour of governments); and social choice theory (a subset of rational choice theory which examines the properties of voting systems and the possibilities of aggregating individual preferences to form a social choice). One leading proponent, Dennis Mueller (1993: 174), went so far as to predict that 'rational choice and political science will be indistinguishable in another generation'; and that rational choice 'will be a field within economics, and will encompass all of political science'. This has not come to pass. Rather than rolling over and learning to think like rational choice theorists, many political scientists reacted to the arrival of rational choice by criticising the shallowness of its assumptions, its political biases and poor predictive record. Economics and politics, they argued, are very different spheres of human activity. Methods that might work for economics will not necessarily work for politics.

In recent years the intensity of the argument over rational choice has started to dissipate (Hindmoor, 2011). Rational choice theory no longer divides the discipline in quite the same way as it once did. One reason why is that rational choice theorists have, in practice, learnt how to relax and so make more palatable some of the assumptions they make. Increasingly, some of the most interesting work in political science does not consist of passionate defences of or attacks upon rational choice theory but, instead, exercises in theoretical 'border crossing' (Thelen, 1999) in which rational choice assumptions and arguments are deployed within and alongside other theoretical approaches (see Chapter 4 on institutionalism, for instance).

In this chapter we start by describing in more detail what the rational choice method consists of. To show what this method looks like and how, in practice, some of its assumptions can be softened and blended with other theoretical approaches we then look at the concept of collective action problems in relation to environmental politics. We conclude by listing some of the more salient criticisms which have been made of the rational choice approach and discuss how rational choice theorists have responded to them.

The methods of economics (and rational choice)

Rational choice theorists think like economists. How do economists think? The simplest answer is that they think deductively. They start from an assumption that people are self-interested and rational. They then go on to work out how, in any particular situation, people might behave given their expectations of how other rational and self-interested people are going to behave. Rationality here means instrumental rationality. People are able to identify the course of action which is most likely to allow them to achieve their goals.

To put some flesh on these bones, economists assume that people respond predictably to incentives. So, to work out what is going to happen in any particular situation you need to work out what incentives people face to behave in particular ways. To do this, economists usually construct models (theoretical, not literal) of particular situations and use these to generate predictions about how people will behave and what kinds of things will happen in particular situations. They can then test these models against real-world data. What is a model? People usually think of models as small objects which, in perfect scale, exactly represent some larger object. Think of model aeroplanes or model cities. Models of this sort are 'isomorphic' in the sense of having a high degree of correspondence with the object of which they are a model. Economic models are not models of this sort. They are, instead, attempts to pick out the *essential* features of some situation. Models are, in this sense, idealisations which, although simple and incomplete, can nevertheless help us understand something about that world. Ariel Rubinstein (2012: 16) sees formal models as 'fables' designed to impart some generally useful lesson. A model, like a story, 'hovers between fantasy and reality ... it can be free from irrelevant details and unnecessary diversions.' According to this view, we learn from rational choice models in the same sense that we learn from literature: 'We will take the tale's message with us when we return from the world of fantasy to the real world, and apply it judiciously when we encounter situations similar to those portrayed in the tale.'

A lot of economic models are going to tell us things that are pretty intuitively obvious. What happens when the price of a product goes up? Demand goes down. What happens when governments announce plans to raise inheritance taxes? More people give gifts to their relatives before they die in the hope of avoiding the tax. But the most interesting economic models show us how incentive structures sometimes lead people to behave in unexpected and often suboptimal ways. Take the issue of car safety. Cars are now built to far higher safety standards than they once were – with features like air bags and crumple zones often coming as standard even in economy cars. At the same time, most countries now require drivers and passengers to wear seat belts. So does this mean we are all a lot safer? Not quite. In the mid-1970s Sam Peltzman, a professor of economics at the University of Chicago, argued that people have an incentive to react to the introduction of a new safety measure or rules by acting in an increasingly risky manner, therefore negating the benefit of the change. If people buy a new and much safer car in which they are much less likely to be killed or seriously injured if they crash, they may suddenly decide to drive more quickly and aggressively in order to get to their destination quicker. This is potentially bad news for pedestrians and cyclists whose chances of surviving a collision are going to depend a lot more upon the speed of the car hitting them than the number of safety features it has protecting its driver.

Or think about consumer and business behaviour. At the start of a recession when confidence is low, growth is falling and jobs are being lost, consumers and businesses have an incentive to rethink their spending plans. Fearing for their own jobs, consumers may well shelve plans to buy a new and safer car in favour of saving more money for a rainy day. Fearing that consumers are going to save rather than spend, business mangers might then cancel proposed investments. From an individual perspective, such behaviour makes perfect sense. It would be pretty foolish not to adjust your behaviour when the world around you is changing. But as John Maynard Keynes argued in *The General Theory of Employment, Interest and Money*, published in the midst of the Great Depression in 1936, if everyone behaves in this way it will simply result in lower consumption, more job losses and a vicious circle of economic contraction. Skip forward a few generations and critics of austerity argue that Keynes' paradox of thrift, as it is known, tells us why it was a mistake for so many governments to cut public expenditure when the global economy was faltering in the aftermath of the 2008 financial crisis. In a recession government needs to spend more to compensate for lower spending in the private sector and to boost confidence. Others disagree. The theory of 'expansionary fiscal contraction' holds that governments can actually kick-start economic recoveries by cutting expenditure, because people will think that cutting expenditure now will result in lower taxes tomorrow – so, encouraging them to spend more money. The disagreement here is as much political as it is economic. But what economists on different sides of this debate will agree is that in their everyday lives, people respond rationally and predictably to incentives and that we can best understand what is happening in the world by building models and testing those models against available data.

Precisely because economics can be defined as a method rather than simply as a subject matter, economics has always had an imperialist edge. Another Chicago economist, the Nobel Prize–winning Gary Becker, first made a name for himself in the 1960s by constructing economic models of marriage, child-rearing and racial discrimination. More recently, Becker's former student Steven Levitt has taken the assumption that 'incentives are the cornerstone of modern life' (Levitt and Dubner, 2005: 11) to explain the behaviour of, among others, drug dealers, prostitutes and terrorists in the bestselling series *Freakonomics*, *Superfreakonomics* and *Think Like a Freak*.

So it should not surprise us that the method of economics has come to be applied to the study of politics. In the following section, we examine one particular area of work: collective action. But the important point to make here is that rational choice theory can be applied to any subject within political science – voting, party competition, security dilemmas in international relations theory, conflict resolution, interest-group lobbying, redistribution, regulation, constitutional change, legislative bargaining, intergovernmental treaty negotiations or the setting of policy agendas.

The logic of collective action

If individuals are rational it makes intuitive sense that groups, being composed of individuals, will also be rational. If a group shares a common goal which everyone agrees is worthwhile, we might expect everyone to contribute to the realisation of this goal. Experience teaches us that this is not always the case, however, and rational choice theory helps explain why.

When waiting for your luggage at an airport, you will normally find a crowd of people packed around the baggage carousel. At the end of a journey this can be quite irritating because it would be a lot easier to spot and then grab your bag if everyone took just two steps back. But there is a problem here. Anyone who takes a step back when the others are already at the front will suddenly find themselves with a poor view and a long wait. Meanwhile, someone who pushes forward a few inches to get an extra bit of space will actually find themselves at an advantage. But of course, when one person pushes forward other people's views will be obscured and they will respond by also pushing forward and, in the end, nobody will be any better off. What is happening here is a collective action problem. No one person has an incentive to act in a way in which it would be best for everyone to act.

Situations like this are the subject of Mancur Olson's (1965) classic work *The Logic of Collective Action* which attempts in a general and abstract way to explain why and predict when such collective action problems arise. A group seeking a collective benefit requires the participation of its members. This could be active participation (signing a petition, joining a protest, doing your share of the cleaning of a shared living space) or passive compliance (as in the case of passengers not crowding the carousel). In either case, individuals need to engage in action which is costly to themselves individually in order to secure a benefit for the group of which they are a part. The danger here is that individuals will perceive their own effort as having little effect on the provision of the collective good. Each passenger concludes that their individual decision of whether or not to step towards the carousel will have little or no effect on the number of other passengers choosing to step forward. Individuals might then attempt to enjoy the benefits of the collective good without contributing to its production – that is, they might 'free ride'. Of course, if too many free ride in this way, the group benefit is not produced. Individual incentives fail to produce the optimal outcome for the group, even if everybody would in principle be willing to do their share in exchange for a promise that others will also do their share.

A useful way of illustrating the problem is by using game theory, a branch of mathematics which allows us to consider strategic interaction among self-interested and rational agents. The most celebrated example in game theory, the prisoner's dilemma, provides a simple illustration of collective action problems. Suppose a pair of criminals, Jake and Keith, are hauled into a police station on suspicion of armed robbery and placed in separate cells. The police lack the evidence for a conviction and require the confession of at least one of the accomplices. If neither prisoner confesses, the police have enough evidence to convict the pair for a lesser crime, for which they will each serve one year in prison. Sensing the need for a confession, the police offer Jake a deal. If he blames everything on Keith and Keith refuses to cooperate, Jake will be allowed to go free and the police will throw the book at Keith, giving him four years in prison. The catch, the police say, is that Keith will be offered exactly the same deal and if they both confess they will both get three years in prison.

What should Jake and Keith do if they want to minimise their prison terms? The prisoner's dilemma is a model allowing us to answer this question. Being a rational choice model it assumes that the people whose behaviour is being modelled are self-interested and rational.

Jake can choose between confessing and not confessing, and his choice determines whether we end up in the top or bottom row in Figure 3.1. Keith has the same options, and his choice determines whether we end up in the left or right column of the figure. The number in the bottom of each cell is the prison sentence Jake serves with this outcome; the number on the top is the sentence Keith serves. Thus if Jake confesses and Keith does not confess, the result is that Jake serves no sentence and Keith serves four years. If both Keith and Jake are interested only in minimising their prison sentence, both believe that the other is similarly motivated, and both trust the police to stick to the deal, then we can use game theory to predict the outcome in this situation.

Jake needs to consider the sentence he will serve given the decision Keith makes. If Keith does not confess (meaning the result will be one of the two cells on the left), Jake can either stay quiet and serve one year in prison or confess and go free. If Keith confesses (meaning the result will

Figure 3.1 *The prisoner's dilemma*

		Keith	
		Don't Confess	Confess
Jake	Don't confess	1 1	0 4
	Confess	4 0	3 3

be one of the two cells on the right), Jake can either stay quiet and serve the full four years or confess and serve three years. No matter what Keith does, Jake has an incentive to confess. In the parlance of game theory, confessing is his dominant strategy. Since Keith faces exactly the same situation, the same reasoning can be used to show that confessing is also his dominant strategy. Thus if the above payoffs accurately represent Keith and Jake's preferences, we know that the outcome will be that Jake and Keith both confess and serve three years in prison (the confess, confess cell – 3,3).

Both Jake and Keith are rationally pursuing their interests, but the outcome is worse for both of them than one of the available alternatives – the don't confess, don't confess cell – 1,1 – where both stay quiet and serve only one year in prison. If Jake and Keith could somehow reach a binding agreement to stay quiet, both would be better off. A non-binding agreement is, however, not going to be enough here because neither Jake nor Keith will have an incentive to stick to it. Keith may well agree to keep quiet hoping to influence Jake's decision, but it will remain in Keith's interest to confess no matter what Jake does. Non-binding agreements are simply 'cheap talk'.

The story about Jake and Keith is a very specific scenario, but the underlying logic of the prisoner's dilemma can be applied to other situations. A large group of people living in a dictatorship may share a collective interest in securing a transition to democracy. But this does not necessarily mean that it is in any one person's interest to be the first to take to the streets in protest. In a crisis situation, countries may all share a joint interest in defusing the tension. But this does not mean that it is necessarily in one country's interest to unilaterally demobilise. In the midst of an economic crisis, people may share an interest in maintaining consumption and investment. But this does not mean that it is necessarily in any one person's interest to spend more.

Collective action poses a problem. But some collective action problems get solved. Why? Olson distinguishes three broad types of group: privileged, intermediate and latent groups. Privileged groups are those in which at least one member values the collective good highly enough to be willing to pay the full cost of providing the collective good themselves regardless of whether anyone else contributes to it. Within international relations theory, for example, it has been argued that 'hegemonic powers' such as Britain in the nineteenth century and the USA in the latter part of the twentieth century and perhaps still today, had such a stake in the maintenance of the global order from which they benefited that they were willing to intervene to resolve collective action problems such as the policing of international sea lanes to ensure free trade (Gilpin, 2001: 93–97). Olson predicts that privileged groups will produce collective goods, since no collective action problem arises.

Intermediate groups lack any individual willing to provide the collective good unilaterally, but the contribution of each individual has a significant and perceptible effect on the provision of the collective good.

This would seem to be the situation facing passengers waiting at a baggage carousel. Nobody can enforce the orderly outcome unilaterally, but passengers are easily able to tell when another person is stepping forward and each passenger stepping forward produces a minor but perceptible inconvenience for others. Olson makes no general prediction about whether intermediate groups will be successful in securing collective goods, but insists that success will depend on formal or informal coordination of some sort. We will discuss the circumstances in which that coordination is most likely to arise presently.

Finally, a latent group is one in which no single individual's action has any perceptible effect on others. Consumers in an economy teetering on the edge of recession are in a latent group. Even if one of the wealthiest of people decides to spend rather than save, this will not make any appreciable difference to aggregate demand and the health of the economy. Olson predicts that latent groups will not be able to produce collective goods except through the use of 'selective incentives' – rewards or punishments which are tied to individual contributions rather than to the group as a whole.

Collective action and the environment

Protection of the environment often poses a collective action problem. In a classic article 'The Tragedy of the Commons', the ecologist Garrett Hardin (1968) offers the example of a pasture on which herdsmen are free to graze their cattle. Each herdsman benefits by using the pasture, but in doing so depletes the pasture for all other herders. By exploiting the commons each herdsman thus receives a sizeable personal benefit while imposing a small cost on everyone else. The policy problem to which Hardin wanted to direct people's attention in writing about the tragedy of the commons was overpopulation. But the logic of his argument – which is essentially a variant of the prisoner's dilemma game – can be applied to other environmental problems such as climate change.

The atmosphere is a common which, in the absence of effective regulation, individuals can use to dispose of greenhouse gases. By emitting carbon into the atmosphere, each individual receives a benefit but imposes a cost on everybody else in the world. This is a classic collective action problem. Each person would be willing to reduce their emissions in an exchange for a similar commitment from everyone else, but without some way of forcing such an agreement, promises are simply 'cheap talk'. Rational choice theorists would predict that self-interested politicians will be happy to talk about the existential threat posed by climate change but will seek to offload the costs on to other countries of either reducing emissions or adapting to climate change, and that this will either result in the failure of climate talks or the conclusion of 'sham' agreements which contain endless loopholes allowing countries to miss their targets and have no enforcement mechanisms.

Rational choice accounts of collection action problems might seem to offer a counsel of despair. But not all efforts to solve global collective action problems have failed. As a result of the 1987 Montreal Protocol, the once-pressing problem of ozone depletion in the earth's upper atmosphere has, for example, been effectively managed. On the face of things, global warming and ozone depletion look like similar problems with similarly grim prognoses for collective action. As with global warming, ozone depletion is a global problem. The emission of chlorofluorocarbon (CFC) into the atmosphere as a by-product of economic activity causes environmental harms, and like greenhouse gas (GHG) emissions, the location of these harms is unrelated to the location of the emissions.

Why, then, has global action been so much more successful for ozone depletion than global warming? One important difference here is the concentration of emissions. When the Montreal Protocol was ratified, 78 per cent of CFC emissions came from just 12 countries. Indeed, the US Environmental Protection Agency calculated that the USA's share of the benefits of cutting emissions would be greater than the cost of cutting *global* emissions by half. To use Olson's term, the group of countries emitting CFCs was 'privileged' because the USA valued the collective good of reduced CFC emissions so highly that it was willing to bear the cost of cutting its emissions unilaterally. GHG emissions, on the other hand, are much less concentrated. China is responsible for around 25 per cent of emissions and the USA around 15 per cent. All countries make significant contributions to climate change and unilateral action by even the largest emitters would have only a modest effect on global emissions (Sandler, 2004: 221–225). The situation here is not hopeless, however. No single country could stabilise climate change by unilaterally drastically cutting its own emissions. But almost every country could make some difference by cutting its emissions and, just as importantly, could be *seen* to be making a difference. In the case of climate change, countries find themselves in an intermediate group in which successful resolution of the collective action problem requires coordination and cooperation.

In what circumstances are actors within an intermediate group most likely to successfully coordinate their actions in order to jointly provide a collective good? One interesting finding from game theory here is that, even within the structure of the prisoner's dilemma game, people can learn to cooperate with each other when they know that the game they are playing is not a one-off. If players are 'conditional cooperators' – that is, if they cooperate only when others are also cooperating – and if people know that they are going to be playing the same game over a prolonged period they will find that they have an incentive to cooperate in order to increase the likelihood of cooperation from others in the future (Hindmoor and Taylor, 2015: 42–43).

In a series of case studies of commons management, Elinor Ostrom (see 1990, 2012) examined how people operating within intermediate groups can sometimes learn to cooperate to preserve common pool resources such as fisheries and scarce water supplies by, for example, developing rotas which specify on which days people are allowed to use a shared resource or quotas limiting how much any one person can take. She also found that time makes a difference. People are more likely to cooperate when they expect to have to interact with each other time and again. What also matters here is whether people can relatively easily monitor whether other people are abiding by any agreements which have been reached. Another focus of her work was on norms of behaviour which operate alongside economic motivations to shape individual behaviour. In a tight-knit community in which people must not only work but live alongside each other, the threat of being ostracised is a powerful deterrent to free riding. In Olson's terms, norms operate as a type of selective incentive. But this is not simply a matter of self-interest. People are also likely to want to cooperate with each other in situations in which they believe others are cooperating because they will want to do the right thing.

What's wrong with rational choice theory?

Rational choice theory provokes strong reactions. Its proponents regard it as having developed insightful, rigorous, parsimonious explanations of political outcomes which other parts of the discipline have not come close to matching. Rational choice theory's opponents argue that it has, at best, been used to restate what everyone already knows in a language few can understand and, at worst, that it has propagated entirely bogus explanations and legitimised disastrous policy choices. Here, we describe six objections.

1. *People are not rational* – Rational choice theory views people as being rational to the extent that they select the best possible means to achieve their goals. But, in practice, people may not always know what consequences of their actions are going to be and so can act in ways that, ultimately, they or other people realise are detrimental to their interests. People do not always have perfect information. They operate in a world of limited information and, sometimes, of radical uncertainty in which, to paraphrase the former US Secretary of State for Defense Donald Rumsfeld, they do not know what they do not know.

   Yet while recognising that individuals may not always have all the information they need to make the best possible decision, rational choice theorists maintain that people always make the best possible use of the information they *do* have. There is, however, a further problem here. People are not always very good at making decisions. Behavioural economists have repeatedly shown that real humans consistently act in suboptimal ways by, for example, heavily discounting the future and being overly influenced in their decisions by the way in which problems are framed (for a recent overview, see Kahneman, 2011). If people behave irrationally, critics argue, rational choice theory is unlikely to make accurate predictions or provide insight into real-world behaviour.

Rational choice theorists can, however, respond by arguing that careful decision-making is itself costly and that poor decision-making can sometimes actually be a rational choice. By gathering information and deliberating on the best course of action, people are able to make better decisions (i.e. make choices which are going to best realise their interests). But searching for information and deliberating about what choices to make are costly activities in terms of time and effort, so a rational person would weigh the value of a better decision against these costs when deciding whether or not to spend time becoming informed. Attempting to make every minor decision in a perfectly optimal way would be highly irrational, since time and cognitive capacity are scarce resources which should be directed to their most valuable use. People can, in this sense, be rationally irrational (Caplan, 2007).

2. *People are not selfish* – A second criticism of rational choice theory is that people are not consistently selfish. Indeed, critics argue that one of the things which distinguishes politics as a sphere of activity from economics is precisely people's willingness to act on the basis of their commitments to other people as well as to general principles of fairness and justice. Politics is frequently a grubby business in which there are tactical advantages in breaking promises and betraying friendships. But politics can sometimes also bring out the best in people. In accounting for apparently altruistic behaviour, rational choice theorists can always impute a self-interested motive. Politicians who are prepared to go to jail for their beliefs are simply seeking a reputation for trustworthiness. Activists who risk their lives to campaign for a cause are simply seeking camaraderie and the adrenaline rush of a violent confrontation. But there is a danger of creating 'as if' explanations here. It is significant that, in experimental settings where people have been deliberately left facing a clear choice between self-interest and fairness, self-interest does not always win out.

   In the ultimatum game two players must decide how to divide a sum of money which has been given to them. The first player makes a proposal about how to divide the money and the second player can either accept or reject this offer. If the second player rejects it then neither player receives anything. If the second player accepts the proposed division the money is split accordingly. The game is only played once and is usually played anonymously. If you are the first player what kind of an offer should you make? If you are entirely selfish you should propose giving yourself 99 per cent of the money so leaving the second player with the choice between getting one percent and getting nothing. But, in practice, the *average* offer made to the second person is actually between 30 and 40 per cent, while many propose a 50–50 split. Furthermore, many of the players who are left with a choice between getting almost nothing and getting nothing choose nothing so as to prevent the first player from getting almost everything (for a recent review, see Mousazadeha and Izadkhah, 2015).

Self-interest remains the standard assumption within rational choice because many of its practitioners continue to believe that people really are self-interested and because it is easier to make definite predictions about how people are going to behave when using this assumption. But rational choice theorists might argue that it is perfectly possible to practice rational choice theory without assuming self-interest. Indeed, several economists and rational choice theorists have included 'other-regarding' preferences into rational choice models, assuming that rational actors can weigh up their material interests against altruism, spite and envy (see, generally, Brennan and Hamlin, 2000).

3. *Rational choice theory ignores individual agency and ideas* – Within political science arguments about the relative significance of structure (underlying conditions) and agency (individuals' capacity to achieve their goals and affect their environment) have given way to more nuanced debates about the interplay between these two factors (see Chapter 12 of this volume). It would be a brave person who today argued that agency is all that matters or that structure is all that matters in explaining political processes and outcomes. Yet rational choice theorists come close to doing just that.

   The problem here is not that rational choice theorists ignore structure or agency. Rational choice theorists recognise that structure affects agency by structuring incentives. At the same time, rational choice institutionalists recognise that agents can consciously create and reform institutions in order to change those incentives (see Chapter 4). The problem instead comes with the way in which agency is conceived. Rational choice theorists assume that groups of actors have the same exogenously given, fixed and self-interested goals which they pursue in the same rational manner. Placed in the same situation, these groups can be relied upon to make the same choices in the same way that different pocket calculators can be relied upon to provide the same answer to a question. The incentive structure agents confront completely determines their behaviour and this has the effect of eliminating the possibility of *individual* choice and active agency.

   In ignoring the possibility of *individual* agency, rational choice is also in danger of ignoring the causal significance of ideas. One obvious way in which agents differ from each other is in terms of the ideas they consciously or subconsciously possess. People have different *normative* ideas about how they ought to behave and how the world ought to be and these ideas lead people to behave in different ways. Of course, we may sometimes be able to explain the normative ideas people possess in terms of their interests. People often believe what it is in their self-interest to believe. But it is not plausible to argue that ideas are always and everywhere explicable in terms of interests. Furthermore, individuals also have different *empirical* ideas about how the world works and these differences can lead people to make contrasting calculations about which course of action *is* in their self-interest (Hay, 2002: 208–209). The bottom line here is that agents do not always act in the same way when placed in the same situation.

Critics make a number of additional criticisms.

4. *Rational choice has a very poor empirical record* – It is argued that, in practice, rational choice actually has a very poor empirical record; that many rational choice explanations have not been tested; and that those which have been tested 'have either failed on their own terms or garnered theoretical support for propositions that, on reflection, can only be characterized as banal' (Green and Shapiro, 1994: 6).
5. *Rational choice depends upon equilibrium explanations* – Critics also argue that rational choice depends upon equilibrium explanations in a world which consistently demonstrates non-equilibrium properties. Equilibrium is a stable outcome. Natural scientists conceive of equilibrium as arising when physical forces interact in such a way that a process is either endlessly repeated (the movement of planets around the sun) or comes to a rest (a hot drink eventually cooling to room temperature). Economists and rational choice theorists conceive of equilibrium as arising when individuals interact in such a way that no individual has any reason to change their actions. Rational choice theorists search for and rely upon the notion of equilibrium because the identification of some outcome as equilibrium provides them with an explanation of why that outcome might be expected to arise. Think back to the prisoner's dilemma. Keith and Jake both confessing is an equilibrium because no matter what the other person does each will find it in their interests to confess if this game is only played once. Because we know the outcome is an equilibrium we can predict that it will occur. But critics argue that the most interesting economic and political processes are frequently characterised by sudden, unexpected and cascading changes which destroy an existing equilibrium and that in spending all its time searching for equilibrium outcomes rational choice entirely misses this feature of the world. Think about events such as the 2007/08 financial crisis, the sudden 'punctuated' arrival of a major issue on the policy agenda or the outbreak of an armed conflict. All of these are interesting and ought to command the attention of political scientists in part because they are profoundly disruptive of equilibrium.
6. *Rational choice is a political project* – Finally, critics argue that behind the technical veil of models and empirical testing rational choice is a stridently political project which uses the assumption of self-interest to venerate competitive markets and denigrate government.

From imperialism to peaceful co-existence

Rational choice theorists can stand and fight their corner on each of these points – arguing that people really are rational and self-interested (and that experimental results which suggest otherwise are misleading because they ignore the costs of gathering and processing information); that agents do, basically, behave in similar ways when confronted with similar incentive structures; that, increasingly, rational choice explanations have been tested against the empirical evidence and shown to perform better than any of their political science rivals; that departures from equilibrium are self-correcting; and that markets really do outperform government.

There is a more productive alternative here. We can view rational choice as an 'organising perspective' (Dowding, 2015) which generates useful insights into the situations in which political actors find themselves and must make choices but which can be refined and supplemented in order to provide more rounded and thorough explanations of particular events. Rational choice models can be refined by either adding additional layers of complexity to initial models (moving from one-shot prisoner's dilemma games to repeated games) or by relaxing the assumption that people are entirely self-interested and completely rational. Increasingly, the most sophisticated and compelling rational choice models of collective action (and of party competition and a range of other political activities) assume that people have 'mixed' motives (that they are partly driven by their own interests and partly by a commitment to particular political causes) and that they operate in an uncertain world in which it is costly to acquire information. Elinor Ostrom's work on the preservation of common pool resources assumes that individuals are driven by social norms and calculations of self-interest. Work of this kind opens the way for the kind of 'border crossing' activity we heralded in the opening part of this chapter in which rational choice is melded with and deployed alongside other theoretical approaches to resolve specific empirical puzzles. Rational choice sets out to conquer political science. But there is no reason why rational choice insights cannot be used alongside institutionalist (see Chapter 4), constructivist (see Chapter 5; and, on collective action narratives, Mayer, 2014), feminist (see Chapter 6 and Driscoll and Krook, 2012) or even Marxist (see Chapter 7 and Elster, 1985) approaches to political science.

Conclusion

Neoclassical economics provides a framework for analysis and a set of tools which have radically increased our understanding of market behaviour. Rational choice theorists have applied these tools to political behaviour and, though the transformation of political science has been far less complete, it has provided some insights on important political questions.

Rational choice theory is not going to colonise the rest of political science. But neither is it simply a passing intellectual fad, and for this reason disputes between rational choice theorists and proponents of other approaches are likely to persist. This is not necessarily a bad thing. Political scientists often express concern about the lack of a theoretical consensus within their discipline. But it is one of the valuable lessons of economics and of rational choice theory that monopolies are inefficient and that competition, while often painful, is beneficial. Vigorous academic debate can identify points of weakness and act as a spur for theoretical and empirical innovation. This is a two-way street. Rational choice theorists have refined (and need to continue to refine) their arguments by, when necessary, relaxing the assumptions of self-interest and perfect rationality. At the same time, critics need to recognise both that rational choice has moved on and that simple insights about how collective action problems can arise when nobody has an incentive to act in ways which are in everyone's interest can illuminate our understanding of complex political events and provide the starting point for more detailed research work.

Further reading

- For a basic introduction to the logic and applications of rational choice theory which assumes no prior knowledge of the subject, see Hindmoor and Taylor (2015).
- For a review of the argument about the value of rational choice theory within politics, see Hindmoor (2011).
- For a more detailed but still accessible examination of the philosophy and methods of rational choice theory, see Eriksson (2011).

Chapter 4

Institutionalism

VIVIEN LOWNDES

Until the 1950s the dominance of the institutional approach within political science was such that its assumptions and practices were rarely specified, let alone subject to sustained critique. Methodological and theoretical premises were left unexamined behind a veil of academic 'common sense'. Outside of political theory, the core activity within political science was the description of constitutions, legal systems and government structures, and their comparison over time and across countries. Institutionalism *was* political science. But this traditional form of institutionalism found itself under attack from a range of quarters. Rather than taking the functions of political institutions at face value, behaviouralists sought to explain how and why individuals acted as they did in 'real life' (see Chapter 2). The behavioural revolutionaries, as Goodin and Klingemann (1996: 11) argue, 'were devoted to dismissing the formalisms of politics – institutions, organizational charts, constitutional myths and legal fictions'. A generation later, rational choice theorists sought to explain politics in terms of the interplay of individuals' self-interest (see Chapter 3). From another direction, neo-Marxist accounts focused upon the role of 'systemic power' (deriving from capital/labour relations) in structuring political action and the organisation of government (see Chapter 7). 'Modern' political scientists of all colours seemed intent upon debunking the institutionalist certainties of their forebears. The clear message was that there was much, much more to politics than the formal arrangements for representation, decision-making and policy implementation.

By the end of the 1980s, however, institutionalism was making a re-appearance as the internal limitations of the new approaches became clear. A 'new institutionalism' has emerged as a reaction to the 'under-socialised' character of what had become the dominant approaches in the discipline; both behaviourism and rational choice theory had dismissed institutions as no more than the simple aggregation of individual preferences. The new institutionalists asserted that 'the organisation of political life makes a difference' (March and Olsen, 1984: 747). Institutions were back in fashion, although not necessarily in their old guise. The 'new institutionalism' operates with a more expansive (yet more sophisticated) definition of its subject matter and with more explicit (if diverse) theoretical frameworks. Political institutions are no longer equated with political organisations; 'institution' is understood more broadly to refer to a 'stable, recurring pattern of behaviour' (Goodin, 1996: 22). The new institutionalists are concerned with the informal conventions of political life as well as with formal constitutions and organisational structures. New attention is paid to the way in which institutions embody values and power relationships, and to the obstacles as well as the opportunities that confront institutional design. Crucially, new institutionalists concern themselves not just with the impact of institutions upon individuals, but with the *interaction* between institutions and individuals. As March and Olsen (2006: 4) explain, institutionalism is a 'set of theoretical ideas and hypotheses concerning the relations between institutional characteristics and political agency, performance, and change'.

The chapter begins by teasing out the implicit theory and methods of the traditional institutional approach within political science. Next the chapter explores 'what's new?' about the 'new institutionalism'. It identifies core characteristics and key distinctions among the different new institutionalist positions. The chapter considers the challenges facing new institutionalism, not least the charge that its many variants are based upon fundamentally incompatible premises. The chapter concludes by arguing that the multi-theoretic character of the new institutionalism may actually prove to be its greatest asset.

The 'traditional' institutional approach

Rod Rhodes has described institutionalism as the 'historic heart' of the subject and 'part of the toolkit of every political scientist' (1997: 5, 64). B. Guy Peters (1999: 2) characterises the methodology of traditional institutionalists as 'that of the intelligent observer attempting to describe and understand the political world around him or her in non-abstract terms'. The silence regarding theory and methods actually tells us something about the approach – that it was generally unreflective on issues of theory and method, took 'facts' (and values) for granted, and flourished as a kind of 'common sense' within political science (Lowndes, 1996: 181).

Critics of traditional institutionalism point to its limitations in terms of both scope and method. It was concerned (of course) with the institutions of government, and yet operated with a restricted understanding of its subject matter. The focus was upon formal rules and organisations rather than informal conventions; and upon official structures of *government* rather than the broader institutional constraints associated with *governance* (outside as well as within the state). Critics have sought to 'out' the assumptions that lurked behind the descriptive method and disdain for theory. Peters (1999: 6–11) characterises the 'proto-theory' of old institutionalism as: normative (concerned with 'good government'), structuralist (structures determine political behaviour), historicist (the central influence of history), legalist (law plays a major role in governing) and holistic (concerned with describing and comparing whole systems of government). John (1998: 40–41) points to a strong functionalist tendency – that is, the assumption that particular institutions are the 'manifestations of the functions of political life', or 'necessary for a democracy'. For the modern reader, the old institutionalists' claims of objectivity and 'science' often sit uneasily alongside their polemical idiom and desire to foster the 'Westminster model' (see Box 4.1).

Rhodes (1995: 49) counsels, however, against setting up a 'straw man'. Many of the 'old' institutionalists adopted a far more sophisticated form of analysis than their critics imply. Herman Finer in the 1930s went out of his way to show that the study of constitutions extended far beyond written documents (Finer, 1932). Nevil Johnson's work in the 1970s reveals a concern with procedural norms as well as formal structures (Johnson, 1975). Exponents of the historical-comparative method from Woodrow Wilson onwards understood that the values underlying one system become clearer when contrasted with another.

Box 4.1 The traditional institutional approach in action

Looking at political institutions in the USA, Britain, France and Germany, Finer (1932) eschewed a country-by-country analysis (more typical of his time) and instead compared institution-by-institution (e.g. parties, electorates, civil service, judiciaries) across countries. Representing an enlightened version of the traditional approach, he grounded his analysis in an understanding of the state as the 'monopoly of coercive power'.

Woodrow Wilson (1956), himself an early president of the USA, studied the problems of 'divided government' that were beginning to affect the presidential system, and analysed the possibilities presented by parliamentary government as an alternative.

Studying the emergence and functioning of nationalised industries in Britain, Robson (1960) provided a comprehensive account of all aspects of the organisation and management of public corporations. Despite the critical climate of the time, Robson was determined to defend the public corporations as 'an outstanding contribution to public administration', and provided prescriptions as to their future reform.

Polsby's (1975) famous essay on legislatures was typical of the reductionist strain of institutionalist analysis; it focused upon 'how a peculiar form, the legislature, embeds itself in a variety of environmental settings'.

Sources: Rothstein (1996), Rhodes (1997), Peters (1999), Lowndes and Roberts (2013)

The emergence of the 'new institutionalism'

In the mid-1980s James March and Johan Olsen, who coined the term 'new institutionalism', observed that political institutions had 'receded in importance from the position they held in the earlier theories of political scientists'(1984: 734). For behaviourists, institutions are simply the aggregation of individual roles, statuses and learned responses. For the first generation of rational choice theorists, institutions were no more than an accumulation of individual choices based on utility-maximising preferences (Shepsle, 1989: 134). March and Olsen (1984: 747) asserted that political institutions played a more autonomous role in shaping political outcomes than was acknowledged by these approaches. They made a deceptively simple, yet at the time arresting, claim: 'The organisation of political life makes a difference.' By way of illustration, March and Olsen (1984: 738) argued that:

> The bureaucratic agency, the legislative committee, the appellate court are arenas for contending social forces, but they are also collections of standards operating procedures and structures that define and defend interests. They are political actors in their own right.

March and Olsen's proposition prompts fascinating questions – about what constitutes a 'political institution', about the way institutions 'do their work' (how can they 'define and defend interests'?) and about the capacity of individual actors to influence the shape and functioning of relatively 'autonomous' political institutions. The questions are of particular interest at a time of rapid institutional change. How have institutional innovations such as privatisation shaped public service outcomes and debates about the future of the welfare state across Europe? How can the UK and Spanish governments contend with the identities and interests that have found expression in, and are increasingly defended by, the devolved administrations of Scotland or Catalonia? How can the secular institutions of France's Fifth Republic respond to the resurgence of religious institutions associated with the migration and settlement of Muslim communities? If political institutions are 'actors in their own right', how easy will it be for reformers to re-shape the European Union (EU) to respond to the growth in Euroscepticism across many member states? And how will Britain fare in disentangling its domestic institutions from EU arrangements, which reflect deep-seated values and identities as well as regulatory requirements?

There is no single 'new institutionalist' response to these questions. What responses do have in common is a commitment to investigating the way in which institutions shape political behaviour and outcomes, and can also be shaped by human action. As such, the new institutionalism is not an approach that is 'about institutions'; rather, it focuses on the role of institutions in explaining politics. Where the old institutionalists were disdainful of theory, the new institutionalists are markedly enthusiastic, developing diverse theoretical projects. Where traditional institutionalists employed a descriptive-inductive method (drawing conclusions from empirical investigation), the new institutionalists experiment with deductive approaches that start from theoretical propositions about the way in which institutions shape politics. The 'institutionalist turn' in political science actually comprises a range of developments which, initially at least, occurred in relative independence from one another. New institutionalism was not only a reaction to old institutionalism; it developed in response to the shortcomings of the new approaches that had come to dominate the political science mainstream. As Chapter 1 explains, approaches develop in dialogue with each other and pass through different iterations, spawning subfields and revisions along the way. Distinctive bodies of work come to cohere over time, but should not be seen as set in stone. This chapter shows how the institutional approach has developed over time in dialogue with many of the approaches featured in this volume – behaviouralism, rational choice, Marxism, feminism, poststructuralism and normative political theory.

The 'three new institutionalisms'

The main cleavage in new institutionalism is between *normative institutionalism* and *rational choice institutionalism*. Normative institutionalists argue that political institutions influence actors' behaviour by shaping their 'values, norms, interests, identities and beliefs' (March and Olsen, 1989: 17). Seemingly neutral rules and structures are seen as embodying values (and power relationships), and determining 'appropriate' behaviour within given settings. Institutions 'simplify' political life by ensuring that 'some things are taken for granted in deciding other things' (March and Olsen, 1989: 17). Rational choice institutionalists, in contrast, deny that institutional factors 'produce behaviour' or shape individuals' preferences, which are seen as endogenously determined and relatively stable (favouring utility maximisation). Political institutions are seen as influencing behaviour by affecting 'the structure of a situation' in which individuals select strategies for the pursuit of their preferences (Ostrom, 1986: 5–7; see also Chapter 3). Institutions provide information about others' likely future behaviour, and about the incentives (and disincentives) attached to different courses of action. While normative institutionalists stress the embeddedness of political institutions within temporal and cultural contexts, rational choice theorists argue that institutions are purposeful human constructions designed to solve collective action problems.

Another variant, *historical institutionalism*, is elaborated by Peter Hall and Rosemary Taylor (1996) in their influential essay on the 'three new institutionalisms'. Historical institutionalism was influenced by the structural functionalist and group conflict theories of the 1960s and 1970s (which had both pluralist and neo-Marxist variants). Historical institutionalists explored how the structures of the state reflected, and reinforced, power relationships between different social and economic groups but did not assume that institutional development followed a functionalist logic. Using an eclectic mix of incentive- and norm-based explanations, historical institutionalists showed how the 'institutional organisation' of the polity works to 'privilege some interests while demobilizing others' (Hall and Taylor, 1996: 937). Institutional change arises when power relations shift, new ideas come to the fore and the costs of maintaining an established institutional path become greater than those involved in change. Historical institutionalists have produced a wide body of empirical work, including detailed studies of institutional effects in policy areas such as taxation, pensions and health services (Steinmo et al., 1992; Fioretos et al., 2016).

Hall and Taylor's article has had a major effect on the development of institutionalism, its application in research and the way it is taught to political science students. Indeed, the idea that there are three new institutionalisms has assumed a canonical status within the discipline. While the article is remembered for the specification of the three schools, the thrust of Hall and Taylor's argument is actually in favour of greater 'interchange' between the positions, and criticises the fact that each camp has 'been assiduously burnishing its own paradigm' in isolation from the others. Hall and Taylor (1996: 955) argues that each approach reveals 'different and genuine dimensions of human behaviour and of the effects institutions can have on behaviour', with each only able to 'provide a partial account of the forces at work in a given situation'. However, in the years following the publication of Hall and Taylor's article, the 'burnishing' of separate positions has increased; Box 4.2 enumerates the many strands of institutionalism.

Core features of new institutionalism

Following the direction of Hall and Taylor's original critique, this chapter argues against the proliferation of separate strains of institutionalism, or any sectarian competition to discover its true essence. The institutional approach is better seen as a broad intellectual trajectory that has passed through distinct phases, sharing many common concepts and grappling with common dilemmas along the way. Because of the variety of positions represented by both the 'old' and the 'new' institutionalism, it is not helpful to draw too sharp a contrast between them. Indeed, in many cases, new institutionalism is built upon the insights of the best of the traditional institutionalists, within the context of more explicit and sophisticated theoretical frameworks. But, in attempting to capture what Bob Goodin (1996: 20) calls 'the moving spirit of the new institutionalism', we can point to five conjectures that are shared among institutionalists of different hues and mark distinctive points of departure when compared with the descriptive and legalistic accounts of the past.

Box 4.2 Different strands of new institutionalism

Normative institutionalists study how the norms and values embodied in political institutions shape the behaviour of individuals (see the seminal work of March and Olsen, 1984, 1989).

Rational choice institutionalists argue that political institutions are systems of rules and inducements within which individuals attempt to maximise their utilities (for a review of rational choice approaches, see Weingast, 1996).

Historical institutionalists look at how choices made about the institutional design of government systems influence the future decision-making of individuals (for a review, see Hall and Taylor, 1996; and for applications, see Pierson, 2004; Streeck and Thelen, 2005; Mahoney and Thelen, 2010).

Empirical institutionalists, who most closely resemble the 'traditional' approach, classify different institutional types and analyse their practical impact upon government performance (for a review, see Peters, 1996).
International institutionalists show that the behaviour of states is steered by the structural constraints (formal and informal) of international political life (for an accessible example, see Rittberger, 1993).

Sociological institutionalists study the way in which institutions create meaning for individuals, providing important theoretical building blocks for normative institutionalism within political science (for the classic statements, see Meyer and Rowan, 1977; DiMaggio and Powell, 1991).

Network institutionalists show how regularised, but often informal, patterns of interaction between individuals and groups shape political behaviour (see Marsh and Rhodes' 1992 edited collection).

Constructivist or discursive institutionalism sees institutions as shaping behaviour through frames of meaning – the ideas and narratives that are used to explain, deliberate or legitimise political action (see Hay, 2006a; Schmidt, 2006, 2009). 'Post-structuralist institutionalists' go further in arguing that institutions actually construct political subjectivities and identities (Sørenson and Torfing, 2008; Moon, 2013).

Feminist institutionalism studies how gender norms operate within institutions and how institutional processes construct and maintain gendered power dynamics (see Chappell, 2006; Kenny, 2007; Krook and Mackay, 2011). Revealing further fragmentation, a 'feminist historical institutionalism' (Waylen, 2011) and 'feminist discursive institutionalism' (Freidenvall and Krook, 2011) have also been identified.

Institutions as rules not organisations

New institutionalism represents a departure from what Fox and Miller (1995: 92) call the 'brass name-plate' tradition of institutional analysis. Political institutions are no longer equated with political organisations;

rather, they are seen as sets of 'rules' that guide and constrain the behaviour of individual actors. Rather than focusing upon Britain's Ministry of Defence as an institution, for example, new institutionalists are more likely to study the decision-making, budgetary or procurement procedures within it. Institutional rules are important because they provide information on others' likely future behaviour and on sanctions for non-compliance (Knight, 1992: 17). For those on the 'normative' wing of the new institutionalism, rules work by determining 'appropriate' behaviour (March and Olsen, 1989); for those influenced by rational choice assumptions, rules determine the basis of exchanges between utility-maximising actors (Weingast, 1996). Institutions, then, provide the 'rules of the game', while organisations – like individuals – are players within that game. The institutional dynamics of the Ministry of Defence are best understood by studying the particular combination of institutions *within* it, which are themselves influenced by the 'rules' that characterise the wider governmental, legal and financial systems. While organisations are not 'the same as' institutions, they remain an important focus for new institutionalist analysis – in their role as collective actors subject to wider institutional constraints (think of a football club competing within the rules of the sport), and also as arenas within which institutional rules are explored and interpreted (the football club is also a place in which players and coaches work with, and seek to adapt, the rules).

Institutions as informal as well as formal

In contrast to the traditional institutional approach, new institutionalism focuses upon informal conventions as well as formal rules. In legislatures, for example, some rules are consciously designed and clearly specified (like speaking rights, voting arrangements or legislative timetables), while others take the form of unwritten conventions (concerning, for instance, the role of the party group in decision-making, the relations between parties in a coalition or the style of parliamentary debate). The informal rules of political life – while hard to research – can be every bit as important in shaping actors' behaviour as formally agreed procedures. Informal conventions may reinforce formal rules; for example, new rules about the separation of the executive and assembly function were introduced to English local government in 2000, but had a far greater impact on political behaviour in those cities that already had a strong tradition of civic leadership. Informal conventions may also override formal rules, as in the fate of many 'equal opportunities' initiatives where customary gender roles persist despite new laws or policies (Waylen, 2017). Studying democratic transitions in Latin America, historical institutionalists Helmke and Levitsky (2006: 1) identify the important role of institutions that are 'created, communicated and enforced outside officially sanctioned channels'. They show how informal institutions (like patronage, paternalism or corruption) may complement, co-exist, compete with, or even substitute for, formal institutions of democracy.

Institutions as dynamic as well as stabilising

Stability is a key characteristic of institutions. Back in 1968, Samuel Huntington described political institutions as 'stable, valued and recurring patterns of behaviour' – a definition that still works well today, even when political scientists are confronted with contemporary institutional developments such as transnational agreements that do not have an organisational home (as with climate change). However, the existence of a set of rules does not imply that all parties comply with their strictures, or that their willingness to do so will not change over time. As March and Olsen (1989: 16) put it, institutions are best seen as 'creating and sustaining islands of imperfect and temporary organisation in potentially inchoate political worlds'. Institutional stability cannot be taken for granted; it is, in fact, only accomplished through human action. Rational choice institutionalists see arrangements as persisting only as long as they serve the interests of utility-seeking rational actors, crucially as a means of solving collective action problems (Shepsle, 1989: 134). The impulse to institutional design is central to political practice, as actors seek to bind others to specific sets of values and priorities (Goodin, 1996: 193–194). However, designers frequently fail to achieve their objectives as we see in so many programmes of stalled, or even abandoned, institutional reform. Normative institutionalists pay special attention to the way in which institutions develop incrementally in response to changing contexts, as individuals seek 'to encode the novelties they encounter into new routines' (March and Olsen, 1989: 34). Historical institutionalists, such as Kathy Thelen and her collaborators, have focused on how transformative change can emerge from gradual processes of institutional adaptation (Streeck and Thelen, 2005; Mahoney and Thelen, 2010).

Institutions as embodying values and power

We saw earlier that the old institutionalism had an explicit concern with 'good government', and an implicit commitment to a particular set of values and model of government. In contrast, new institutionalists seek to identify the various ways in which institutions embody (and shape) societal values, which may themselves be contested and in flux. On the normative wing, seemingly neutral procedures and arrangements are seen as embodying particular values, interests and identities (March and Olsen, 1989: 17). For those influenced by rational choice theory, institutions are not seen as affecting preferences and yet, as Peters (1999: 19) argues, they must reflect some relatively common set of values if incentives are to function equally well for all participants. Reflecting on democratic transitions in Eastern Europe, Claus Offe (1996: 685) has observed that institutions typically change when 'their value premises have changed or because they are considered incompatible with other values'. Theorists such as Bo Rothstein (1998) have set out to specify what 'just institutions' might look like. The value-critical stance of new institutionalism is well summed up by Pierre (1999: 390) who argues that 'the structure of governance – the inclusion or exclusion of different actors and the selection of instruments – is not value neutral but embedded in and sustains political values'. Political institutions distribute power, because they specify who has access to resources and decision-making. This may be a technical matter set out in formal rules, but informal conventions may also have distributional effects. For example, 'institutional racism' was detected in London's metropolitan police in the 1990s; despite the abolition of discriminatory rules, black and white police officers still had access to different opportunities, while suspects from different ethnic groups could expect to receive markedly different treatment (Lowndes and Roberts, 2013: 74). In a similar vein, feminist institutionalists have been studying the discriminatory effects of the gendered norms that characterise processes of candidate selection and political recruitment (see Chapter 6). Research shows how such norms can operate to neutralise the impact of formal rule change, like the introduction of gender quotas (Waylen, 2017). But, historical institutionalists point out that the unequal power relationships that are built into political institutions can actually provide an important dynamic for change, as different interests seek over time to shift the power balance in their favour through strategies for institutional change (Mahoney and Thelen, 2010).

Institutions as contextually embedded

Building on the insights of the best of the traditional institutionalists, new institutionalists stress that political institutions are not independent entities, existing out of space and time. Even within the so-called Westminster system, legislatures and executives look very different in the UK, Kenya and Australia. Or federalism is instituted quite differently in Germany, Brazil or India. Understanding how institutions are contextually embedded is vital to explaining their role in politics. Institutional rules tend to be nested vertically, 'within an ever-ascending hierarchy of yet-more-fundamental, yet-more-authoritative rules and regimes and practices and procedures' (Goodin and Klingeman, 1996: 18). Kiser and Ostrom (1982) distinguish between operational (day-to-day), collective (legislative or policy based) and constitutional rules. The scope of rules at each level is constrained by those above. But institutional rules are also horizontally embedded within wider institutional contexts. Historical institutionalists have studied 'varieties of capitalism', for instance, demonstrating how capitalism is differently institutionalised in (groups of) countries that have different social and political institutions (e.g. parties, trades unions, religious blocks) (Hall and Thelen, 2008). Explaining processes of institutional development requires that we understand not just path dependency but also spatial contingency. Institutional choices in the past may influence a particular process of institutional formation (Pierson, 2004), but so might contemporaneous linkages with 'neighbouring' institutions (e.g. between health care and taxation institutions at the national level, or locally between the institutions of municipal government and civil society). New institutionalists recognise that no institution stands alone; rather, it is connected to a range of other institutions (political and non-political), which may either reinforce or undermine its effects (Mahoney and Thelen, 2010: 22; Lowndes and Roberts, 2013: 42).

New institutionalist dilemmas

New institutionalism reasserts what the best of the old institutionalists also knew: that political structures shape political behaviour and are themselves normatively and historically embedded. New institutionalists take care not to equate political institutions with political organisations; 'institution' is understood more broadly to refer to a 'stable, recurring pattern of behaviour' (Goodin, 1996: 22). The new institutionalists are concerned with the informal conventions of political life as well as with formal constitutions and organisational structures. New attention is paid to the way in which institutions embody values and power relationships, and to the obstacles as well as the opportunities that confront institutional design. Crucially, new institutionalists concern themselves not just with the impact of institutions upon individuals, but with the *interaction* between institutions and individuals. In contrast to the traditional approach, the new institutionalists are interested in testing theoretical models of how institutions shape behaviour, rather than relying upon a descriptive-inductive method to generate conclusions. Box 4.3 provides a selection of examples of new institutionalist approaches in action.

There are, however, many areas of disagreement among self-styled 'new institutionalists', and between institutionalists and sceptics in other parts of the discipline. In what follows we review three of the most hotly debated issues, finishing with the most fundamental – can the 'big tent' of new institutionalism really span the different ontologies of its normative and rational choice versions?

What is an institution anyway?

New institutionalists are all agreed that political institutions are 'the rules of the game' – but what should be included in the category of rules? By including informal conventions as well as formal procedures, the new institutionalists are able to build a more fine-grained, and realistic, picture of what *really* constrains political behaviour and decision-making. An expanded definition of 'institution' runs the risk,

Box 4.3 New institutionalist analysis in action

Comparing Britain, Sweden and the USA, Steinmo (1993) shows that constitutions influenced the distribution of tax burdens more than the organisational strength of different social classes.

In a comparison of health policy in France, Sweden and Switzerland, Immergut (1992) shows how the institutionalised 'veto points' explained the influence of pressure groups better than the initial strength of the groups themselves. Pierson (2004) studies the way in which 'institutional resilience' is related to self-interested actors seeking to preserve veto points over time.

Explaining the shift from Keynesianism to monetarism in Britain, Hall (1992) argues that political institutions structured policy by influencing how new ideas came to the surface and became expressed in government decisions. Schmidt (2002) builds on this work to compare the interaction of ideas and institutions in shaping the market economies of France, Britain and Germany.

In research in Southern California, Ostrom (1990) shows how voluntary associations established for the management of scarce resources (like water) changed the view of individual famers about where their self-interest lay.

Explaining variations in British policy-making, Marsh and Rhodes (1992) argue that relationships between political actors were differently institutionalised in different sectors, being more or less stable and exclusive.

Comparing presidential and parliamentary systems, Weaver and Rockman (1993) show that division of powers inherent in the former made legislation more difficult.

The role of creative actors ('institutional entrepreneurs') in seeking to achieve institutional change through combining different modes of governance is considered by Crouch (2005) in relation to economic policy and by Lowndes (2005) in terms of local government.

In international relations, Rittberger (1993) argues that states accepted treaties and conventions in order to reduce uncertainty about the behaviour of other nations, whether friends or adversaries. Duffield (2006) looks at the role of international institutions in conferring legitimacy upon states seeking to maximise others' cooperation and limit potential opposition, using the case of US action in Iraq.

however, of 'conceptual stretching' (Peters, 1996: 216) – its meaning and impact diluted as it comes to include everything that guides individual behaviour. North (1990: 83) goes as far as to include tradition, custom, culture and habit as informal 'institutions', and for March and Olsen (1989: 17) there seems to be no clear distinction between institutions and norms in general. As Rothstein (1996: 145) notes, if the concept of institution 'means everything, then it means nothing' – how can political institutions be distinguished from other social facts? John (1998: 64) argues that the new institutionalists 'include too many aspects of political life under one category ... (which) disguises the variety of interactions and causal mechanisms that occur'. On a practical level, how can political scientists recognise (and measure) an institution when they see one? On a theoretical level, how can they avoid the traps of reductionism and tautology? As Peters (1996: 215) notes:

> If the rules that shape behaviour are expanded to include implicit rules and vague understandings, in order to cover instances in which observed behaviours do not correspond to the formal rules of any institution, then the theory may not be falsifiable. If we observe behaviours that do not conform to the strictures of the formal rules then there must be other rules that were not identifiable.

Peter Hall's (1986) concept of 'standard operating procedures' ('SOPs') offers a helpful way forward: the researcher's aim should be to identify the specific rules of behaviour that are agreed upon and (in general) followed by agents, whether explicitly or tacitly agreed (see Rothstein, 1996: 146). Informal institutional rules are, in this formulation, distinct from personal habits or 'rules of thumb'. The style and form of questioning in a UK Parliamentary Select Committee, for example, may not be set down in writing; however, it is clearly identifiable as a SOP that structures political behaviour, while expressing particular values and power relationships. This SOP can be described, evaluated and compared with alternative arrangements for scrutiny. In contrast, the way that a Select Committee member organises his or her papers (however regularly and systematically) is a matter of personal habit or routine, and does not qualify as an informal institution or SOP.

SOPs may be circumvented or manipulated by certain individuals or groups of actors, but actors in general are still able to identify, and reflect upon, the nature of such 'rules'. In politics, as elsewhere, rules exist to be broken as well as to be obeyed! Peters' (1999: 144) charge of tautology only really applies to those rational choice perspectives that *define* institutions by the creation of regularity, that is, by the acceptance of rules of behaviour. Institutional rules are subject to some form of 'third-party enforcement' – either via formal sanctions or informal displays of disapproval (this is what makes them different from personal habits or broader cultural concerns). The notion of SOPs offers institutionalists a way of combining a concern for formal and informal 'rules', and yet distinguishing political institutions from broader customs and habits. Elinor Ostrom (2005) helpfully distinguishes between rules-in-form and rules-in-use, with the latter referring to the distinctive ensemble of 'dos and don'ts that one learns on the ground'. Rules-in-use are typically a mix of formal and informal elements, as we know from studying constitutions, legislatures, executives, legislatures and institutions of civil society.

To summarise, the researcher's aim should be to identify the specific rules of behaviour that are agreed upon, whether explicitly or tacitly, and (in general) followed by agents. Such institutional rules are:

- specific to a particular political or governmental setting,
- recognised by actors (if not always adhered to),
- collective (rather than personal) in their effect, and
- subject to some sort of third-party enforcement (formal or informal).

The difficulty of identifying and measuring rules-in-use is, however, considerable. Peters (1999: 145) is right to remind new institutionalists of the 'need for more rigour in conceptualisation and then measurement of the phenomena that are assumed to make up institutions'. Box 4.4 sets out the broad repertoire of techniques with which new institutionalists are responding to this challenge. While historical, comparative and case study methods (not so very different from those of the better 'traditionalists') continue to dominate, new methods are also developing, from ethnography to experiments and game theory.

Where do institutions come from, and how do they change?

As we noted earlier, stability is a defining feature of institutions. It is often said that new institutionalism is at its weakest when trying to explain the genesis and transformation of institutions (Mahoney and Thelen, 2010; Koning, 2015). The way that change is conceptualised depends upon how the relationship between the individual and the institution is understood. While rational choice theorists see individual preferences as prior to institutions, other forms of new institutionalism see preferences as shaped by institutions. Rational choice theory tells us that political institutions are human constructions, designed to solve collective action problems – to maximise gains from cooperation. Institutions can be 'undone' when they no longer serve actors' interests – they provide only short-term constraints on individuals' behaviour (Peters, 1999: 148). It has not, of course, escaped the notice of more sophisticated rational choice theorists that institutions tend to be self-reinforcing, and remarkably enduring. These theorists argue that actors will only change institutions where the likely benefits outweigh the expected costs of change itself – which include the costs of learning how to operate within a new structure, of dealing with new sources of uncertainty, and of engaging in change (which itself presents a collective action problem!) (Rothstein, 1996: 152). Explaining change has tended to rely on 'stop-go' models, notably through the concept of 'punctuated equilibrium' (originally from Krasner, 1984). While path dependency persists during 'normal' times, critical junctures emerge at moments of political upheaval which are typically stimulated by external shocks.

Box 4.4 New institutionalist methods

Mathematical modelling: Colin Crouch (2005) uses modelling to show that institutional heterogeneity facilitates innovation in economic policy, by presenting new opportunities when existing 'paths' are blocked, and by allowing for new combinations of elements from existing paths.

Game theory: Patrick Dunleavy (1991) uses game theory to develop his theory of 'bureau shaping' as an alternative to conventional 'budget maximising' assumptions in explaining how self-interested bureaucrats seek to influence the institutions they work through.

Experimental methods: Elinor Ostrom and colleagues (1994) work both in the laboratory and through field experiments to investigate the institutional and physical variables that affect whether cooperation can be achieved (and overexploitation avoided) in the use of 'common pool resources' such as forests or grazing lands. Sven Steinmo (2016) uses experiments to 'get inside the black box' and better understand how individuals formulate strategies within institutional frameworks, focusing on the types of taxes citizens might be willing to pay in different countries for welfare benefits.

Ethnography: Mary Douglas (1987) uses anthropological and ethnographic methods to develop her theory of 'how institutions think', differentially structuring categories of thought across cultures, whether in law, religion or science.

Process tracing: Sven Steinmo and colleagues' (1992) classic collection on 'structuring politics' uses process tracing to investigate the sequencing of key decisions and events, and identify episodes for particular study. It is a method for in-case analysis using qualitative data, notably historical documents but also interviews in contemporary work. Peter Hall (2013), a pioneer of the technique, reviews its development over time.

Case studies: Kathleen Thelen's collections of case studies analyse macro-economic trends and policy development to compare the different ways in which incremental change leads to institutional transformation (Streeck and Thelen, 2005; Mahoney and Thelen, 2010) Taking a bottom-up approach, Lowndes and colleagues (2006) collect micro-level data via surveys, interviews and focus groups to analyse the rules-in-use that shape citizen participation in a sample of English cities.

Narrative analysis: Lisa Freidenvall and Mona Krook (2011) analyse the phrasing, imagery and layout of official documents (manifestos, legal decisions, technical guidance) associated with the introduction of gender quotas in different countries, looking also at the ways in which they articulate with discourses in popular culture.

Normative institutionalists, who see individuals' preferences as shaped by institutions, do not have an easy answer as to *why* institutions in general (or particular political institutions) come into being. They are better at describing how they persist and exercise their ongoing influence over actors. As March and Olsen (1989: 17) explain, institutions 'increase capability by reducing comprehensiveness'; they 'simplify' political life by ensuring that 'some things are taken as given in deciding other things'. But if, as March and Olsen (1989: 159) insist, 'institutional actors are driven by institutional duties', how is it that they 'break out' in order to criticise existing arrangements or design new political institutions? Normative institutionalism actually allows more room for reflexivity and human agency than might initially seem to be the case. Normative institutionalists expect institutions continually to evolve. Rules are seen as producing variation and deviation as well as conformity and standardisation; this is because there are always areas of ambiguity in the interpretation and application of rules (not least because individuals vary in terms of their own values and experiences), and because rules are adapted by actors seeking to make sense of changing environments. As Peters (1999: 149) notes, normative institutionalism 'permits the mutual influence of individuals and institutions'.

Goodin (1996: 24–25) distinguishes between three basic ways in which institutions emerge: intentional design, accident or evolution. While rational choice approaches prioritise intentional design, normative institutionalists do not rule it out. They argue, however, that attempts at institutional reform are hard to control. Once one 'logic of appropriateness' is destabilised, space opens up for deliberation over competing norms and values; institutional change 'rarely satisfies the prior intentions of those who initiate it' (March and Olsen, 1989: 65). Indeed, research suggests that change in political institutions may be better understood as an emergent process, in which endogenous and exogenous factors combine in the fashioning of new forms of 'recombinant governance' (Crouch, 2005). James Mahoney and Kathleen Thelen (2010: 15–18) argue that gradual processes of adjustment can lead, over time, to transformational change. Because 'dynamic tensions and pressures for change are built into institutions', transformation can occur through strategies that fall short of all-out reform. For instance, where the costs of getting rid of old rules is simply too great, new ones may be introduced 'on top'; such processes of 'institutional layering' lead, over time, to a situation in which the 'new fringe eats into the old core'. 'Institutional conversion', on the other hand, occurs when 'rules remain formally the same but are interpreted and enacted in new ways'. Tulia Falleti (2010) provides evidence of such processes in health care reform in Brazil, where the 'sanitarista' movement had introduced preventative and social medicine 'under the radar' during the military dictatorship. As she explains: 'Although radical changes in the health care system were codified in the Constitution of 1988, they only brought to light changes that had been percolating beneath the surface' for more than a decade (Falleti, 2010: 58).

So there exist creative spaces between institutional stability and volatility, in which 'institutional entrepreneurs' seek to adapt 'the rules of the game' in order to meet the demands of uncertain and changing environments, and to further their own interests or values (as in the case of Brazil's left-wing health practitioners). Institutional change involves active processes of experimentation – or what Lanzara (1998) calls 'institutional *bricolage*' – through which diverse institutional elements are patched together (old and new, formal and informal, external and internal) in elaborating new rules. Mahoney and Thelen (2010: 22) argue that ambiguity and compromise in institutional design can actually be a resource for future rounds of institutional development. While rational choice theory provides us with a valuable hypothesis about why political institutions emerge (i.e. to solve collective action problems), normative and historical approaches help explain why all political institutions are not alike. New institutionalists of all colours remain preoccupied with the central paradox, or 'double life', of institutions, which are both 'human products' and 'social forces in their own right' (Grafstein, 1988: 577–578).

Are the normative and rational choice approaches compatible?

We have referred throughout our discussion of new institutionalism, to the 'normative' and 'rational choice' variants. We have argued that they share characteristics of a distinct 'new institutionalist' movement within political science, but are built upon different theoretical assumptions about the impact of institutions upon political behaviour, and about the interaction between individual actors and institutions. Is this a sleight of hand?

Some critics have objected to any attempt to seek common purpose, or even complementarity, between such diverse theoretical positions. In 1998, Hay and Wincott argued that the distinction between 'calculus' (rational choice) and 'cultural' (normative) approaches 'represents an intractable divide between two contending and incompatible approaches to institutional analysis'. They counselled against the 'cobbling together of institutional insights from differently-informed institutionalisms', and urged historical institutionalists, in particular, to develop a new and distinctive social ontology that could *overcome* rather than reproduce traditional binary thinking (Hay and Wincott, 1998: 953). In 2006, Colin Hay responded to his own challenge with the elaboration of 'constructivist institutionalism as a new addition to the family of institutionalisms' (2006a: 62; see also Chapter 12). Hay expresses his concern that historical institutionalists like Pierson and Hall have drifted towards a rational choice settlement of their ontological dilemma. But, while claiming ontological distinctiveness for the approach, Hay's constructivist institutionalism falls back on the additive, binary formulations he previously criticised: 'actors are both strategic and socialised'; both 'ideas and practices' matter; and attention should be paid to both 'institutional creation and post-formative institutional change' (Hay, 2006a: 58–59).

Such statements serve simply to remind researchers of the premises of a good institutionalist analysis – and of the dangers of searching for the political scientist's equivalent of 'an alchemist's stone' (Hall and Taylor, 1998: 960). The real contribution of constructivist, or discursive, institutionalism is its conceptualisation of institutions as 'codified systems of ideas' (Hay, 2006a: 59). Institutions shape behaviour through the frames of meaning they embody – the ideas and narratives that are used to explain or legitimise political action. At the same time, actors themselves use ideas 'to (re)conceptualise interests and values as well as (re)shape institutions' (Schmidt, 2009: 530). Explaining the origins and subsequent development of political institutions requires an understanding of how ideas become codified over time, and the conditions under which underlying ideas are 'contested, challenged, and replaced' (Hay, 2006a: 65). Mark Blyth's (2002) work on 'great transformations' in economic policy, for example, shows how new ideas become 'weapons' at times of institutional crisis, enabling actors to build replacements. In the USA liberalism was 'embedded' institutionally after the Great Depression of the 1930s, but challenged by business interests in the context of the oil price shock of the 1970s. At the present time, austerity (described by Blyth as a 'dangerous idea') is underpinning further restructuring of the relationship between state and economy (Blyth, 2013).

But do we need to choose between normative, rational choice and discursive accounts? Perhaps the special character of institutions lies precisely in the fact that institutions are 'over-determined'. In robust institutional arrangements, regulative, normative and cognitive mechanisms all work together to shape behaviour (Scott, 2008). Indeed, it is this combination of characteristics that constitutes an 'institution' – a set of valued, meaningful and recurring patterns of behaviour – and distinguishes it from an 'organisation' or a 'rule book' or a set of personal habits. While theoreticians inevitably emphasise the distinctive features of each variant, Vivien Schmidt (2006: 116) reminds us that 'problem-oriented scholars tend to mix approaches all the time, using whichever approaches seem the most appropriate to explaining their object of study'. Given that political actors and institutional designers are themselves subject to mixed motivations, we have to be aware of the artificial nature of 'pure' ontological constructs. As Garret Hardin (1968) observed: 'We can never do merely one thing.' As actors encounter institutions (as rule-takers or rule-makers), they are likely to be motivated by (some combination of) their selfish interests, their 'need to belong', and their underlying ideas and values.

Rather than trying to win an argument about 'what counts most', Lowndes and Roberts (2013: 50) propose that institutions actually work

Table 4.1 *Modes of institutional constraint*

	Rules	*Practices*	*Narratives*
How we recognise them:	Formally constructed and recorded	Demonstrated through conduct	Expressed through words and symbols
Empirical examples:	Clauses in a constitution, terms of reference, national and international laws	How elected members conduct themselves in parliaments, assemblies or local councils	Speeches by politicians explaining the need for change; the collections of stories in an organisation which justify the status quo
Enactment by actors through:	Writing and formal interpretation (e.g. law to policy documents to guidance)	The consistent rehearsal of 'the ways in which we *do* things around here'	The linking together and spoken expression of ideas into explanation and persuasion
Impact on actors through:	Reading representations and interpretations of rules (e.g. following instructions on signs or specifications of procedure manuals)	Observing the routinised actions of members of the group and seeking to recreate those actions (e.g. mimicking how to act in a legislature)	Hearing familiar stories and recognising shared understandings to the point where the normative implications are taken for granted (e.g. looking for policy ideas that fit dominant frames)
Sanctioned by:	Coercive action through formal rewards and punishments (e.g. fines, bonus for performance)	Displays of disapproval, social isolation and threats of violence (e.g. refusing access to a minister)	Incomprehension and ridicule, and attempts to undermine the reputation and credibility of non-conformists (e.g. briefing against political rivals)
Interconnections between modes of constraint:	Narratives are often used to justify the existence of rules; rules often formalise well-established practices	Practices often form the basis of narrative; rules may specify practices required for compliance	The case for changing the rules is usually made in narrative form; narrative accounts can present prevalent practices in a positive or negative light
Indicative research methodologies:	Documentary analysis, process tracing, laboratory studies, game theory and mathematical modelling	Observation of conduct in formal meetings and behind the scenes, ethnographic approaches	Interviewing actors and recording their stories, seeking verbalised explanations for policies, narrative analysis of speeches and interviews

Source: Adapted from Lowndes and Roberts (2013: 52–53)

through three distinct, but interconnected, modes of constraint: rules, practices and narratives. The real agenda for institutionalism is to better understand how these distinctive modes of constraint work together in practice, and to establish what this means for processes of institutional design and change. Where gaps open up between modes of constraint (for example, the 'story' no longer reflects day-to-day practice, or formal rules are imposed without justification), institutions become less stable and more susceptible to change. Table 4.1 identifies the key features of each mode of constraint, including the different ways in which they shape political behaviour and the varied forms of enforcement to which they are subject. It also shows how each mode of constraint can be identified and through which research methods.

Conclusion

Discipline-watchers Goodin and Klingemann have argued that the special significance of the new institutionalism lay precisely in its capacity to defuse the unconstructive stand-off between structuralists and behaviouralists that has bedevilled political science. In a pragmatic rather than a heroic vein, they observed that:

> Political scientists no longer think in the either/or terms of agency or structure, interests or institutions as the driving forces: now, virtually all serious students of the discipline would say it is a matter of a judicious blend of both ... it is a matter of analyzing behaviour within the parameters set by institutional facts and opportunity structures. (Goodin and Klingemann, 1996: 10–11)

We can conclude that new institutionalism is best understood as an 'organising perspective' (Gamble, 1990: 405). It is not a causal theory in the behavioural sense; instead it 'provides a map of the subject and signposts to its central questions' (Rhodes, 1995: 49). Where traditional institutionalists were silent on matters of theory (smuggling in their assumptions under a veil of 'common sense'), the new institutionalists are highly vocal. New institutionalism does not require any one particular theory, but it does demand a critical stance towards theory. The strength of new institutionalism may be found precisely in its multi-theoretic character, which allows for the assessment of competing propositions drawn from different political theories. As Rod Rhodes (1995: 56) pointed out in the first edition of this volume:

> No theory is ever true, it is only more or less instructive. You can learn from the critical assessment of one theory; you can learn much more from a comparative critical assessment of several theories brought to bear on a single topic. The study of political institutions will benefit greatly from such multi-theoretic research.

The contribution of new institutional approaches within political science is perhaps best understood in terms of 'epistemic gain'. Such a gain is constituted by the 'movement from a problematic position to a more adequate one within a field of available alternatives', and can be contrasted with 'epistemology's mythical movement from falsity to truth' (Calhoun, 2000: 538). In reviewing, twenty years on, their pioneering contribution, March and Olsen (2006: 16) agree that the institutionalist project is a work in progress: 'The spirit is to supplement rather than reject alternative approaches ... Much remains, however, before the different conceptions of political institutions, action, and change can be reconciled meaningfully.'

Further reading

- For an in-depth critical review of institutionalism, with illustrative case studies, see Lowndes and Roberts (2013).
- For collected essays using an institutional approach to investigate different aspects of politics, see *The Oxford Handbook of Political Institutions* (Rhodes et al., 2006) and *The Oxford Handbook of Historical Institutionalism* (Fioretos et al., 2016).
- March and Olsen (1989) and Hall and Taylor (1996) remain the field-shaping works on new institutionalism.
- On the variety of institutional approaches, see Peters (2005).

Chapter 5

Constructivism and Interpretive Theory

CRAIG PARSONS

A constructivist argument claims that people do one thing and not another due to certain 'social constructs': ideas, beliefs, norms, identities or some other interpretive filter through which people perceive the world. We inhabit a 'world of our making' (Onuf, 1989), and action is structured by meanings that groups of people develop to interpret and organise their identities, relationships and environment. Non-constructivist scholarship, by contrast, like that surveyed in Chapters 2 (behaviouralism), 3 (rational choice) and 7 (Marxism), suggests that our interpretive filters do not greatly affect action. Instead we inhabit a 'real' landscape of features like geography, resources and relative power, to which we respond fairly directly. Some institutionalists (Chapter 4) also make non-constructivist arguments. Even though organisations and rules are obviously 'social constructs' as well – institutions are created by people – many institutionalists treat organisations and rules as fairly clear, 'real' objective obstacle courses to which we respond directly. An argument is only constructivist to the extent that it argues that subjective interpretation of some sort affects what people do.

At a more meta-theoretical level, constructivism has a contested relationship to other approaches. Many constructivists espouse an interpretive epistemology, as discussed in Chapter 11. If our world is socially constructed, they reason, there is little 'real world' for political scientists to study. The social sciences thus amount to an interpretive (or 'hermeneutic') search for meanings rather than a scientific search for causal relations. This view downplays debate between constructivists and non-constructivist scholarship, since the latter is portrayed as illegitimate. On the other hand, many constructivists do not break with science and causality. They argue that social construction does not eliminate the possibility of fruitful debate over why certain people do certain things. Perhaps the most compelling truth about human action is that people act within meaningful social constructs – and perhaps a careful observer can show it persuasively in competition with non-constructivist theories. Constructivists who take this position see their approach as a new kind of alternative within older, traditional political science debates.

Not only do constructivists vary epistemologically in how they think their claims relate to reality, science and causality, but they vary substantively and methodologically as well. Just as there are many different rational choice theories, or many different behaviouralist claims, so there are many constructivisms. They address different levels of action, from 'world culture' (Meyer et al., 1997) to discrete policy arenas (Hall, 1989) and 'everyday politics' (Hobson and Seabrooke, 2007), and invoke different mechanisms of social construction. They draw on many kinds of methods, from interpretive ethnography and process-tracing narrative to conventional comparisons and even quantitative studies. The chapter begins with a short historical survey of constructivism, and then discusses these variations.

Origins of constructivism

The basic notion of constructivism originated along with the discipline of sociology in the late nineteenth century. One celebrated source was the work of Émile Durkheim (1984 [1893]). He argued that societies are held together by the 'social facts' of culture, not just objectively rational responses to 'natural' or 'material facts', and that societies creatively invent different socially constructed identities and beliefs. Durkheim's work and that of his students (i.e. Mauss, 1954 [1923]) set the concept of culture at the centre of sociology, and also of the closely related new discipline of anthropology.

An even more celebrated father of constructivist thinking is Max Weber, a German sociologist who attempted to synthesise a Durkheim-style emphasis on ideas and culture with more Marx-style attention to the material landscape – but with a priority for the former. He suggested that ideas are like 'switchmen' which often 'determined the tracks along which action has been pushed by the dynamics of interest' (Weber, 1958 [1922]: 280). In his most famous work, *The Protestant Ethic and the Spirit of Capitalism*, Weber argued that it was the religious ideas of Protestantism that led indirectly to the rise of capitalism (Weber, 1992 [1930]). This claim 'turned Marx on his head', reversing Marx's view that ideas and ideology were just rationalisations that people made up as they pursued wealth and power in a material landscape. For Weber, ideas and culture deeply defined what people saw as their 'interests'.

Durkheim and Weber's focus on the impact of socially constructed ideas, norms and culture first entered the emerging discipline of political science mainly through the scholar who initially translated Weber into English, Talcott Parsons. A professor of sociology at Harvard, Parsons was enormously influential across the social sciences in the 1950s and 1960s, and his students developed the first distinctively political science literature on 'political culture'. The best-known example was *The Civic Culture* (Almond and Verba, 1963), which used surveys to judge how well attitudes and values in various countries might sustain democracy.

After a brief heyday, however, the Parsonian school fell out of favour. Critics pointed out that the 'political culture' approach was often tautological (Barry, 1970). Whatever people said they valued politically, or whatever they displayed in their political actions, was portrayed as their 'political culture'. These scholars then argued that political culture explained their values and actions. Partly because the study of ideas and culture in political science became associated with these circular problems, it largely dropped out of the mainstream of the discipline in the 1970s.

It was not until the late 1980s that scholarship on ideas, norms and culture re-entered political science in force. Over the next decade came an explosion of such work. As part of a reaction to the perceived failures of non-constructivist theorising in international relations (IR) – most notably in failing to predict or account for the end of the Cold War – a movement arose with the new name 'constructivism'. Drawing on cultural theorists in sociology, Alexander Wendt argued that the apparently 'anarchic' structure of international politics did not result from a natural, material system; instead, 'anarchy is what states make of it', and the rules and identities of IR are socially constructed (Wendt, 1992, 1998; also Onuf, 1989). At roughly the same time, related movements developed elsewhere in political science. They usually did not use the label 'constructivist', but similarly directed attention to social constructs. Scholars of comparative politics argued that they could not understand changing domestic policies and institutions without tracing the introduction of new ideas (Hall, 1989; Sikkink, 1991; Berman, 1998; Blyth, 2002). Political scientists also discovered the large literature in sociology on 'sociological institutionalism', which is (despite its name) a variety of constructivism (Powell and DiMaggio, 1991; Finnemore, 1996; Katzenstein, 1996; Swedberg, and Granovetter, 2001). Yet another related school of thought grew up mainly in Britain, where scholars drew on the ideologically focused Marxism of Antonio Gramsci to analyse the social construction and 'hegemony' of neoliberalism and globalisation (Cox, 1987; Jessop, 1990; Gil, 1993). And another strand appeared mostly in continental Europe, drawing on theorists such as Derrida (1976), Michel Foucault (1975) and Lacan (1977) to advance what became known as 'poststructuralist' or 'postmodern' constructivism (Jachtenfuchs, 1995; Waever, 1995; Diez, 1999; Rosamond, 1999; Jørgensen, 2000; Zehfuss, 2002; Epstein, 2008; see Chapter 6 in this volume).

By the turn of the millennium, constructivism was better established in political science than ever. Scholars of social construction from all these different lineages held prestigious faculty posts and published in highly regarded venues. On one hand, the thriving variety in constructivism was a sign of strength; much like different rational choice theories, the many different kinds of constructivist arguments displayed the rich range of tools and logics that could be developed from its basic insights. On the other hand, some of these differences amounted to fierce fights over what constructivism is and how it is distinctive from other approaches.

What is and isn't distinctive about constructivism?

At a basic level, no one contests the first paragraph of this chapter: the core distinctiveness of constructivism lies in its attention to the role of interpretation in action. But there is considerable contestation about whether and how arguments about interpretive social constructs can engage with other work in the social sciences. Many theorists argue that a focus on social construction implies even deeper kinds of distinctiveness that set constructivism apart from other scholarship.

The best-known argument traces to another observation from Max Weber. He distinguished between two modes of argument about action. *Explanation* is concerned with an argument's 'adequacy on a causal level': how well it shows that someone's actions followed predictably from certain conditions. *Understanding* concerns an argument's 'adequacy on the level of meaning': how well it captures how the actor interpreted what she was doing. Weber saw these two components as somewhat separate – suggesting that we might 'explain' someone's actions without really understanding her thinking – but argued that a valid 'causal interpretation' of action always covers both (Weber, 1978 [1922]: 11).

Later scholars developed the Explanation/Understanding line into two views that set constructivism apart from non-constructivist social science. One hardens Weber's line into two valid but incommensurable modes of argument, 'each persuasive but not readily combined' (Hollis and Smith, 1990: v–vi). Some scholars seek 'outsider' accounts that present natural science-style causal explanations of patterns in action. Others seek 'insider' accounts that interpret meanings, perceptions and the process of action. By this logic, constructivists and non-constructivists make separate contributions within a division of labour. We 'always and inevitably' have 'two stories to tell' about action (Hollis and Smith, 1990: 210). The second, more aggressive view draws the same line but argues that only 'insider', Understanding arguments apply to action. It suggests that human action never responds to conditions in an automatic stimulus–response causal relationship; people always act through meanings, and have some free will to choose (Winch, 1958). Thus we do not 'explain' action; all scholars can do is offer meaningful interpretations of actors' interpretations (sometimes called a 'double hermeneutic': Taylor, 1971; see also Chapter 1 in this volume). The upshot is that constructivism is the only valid approach to study action (Bevir and Kedar, 2008; see also Box 5.1 below).

Many scholars today subscribe to one of these views, and make constructivist arguments without directly confronting non-constructivist theories. But in recent years the Explanation/Understanding line has attracted much criticism (Kurki, 2008; Wight, 2006). The trouble with Weber's distinction is that it creates the 'Understanding' category by using a debatable definition of 'Explanation'. This old, long-dominant definition originated with David Hume (1975 [1748]). He argued that we can never actually observe the process by which something causes something else; we just see snapshots of conditions that seem to follow from others. For

Box 5.1 'Interpretivists' in political science and international relations (IR)

All constructivists place a core emphasis on interpretation; they argue that actors are always interpreting things through social constructs, and thus also that observers must learn to interpret social constructs to understand action. But the subset of constructivists who explicitly take the 'interpretivist' label are signalling a particular epistemological position. They argue strongly that since all human action passes through interpretation, and since scholars themselves are also interpreting through their own filters, we should not ever pretend that we can access 'the real world'. They criticise 'modern' constructivists, such as Alexander Wendt or Peter Katzenstein in IR or like Mark Blyth or Sheri Berman in comparative politics, for engaging debates with non-constructivists who dispute the role of social construction in political action. Accepting a debate with non-constructivists means accepting that there is a 'real world' out there to debate about, which these theorists see as rejecting the core insight of constructivism.

This view is shared by postmodern constructivists, but scholars who use the 'interpretivist' label usually place a somewhat higher priority on analytical goals – asking, 'What are the social constructs at work here, and how have they evolved?' – relative to the more normative, critical theory focus of similar scholars who call themselves postmodernists. In IR, one leading example is Cecilia Lynch's (1999) work on the interwar peace movements that preceded the construction of the United Nations after World War II. Another is Vincent Pouliot's research (2010) on norms and social practices in the evolving relationship between Russia and the West. Most scholars who use the 'interpretivist' label fall outside IR, however. Celebrated examples are Timothy Mitchell's (1991) *Colonizing Egypt*, Lisa Wedeen's (1999, 2008) studies of politics in Syria and Yemen, Mark Bevir and Rod Rhodes' (2003) work on interpreting British governance, and Timothy Pachirat's (2013) research on industrial slaughterhouses. Important broad statements of versions of this position – with some internal variations – are Winch (1958), Flyvbjerg (2001), Yanow and Schwartz-Shea (2006), Schram and Caterino (2006), Bevir and Kedar (2008) and Adler and Pouliot (2011).

Hume, then, 'to explain' meant to provide a set of patterns across cases in which A (the cause) always precedes B (the effect). In other words, we explain by offering correlations across many instances, not by specifying a mechanism or process by which one thing produces another (which, he said, we can't see or document in any case). Weber relied on this definition in drawing his line. Explanation subsumes an action in a pattern of correlated conditions, but glosses over the process that produced it. 'Understanding' traces how people arrived at their action.

As many philosophers have pointed out, however, Hume's definition of explanation has problems. Rarely can we infer causation from correlations. The mercury in a barometer drops regularly and predictably before a storm, but no one would say that our barometer causes or 'explains' the storm. At a common-sense level, too, what most people want from an 'explanation' is exactly what Hume leaves out: a mechanism or process by which one set of conditions produced another. Over time, then, most philosophers of explanation and most social scientists have moved to different definitions. While many still say that a good explanation includes correlations – it shows that B does indeed tend to follow A – it also offers a plausible mechanism by which A produces B. This is what most of our theoretical arguments in political science try to do today: to capture some mechanisms in the world, and show that they produce some patterns. We often expect good arguments to offer some evidence that they get some patterns right, *and* (breaking with Hume) that we can see at least some evidence for certain mechanisms.

This is important for constructivism because a post-Humean view of explanation erases the Explanation/Understanding line between constructivist and non-constructivist scholarship. Consider a rational choice explanation that some people enacted a certain policy owing to their objectively rational interests in certain economic benefits. If we took an old Humean view of explanation, such an argument might just correlate the pattern of action to some pattern of benefits – the supporters stood to benefit, the opponents did not – and rest its case. But by the definitions of explanation that most political scientists espouse today, we would also demand some evidence that the actors actually perceived the benefits and reasoned in a certain way. In other words, we would want evidence of the right mechanism. Crucially, any mechanism involving 'rational choice' obviously makes claims about meanings and perceptions (or, in Weber's terms, 'understandings'); to say that certain choices were rational under certain constraints is quite a strong claim about how actors perceived and decided. In my example the author would try to show us, at least roughly, that people perceived certain constraints and incentives and used a particular logic to arrive at their choices. Once we make that observation, the Explanation/Understanding breaks down. The difference between this economic interests argument and a constructivist one is not that one features understandings and the other ignores them; it is that they portray understandings in different ways (respectively as objective readings of external conditions or as meaningfully interpreted readings). Thus an updated definition of explanation suggests that constructivist accounts can compete directly with non-constructivist ones. This re-characterisation does not diminish the substantive difference between these approaches, but it suggests that they assert competing accounts on the same territory.

Even for readers who find this position persuasive, another major argument exists that locates constructivism in a separate realm of enquiry (at least partly). It draws a line between causal and 'constitutive' arguments, and has been set out most forcefully by Wendt (1998, 1999). Wendt argues that traditional causal-explanatory scholarship asks 'why' questions about how one set of conditions dynamically produced another, whereas constructivist-style 'constitutive' scholarship asks 'how' or 'what' questions about the static properties that constitute things. Culture, norms, ideas and identities do not usually cause things in a dynamic, one-thing-knocks-into-another way; they define the properties of the world we perceive. For example, Wendt notes that it doesn't make sense to say that the norm of sovereignty preceded and *caused* the rise of the modern state system. At the very moment that people took up the norm of sovereignty, they looked around and saw modern states. This is a relationship of static identity, not causality. Wendt does not insist that all constructivist work is constitutive rather than causal; some constructivists may argue that people invented new ideas and that we can see these ideas leading to new actions in a rather traditional, dynamic, causal-explanatory way. But he suggests that constructivism, more broadly, is distinctive because it is mainly interested in constitutive relationships rather than causal ones. 'So even though I have framed the issue differently than Hollis and Smith' (who authored the most famous account of Explanation/Understanding), Wendt writes, 'I agree with them that there are always "two stories to tell" in social inquiry' (1999: 85). He, too, thinks that most constructivists pursue a separate kind of enquiry from non-constructivists.

There can be no doubt that constitutiveness, like Weber's more basic point about 'understanding', is central to constructivism. The deepest point of constructivism is that the natural world is meaningless and indeterminate for human action until we begin to socially construct some shared meanings about it. From a natural world in which we could do many things, we construct certain meanings and so 'constitute' certain political arenas, actors and actions. But just as constructivists can all accept the fundamental importance of 'understanding' but disagree over whether it sets constructivist claims in their own scholarly realm, so they can all accept the basic role of constitutiveness in constructivism while disagreeing over Wendt's portrayal of separate spaces of enquiry.

The most forceful criticism of Wendt's account suggests that constructivists' constitutive arguments do not just address static properties, but always directly imply certain accounts of processes that compete with non-constructivist explanations (Parsons, 2015). To see why this might be the case, it is important to see that non-interpretive theories like Marxism, realism in IR or the variety of rational choice theories do not actually claim that people have no ideas, norms, identities or culture. That is an absurd claim (especially coming from academics who spend their lives playing with ideas). Instead non-constructivist theories suggest that the ideas and norms we appear to 'believe' in – the rhetoric political actors spout about principles, rules and identity – are congealed rationalisations of some set of roughly rational responses to some 'real', non-socially constructed incentives and constraints. In other words, they claim that we arrived at our apparent ideas, norms and identities by a roughly rational and objective process. Thus non-constructivists argue that ideas and norms are not 'constitutive' of anything; they are by-products of rational political action, or what Marx called 'superstructure'. Constructivists' disagreement with this kind of view is not, as Wendt seems to suggest, primarily about the presence of certain static ideas and norms; both sides agree that people have some ideas in their heads and social norms around them. The debate is about whether people *arrived at* these ideas or norms as a roughly rational reaction to objective conditions or through a *process of social construction*. It follows that a key part of making a claim that certain ideas, norms or identities have constitutive power – constituting the difference between worlds – is to trace a dynamic account of social construction that is presumably different from the dynamic accounts of the same actions offered by non-constructivist 'superstructure'-style arguments.

These are complex issues, and there is room for disagreement about them. My own view is that constructivist arguments can and should debate non-constructivist alternatives; all valid explanations require some 'understanding', and all constitutive arguments imply dynamic claims about process that compete with more traditional causal accounts (Parsons, 2015). That is not to say, however, that constructivism is just like other political science arguments but with different causes – like we might say about a contrast between Marxism (with objective materialist causes located in an economic landscape) and realism in IR (with objective materialist causes located in a security landscape). There *is* something special about constructivism that follows from its focus on distinctively social and interpretive aspects of action. To show a process of social construction that supports claims about the constitutive power of meanings and understandings, we must make a kind of argument that is qualitatively different from standard non-constructivist arguments.

How is it different? It seems to me that the core distinctiveness of constructivism lies not in addressing 'understandings', nor in focusing on static constitutive properties, but in its relationship to *contingency*. Contingency's role in constructivism is no secret; constructivists such as Onuf and Wendt are famous for portraying a 'world of our making', in which politics 'is what we make of it'. But the importance of contingency for how constructivism relates to other approaches may have been obscured by the contested lines discussed above.

To see why contingency puts constructivism in a special position, consider that standard non-constructivist explanations are enemies of contingency. They look for reasons why some set of conditions – in geography, economics, security competitions and so on – required a certain response that we see in action. To the extent real-world conditions were indeterminate, leaving some real openness for agency or accident in action, they have nothing to say. That does not mean that they cannot acknowledge contingency, of course. They can coherently allow that conditions were underdetermined over some range of possibilities, or that their causes have a probabilistic relationship to outcomes rather than a deterministic one. But contingency is not an integral part of their theorising.

Constructivists, by contrast, root their arguments in contingency. The basic logical format of any constructivist argument is that certain people faced an indeterminate set of 'real' conditions – at least across some range of options – and only arrived at a course of action as they adopted certain social constructs. By creativity or accident, they chose one of many imaginable sets of meanings, thereby building certain interpretations around themselves and 'constituting' one world from many that were otherwise possible.

Once certain social constructs are in place, some constructivist arguments may seem just as deterministic as others. Indeed, many constructivists who focus on a late stage of social construction – past initial acts of construction, when social constructs may become deeply embedded – are often criticised for exaggerating how tightly our ideas, norms and cultures lock us into certain worlds (just as critics say that realists exaggerate the importance of the international distribution of power, or that Marxists exaggerate the importance of class conflict, and that institutionalists exaggerate the channelling power of institutions). But at their roots, even the most seemingly deterministic cultural arguments have a different overall relationship to contingency than do standard non-constructivist theories. Even if a constructivist argues (for example) that we have all slavishly adopted ideas of globalisation and neoliberalism, binding ourselves into an invented world of 'market pressures', a fundamental implication of labelling such ideas 'socially constructed' is that *it did not have to be this way*. There was a time when people could have made many choices, but their creative or accidental adoption of certain ideas or norms engaged a series of social mechanisms that embedded them in one world. Another implication is that such a time may come again. If this is deeply a 'world of our making', though changing it may be difficult, it is imaginable that we can remake it.

Variations within constructivism

For students, the crucial point of the preceding section is that there is no single constructivist orthodoxy, but rather a set of debates about what the study of interpretive social constructs entails. Moreover, in addition to these epistemological fights there are substantive variations in the kinds of social construction we might theorise in the world, and a variety of methods we could use to highlight them. This section considers examples from constructivism's many strands.

Epistemological variations

Much of the preceding discussion has concerned epistemology: debates about how to define 'explanation' and the relationship between causality and constitutiveness are debates about how we construct knowledge about the world. Unsurprisingly, contrasting positions in these debates define the main distinctions in most surveys of constructivism.

The most common line is between 'modern' and 'postmodern' constructivists (Hopf, 1998; Adler, 2002; Jacobsen, 2003; Checkel, 2005; see also Chapter 8 in this volume). Certain constructivists who share much of the 'postmodern' position often call their view 'interpretivism' (see Box 5.1).

This division concerns views about how much the subjectivity of social constructs affects not just political actors but also academic observers. If political actors are bound within certain interpretations, why should we expect academics to be any less subjective? Postmodern constructivists and interpretivists tend to argue that the very notion of social construction means that science itself (and especially science about human action) is more a political, power-focused clash of interpretive agendas than anything that can relate to remotely 'true' claims about a 'real' world. In other words, they connect substantive views of social construction to an interpretivist epistemology. 'Modern' constructivists, on the other hand, tend to think that we can posit social construction among actors but still manage to make some acceptable (if modestly tentative) claims about how the socially constructed world 'really' works. The core of their position is usually quite simple (and is also a standard position in non-constructivist scholarship): just being aware of our inclination to interpretive bias helps us to solve the problem. If we set up careful research designs, and submit our arguments to open debate among many people with different views, then we can arrive at pragmatically acceptable claims about how the world really works. In short, for modern constructivists – like for other 'modern' scholars – how much the world is socially constructed is something we can show.

As one might expect, this difference between constructivists shows up most obviously in their engagement with non-constructivist alternatives. For example, in his book *Capital Rules* the modern constructivist Rawi Abdelal (2007) tries to show that traditional theories of power or economic interest fail to offer convincing explanations of the emergence and shape of the rules of international finance. Instead he offers evidence in the content, timing and patterns of support for various international agreements that traces much of today's financial world to the ideas and entrepreneurial leadership of (counterintuitively) some key leaders from the European Left. In a book on similar subjects but from a postmodern constructivist approach, Marike de Goede (2005) traces the 'genealogy' of the discourse and meanings surrounding international finance. She is especially interested in how activities that were perceived as corruption or gambling in the past became valued strategies of investment and risk management in the present day. Though she engages to a certain degree with non-constructivist thinking on finance, she is not directly concerned with claiming to offer a superior argument to account for specific international developments. Her emphasis is more that non-constructivist scholarship simply ignores the meanings and normative bases of financial dealings, and that she offers a different kind of narrative about the evolution of 'the moral dimension of money'.

Different mechanisms and different social constructs

Beyond epistemological differences, constructivists vary just as widely in terms of their concrete arguments about how social construction works. One of the clearest kinds of distinctions lies in the kinds of mechanisms that scholars emphasise in the process of social construction. I cannot discuss all the mechanisms they use, nor do distinctions between mechanisms exhaust the concrete variations in constructivist arguments, but a few examples provide some sense of the variety within this approach. Depending on which mechanism scholars prioritise, they also tend to evoke different views of the results of social construction: how people relate to the social constructs around them.

Socialisation

Socialisation is probably the most common mechanism in today's constructivist literature, and is even sometimes presented as a synonym for social construction overall (Checkel, 2005). In my view, however, scholarship since Durkheim has tended to imply a certain kind of mechanism in using this term. It suggests that norms or ideas spread in a relatively incremental, evolutionary way generated by repeated interaction within groups. A group of people come together in interaction. They could interact in a wide variety of ways, but through either accident, deliberation or initial innovative leadership, they orient themselves around certain norms or beliefs. Action becomes increasingly robustly embedded in the norms or beliefs over time, though the norms and beliefs are also constantly reshaped on the margins as they are reproduced.

To the extent that we see social construction operating by socialisation mechanisms, we also take on a certain view of what the resulting socially constructed world is like. Socialisation suggests a diffused, decentralised, collective and consensual process in which a group of people work their way to certain norms or ideas. It implies relatively low levels of contestation and variation within groups, since such irregularities would disrupt the repetitive rehearsing or social learning by which norms and ideas enter individual thinking. This in turn makes socialisation fairly distinct from power and politicking; it does not depend on 'carriers' with special authority, entrepreneurial spirit or charisma for social construction to happen. It need not be limited, however, to small groups, or to arenas where considerations of power are not in play. Wendt (1992) portrays the worldwide perception of international politics as an arena of anarchy and distinct 'national interests' as the result of long-term socialisation processes. In a much more specific empirical argument, Lewis (2005) shows how national diplomats in the European Union (EU) have become socialised into patterns of rhetoric and bargaining that produce more cooperative, consensual deal-making than rational choice theory would predict.

Persuasion

Another common line of constructivist argument focuses on entrepreneurial people who invent new ideas and sell them to others. These 'carriers' bring new interpretations into an arena and persuade others to take them up. These arguments tend to be much more explicitly political than socialisation arguments. Rather than portraying social construction as something that evolves almost without the consciousness of the actors, persuasion arguments rely on explicit advocates, who clearly believe in their new ideas or norms at a time before the ideas in question are embedded in broader action. Then the 'carriers' purposefully manage to spread the new ideas to others – due to either some qualities of the carriers (like charisma), the sheer force of their new concepts or frequently the indirect 'fit' of the new ideas with existing ideas or norms. To take another example from the context of the EU, advocates of the creation of a European single currency (the euro) in the 1990s tended to argue that the euro and a highly independent European Central Bank would deliver credible and stable monetary policies for all of Europe. Economists at the time often pointed out that these two things did not have to go together; national-level central banks could also provide credible, stable policies. But by connecting the euro project to widely shared notions of good monetary policy – an indirect 'fit' of ideas – champions of a single currency helped legitimise and sell their idea (Jabko, 1999).

Persuasion mechanisms imply quite a different socially constructed world from socialisation mechanisms. The more social construction operates by persuasion, the more we should see a world of conscious advocates of competing ideas, jockeying to persuade other key actors to adopt their agenda (for example, Finnemore and Sikkink, 1998). At the same time, we should see groups or networks of people with relatively coherent, conscious ideologies. The notion of persuasion and 'fit' tends to imply that people consciously consider and knit together their ideas, seeking at least some coherence in their overall mix of ideas and norms.

Bricolage

A third mechanism of social construction has some of the bottom-up, incremental feel of socialisation, some of the notion of entrepreneurial 'carriers' of persuasion, and an emphasis on complexity and incoherence that is somewhat different from both. The French verb *bricoler* means 'to tinker'. Bricolage arguments start from a view of a messy world of overlapping social constructs. In this view, we tend to develop ideas and norms and practices to suit rather discrete problems and goals, and we end up with a complex landscape of overlapping realms of action. At a daily level, our norms and ideas in schools, as consumers, as producers, within families, with friends or in politics may in fact be quite separate, though many of our actions have implications in more than one of these arenas. The same is true of political action more specifically;

it often engages considerations at many levels, and encounters 'friction between multiple political orders' (Lieberman, 2002). While this complexity of norms defines many actions as illegitimate, its overlaps and contradictions create space for actors to tinker with the available social constructs and recombine them in novel ways. Innovative recombinations alter the 'toolkit' of 'strategies of action' available to other actors in similar positions, changing the limits and possible overlaps for future action or further bricolage (Swidler, 1986). The overall result is a fairly decentralised, incremental mechanism of socially constructed change (Lévi-Strauss, 1966[1962]; Campbell, 2004). People who are placed at intersections of a landscape of incoherent norms and ideas generate new lines of action in an entrepreneurial way, but do not necessarily persuade others to take them up or impose them. Instead they simply feed back to alter future possibilities in the shared toolkit.

This emphasis on incremental change may sound similar to socialisation, but to the extent we see social construction through bricolage, it tends to imply quite a different view of the resulting socially constructed landscape. This is a world of incoherence – not consensual, collective identities. It is a world where people have a very 'externalised' relationship to ideas and norms. Unlike in most socialisation arguments, where the notion is that collective norms seep into our internal consciousness, actors encounter the hodgepodge of norms and practices as a set of external concepts. They are just 'the way things are done' in certain areas, whether or not we value or even consciously recognise them. We tinker with them to suit our immediate purposes.

Again, these alternative mechanisms only begin to touch on the variations between different kinds of constructivist arguments. The broader take-away point is one made in Chapter 1 in this book: constructivism, like rational choice theory or institutionalism, is a broad approach within which we can make many theoretical arguments. These arguments share some characteristics, but need not be consistent with each other: some constructivists think that socialisation processes are important in international bargaining within the EU, for example, and others do not. The basic notion that people create and act within social constructs can be built into a very wide range of more concrete theoretical claims.

Different methods

The methods with which constructivists specify and support their claims are almost as diverse as the arguments they make. Choices constructivists make in methods connect most strongly to the kind of constructivism in which they were trained, which carry certain kinds of methodological training as well. Constructivists with IR-focused training usually undertake close process-tracing over time to show how certain ideas or norms inform certain actions. Constructivists in comparative political economy tend to set up small-N cross-national comparisons to show how particular ideas or norms generate certain similar or different modes of action across cases. Poststructural scholars focus first and foremost on discourse analysis and deconstructionist critique. The constructivist school of 'sociological institutionalists' (see Chapter 4) are often trained in multiple methods, and frequently build their studies around quantitative analysis of changing patterns in norms, models and action over time.

This methodological diversity belies the common view of constructivist scholarship, especially among non-constructivists in political science, as a pure exercise in process-tracing or narrative storytelling. Process-tracing is indeed a central part of every constructivist methodology. But it is not as distinctive to constructivism as many scholars seem to think, and most constructivists combine process-tracing with other methodological steps.

Process-tracing has recently attracted complex discussions from methodologists, but its core dictum is rather simply to seek evidence of the pressures, incentives, motivations and decision-making calculus in any given instance of action (Bennett and Checkel, 2015). It instructs us to provide 'within-case' evidence of mechanisms that stands independently from cross-case patterns of initial conditions and outcomes (Brady and Collier, 2004). If one explanation of a deregulatory reform privileges sectoral business interests, did relevant business people perceive these interests and have contact with government officials? If another explanation focuses on deregulatory ideology of party-political actors, what evidence do we have that these actors held these views? Did the push to reform largely circumvent business people or bureaucratic experts? If another explanation focuses on the influence of international organisations (IO), what evidence do we have that IO actors held certain views, and did IO contacts or actions feature prominently in the process and timing of regulatory change? These examples of process-tracing for diverse arguments (some constructivist, some not) effectively echo a point made earlier: whatever kind of explanation they offer, political scientists today tend to ask for some evidence of mechanisms and processes. All kinds of plausible mechanisms in human action – rational choice, constructivist or otherwise – make interpretive claims about what people perceived and thought. Thus constructivist methods are not fundamentally distinctive for including interpretive process-tracing.

If constructivist scholarship seems distinctive in its strong reliance on narrative process-tracing, this is a question of degree. Once we posit the plausibility of social construction – variation in actors' interpretations that is autonomous, to some degree, from a 'real' environment – we are certainly driven to pay fine attention to evidence of rhetoric, discourse and apparent rules in decision-making. Besides just seeking thicker evidence of actors' understandings or discourse and decision-making processes than in typical rationalist accounts, however, the moves most constructivists make fit at a basic logical level with classic methodological orthodoxy. In particular, they hold up thickly interpretive accounts of processes to various kinds of comparisons across patterns of action and environmental conditions. Like non-constructivist scholars, they use either counterfactual comparisons, small-N comparisons or large-N comparisons to highlight the emergence and/or distinctive effects of particular social constructs.

IR-trained constructivists and poststructuralists tend to rely the most heavily on counterfactual comparisons. Their most common approach is to argue, on the basis of close interpretive process-tracing, that certain people could have (or, more aggressively, would have) acted quite differently given the presence of other imaginable social constructs. Poststructuralists tend to pay less attention to documenting the indeterminacy of objective conditions that feature in non-constructivist arguments, but by the same basic process they often reach insightful observations about how certain actions depended on particular discursive foundations. This is not to say that counterfactual thinking is unproblematic, but it has been increasingly accepted by mainstream methodologists (Tetlock and Belkin, 1996). Even if all we have is one case, we can use contrasts to counterfactual 'cases' (scenarios where conditions were different) to formulate and even support accounts of action.

Like many non-constructivist scholars in political economy, many comparative constructivists turn to small-N comparison as a middle ground between the pitfalls of single-case counterfactuals and abstract large-N studies. They tend to seek closely matched cases to show that the interpretations they reveal in process-tracing make a substantial difference in otherwise similar contexts. In studies ranging from the early Industrial Revolution to the emergence of workers' movements and twentieth-century economic policy-making, scholars have shown that actors in comparable situations adopted different strategies due to different ideas (Dobbin, 1994; Biernacki, 1995; Berman, 1998; Blyth, 2002). The reverse strategy is to show that similar interpretations prevail across strikingly different material contexts, as in Finnemore's (1996) study of UNESCO's diffusion of science bureaucracies (see also Meyer et al., 1997). Another inversion of the same logic is to turn comparisons inward on standard national cases, moving downward analytically to see how small groups or individuals within a shared context held similar or different interpretations of collective problems and action (Parsons, 2002).

Demonstration of constructivist claims through large-N comparisons, finally, is common in sociology and is beginning to appear in political science. Economic sociologists tend to use process-tracing-based interpretation to uncover what they suspect are socially constructed norms, models or practices, and then turn to sophisticated quantitative tools to show why these norms or models fit with constructivist-style arguments better than alternatives. They typically gather datasets on organisational models, norms or behaviour, or on network links between individuals or organisations, to show how changing patterns over time reflect the diffusion of certain social constructs rather than patterns of technical competition or material resources (Powell and DiMaggio, 1991). Such methods are still rare among political science constructivists, but they are beginning to spread (Darden and Grzymala-Busse, 2006; Chweiroth, 2007). Chweiroth (2007), for example, shows that the extent of neoliberal economic reforms across Latin America correlates more strongly to the presence of nodes of elites trained in neoliberal economics than to the material or organisational conditions that non-constructivists would expect to see behind patterns of liberalisation.

Conclusion

Constructivism is a broad family of arguments built on the notion that people only arrive at certain actions due to their adoption of certain 'social constructs' to interpret their world. It provides a distinct substantive view of how and why the political world forms and 'hangs together' (Ruggie, 1998). As such, we might think of it as just adding another kind of approach alongside more traditional approaches in political science, which tend to debate the relative influence of various kinds of causes. To take some of the usual suspects, Marxists explain the world as a function of an economic landscape, realists as a function of a landscape of security competition, (most) institutionalists as a function of an organisational landscape – and constructivists as a function of a 'landscape' of ideas, norms, identities and practices.

But social constructs are not just another kind of cause. Since this 'landscape' of social constructs is created by actors themselves, and since it is a relatively intangible kind of 'landscape' that interacts profoundly with the nature and inclinations of the actors, constructivists have long debated whether their arguments even operate in the same realm as non-constructivist arguments. For some, once we posit a socially constructed world, we must recognise that the Understanding/Explanation distinction, the Causal/Constitutive line, and/or the basic problem of observers' subjectivity shift our focus away from causal explanation and social 'science'. Powerful lines of constructivist thinking develop these moves into the assertion that human action cannot be studied like other scientific topics: scholarship about politics should aim at interpretations of actors' interpretations, not the chimerical lures of causality and explanation.

Others, including me, hold that we can advance constructivist arguments about understanding, constitutiveness and contingency in ways that engage with non-constructivist theories. In my own view this does not mean we must concede anything to non-constructivist approaches; the reason to engage with more orthodox alternatives is not necessarily to find some 'middle ground', but to use their different views of the world as foils to highlight how constructivism tells a different kind of story (Parsons, 2015). It is difficult to advance a set of interesting claims about how social construction shapes the world unless we at least entertain, for argument's sake, the non-constructivist alternative that social construction does *not* shape the world.

Whether we conceive of constructivism as a distinctive competitive within the social sciences or as a separate scholarly endeavour, it is now well established as a major way of thinking about politics. Its diversity is one sign of its vitality, and we can confidently expect that constructivism will play an increasingly prominent role in the future of political science.

Further reading

- For a short summary of Durkheim and Weber in historical context, see Andrew Janos (1986), chapter 1. Two classics of constructivist thought – both remarkably readable – are Weber (1992 [1930]) and Polanyi (1944).
- For a relatively accessible entry point to constructivist thinking from a philosopher, see Searle (1995).
- For a broader and deeper discussion and 'mapping' of constructivist thinking, see Parsons (2007), chapter 4.
- Very accessible major discussions of the basic notion of constructivism, though they may conflict partly with some views offered here, are Winch (1958) and Geertz (1973).
- The best-known landmark in contemporary constructivist theory remains Wendt (1999).

Chapter 6

Feminist and Gendered Approaches

MERYL KENNY AND FIONA MACKAY

Taking women and gender seriously fundamentally transforms how we understand and approach the study of politics. Feminist approaches are both corrective – in that they have sought to rectify the gendered 'blinkers and biases' of mainstream political science – and transformative – in that they aim not only to expose gender power inequalities, but also to change them (Lovenduski, 1998; Hawkesworth, 2005).

In this chapter, we evaluate the implications of a feminist perspective for political analysis, focusing in particular on empirically based political science, rather than the prescriptive or normative side of the discipline (see Randall, 2010; Disch and Hawkesworth, 2016). We begin with a brief overview of feminism, before moving on to assess what it means to argue that political science is a historically 'gendered' discipline. We then evaluate two main trends in feminist approaches to political analysis: first, foundational and ongoing work on 'women *in* politics'; and, second, the growing body of work on 'gender *and* politics', which has raised crucial questions about the gendered nature of political institutions and power dynamics. We conclude by discussing some of the dilemmas and challenges that remain in the field, evaluating the overall impact of feminism on political science, and looking towards the future.

What is feminism?

Defining feminism is not an easy task. Its origins lie outside academia, as the ideology of a 'critical and disruptive social movement' (Randall, 2010: 114). Most definitions of feminism share a common concern with women's unequal position in society, calling into question power relations between women and men traditionally defended as 'natural' (Bryson, 1999; Lovenduski, 2005; Randall, 2010). Most would also agree that feminist theories are 'tools designed for a purpose' (Jaggar and Rothenberg, 1993: xvii). Feminist approaches are explicitly political in that they seek not only to recognise and understand gender power relations, but also to change and transform them.

Beyond this, however, there is considerable debate and disagreement over political priorities, framing, strategies and goals. Feminist approaches encapsulate a range of positions and interests, shaped by different theoretical perspectives, but also by the 'diverse experiences of different groups of women' (Bryson, 1999: 8). Most categorisations focus on different historical strands or 'waves' of feminism, classifications that are sometimes artificially delineated and applied (Randall, 2010; Evans, 2015). First-wave feminism generally refers to movements focused on legal and constitutional rights and suffrage in the nineteenth and early twentieth centuries; while second-wave feminism (1960s–1980s) brought attention to broader issues of equality, including in the workplace and the family, and in relation to domestic violence and reproductive rights. The resurgence of feminist activism in the USA and UK from the 1990s is often referred to as the 'third wave' of feminism; yet the term has been used in differing ways, including as a response to the second wave's perceived failure to address diversity and include women of colour, as a neoliberal brand of feminism, or as a generational frame (Evans, 2015).

It is, therefore, more accurate to speak of 'feminisms' in the plural, rather than feminism as a single coherent project. As Vicky Randall (2010: 114) notes, 'rather than maintain that feminism offers a coherent account or meta-theory of its own ... it is more appropriately viewed as a developing dialogue around a common but evolving agenda'. In political science, this agenda centres on the shared objective of correcting gender biases in the 'mainstream' of the discipline.

Political science: gendered foundations

Historically, most political scientists were men, and the spheres of public politics that they studied were likewise overwhelmingly male (Lovenduski, 1981; Sapiro, 1998; Randall, 2010). Some decades later, the balance has shifted, yet political science remains a relatively 'inhospitable' discipline to women and gender, particularly compared to other social science fields. While there has been a steady and long-term increase in numbers, women are still only 30 per cent of the discipline overall and are particularly under-represented among the professoriate (Bates et al., 2012). Meanwhile, feminist approaches are still often sidelined in political science research and teaching (Childs and Krook, 2006; Foster et al., 2012; Evans and Amery, 2016).

In one of the first comprehensive discussions of the relationship between feminism and politics, Joni Lovenduski notes that 'there never was any way that the modern study of politics could fail to be sexist', given that 'women usually do not dispose of public power' (1981: 89). Political science was 'about' politics and public life (Sapiro, 1998: 70). Issues of women and gender were, therefore, usually ignored, with women relegated to the private sphere and 'low politics', while men were associated with the public sphere and 'high politics', the central focus of political science enquiry.

In those few early instances when political scientists did address women, they often fell back on sexist stereotypes of women's essential 'nature' (Randall, 2010: 117). The most cited example of this is the American political scientist Robert Lane's infamous reflections on women's political participation in his book *Political Life*:

> [I]t is too seldom remembered in the American society that working girls and career women who insistently serve the community in volunteer capacities, and women with extracurricular interests of an absorbing kind are often borrowing their time and attention and capacity for relaxed play and love from their children to whom it rightfully belongs. As Kardiner points out, the rise in juvenile delinquency (and, he says, homosexuality) is partly to be attributed to the feminist movement and what it did to the American mother. (Lane, 1959: 354–355)

In a classic article, Susan Bourque and Jean Grossholtz (1974) identify four categories of distortion of the participation of women in politics:

1. 'Fudging the footnotes', in which inaccurate statements are made which are not substantiated by the cited material;
2. The assumption of male dominance without critical examination;
3. The acceptance of masculinity as ideal political behaviour;
4. A commitment to the 'eternal feminine', basing explanations of political behaviour on unexamined stereotypes of women's domestic roles.

These kinds of distortions served to perpetuate gendered 'myths' about women's political behaviour – most notably the stereotype of the 'a-political woman', encapsulated here in Almond and Verba's text *The Civic Culture*:

> It would appear that women differ from men in their political behavior only in being somewhat more frequently apathetic, parochial, conservative, and sensitive to personality, emotional, and aesthetic aspects of political life and electoral campaigns. (Almond and Verba, 1963: 325)

On further examination, however, these explanations were often based on 'minute political differences between men and women', inconsistently supported by data, or not supported at all (Lovenduski, 1981: 93–94; see also Bourque and Grossholtz, 1974). Decades later, arguably no political scientist would make a statement on par with Robert Lane's, but gendered stereotypes about women's political participation persist in some academic and political commentary (see Box 6.1 for a recent case study).

Political science was also heavily shaped by the legacy of positivism and the understanding that 'good' social science was supposed to be

BOX 6.1 Gender, voting and the Scottish independence referendum

A referendum on Scottish independence took place on 18 September 2014. The referendum question, which voters answered with 'Yes' or 'No', was 'Should Scotland be an independent country?' In the run-up to the vote, polling evidence pointed to a gender gap in support for independence, with men more likely than women to say they were going to vote Yes (Ormston, 2014).

What explains this disparity? Some pollsters attributed the gender gap to psychological and evolutionary predispositions, arguing that women were somehow 'naturally' more hesitant and less political than men, and therefore unable to take a 'clear view' towards independence (Curtice, 2012). These kinds of gendered assumptions were also reflected in campaign messaging, most notably in an infamous 'Better Together' ad entitled 'The Woman Who Made Up Her Mind', featuring an undecided woman voter weighing up the pros and cons of independence at her kitchen table.

Feminist scholars, however, have asked whether the gender gap expressed in polling might instead be explained as a rational reaction to the uncertainty of independence. For example, Verge, Guinjoan and Rodon (2015) find that women's support for independence is moderated by the hypothetical 'futures' and possibilities of the independent state that they are presented with. While positive scenarios do not produce significant gender differences in support for independence, in negative scenarios (like being expelled from the European Union or economic problems) risk-averse women are significantly less likely to vote for independence than men with similar risk-taking attitudes. The authors suggest that risk-aversion might well be overcome in circumstances where political actors frame constitutional change as a means to address women's policy concerns, and where women are visible participants in independence campaigns.

'objective' and 'value-free' (Sapiro, 1998). Many early feminist political scientists positioned their critique within this positivist frame, challenging the masculine biases that shaped this supposedly 'scientific' method. Focusing only on measurable political behaviour, they argued, prevented the identification and recognition of 'not only the ... exclusion of women from what is traditionally political, but also the inclusion of politics in what women have traditionally done' (Nelson, 1989: 21). Feminist scholars therefore sought to expand the definition of politics, incorporating actors, activities and questions usually sidelined in existing research in the field (Lovenduski, 1998; Sapiro, 1998).

Similar critiques were made by feminist scholars in the field of International Relations (IR) from the late 1980s onwards (Elshtain, 1987; Enloe, 1989; Tickner, 1992). Early feminist IR scholars highlighted the gendered assumptions underpinning the field, and asked what the discipline of IR might look like if women's day-to-day lives were included. For example, in her groundbreaking work *Bananas, Beaches and Bases*, Cynthia Enloe (1989) explores the ways in which international politics – including tourism, nationalism, military bases, diplomacy and the international economy – are dependent upon women's work. Arguing that the 'personal is international', she also highlights the ways in which the international is personal, demonstrating the extent to which governments depend upon certain kinds of private relationships to conduct their foreign affairs.

Women *in* political science

In the stories we tell about feminist political science, distinctions are often made between different 'stages' in the development of the subfield, progressively moving from simpler to more complex ideas. The first stage, as discussed in the previous section, critiqued mainstream political science's exclusion of women as political actors. The second stage focused more explicitly on 'women *in* politics', integrating women into the theories, frameworks and research areas from which they had been excluded. Subsequently, the question of 'where are the women?' has expanded into questions of 'which women?', driven by feminist theory and a growing body of scholarship on women of colour and intersectionality (cf. Crenshaw, 1989).

Historical reviews of feminist political science often highlight the limitations of these kinds of second-stage analyses, referring to it as an 'add women and stir' approach and suggesting that filling the gaps is a relatively uncomplicated task, or a minor change or addition. But asking the question of 'where are the women' remains an essential component of feminist research. Moreover, 'adding' women in can have significant effects, radically transforming the original mixture into something quite new (Goertz and Mazur, 2008).

Take, for example, the concept of democracy. There is a long history of scholarship and debate on how democracy should be defined and measured. Yet little of this research has made mention of gender or, more specifically, women (Waylen, 1994). In principle, however, as Pamela Paxton (2000, 2008) argues, the concept of democracy is gendered. Women are implicitly (and, indeed, sometimes explicitly) part of the definition of democracy, in that most definitions of democracy emphasise the importance of universal suffrage and the participation of all major adult social groups (Paxton, 2008; see Box 6.2). As such, women – as a major social group, comprising roughly half of the population – should be included as part of a universal suffrage requirement.

In practice, however, women are often 'deliberately excluded or simply overlooked' in the measurement of democracy (Paxton, 2008: 52; see also Lovenduski, 1981). As Paxton highlights, measurements commonly use male suffrage as the sole indicator of a country's transition to democracy, or assume that the achievement of female suffrage will not change a country's 'score' on a graded measure of democracy. Huntington (1991: 16), for example, operationalises his definition of democracy

BOX 6.2 Defining democracy

Democracy is a system of government that features 'a highly inclusive level of political participation in the selection of leaders and policies, at least through regular and fair elections, *such that no major (adult) social group is excluded*' (Diamond et al., 1990: 6–7, emphasis added).

Democracy provides '*all citizens* with both the opportunity to participate in the governing process, as manifested by *universal adult suffrage* and free and fair elections' (Muller, 1988: 65, emphasis added).

A political system is democratic when 'its most powerful collective decision-makers are selected through fair, honest and periodic elections in which candidates freely compete for votes and in which *virtually all the adult population is eligible to vote*' (Huntington, 1991: 7, emphasis added).

using the criteria that 50 per cent of adult males are eligible to vote – a voting population made up of roughly 25 per cent of a typical adult population. This, of course, allows countries to transition to democracy without women having the right to vote.

What difference does 'adding women' make? Paxton's analysis demonstrates that simply adding the variable of women's suffrage can have dramatic consequences, changing existing regime classifications, and challenging existing theories that explain democratisation. Many authors, for example, give Switzerland a democratic transition date of 1848, but adding in the variable of women's suffrage moves this date forward 123 years to 1971 (and in some Swiss cantons, women didn't receive the right to vote on local issues until 1990). Meanwhile, Samuel Huntington's (1991) conceptualisation of 'waves' of democracy changes significantly once women's suffrage is taken into account, with many countries moving from one wave to another. When women are included, only sixteen countries remain in the 'first wave' of democracy, compared to Huntington's original thirty (see Table 6.1). The first wave of democracy also changes to a much shorter time period. This, in turn, challenges existing assumptions about the age and regional prevalence of democracy and points to alternative factors that shape processes of democratisation, including social movements and international actors (Paxton, 2000, 2008).

Gender *and* political science

This foundational and ongoing work on women *in* politics has been joined – but not supplanted by – a focus on gender *and* politics. As Lovenduski (1998: 338) highlights, feminist political scientists have become

Table 6.1 *Waves of democracy with and without women's suffrage*

Countries	*Transition Dates* (Without Women's Suffrage)*	*Transition Dates** (With Women's Suffrage)*
Australia, Canada, Finland, Iceland, Ireland, New Zealand, Sweden, UK, USA, Austria, Denmark, Netherlands, Norway, Czechoslovakia, Poland, Spain	First Wave (1828–1926)	First Wave (1893–1931)
Chile, Belgium, Colombia, France, West Germany, Italy, Japan, Argentina, Greece, Hungary, Uruguay	First Wave (1828–1926)	Second Wave (1943–1966)
Switzerland, Portugal, East Germany	First Wave (1828–1926)	Third Wave (1971–)

**Source*: Huntington (1991: 14). Huntington argues that there are three distinct waves of democracy, with reverse waves in between, in which some (but not all) of the countries that had previously transitioned reverted to non-democratic rule.
***Source*: Paxton (2000, 2008).

increasingly dissatisfied with the 'analytical utility of the concept of sex', understood as a discrete and dichotomous variable separating the categories man and woman, preferring 'gender' instead as an organising term. This shift in the field has been accompanied by calls for innovative approaches, methods and toolkits that not only enumerate gender and sex differences, but also contextualise them; that can capture gendered dynamics between women and men in political institutions; and that can identify and expose the gendered rules, norms and practices that underpin seemingly gender-neutral institutions (Mackay, 2004: 111).

However, there are still inconsistencies in the ways in which feminist approaches define and operationalise the concept of gender, ranging from studies which use gender as a simple synonym for sex to more dynamic understandings of gender as relational (Randall, 2010). The general movement to 'rethink' gender has also been influenced by poststructuralist approaches, challenging the assumption that binary sex/gender is a natural or given division, and arguing that bodies are constructed as male and female through the repeated 'performance' of gender (Butler, 1990). Yet, as Karen Beckwith (2005) argues, a 'common language' of gender does exist in the field, even if it is not always explicitly articulated (see Box 6.3).

In a widely used definition set out by Joan Scott (1986: 1067), gender can be understood as a constitutive element of social relations based upon perceived differences between women and men. From an

BOX 6.3 Defining gender

Gender must be understood as 'an analytic category within which humans think about and organize their social activity rather than as a natural consequence of sex difference' (Harding, 1986: 17).

'Gender is a constitutive element of social relationships based on perceived differences between the sexes, and gender is a primary way of signifying relationships of power' (Scott, 1986: 1067).

'Gender must be understood as a social structure. It is not an expression of biology, nor a fixed dichotomy in human life or character. It is a pattern in our social arrangements, and the everyday activities shaped by those arrangements' (Connell and Pearse, 2015: 11).

Gender is 'a way of categorizing, ordering, and symbolizing power, or hierarchically structuring relationships among different categories of people, and different human activities symbolically associated with masculinity or femininity' (Cohn, 2013: 3).

analytical perspective, gender can therefore be seen as a useful 'category' to examine and identify the socially constructed (rather than natural or given) institutional roles, identities and practices conceived of as 'masculine' or 'feminine' in particular contexts (Beckwith, 2005: 131; see also Harding, 1986).

Gender does not, therefore, map onto a simple dichotomy of 'male and female, men and women' (Beckwith, 2005: 131). Indeed, employing gender in this way means that gender remains a relevant analytical category for analysis, even in contexts where women's agency is deemed an irrelevant causal factor, or where women are not present. An example of this can be seen in the small but emerging body of work on men and masculinities in politics (see, for example, Bjarnegård, 2013; Murray, 2014). While other branches of the social sciences have generated a substantial literature on the social construction of masculinity (cf. Connell, 1995), feminist political scientists have been less interested in directly examining men and masculinity, particularly compared to their counterparts in feminist IR. For example, many feminist IR scholars highlight the ways in which militarism and masculinity are intertwined, arguing that militaries are crucial sites for the construction of particular forms of masculinity – associated with toughness, aggression, physical and psychological strength – which, in turn, make war, violence and military solutions more likely (see, for example, Enloe, 1993; Cockburn, 2010; Duncanson, 2013).

This, however, is changing in political science. Murray's work (2014), for example, shifts the question from women's political under-representation to male over-representation, examining how male dominance in politics affects the quality of representation for both men and women. Meanwhile, Bjarnegård (2013) offers an in-depth investigation of the causes of male dominance in politics, focusing in particular on clientelist political networks in developing democracies such as Thailand (see Box 6.4).

What holds these different feminist approaches together is the recognition that gender is a 'primary way of signifying relationships of power' (Scott, 1986: 1067) – intersecting with race, class and other structural power relations. Gender makes 'distinctions between different categories of people, valorizes some over others, and organizes access to resources, rights, responsibilities, authority, and life options along the lines demarcating these groups' (Cohn, 2013: 4). Gender can, therefore, also be conceived as a 'process' through which structures and policies may have a differential impact upon women and men, while also providing different opportunities to actors seeking favourable gendered outcomes (Beckwith, 2005: 132).

These more complex understandings of gender have shifted the focus from women at the individual level to an increasing interest in institutional-level analysis, focusing on the underlying structures which underpin 'institu tionalised advantages and disadvantages' (Duerst-Lahti and Kelly, 1995: 44; see also Kenny, 2007; Krook and Mackay, 2011). The institutional 'turn' in the field has been both theoretically and empirically eclectic, frequently drawing upon insights from other disciplines, most notably

BOX 6.4 Men and masculinities in politics

Who runs the world? The short answer is: men. Despite a global upwards trend in women's representation, 77 per cent of parliamentarians worldwide are men (Inter-Parliamentary Union, 2017). New work in the field asks why this is the case, shifting the focus from women's under-representation to male over-representation and problematising the role of men and masculinities in politics. An excellent example of this is Elin Bjarnegård's (2013) study of gender and political recruitment in Thailand, which takes a closer look at the political practices that facilitate and reinforce male dominance in politics.

The Thai political landscape is marked by patronage and clientelism, particularly in rural areas. Clientelism – understood as the exchange of personal favours for personal support – requires the building and maintenance of close-knit personal informal networks. These networks are crucial for social acceptance and for being considered a suitable candidate for political office. But they are also highly gendered. Indeed, Bjarnegård finds that Thai male politicians largely cooperate with other men, as male political actors are more likely to have access to the political resources and networks needed to ensure electoral success. Women, in contrast, do not have access to the crucial (and gendered) 'homosocial capital' needed to build political networks and gain electoral power.

from work on gender and organisations in the field of sociology (see, for example, Acker, 1990; Savage and Witz, 1992). But, while institutionally focused feminist political science is internally diverse, work in the field shares a foundational concern with both 'the *gendered character* and the *gendering effects*' of political institutions (Mackay, 2011: 181; emphasis added; also see Chapter 4).

To say that an institution is 'gendered' means that constructions of masculinity and femininity are intertwined in the daily culture or 'logic' of political institutions, rather than 'existing out in society or fixed within individuals which they then bring whole to the institution' (Kenney, 1996: 456). Thus institutions rely on particular ideas about gender in order to function, but they are also producers of ideas about appropriate masculinities and femininities; they prescribe acceptable forms of behaviour, rules and values for men and women within institutions (Chappell, 2006). Institutions are not, of course, only gendered. They are also shaped by – and reproduce – other intersecting categories of 'race' and ethnicity, class, caste, dis/ability and sexuality (see Box 6.5). Intersectionality – a term first coined by Kimberlé Crenshaw (1989) – has, therefore, become a key analytic framework for studying not only identity politics but, importantly for gender and politics scholars, the effects of interlocking structures of power (Weldon, 2006).

Next, we briefly review three key areas of feminist research, focusing on international and comparative trends: political representation, political parties and the state. While the full range and breadth of feminist political science is beyond the scope of this chapter, these three areas provide an illustration of the institutional 'turn' in feminist political science, and the significant (if at times incomplete) shift from

BOX 6.5 Race-gendered institutions

In a landmark study, Mary Hawkesworth (2003) draws on the concepts of both gendered institutions and intersectionality to present a theory of the US Congress as a 'race-gendered' institution. Inequalities of race and gender are perpetuated through everyday processes and institutional dynamics, despite formal rules and procedures of political equality. At the intersection of race and gender, congresswomen of colour face particular constraints that are qualitatively and quantitatively different from those faced by either male congressmen of colour or white women.

Analysing congressional records and personal accounts of the 103rd and 104th Congress, Hawkesworth identifies political mechanisms of 'race-gendering' that combine to marginalise and disempower congresswomen of colour and the interests they seek to represent. These practices include *silencing*, *stereotyping*, *invisibility*, *exclusion*, *discrediting*, and demanding higher standards of evidence and expertise from women of colour than from other groups. Such practices persist regardless of partisan composition or party regime.

'women *in*' to 'gender *and*' politics in the field (for an extended review, see also Lovenduski, 1998).

Political representation

Political representation is a central concern of feminist politics and gender and politics research. In particular, scholarship has focused on the questions of the descriptive representation of women (the presence of women 'standing for' women), and the substantive representation of women ('acting for' women, and promoting women's interests). A central puzzle for scholars is the relationship between 'representativeness' and 'representation' – that is, between descriptive and substantive representation. Normative, conceptual and empirical dimensions are intertwined; empirical studies take place against a backdrop of complex theorising about political representation (Phillips, 1995; Mansbridge, 1999), gender (Lovenduski, 1998), intersectionality (Smooth, 2011), the nature of identities and poststructuralist concerns about whether the category 'women' is sufficiently stable to have collective interests at all (Butler, 1990; Pringle and Watson, 1992).

Much of the early work in this area focused on the political, socio-economic and cultural variables that explain cross-national variations in women's descriptive representation, including systematic factors (such as electoral systems), party political factors (see following section) and individual factors (including resources and status) (for a comprehensive overview, see Paxton and Hughes, 2017). Counting women is relatively simple; however, capturing the links between descriptive and substantive representation is more complicated. Investigations of attitudes, legislative activities and priorities, using a variety of methods including surveys, interviews and policy case studies, tend to find that female legislators are more likely than their male counterparts to 'act for' women, although within constraints (see, for example, Wängnerud, 2000; Swers, 2002; Mateo Diaz, 2005; Dodson, 2006). However, presence – at whatever numerical strength – is mediated by political party affiliation, intersectional identities, individual and collective capacities and inclinations, and institutional environments. As such, there is an increasing recognition that answering questions about the difference women representatives make requires that theories of representation be integrated with theories of institutions and institutional change (Lovenduski, 2005: 145; see also Mackay, 2004, 2008; Krook, 2009).

Over time, the central focus of empirical research has shifted from what 'difference' the presence of women representatives makes to questions of 'how the substantive representation of women occurs' (Childs and Krook, 2008). Contemporary scholarship has moved on from a near-exclusive focus on parliaments and legislatures and increasingly recognises the multiple sites and actors involved in interest representation and policy-making, including executives (Annesley and Gains, 2010), bureaucracies (particularly women's policy machineries) (Chappell, 2002, McBride and

Mazur, 2010) and judiciaries (Hoekstra et al., 2014), as well as extra-institutional spaces such as civil society (Weldon, 2002). More recently, feminist scholars have also begun to consider the challenge posed by conservative and anti-feminist representatives who claim to act for women (see, for example, Celis and Childs, 2014).

Feminising political parties

Political parties have notably been described as the 'missing variable' in gender politics research (Baer, 1993), a lacuna rectified in the early 1990s with the publication of Joni Lovenduski and Pippa Norris's classic edited collection *Gender and Party Politics* (1993). Across its eleven substantive chapters, this comparative text evaluated women's demands for inclusion, and the responses parties made to those demands, not only in terms of women's numerical representation, but also the representation of women's policy concerns. Subsequent research in the field has continued to explore the interactive relationship between gender and party politics, conceptualising parties as both *gendered* and *gendering* (Celis et al., 2016: 572; see also Lovenduski, 2005; Bjarnegård, 2013; Kenny, 2013). In doing so, this rapidly growing body of literature has moved from focusing on women's (and men's) activities within parties, to evaluating the institutional conditions under which women can achieve concrete gains (Kittilson, 2006).

Much of this work continues to focus on women's descriptive representation, including the relationship between gender, voting behaviour and political parties (see, for example, Campbell, 2006); party strategies to increase the selection and election of women candidates, including gender quotas (Dahlerup, 2006; Krook, 2009; Franceschet et al., 2012); and processes of candidate selection and recruitment within parties (Norris and Lovenduski, 1995; Bjarnegård, 2013; Kenny, 2013). In particular, the growing body of work on gender and political recruitment has put the focus squarely on parties as gendered organisations, investigating the ways in which gender shapes the structures, practices and rules of candidate selection and recruitment (both formal and informal) (for a review, see Kenny and Verge, 2016). This literature provides ample evidence of the ways in which parties often resist or block women's access to political office, identifying practices ranging from running women in 'no-hope' seats where they have little chance of winning to practices of local patronage and the privileging of 'favourite sons', and, even in some cases, committing electoral fraud in order to sidestep formal gender equality reforms (Ryan et al., 2010; Hinojosa, 2012; Bjarnegård and Kenny, 2015).

A second, and related, body of party politics research focuses on substantive representation, arguing that a gendered perspective can offer important insights for theories and frameworks of party characteristics, competition and change. Childs (2008), for example, develops a typology of feminisation and party types, evaluating the extent to which political parties integrate women as political actors and address women's policy concerns (cf. Young, 2000; Lovenduski, 2005).

Gendering the state and state feminism

As in other subfields of enquiry, feminist conceptions of the state have changed markedly since the 1980s. We can trace important shifts from a patriarchal to a gendered conception of the state; from preoccupations with descriptive to substantive dimensions; and from notions of a monolithic state to a differentiated one, comprising a complex set of gendered institutions and discourses, which in turn have gendering effects (for comprehensive reviews, see Chappell, 2013; Kantola, 2006; for similar discussions in feminist IR, see Kantola, 2007). These shifts have happened in parallel with the increasing adoption of gender equality norms and policy goals by states, through global processes of norm diffusion (Krook and True, 2012), and the growth of state feminism including though the proliferation of state women's policy agencies (Squires, 2007). The Research Network on Gender, Politics and the State (RNGS), for example, has studied the state-women's movement nexus in comparative perspective, tracing the conditions under which women's movements influence the state through their interaction with women's policy agencies in areas as diverse as job training and abortion (see McBride and Mazur, 2010).

Scholarship continues to expose the relative exclusion of women from the state, especially from positions of power in its economic, political, cultural and military institutions. But, more important are conceptions – influenced to a lesser or greater degree by post-structuralism – of the state not as a single or coherent entity, but as a differentiated set of institutions, agencies and discourses through which specific gender power relations are constructed and reproduced (Pringle and Watson, 1992; see also Chapter 8). While some work gives primacy to discourse, other studies combine institutional and discursive approaches to understand the gendered dynamics of continuity and change within and across states (Kantola, 2006; Krook and Mackay, 2011). Louise Chappell's (2002) 'most-similar' comparative study of Australia and Canada is a good example of such a combination. Her study highlighted the obstacles and opportunities created by the differentiated state for feminist engagement, pointing to similar gendered institutional logics operating across different institutional arenas in the same polity, as well as differences between similar institutions in the two states. Institutional contexts present constraints but also openings, leading feminists in Canada to focus on legal and constitutional arenas, compared with strategies of state feminism and multilevel advocacy by their Australian counterparts.

Most extant work has focused on Western democratic states; however, feminist scholars drawing on experiences in postcolonial contexts in Africa, Asia and Latin America challenge the degree of influence attributed to the state by Western scholarship (Goetz, 2007; Mukhopadhyay, 2007; Htun and Weldon, 2011). Meanwhile, working in the intersection between politics and IR, researchers are increasingly grappling with the gendered dimensions and consequences of state reconfiguration in an era of neoliberal globalisation (Banaszak et al., 2003), and the apparent shift from state-centric modes of government to diffuse and interdependent forms of governance involving multiple state and non-state actors at local, national and global scales (Kantola, 2007; Rai and Waylen, 2008; Caglar et al., 2013).

Dilemmas and challenges

Over the past several decades of gender politics research, we have seen the production of many – as Sapiro (1998) notes, probably too many – critical reviews of the continuing marginalisation of women and gender in political science research. Indeed, as Lovenduski (2015) provocatively asks in a recent essay, is political science still worthwhile for feminists? Why should gender politics scholars continue to engage with a discipline that largely ignores their concerns?

At the same time, gender politics scholarship faces criticisms from a feminist perspective – that it is not 'bold' enough, and that it has not pursued 'the feminist analysis of politics to its most radical conclusions' (Randall, 2010: 133). Feminist political science has 'never abandoned its interest in the political', conventionally defined (Mackay, 2004: 100; see also Lovenduski, 1998). Instead, it has insisted that gender is central to political processes and institutions, posing a fundamental challenge to conventional understandings of political life, and linking public and private and formal and informal spheres (Mackay, 2004: 100). Most gender politics scholarship sits squarely within 'mainstream' political science and (sometimes uncritically) adopts traditional methods – despite a tendency to interdisciplinarity in feminist research more generally (Lovenduski, 1981; Kenney, 1996; Randall, 2010).

In grappling with this 'double bind', research in feminist political science has generally taken a problem-driven rather than a method-driven approach, employing a broad range of theoretical and methodological frames and synthesising different types of methods in innovative ways to answer specific questions (Childs and Krook, 2006). As such (and in contrast to their counterparts in feminist IR) feminist political scientists are generally open to combining more interpretive and discursive approaches with traditional positivist methods and tools, often for strategic reasons (cf. Childs and Krook, 2006; Kantola, 2006). Yet this research continues to be critical, arguing that supposedly 'value-free' research needs to take gender and context into account and be used with clearer understandings of the gendered assumptions undergirding these analyses (Duerst-Lahti and Kelly, 1995; Lovenduski, 1998; Randall, 2010).

Challenges, however, remain. The first challenge is to continue to gender political science research. Significant progress has been made on this front, as this chapter highlights. Yet, as Lovenduski (2015) reminds us, it is not enough to simply assert that gender bias exists in institutions; rather, researchers must move beyond the description stage and systematically identify particular gendered institutional processes and mechanisms and their gendering effects (see also Mackay et al., 2010). This call has been taken up, in part, by the rapidly growing and diverse field of 'feminist institutionalism', which combines insights from institutionally focused feminist political science and new institutional theory to investigate the interplay between gender and the operation and effect of political institutions (Mackay et al., 2010; Krook and Mackay, 2011; Kenny, 2013). In illuminating institutional patterns of advantage and disadvantage, feminist researchers must also address the research imperative of intersectionality, incorporating analyses of race, class, sexuality and other axes of disadvantage, and exploring interactions between them (Weldon, 2006; Smooth, 2011). This kind of research is crucial not only to advance theory building on gender and institutions, but also, strategically, to continue to make the case to mainstream scholars of the importance of gender in political analysis.

The second challenge is that of incorporating the concept of gender into quantitative research. Recent debates in the field have highlighted the perceived shortcomings of standard methods and frameworks, for example arguing that behavioural measures and quantitative methods are often 'ill-equipped to deal with "messy" and "complex" issues of gender' (Mackay, 2004: 110; see also Duerst-Lahti and Kelly, 1995; Sapiro, 1998). Others, however, argue that feminist political scientists can and should use a more diverse range of measures and methods to study institutions, including statistical methods and large-scale cross-national studies that may provide unique insights into wider trends and patterns (Weldon, 2014). Indeed, feminist political science has increasingly drawn on quantitative methods, often as a springboard to more in-depth qualitative analyses (see, for example, Bjarnegård, 2013; Tripp, 2015).

A third challenge is that of comparison and its role in theory building. While all institutions are gendered, gender relations play out differently within and across particular institutions over time (Lovenduski, 1998; see also Chappell, 2002, 2006), pointing to the need for comparative research. Work on gender in comparative politics has expanded dramatically over the last few decades, including work on women's representation, women's movements and gender quotas in particular. Yet, as Schwindt-Bayer (2010) highlights, this has become to some degree a study of gender *and* comparative politics, in that it is neither fully comparative, nor fully integrated into the subfield of comparative politics. More recent debates in the field have focused on developing a 'comparative politics of gender', moving beyond comparing women to integrating gender as a central concept in comparative political research (see, in particular, Beckwith, 2010).

Conclusion

Gender and politics research is now a well-established, and rapidly growing, subfield in political science. There is still much work to be done, and the impact of feminism on the discipline continues to be hard fought for and contested, often in the face of ongoing resistance and marginalisation. Nevertheless, the achievements of feminist political science have been substantial, making important contributions to the study of both 'women *in* politics' and 'gender *and* politics'. Work in both areas is ongoing – and often overlapping – and is growing ever more sophisticated, as the result of a productive tension and iterative relationship between theoretical and empirical research in the field.

Does political science still need feminism? We would answer that, despite (or indeed, because of) its internal diversity and debates, feminist and gendered approaches are essential for the study of politics. Politics is, at its heart, the study of power. Feminist approaches illuminate gender power and gendered institutions, challenge the foundational assumptions and preoccupations of political science, and open up new questions and directions for research. Failing to engage with issues of women and gender therefore limits the ability of the discipline to understand and explain the political world (cf. Hawkesworth, 2005). We leave the last word to pioneering feminist political scientist Joni Lovenduski, who states:

> Good feminist social science is simply good social science; it is no more or less than good practice. It should concomitantly be impossible to imagine a good social science that ignores gender. (Lovenduski, 2011: vii)

Further reading

- For a highly accessible introduction to the concept of gender that combines empirical research with theory, see Connell and Pearse (2015). For more advanced texts, see Goertz and Mazur (2008) or *The Oxford Handbook of Gender and Politics* (Waylen et al., 2013), among others.
- Lovenduski's (1998) classic review of the state of the discipline is a must-read, while her later work *Feminizing Politics* (2005) provides an essential overview of key debates and issues in the study of women's political representation.
- The Critical Perspectives section of the journal *Politics & Gender* brings together accessible short symposiums on fundamental questions in gender politics scholarship, as well as new approaches and methods. See, in

particular, the very first Critical Perspectives published in 2005 (Volume 1, Issue 1), which includes foundational pieces from Karen Beckwith and Mary Hawkesworth among others.

- Krook and Mackay (2011) is an excellent starting point for reading more about gender and political institutions, and in particular, feminist institutionalist approaches. Beckwith and contributors (2010) also provide an essential introduction to a comparative politics of gender.

Chapter 7

Marxism: A Global Perspective

RAY KIELY

A chapter on Marxism may seem odd in a book on contemporary politics. The former Communist world has collapsed and, some would argue, good riddance to a body of thought which provided an apology for the existence of highly repressive governments. This point might be applied to other political ideologies, not least in terms of the West's treatment of the colonial world, and ignores the important Marxist critiques of, and opposition to, these regimes. More important, Marxist analyses of capitalism remain relevant, as they highlight the exploitation and hierarchy that exists within global capitalism, the focus of this chapter. The chapter aims: (1) to show the utility of some of Marx's analysis of the expansion of capitalism for understanding contemporary globalisation, with particular reference to political economy; and (2) to assess the contemporary political economy of globalisation, with particular attention paid to the question of whether the world is becoming 'flatter' and therefore converging, or actually becoming more uneven and therefore diverging. The two questions will be linked because it will be suggested that Marx and the Marxist tradition contains arguments supportive of both positions, and this is linked to how Marx understood both capitalism and its expansion beyond national borders.

The chapter will outline its contentions in three main sections. First, it will introduce the reader to Marx's arguments concerning capitalism and show how Marx saw it as both exploitative and progressive. The second section's focus is on 'globalisation' and how Marx and later Marxists attempted to understand the expansion of capitalism beyond its 'heartlands' in Europe. It particularly focuses on the extent to which this expansion leads to divergence between countries in the world economy, but also how it might lead to uneven development between these countries. The third relates to the 'capitalist convergence versus uneven development' controversy to contemporary globalisation and shows the ways in which different perspectives – Marxist and non-Marxist – have understood it. The conclusion will then summarise the chapter and consider the question of the continued relevance of Marxism for understanding contemporary globalisation.

Marxism and capitalism: structuralist economism or agency-led contingency?

Marxist economism and base and superstructure

Karl Marx (1818–83) is rightly regarded as the nineteenth century's greatest critic of capitalism, one whose influence spread into the twentieth century, which saw the rise of several political regimes that (somewhat problematically) claimed allegiance to the doctrine of Marxism. Although we will briefly touch on these regimes in the discussion below, here we want to focus mainly on Marx and Marxism as a critical body of thought, and therefore understand what Marx and his later followers had to say about capitalist societies, not just in the Western world, but across the globe. Marx argued that capitalism was a mode of production in which one class of people – the bourgeoisie or capitalist class – exploited another class of people – the proletariat or working class. He believed that this was the essence of the capitalist mode of production, and that this basic division in capitalist society would become starker as capitalism further developed, and would eventually lead to socialist revolution, as occurred in Russia (1917), China (1949) and elsewhere.

The exploitation that was central to the capitalist (and other class-based) modes of production reflected Marx's belief that social analysis needed to first focus on the way in which production is organised. This is because the production of goods and wealth is necessary for societies, and individuals in those societies, to exist. If we do not produce things (above all food, clothing and shelter) then we cannot exist. This basic point is why Marx is sometimes called a materialist thinker, in that his starting point is material social relations. This is in contrast to other traditions of political and social analysis which might take ideas as their starting point, and which is sometimes called the idealist tradition.

This dichotomy between materialism and idealism is not quite as straightforward as this however. Specifically, in terms of Marx's account of capitalism, we might indeed recognise that exploitation of the working class by the capitalist class is a central feature of capitalism, but this begs lots of questions. For example, where does this leave the role of the state in capitalist society? Is it simply a mechanism or instrument by which the capitalist class exploits the proletariat? Marx wrote at a time when workers did not have the vote but the later extension of the franchise suggests that a more nuanced account of the state is necessary. This point seems all the more relevant when most of the developed world gradually introduced some forms of welfare state in the twentieth century. Not unrelated to this, how did the rise of mass labour movements and parties, which won significant concessions from the state, fit into this picture? As a materialist, Marx and (especially) his collaborator, Friedrich Engels (1820–95) had sometimes used a metaphor to describe how the economic base determined the political, ideological and cultural superstructure. In this account the forces and relations of production, or mode of production, determines the superstructure, which is made up of culture, norms, ideas, institutions and the state. The mode of production refers to the technologies and instruments, or forces of production, and the social (class) relations which characterise the way in which goods are produced. If we accept that this metaphor was being used in this way, then essentially the state is part of the superstructure and is in some sense an epiphenomenon of the economic structure of capitalist society, which we might call a *structuralist* analysis (Engels, 1890). The state is seen as purely an instrument of the powerful interests that dominate the economic base. Using this base-superstructure metaphor, the welfare state can then be explained away by saying that it was in the interests of the capitalist class to expand welfare, so that capitalists could exploit a healthy and therefore more productive workforce. Similarly, more recent attempts to roll back the welfare state also reflect the interests of the capitalist class who have no longer deemed the welfare state as either necessary or affordable. We might note here that the origins of demands for welfare originated not with the capitalist class but with labour movements and the rise of labour parties. Moreover, to argue that the welfare state arose because capitalists wanted it, and that it has been under attack since the 1970s and 1980s because capitalists want that too, does beg the question of how and why they have changed their mind and how this has been sold to electorates and political parties in liberal democracies. Furthermore, where does this leave another key argument in Marxist analysis, namely that history is driven by class struggle? And even though we may recognise the existence of class struggle, what direction might such struggle move towards? To simply assume that the working class is moving unproblematically towards socialism ignores the ways in which some kind of compromise or consensus might be reached between capital and labour – which brings us closer to Gramsci's understanding of hegemony. In capitalist society particular political outcomes are not simply driven by changing capitalist interests, or what might be called the *structural logic of capital*, but by more contingent outcomes of political mobilisation. Box 7.1 explores the relationship between structure and agency in Marxist explanations of the abolition of slavery.

What all this suggests then is that we need a more nuanced account of politics, one which rejects a simplistic economism (in which dominant interests at the base supposedly determine the superstructure) or *structuralism* (in which agents are reduced to simply following a logic of the structure of capitalism) and which gives much greater space to 'superstructural' phenomena such as state reforms, political movements and mobilisation, and indeed to ideas. We have already noted that the (problematic) extension of Marxism in the twentieth century was in part a product of socialist revolution in countries such as Russia and China. These were places where the size of the proletariat, the revolutionary class, was very small, and (for reasons we will explore in a moment) Marx expected revolution to take place in more developed societies. The rise of socialism in the twentieth century is surely an example of change

Box 7.1 Structure and agency: the case of slavery and abolition

We can contrast structure and agency by thinking about the abolition of slavery in the British Empire, which eventually came into force in 1838. If we focus on Williams (1964), the structuralist argument is that the system of slavery broke down because its structural requirements no longer made sense. Put more concretely, slavery was less profitable to the British Empire than it once had been, and so the system was replaced, as part of a new structure in which British hegemony was secured by free trade (though unfree labour persisted). A different approach (see James, 2001) emphasises the agency of the slaves in bringing about abolition, and stresses the significance of slave revolts across the New World, not only in the British Empire, and above all in Haiti. The structuralist approach is top-down while the agency approach is bottom-up. Nonetheless, they can complement rather than contradict each other. In this example agency is implicit in the structuralist approach in that dominant interests ultimately produced abolition, and increased costs of slavery were in part a product of agency from below, namely slave rebellion. Seen in this way, structure and agency are not necessarily diametrically opposed methodologies.

by agency other than capitalist interests. Also, the fact that *socialist ideas* became so significant in societies with small working classes again suggests that we need to move away from a crude materialism or economism, in which ideas are simply reflections of the so-called economic base. We return to this point below when we consider the ideas of two of the most significant Marxists of the twentieth century, the Italian theorist Antonio Gramsci and the Russian revolutionary Leon Trotsky. First, however, we need to consider Marx's account of capitalism in more depth.

Marx and capitalism

This somewhat abstract discussion of materialism and economism can now be concretised by focusing in more depth on Marx's analysis of capitalism. Marx argued that in capitalist societies, commodity production is generalised, which essentially means that the goods that are produced then enter the marketplace where they are bought and sold. This is in contrast to feudal societies, for example, where some production may be for direct use – producers grow a product not in order to sell it but so that they might directly consume it. Under capitalism, however, goods are produced for a competitive market. This means that the owners of the means of production must compete with other owners in order to survive in the marketplace. In order to stay ahead of competitors, individual capitalists each attempt to produce goods more profitably, which leads to attempts to keep the value of wages down or increase the working day. While these strategies persist, they also have real limits, based on the fact that wages cannot be paid below the value of zero, and the working day cannot be extended beyond twenty-four hours. Therefore, other strategies are deployed, which include attempts to increase the productivity of labour, investment in new technology and the search for new markets. This gives capitalism a dynamism which does not exist, at least to the same extent, in pre-capitalist modes of production. And it is this dynamic which lays the basis for globalisation, which in essence means the expansion of capitalist social relations beyond national borders.

Thus, according to Marx and Engels (2000: 246):

> The bourgeoisie cannot exist without constantly revolutionizing the instruments of production, and thereby the relations of production, and with them the whole relations of society ... All fixed, fast frozen relations ... are swept away ... All that is solid melts into air.

Marx believed that capitalism was a more dynamic mode of production in comparison to previous modes, and it had the effect of incorporating all countries, localities and regions into the world market. In this sense capitalism was progressive in that it expanded the wealth that was produced across the globe, and laid the foundations for socialism. It did so in two ways: first, it was based on the exploitation of the working class, and this class was unique in its capacity to overthrow a mode of production (capitalism) based on exploitation; and second, because of the competition between capitalist companies led to the development of what Marx called the productive forces (which essentially meant a combination of machinery, technology and labour). This meant that the total wealth in society, or social surplus product, massively increased. Marx had argued that class societies emerged when a social surplus product developed and allowed some people to live off this. However, the total social surplus product was not great enough for everyone to live off, and so class society persisted. However, with capitalism, the social surplus product increased so much that potentially everyone could live off it – but this potential was not fulfilled because the capitalist class own the means of production and so gained a disproportionate amount of this product in the form of profit. Socialism would allow everyone to live off this social surplus, but this could only come about through the agency of the working class. This class was unique in history because, in contrast to previous exploited classes, the proletariat came together in the production process far more than, say, the peasantry (Marx and Engels, 2000: 250). This allowed them to become aware of their common condition of exploitation, and thereby make the transition from being a class in itself (an exploited class) to a class for itself (a class consciously committed to ending its shared exploitation).

Marx argued along these lines in the famous 1859 'Preface to a Critique of Political Economy'.

> In the social production of their existence, men inevitably enter into definite relations, which are independent of their will, namely relations of production appropriate to a given stage in the development of

> their material forces of production. No social order is ever destroyed before all the productive forces for which it is sufficient have been developed, and new superior relations of production never replace older ones before the material conditions for their existence have matured within the framework of the old society. (Marx, 2000b: 425)

In this account then, Marxism assigns a central role to the working class in bringing about socialism. But equally economistic Marxism believes that capitalist expansion is progressive and socialism could only emerge at a particular stage of development in history. Where then does this leave 'superstructural phenomena' such as nationalism?

Marxism, capitalism and nationalism

This account of history and the progressiveness of capitalism is both useful and problematic. There is little doubt that capitalism has developed the productive forces in unprecedented ways, and that socialist and labour movements emerged in response to the inequalities and exploitation generated by capitalism. But it is also problematic in that it again can be seen to be guilty of an excessive materialism economism, and structuralism. What does it mean to say that no social order is destroyed before 'all the productive forces for which it is sufficient have been developed'? Should a political or social movement somehow 'wait' for the 'sufficient' development of the productive forces, an argument made in different ways by the Mensheviks, a faction of Russian Marxism which opposed the 1917 Bolshevik Revolution, and by Stalin once he had emerged as the leader of the Soviet Union after the revolution? In any case how would one measure 'sufficient' development? Not unrelated to this point, is revolution then simply a question of taking over the wealth produced by capitalist society, when much of this wealth may in fact be socially (or environmentally) dysfunctional, as in the case of, say, massive private transport systems as opposed to more public transport? More-over, how does one consider the transition from the proletariat being a class in itself to becoming a class for itself – surely this involves some consideration of ideas that might influence this process, and thus not reduce ideas and consciousness to a simple reflection of the economic base or the level of development of the productive forces? And how do these questions influence our understanding of global political economy?

Thus, in keeping with the argument that capitalism progressively expands beyond nation states and creates a world market, Marx and Engels argued that nationalism will gradually diminish in the face of the unifying logic of a global capitalist political economy. In particular, they argued that:

> The working men have no country ... National differences and antagonisms between peoples are vanishing gradually from day to day, owing to the development of the bourgeoisie, to freedom of commerce, to the world market. (Marx and Engels, 2000: 270)

Marxism and globalisation: economistic unilinearity or contingent uneven development?

The previous section outlined the broad themes of Marxism and identified two possible interpretations – one was more economistic and structuralist, the other, considered more implicitly, gave more room to agency and contingency while still recognising the hierarchy and exploitation that is central to capitalism. This section applies these two interpretations to understanding 'globalisation'.

Marxist economism and capitalist diffusion

Marxists regard globalisation as the spread of capitalist social relations beyond its core heartlands. It should therefore come as little surprise that the economistic and structuralist approach thus tends towards the views that this is a progressive development in human history. As we saw above, capitalism may be exploitative but it is also progressive compared to previous modes of production, because it develops the productive forces and creates the working class, the gravediggers of class society. Given that globalisation spreads capitalism, this can be seen as regrettable in that it is exploitative, but also it is necessary because it overthrew pre-capitalist modes of production and replaced it with capitalism. Indeed, at times Marx even argued that colonialism was progressive and that 'English interference ... produced the greatest, and to speak the truth, the only *social* revolution ever heard of in Asia' (Marx and Engels, 1974: 40). England thus played a 'destructive' but 'regenerating' role in Asia, the latter of which meant 'laying the material foundations of Western society in Asia' (Marx and Engels, 1974: 82). This accords with Marx's (1976: 91) famous statement that '(t)he country that is more developed industrially shows to the less developed, the image of its own future'.

Marx (2000a: 295) argued that the free trade system is progressive because it 'breaks up old nationalities and pushes the antagonism of the proletariat and the bourgeoisie to the extreme point. In a word the free trade system hastens the social revolution.' This statement is consistent with Marx's view that like capitalism and colonialism, globalisation was a tragic necessity. Some nation states were deemed to be at a more advanced stage of development (capitalism), while other places – often colonies – were said to be at a lower stage of development (pre-capitalism). Globalisation facilitated a process whereby the backward locations gradually caught up with the more advanced ones. This kind of argument was central to various strands of liberal thought, such as John Locke's (1980: chapter 16) argument in the seventeenth century that the commercial colonisation of North America should be supported on the grounds that it would lead to a more productive use of private land and hence 'improvement'. John Stuart Mill (1984: 121) argued in the nineteenth century that 'nations which are still barbarous have not got beyond the period during which it is likely to be for their benefit that they should be conquered and held in subjection to foreigners'. It was this kind of thinking that led to apparent apologies by Marx and Engels for colonialism in India (above) and Algeria, and for the annexation of part of Mexico by the USA (Marx and Engels, 1974: 81–82; see Larrain, 1989: 57)

Marx and the unequal international order

But in the same speech, Marx (2000a: 295–296) also argued that 'If the free traders cannot understand how one nation can grow rich at the expense of another, we need not wonder, since these same gentlemen also refuse to understand how within one country one class can enrich itself at the expense of another'; and that protectionist measures might 'serve the bourgeoisie as weapons against feudalism and absolute government, as a means for the concentration of its own power and for the realization of free trade within the same country'.

What this suggests is that while protectionism may not enable states to avoid globalisation, it might constitute an alternative strategy for countries in the international order which differs from a simple embrace of free trade. For our purposes, what it also at least implies is that free trade – and globalisation – might serve the interests of already powerful states against weaker ones. Though Marx was a critic of Friedrich List (1789–1846), the latter made a similar and probably more substantial argument when he argued that free trade policies in effect undermined the development possibilities for later developers as it 'kicked away the ladder' that had enabled the already developed countries to develop (List, 1966). In the context of the unequal development of productive powers between countries, free trade will exacerbate uneven development between them (List, 1966: 102).

What this suggests then is an account of the international order which highlights unevenness and inequality, not just as features of the capital–labour relation, but as constituent features of globalisation. Marx was acutely aware of this in his writings. For example, he suggested that the construction of an international division of labour dominated by Western, colonial powers altered the context in which 'late developers' might attempt to catch up. For instance, he argued that 'the veiled slavery of the wage earners in Europe needed the unqualified slavery of the New World as its pedestal' (Marx, 1976: 925). Even when apparently 'apologising' for colonialism, Marx was under no illusions about the real beneficiaries of this process. In 1881, Marx went so far as to argue that the abolition of the communal ownership of land in India 'was only an act of English vandalism which pushed the indigenous people not forward but backward' (cited in Larrain, 1989: 49). This was consistent with his earlier argument that British colonialism in India represented a 'bleeding process' in which resources were sucked out of India for the benefit of the colonising country (Marx and Engels, 1974: 340).

What is central here then is a distinction between the progressiveness of capitalism in particular places, and its uneven global diffusion beyond the core countries (Gulalp, 1986). In other words, the capitalist mode of production also entailed the construction of a capitalist world market and an international division of labour, which were themselves hierarchical, not only in terms of the capital–labour relation, but also in terms of location, empire and colony, and the persistence of unfree forms of labour. In making this distinction, Marx was also suggesting that his account of the transition was specific to a particular location, and that transitions elsewhere would take different forms. This was because he in effect challenged the view that globalisation meant the expansion of capitalist social relations in ways that replicated the British, and more specifically, English experience (Marx, 1982: 109–110; 1984: 124).

This is consistent with Marx's argument that capitalist social relations are a product of specific *relations of production*. The argument that globalisation will lead to the progressive diffusion of capitalist social relations tends to imply that the expansion of the capitalist *world market* alone will lead to the progressive diffusion of capitalism throughout the globe. This argument is based on an implicit account in which capitalism is defined as the expansion of exchange relations, rather than the social relations of production. Capitalist exchange relations will of course impact on social relations of production in capitalism's peripheries, but this alone will not lead either to the emergence of the capital–labour relation as emerged in the core areas of capital accumulation, or to the development of the productive forces. One possible implication of this argument might be that if capitalist social relations do emerge, in part because of globalisation but also because of the universalisation of the process whereby the direct producers are separated from direct access to the means of production (for instance, through state-directed private enclosures of land), then this will lead to a process of convergence around the globalisation of the capital–labour relation. As we will see in the final section, this is the assumption of several (Marxist and non-Marxist) approaches to understanding globalisation in the twenty-first century. However, in Marx's work there is clear evidence that even in the case of 'mature capitalisms' developing across the globe, this would not lead to convergence and uneven development would persist. There are two reasons for this. First, Marx argued that the competitive accumulation of capital was based on the ongoing search for surplus profit, which leads to a process whereby capital increasingly concentrates and centralises in the hands of fewer and larger capitals, a process reinforced by state legislation (for instance, to encourage limited liability). This process of concentration also encourages the agglomeration of capital, so that it tends to concentrate or cluster in certain locations. Though Marx's statements on these processes are relatively rudimentary and tentative, it is quite clear that this process took off enormously from the late nineteenth century, even in places such as the USA which in some respects discouraged the formation of 'capitalist trusts'. What is relevant for our purposes is that this process impacted beyond national boundaries, and so the effects of global capital accumulation were such that uneven development, and cores and peripheries, emerged through globalisation.

Marxism, imperialism and uneven development as dependency

What is central to this more nuanced account of globalisation is that, first, the effects of globalisation will vary across time and space and do not amount to a progressive diffusion of capitalist social relations, at least in ways which replicate earlier transitions. This approach rejects simplistic unilinear analyses of capitalist globalisation, as well as wider processes of history and development. These debates were taken up and developed by later Marxists. For instance, the Austrian Marxist Rudolf Hilferding (1981) and two leading Bolsheviks, Lenin (1977) and Bukharin (2003), argued that from the late nineteenth century capitalism had entered a new stage of development, based on the growing concentration and centralisation of capital, increasingly close ties between financial and industrial capital, and the division of the world into various spheres of influence. Capitalism had developed into a new *imperialist* phase based on the effective fusion of economic competition between capitals and geopolitical competition between states (Lenin, Bukharin). There were enormous problems with these theories. For example, while there were growing tensions between capitalist states, it was less clear that this was an inevitable consequence of capitalist expansion (Kautsky, 1970), an argument all the more relevant after the end of the Second World War and growing cooperation between capitalist states (Panitch and Gindin, 2012). Most important for our purposes, classical Marxist theories of imperialism argued that the export of capital from the core countries led to the development of a division of the world into core countries, and subordinate, peripheral and semi-peripheral countries (Lenin, 1977). These theories were ambiguous on the mechanisms through which such a division was sustained, and in fact in some respects it was less the export of capital to the periphery and more its concentration in core countries that led to the division into core and periphery. Nonetheless, recognition of this core/periphery division constituted an important break from any unilinear approaches by which 'backward' countries simply caught up with 'advanced' ones through capitalist diffusion. Lenin thus argued, in sharp contrast to Marx and Engels in 1848 (above), that recognising the right of nations to self-determination was an important, progressive demand that should be supported by socialists. This was a long way from capitalist diffusion emanating from the (global) 'economic base' eroding supposedly 'superstructural' national differences.

These kinds of arguments were further developed by the Russian Marxist and Bolshevik Leon Trotsky (1879–1940), who argued that capitalist diffusion was a far from uniform process. Focusing initially on the combination of 'advanced' and 'backward' features of capitalist development in Russia, Trotsky argued that, in some respects, capitalism 'equalizes the economic and cultural levels of the most progressive and the most backward countries' (Trotsky, 1970: 18). However, in contrast to excessively economistic and unilinear accounts, he also argued that it does so by 'developing some parts of world economy while hampering and throwing back the development of others' (Trotsky, 1970: 19). This has echoes of Marx's distinction between the extension of capitalist social relations and the hierarchical international division of labour and world market. It was also an argument developed by a number of important intellectuals after the Second World War, many originating from the global South, who argued in differing ways that the 'third world' as it came to be known was in a peripheral and subordinate position in the capitalist world economy (Rodney, 1972; Amin, 1974).

Marxism and hegemony: the significance of Gramsci

Much of these debates were still very much focused on political *economy*. Nonetheless, these kinds of accounts gave far more room for contingency and agency than more structuralist and unilinear economistic accounts. And this focus on contingency was extended further by the work of the Italian Marxist Antonio Gramsci (1891–1937). His concept of hegemony was developed to challenge economistic Marxism, and in particular to explain the relative absence of working-class revolution in the developed capitalist countries. The ruling class, the bourgeoisie, did not rule simply through coercion and violence, but through ideological means. This meant the development of a hegemonic culture which presented itself as the common sense of the age. Gramsci (2005: 277–316) also made brief but highly suggestive comments about the rise of 'Fordist' mass production techniques, and a useful example of a hegemonic statement is Henry Ford's claim that 'what is good for Ford is good for America'. For a time this was in some respects the 'common sense' view of sections of the US working class, and given their dependence on investment decisions made by the Ford motor company, it can be considered an idea that carried material weight. On the other hand, a counter-hegemonic position would be one that questioned why workers are so dependent on investment decisions in the first place, and that means a challenge to the social relations associated with capitalism, and specifically the situation where the property-less proletariat come to depend on the propertied few for their livelihood. We might also note that with technological change, increased amounts of profits going to shareholders instead of being reinvested, and the growing use of overseas outsourcing, this statement has been increasingly challenged in an age of globalisation. This brings us nicely to a wider consideration of contemporary globalisation, and this is the subject of the third and final section. But before doing so, we should note here that Gramsci's account of hegemony again highlights the limits of economism. This is because hegemonic or ideological battles have political consequences, and these are ones that are in part forged at the level of ideas, which is supposed to be part of the 'superstructure'.

Debating globalisation in the twenty-first century

Contemporary globalisation defined

Held and McGrew (2007: 2) define globalisation as 'the intensification of worldwide social relations and interactions', and the contemporary Marxist thinker Bill Robinson argues that it is characterised as referring to 'fundamental worldwide changes in social structure that modify and even transform the very functioning of the system in which we live' (Robinson, 2004: 4). These changes include an intensification of capital mobility, globalised circuits of accumulation and the fragmentation of production. Thus globalisation is distinguished from earlier periods of internationalisation, and there is now an increase in direct foreign investment, including mergers and acquisitions between firms originating in different countries, the increased practice of subcontracting and outsourcing by companies to (local and foreign) suppliers, and the increase in trade between two or more subsidiaries of the same parent company. In addition there has been a massive increase in the significance of financial circuits of capitalism, both within and between countries.

How, then, should we think about the effects of these globalising processes? One way would be to revive the linear and economistic Marxism outlined above, and suggest that the globalisation of capitalism has led to a diffusion of capitalism throughout the globe, thus leading to a straightforward global division between bourgeoisie and proletariat (Robinson, 2004; though see Robinson, 2015). This is because the diffusion of capitalism is indeed at long last creating a world market and thus 'evening up' inequalities *between* countries, even if inequality within countries and between global classes is increasing (see Warren, 1980; Desai, 2002). The argument that global diffusion is encouraging some kind of economic convergence between countries is also made by non-Marxist accounts of globalisation, such as that associated with neoliberalism. Those countries that have most integrated into the global economy through economic liberalisation policies have experienced high rates of growth and poverty reduction (World Bank, 2002). The World Bank (1996) has even used Marx's famous 'all that is solid melts into air' quotation (cited above) to recognise the growth of formal labour employment relations in the world today, and at least implied that this represents a growing process of incorporation of the world labour force into the benefits of globalisation. This argument is based on the assumption that globalisation is inclusive, thus a priori ruling out the argument that globalisation is exclusionary and that poverty may be relational, and thus in part be caused by unequal social relations. In other words, in economic terms, the world is increasingly flat (Bhagwati, 2004; Friedman, 2005). Advocates of this argument point to the growth of manufacturing in parts of the developing world, measures which suggest significant poverty reduction in recent years, and the rise of countries such as China and India, which are said to have embraced the opportunities presented by the world market (O'Neill, 2013).

The continued relevance of Marxist ideas I: globalisation as uneven and combined development

However, drawing on the arguments made earlier in this chapter, there is an alternative interpretation of the political economy of contemporary globalisation, especially if we revisit the arguments concerning both the hierarchical international division of labour, and the concentration and centralisation of capital. The political economy of globalisation has indeed seen the rise of multinational corporations (MNCs) and foreign investment, subcontracting and so on, and this has encouraged the selective industrialisation of parts of the developing world, which are integrated into global networks of production whereby different locations are used for different stages of the production process (Dicken, 2015). However, this diffusion has not eroded, and indeed in some ways has intensified uneven development, as higher value-added components of production still tend to cluster in selected regions of the world, mainly in the 'global North' (and parts of East Asia), while lower value-added production is increasingly deployed in the 'global South', attracted by (among other factors) low labour costs (see Box 7.2).

Box 7.2 The case of Apple

Apple products are designed in the USA and assembled in China. The Apple iPod Classic cost $299 in the USA in 2005, and Apple paid around $144 to Hon Hai Precision Industry, a Taiwanese-owned, company which used its Chinese subsidiary, Foxconn. Of this amount, about 3 per cent went to the Taiwanese assembler operating in China, 51 per cent to the Japanese hard drive producer (assembled in China using imported inputs), 3 per cent to the US semi-conductor designer, and 2 per cent to the South Korean (owned and located) memory chip producer (see Linden et al., 2007: 6). The Apple iPhone, launched in 2007, sold for $500 while the cost of manufacturing stood at $178.96. Chinese labour costs were around $6.50 for each phone, which constitutes just 3.6 per cent of the manufacturing cost (Xing and Detert, 2010: 8). In 2011, Hon Hai Precision Industry's total profit was $2.6 billion, while Apple's was $33 billion (Starrs, 2013: 819). In other words, the parent company produced goods (or more accurately, had goods produced for them) through a global production network, but this network did not end uneven development; indeed, contrary to the flat earth globalisation position, its corporate strategy intensified it.

Uneven development and continued divergence is also clear if we examine data on poverty and global inequality. If we define those in absolute poverty as people living on less than $2 a day, adjusted to take account of local purchasing power, and those living on between $2 and $10 a day as global insecure then we can put global inequality into some kind of perspective. According to Edward and Sumner (2013: 37) for 2011–12, 1 million out of the 2,407 million global absolute poor lived in the developed countries, compared to 2,406 million in the developing countries, and 148 million of the 2,914 million global insecure live in the developed world, compared to 2,766 million in the global South. If this is a story of capitalist diffusion then it is equally a story of continued divergence and uneven development, and so uneven and combined development is an idea which remains useful for framing continued global divergence.

Uneven and combined development has, however, been used in a different way in some Marxist-inspired international relations (IR) scholarship in recent years, which focuses on the geopolitics of relations between states (Anievas, 2010). The argument here is essentially an update of Lenin's theory of imperialism and his argument that the uneven development of international capitalism gives rise not only to economic competition between capitals, but geopolitical conflict between states. Although advocates of this position are careful not to draw direct parallels between Anglo-German relations before 1914 and US-Chinese relations in the current era, they do argue that conflict is bound to occur within the context of the uneven development of the international capitalist order (Callinicos, 2009). Empirically, there is indeed evidence that there is some degree of conflict between China and the USA, over Taiwan, the South China Sea and so on. But theoretically, it is far less convincing to argue that this conflict is somehow more significant than cooperation between these states because of the uneven development of capitalism. There is plenty of evidence of cooperation and mutual interdependence between China and the USA, in terms of foreign investment, reliance on Chinese imports, Chinese willingness to finance US debt and so on, as the Apple example in Box 7.2 demonstrates. This does not mean of course that such cooperation will always be more important than conflict. Rather, in keeping with the argument of this chapter, we need to see such relations as more contingent, and less determined by economistic laws or the structure of the international system. In other words, to borrow from another IR theory, uneven and combined development does not simply determine state behaviour and in part it is the product of 'what states make of it' (Wendt, 1992).

The continued relevance of Marxist ideas II: hegemony and the international order

So far, then, we have argued against the idea that (economic) globalisation has led to anything like convergence in the international order, and in doing so challenged some of the crude economistic and unilinear accounts of Marxism and flat earth, neoliberal accounts of globalisation. But this leaves one last question, and here we might usefully revisit Gramsci's account of hegemony. Some Marxist-inspired accounts of IR have attempted to apply this concept to the role of leading states in the international order, and the question of whether or not the US state remains hegemonic, not least in the face of China's rise (Cox, 1981; Gill, 2003). In terms of the specifics of US hegemony, we might argue that in contrast to all previous hegemonic powers (with the partial exception of Britain), the USA has attempted to promote a specifically global capitalism, as opposed to say expanding German or French capitalism overseas. The Apple example (Box 7.2) demonstrates that diffusion has not led to an evening up of capitalist development throughout the globe. Nonetheless, the promotion of such a globalised capitalism has in effect incorporated dominant classes and elites from other countries into these globalised circuits of capitalism (Panitch and Gindin, 2012). This is one way in which the USA exercises its hegemony, and we might add, continues to do so, even as global capitalism has entered a period of great uncertainty since the financial crisis of 2008. Second, hegemony is not exercised only through the political economy of global capitalism, but through what some liberal writers have called soft power (Nye, 2004). While nationalist resistance against specific US (military) actions does exist and intensified after 2001, it remains the case that the USA is still a significant pole of attraction for other countries. This is not only because of the need to access global circuits of capital, but also because of wider cultural products, from liberal ideas of human rights through to consumer capitalism. Seen in this way, hegemony is once again exercised not just through political economy. These of course might be challenged, not least in terms of much of the hypocrisy around human rights implementation through to the questionable capacity of US consumers to continue debt-driven consumption since the 2008 financial crisis. Nonetheless, these ideas have been central features of US hegemony, both in the international order and within the domestic economy.

Conclusion

This chapter has both considered Marxism as a theory and considered its applicability in terms of understanding the contemporary global political economy. In some respects the collapse of Communism in the period from 1989 to 1991 did undermine Marxism as an ideology that influenced a number of authoritarian political regimes throughout the world. Recent years have, however, seen something of a revival of interest in Marxism as a critical mode of analysis for understanding contemporary capitalism. When one considers recent events it is not hard to see why, and so we should take stock here and summarise the strengths of Marxism as a critical theory. First, Marxism shows how capitalism and the capital-labour relation is something that was historically created as producers were divorced from direct access to the means of production and therefore compelled to work for a wage in order to live. Struggles over access to land continue to this day, particularly in the developing world, as do urbanisation processes where people forced off the land enter towns desperate to find work. Second, capitalism is a process which is unequal precisely because the ownership of the means of production by some gives them power over others, and their constant drive for profit forces them to keep wages down. Third, this is a dynamic process as capitalists compete and so may innovate through investment in new technology. But at the same time it is a process which is also prone to crisis. The precise reasons for particular crises vary, but the general root of crises is the fact that capitalists aim to maximise profits but also need a market for their goods, and the workers paid low wages are precisely that market. There are a number of ways in which crises may be averted (state spending, luxury consumption by capitalists), and in the run-up to the 2008 financial crisis there was a sharp increase in household and mortgage debt in a wider context of stagnant real wages in the USA and Britain. But a crisis still emerged, and we continue to live with the consequences almost ten years later. It is therefore not surprising that in the era of contemporary globalisation, we have also seen the rise and resurgence of movements that challenge globalisation in its current form, and the rise of a class of capitalists which makes much of its money not through innovation in production, but through innovation – and in many cases, this means speculation – in finance. The rise of the so-called global justice movement or anti-globalisation movement after 1999, the Occupy Movement following the 2008 financial crisis, and new political parties such as Podemos in Spain and Syriza in Greece should be seen in this light. Used in an open fashion, and in constructive dialogue with other (feminist, postcolonial, poststructuralist) approaches, Marxism remains a powerful tool of political analysis.

Further reading

- Anievas (2010) is a useful collection of Marxist writings on uneven and combined development.
- Dicken (2015) is an excellent account of contemporary globalisation, with particular emphasis on global commodity chains.
- Kiely (2010) examines Marxist and non-Marxist theories of imperialism and contemporary globalisation.
- McLellan (1977) and Sayer (1989) are both excellent collections of many of Marx's key writings.
- Panitch and Gindin (2012) theorise global capitalism and stress the central role of the US state in its making.
- Robinson (2004) is a sophisticated Marxist theory of globalisation as transnational capitalism.

Chapter 8

Poststructuralism

MARK WENMAN

The term 'poststructuralism' refers to movements in French theory that emerged from the late 1960s. This was a time of political instability in France, which culminated in 'May 68', when radical student groups took over the campuses, workers shut down factories and for a while these militant 'assemblages' occupied significant parts of Paris. These events almost toppled the De Gaulle government, and in retrospect they can be seen as the focal point of the widespread social changes of the 1960s, associated with youth countercultural movements, the politicisation of sexuality, the rise of second-wave feminism and of the 'new social movements'. The key figures associated with 'poststructuralism' came of age during these times, and emphases on contingency and unpredictability, as well as on a diversity that extends beyond class-based politics, have become abiding themes in poststructuralist theory, as they have likewise become key characteristics of our increasingly post-industrial societies.

However, beyond this initial characterisation, 'poststructuralism' is difficult to define. Like perhaps all significant movements in social and political theory, poststructuralism is identified with a number of prodigious thinkers. The advent of poststructuralism is associated with those who would become major figures in the Parisian academy, such as Michel Foucault, Jacques Derrida, Julia Kristeva and (more tangentially) Gilles Deleuze (for some of their most influential works, see Foucault, 2007, 2008, 1991; Derrida, 1976, 1978; Kristeva, 1986; Deleuze, 1983, 1994). Nevertheless, the differences between these thinkers are almost as intense as their commonality, and so we begin to see why 'poststructuralism' resists easy designation. Poststructuralism is not a unified body of theory, has no self-conscious avant-garde, and there is no 'poststructuralist manifesto'. Unlike rational choice theorists, poststructuralists do not share a precise methodology, and in contrast to behaviouralism and neo-behaviouralism, poststructuralists do not advocate specific criteria for data collection. To the extent that poststructuralism is a tradition, this is not in a conventional sense. In contrast to Marxism, for example, there is no reverence here for the unsurpassable authority of a single progenitor.

In some ways, poststructuralism is identified by the positions it pits itself against. Poststructuralism is often described as 'anti-essentialism' and 'anti-foundationalism'. These terms indicate that poststructuralists have criticised attempts to provide rational foundations for work in the social and political sciences. It would be fair to say that poststructuralists are anti-positivist, and their arguments connect with the 'postmodern' attitudes that have pervaded Western societies since the late twentieth century, which draw into question core assumptions of modernity about the privileged status of scientific knowledge and the inevitability of scientific progress (see Lyotard, 1986). Those who are committed to various forms of positivism have therefore been strongly resistant to poststructuralism. However, even the most hardened critics will acknowledge the deep impact of poststructuralism across the humanities and social sciences, as poststructuralism has recurrently permeated and been combined with alternate approaches. As we will see, this influence has extended into the disciplines of politics and international relations. Although, political science in particular has remained more impervious to the infusion of poststructuralism than other disciplines, and this is symptomatic of the ongoing grip of positivism on the core of the discipline, and perhaps especially in the USA.

With some irony, the difficulty in defining 'poststructuralism' has been compounded by its influence. This has given rise to new sub-disciplines, such as poststructuralist feminism, poststructuralist cultural studies, post-Marxism, post-anarchism and postcolonialism, to name only a few. At first sight, these various 'post-isms' appear mystifying (Mackenzie, 2010). Despite this, I think the core assumptions of poststructuralism can be presented fairly succinctly (there is nothing too difficult or esoteric about them), and constructively (that is, they do not *only* take the form of a critique of other viewpoints, they also have an affirmative content). According to David Howarth (2013: 6), poststructuralism is defined by a 'particular style of theorising, and a specific way of doing social and political theory, which is informed by a distinctive ethos'. This formulation perhaps overstates the commonality between different strands of poststructuralism. Nevertheless, if there is something like a shared disposition behind the collection of theories that make up 'poststructuralism', it is to draw into question notions of system, unity and closure, in the name of contingency, openness and disruption, and this in part brought about through a strategy of tenacious questioning.

In this chapter, I first provide an account of the movement in French theory from structuralism to poststructuralism. Following this, I outline two prominent examples of the application of poststructuralism to the study of politics in the work of Foucault and Ernesto Laclau, and consider the wider impact of poststructuralism on the study of politics and international relations. I then examine the ontological and epistemological assumptions of poststructuralism, and show how they differ from other approaches covered in this volume. Finally, I evaluate some of the key criticisms, and conclude by stressing the ongoing importance of poststructuralism.

French structuralism

The emergence of poststructuralism is indebted to earlier traditions of structuralism, as the name clearly indicates. In a broad sense, 'structuralism' is invoked to characterise perspectives that highlight the role of background structures in conditioning the behaviour of social and political actors. So, for example, the 'old institutionalism' in political science is akin to structuralism and so too are the classical traditions of Marxism. More narrowly, however, 'structuralism' refers to a particular tradition within French theory that was at its peak in the late 1950s and early 1960s. In the same manner as poststructuralism, the earlier traditions of structuralism were similarly characterised by a diffusion of their core ideas into adjacent disciplines, and most notably into anthropology in the work of Claude Lévi-Strauss, into psychoanalysis with the contribution of Jacques Lacan, and into Marxism in the thought of Louis Althusser (see, for example, Lévi-Strauss, 1971; Lacan, 1998; Althusser and Balibar, 2009). Each of these theorists was influenced by structural linguistics, which was developed in the early twentieth century by a number of thinkers, but most notably by the Swiss linguist Ferdinand de Saussure. It is therefore to Saussure's thought that we go first in order to understand structuralism and in turn poststructuralism.

Saussure broke with established ways of thinking about language, or of the relationship between language and 'objects' in the world. In more conventional approaches, individual words are often presented as the basic units of language and these are said to have an intrinsic relationship with their corresponding objects, or – to use Saussure's terminology – with the 'referent' (that is, the thing the word refers to). So, for example, in the conventional model when I say 'cup' this word refers to essential characteristics that reside in the object (or referent) which is currently sitting on my desk half-full of coffee. This interpretation of language also fits with conventional understandings about the status of truth claims, that is, with the so-called 'correspondence theory of truth'. On this account, a given statement about the world – for example a scientific hypothesis – is considered to be 'objectively' true when it accurately *refers* to some thing or state of affairs, or when it captures the 'object' (referent) as it 'really is'. Saussure's theory departs fundamentally from these assumptions about language, and also by implication about the construction of truth claims.

First, Saussure does not present the word as the basic unit of language. Instead, he understands language as a set of relationships between signs. His approach is described as semiotics, or a science of signs. Second, Saussure comprehends the sign as composed of two elements, what he called the 'signifier' and the 'signified'. The signifier could be a written or spoken word or collection of words, but it could equally be an image or a gesture; think of Winston Churchill's famous

V sign for example. The signified is the corresponding concept that is attached to a given signifier, for instance, Churchill's confidence that the Allied Powers would eventually secure 'victory' over Nazi Germany. One of the central points in Saussure's approach was his insistence on the 'arbitrary nature of the signifier'. In other words, there is no intrinsic relationship between a given signifier and the signified, that is, between a word, image, gesture and so on, and its corresponding concept. For example, Churchill could have invoked a different signifier to convey this same message.

This approach raises various questions. Most importantly: if the signifier is no longer a label for a pre-given object, how is meaning established? Indeed, Saussure's other central insight was to insist on the *relationships* between signs as key to understanding the production of meaning. Saussure described language as a 'system of differences without positive terms'. He stressed, if we want to grasp the meaning of a given term we need to appreciate the situated significance of the term in its relationships with other terms, in the context of a particular linguistic structure (Saussure, 1998: 110–120). So, for example, the meaning of 'table' is dependent on its commonality and difference with/from other items of domestic furniture, such as 'chairs', 'beds', 'chest of drawers' and so on. Crucially, this relationality operates in much the same way as the relationships between counters in a board game, that is, where each has a particular significance but only in relation to one another. Take one of the chess pieces away from the board and it becomes more or less meaningless; its significance is entirely dependent on the part it plays in relation to the other pieces.

This is why Saussure's approach is an example of linguistic 'structuralism'. His insight is that the production of meaning is 'differential and not referential' (Belsey, 2002: 10). He taught subsequent thinkers to pay attention to the ways in which signifiers combine, to examine the particular system of differences within a given linguistic structure. To take a quick but pertinent example, in order to understand the meaning of 'Brexit' we might examine the precise relationship between this signifier and a series of related signifiers in the respective discourses of 'leave' and 'remain'. In the first of these linguistic structures, 'Brexit' is understood as an opportunity, in relation to Britain's independence from the 'Brussels bureaucracy', for 'taking our country back', for a reasonable control of immigration, and for a future of openness and global trade. In the latter, 'Brexit' signifies instead a dangerous leap in the dark, a retrograde step, a kind of narrow nationalism that is predicated on unwarranted fear of foreigners, and one that will threaten the good will of our immediate continental neighbours. Note that it follows from this approach that there is no intrinsic meaning to the signifier 'Brexit'. It is rather a question of understanding the particular relationships that surround this term in these competing sets of linguistic structures, and this despite the Prime Minister's efforts to close down this contestability with her infamous assertion that 'Brexit means Brexit'.

From structuralism to poststructuralism

To grasp the emergence of poststructuralism we first need to acknowledge another dimension of Saussure's approach, which was his emphasis on the relative fixity of linguistic structures. To use the technical idioms, Saussure took a 'synchronic approach', highlighting the relations between signifiers at a given moment in time, rather than a 'diachronic approach' which would trace the development of meaning over time. Moreover, as Saussure's ideas began to impact across the social sciences, this emphasis on synchronic closure became a defining feature of French structuralism. For example, in *The Elementary Structures of Kinship*, in 1949, Lévi-Strauss identified the underlying structures of kinship and exchange, which – he claimed – were present in all historical and cultural contexts (Lévi-Strauss, 1971). In Marxism, Althusser likewise drew on structuralism to challenge overly deterministic readings of the base/superstructure distinction. Rather than seeing the legal, political and ideological superstructures as simply a reflection of the essential contradictions played out at the level of the economy, Althusser stressed instead their 'relative autonomy'. However, he also remained within the framework of classical Marxism, as well as the closed logic of linguistic structuralism, with his further insistence that together the various structures formed a relatively closed totality in which the economy was the determining structure 'in the last instance' (Althusser and Balibar, 2009).

It was against this background that poststructuralism emerged in the late 1960s. The interface between structuralism and poststructuralism is fluid, and it is important to see post*structuralism* as an internal reworking rather than something that simply comes after structuralism. The advent of poststructuralism had numerous sources. Nevertheless, we can now see Derrida's early work as a pivotal turning point. This was set out in *Of Grammatology* and the essays collected in *Writing and Difference*, both published in 1967 (Derrida, 1976, 1978). In these works, Derrida linked the emphasis on the fixity characteristic of structuralism to a more general concern with surety, grounding and closure running through the entire Western tradition, which he called the 'metaphysics of presence'. In effect, Derrida sees an underlying need for certitude expressed in Western modes of thought (Derrida, 1978: 353). This takes distinct forms in philosophy, religion, and in the modern hard and social sciences; but despite their important differences each of these predominant modes of thought attempts to contain the experience of contingency with reference to some 'invariable centre', 'fixed presence' or what Derrida called the 'transcendental signified'. This goes variously by the name of 'reason', God, and natural or scientific laws (Derrida, 1978: 352–353).

However, these observations do not lead to an outright rejection of structuralism. Instead, Derrida saw resources in structural linguistics to develop a renewed account of meaning and significance, one that is attentive to the constitutive character of temporal displacement, deferral and disruption. Indeed, Derrida extended the idea of the arbitrary nature of the signifier to draw attention to the playful openness and instability, or the 'rupture and a redoubling', that is characteristic of language use (Derrida, 1978: 351). The meaning of a given signifier can never be fixed, but is 'permanently deferred', because the signifier can always be re-signified or reiterated, that is, cut and pasted from a particular context and employed in innovative ways. Think, for example, of the inventive use of terms such as 'wicked', 'minted' or 'random' in youth subcultures. This is indicative of the role that metaphors play, not just in poetic language but in everyday speech, as well as in more technical discourses. In other words, signifiers have a performative quality that can never be closed down by some definitive or literal meaning. This does not mean we should abandon the notion of structure altogether, but leads instead to the more considered view that linguistic structures are inherently unstable (or to use the Derridean terminology 'undecidable'), that is, forever subject to the possibility of disruption and displacement, through a creative (re)appropriation of their key terms. Again, it is important to stress that these points of emphasis emerged from several quarters. For example, similar claims can be found in Roland Barthes' work, as well as in Lacan's emphasis on what he called the 'permanent sliding of the signified under the signifier', but it is Derrida who first gave systematic expression to these tenets of poststructuralism.

Poststructuralism in politics and international relations

As we noted in the introduction, these poststructuralist insights have impacted across the social sciences, including on the study of politics and international relations. However, we should also note at this point that poststructuralism is antithetical to the typical conceptions of politics representative of these disciplines. For example, poststructuralists reject the idea that we can delimit 'politics' to a self-contained area of activity, associated for example with the activities of the government or the state, or with various inputs into the 'political system'. Like Marxists and feminists, poststructuralists have maintained instead a more extended conception of 'the political'. Where Marxism draws attention to the political character of economic class relations and feminists identify the operations of patriarchy in the private realm and assert the 'personal is political', poststructuralists see power and resistance (that is, politics) in the prevailing frameworks of meaning, that is, in the dominant 'discourses' that shape our identities and sense of who we are. This suggests a very broad conception of 'the political'. Politics can be found more or less anywhere, and so it is not surprising that much of what poststructuralists tend to focus on is not regarded as a legitimate object of political study by those working with a more narrow conception of politics, that is, within the political science mainstream (on this point, see Finlayson and Valentine, 2002: 5).

It is nonetheless possible to discern those poststructuralists who have focused most directly on overtly political questions. Howarth (2013: 13–16) makes a distinction between three generations of poststructuralism. The first is the '68 generation' and from this original cohort, the most systematic and lasting contribution for the study of politics is arguably Foucault's analyses of power relations. The second generation, from the mid-1980s to the end of the century, saw poststructuralist ideas being mobilised by a number of leading political thinkers in the UK and the USA, including the publication of Ernesto Laclau and Chantal Mouffe's influential *Hegemony and Socialist Strategy* (1985), which explicitly reworked Marxist categories from a poststructuralist perspective, and Judith Butler's similarly influential *Gender Trouble* (1990), which mobilised poststructuralism to critique heterosexual normativity and the construction of gender identities. The early 1990s also saw William Connolly rework categories in political science, such as 'power', 'authority' and 'interests' from a poststructuralist perspective, as well as pioneering an approach to normative questions and political ethics drawing mostly on Friedrich Nietzsche and Foucault (Connolly, 1991, 1995). This generation also included important applications of poststructuralism to the study of international relations (Der Derian and Schapiro, 1989; Connolly, 1991; Walker, 1993). More recently, from around the turn of the century, a third generation has extended poststructuralist analyses to a wider range of political issues and topics, including the publication of new theoretical works by the 'Essex School' (Glynos and Howarth, 2007) (see Box 8.1), the emergence of a distinctly poststructuralist analysis of political speeches and the role of rhetoric (Finlayson, 2014), debates between different strands of poststructuralism about politics and 'representation' (Tormey, 2006; Thomassen, 2007; Robinson and Tormey, 2007), and the further development of a distinctly poststructuralist approach to normative theory in the mode of 'agonistic democracy' (Norval, 2007; Wenman, 2013). For now, I provide a brief account and comparison of Foucault and Laclau's contributions. These can be seen as representative of two distinct poststructuralist renditions of the operations of power, as well as two different understandings of the role of 'discourse'.

The title of Foucault's Chair at the Collège de France was Professor of 'History of Systems of Thought', and this describes the orientation of his key works. In *Madness and Civilisation* (1960) and *Discipline and Publish* (1975) Foucault presented accounts of the historical emergence of forms of knowledge such as psychiatry, medicine and political economy, as well as key modern institutions such as the prison (Foucault, 1991, 2007). He variously described his method as 'archaeology' and 'genealogy', and one of the central objectives was to trace the contingent formation of truth claims and institutions that today we take for granted. In other words, he sought to de-naturalise our current practices, like the medicalisation of those deemed 'mentally ill' and the role of incarceration

Box 8.1 The Essex School

Laclau taught at the Department of Government at the University of Essex for nearly thirty years. Laclau's approach is characterised by a distinctive set of conceptual categories which he refined over many years. These concepts have also been further enhanced and developed by his former students, and this body of work denotes a distinctive 'Essex School' of poststructuralist political analysis.

The main thrust of this approach is concerned with analysing the mobilisation of collective identities (or forms of 'hegemony'), and this through a politics of building alliances (or 'chains of equivalence') between an assortment of competing political demands.

The Essex School have applied these ideas to a wide range of case studies; including the rise of Thatcherism, the phenomena of left- and right-wing populism (including the emergence of movements such as Syriza and Podemos) and the politics of more localised struggles, for example resistance to airport expansion in the UK (see, for example, the essays collected in Howarth et al., 2000, and those in Panizza, 2005).

as the centrepiece of our criminal justice system. In contrast to Derrida, there is less direct influence of Saussure in Foucault's approach. Nevertheless, Foucault shared Saussure's emphasis on the internal relations between elements as key to understanding the reproduction of social structures, which he presented as 'heterogonous ensemble[s] consisting of discourses, institutions, architectural forms, regulatory decisions, laws, administrative measures, scientific statements, philosophical, moral and philanthropic propositions' (Gordon, 1980). His *post*structuralism is evident in his rejection of the idea that these 'ensembles' ever form anything like a closed totality. Instead, they are historically contingent formations, ultimately held together by power relations, and subject to the possibility of disruption and change.

Indeed, Foucault's interest in the historical emergence of particular institutions leads to his more general reflections on the operations of power, for which he is best known. One way into these ideas is to see what Foucault rejects, which is the commonly held view that power emanates from a single source, is homogeneous in its effects and is essentially repressive. These claims are associated above all with what Foucault calls the predominant 'juridical conception' of power, which he sees in the various doctrines of 'sovereignty' (Gordon, 1980: 96). However, Foucault also had in mind for critique certain forms of Marxism and feminism, which also tend to see power in terms of a single logic or system of domination, exploitation or patriarchy. By way of contrast, Foucault describes power as a 'productive network', as a set of diverse relations that produce knowledge, discourse and forms of subjectivity (Gordon, 1980: 119). Indeed, Foucault was primarily interested in what he described as the 'different modes by which, in our culture, human beings are made subjects' (Gordon, 1980: 208). This leads to a focus on the specific power relations, or on the modes of 'governmentality', that function in particular institutions such as prisons, factories and schools. Foucault explores the way in which in these institutions certain forms of knowledge come together with more physical strategies and techniques to produce forms of discipline, norms or modes of 'bio-power' that are 'intimately related to our bodies and [seek to shape and direct] our everyday behaviour' (Gordon, 1980: 142).

Foucault's work has been extremely influential, but has also been criticised and not only from those outside poststructuralism. Despite core sympathies, Laclau was concerned that Foucault's approach focused too extensively on the diffusion of power in particular institutions and consequently blinds political analysis to the 'partial concentrations of power existing in every concrete social formation' (Laclau and Mouffe, 1985: 142). Taking his inspiration from Derrida, Laclau also worked with a broader conception of 'discourse' which he extended to account for what are often considered non-linguistic or extra-linguistic phenomena. Indeed, taking Derrida's account of the disruptive movement of signification as his starting point, Laclau was primarily interested in explicating the political strategies that temporarily arrest the flow of meaning, and momentarily fix social or 'discursive' structures around privileged 'nodal points'. In order to account for this aspect of politics, Laclau developed a detailed set of conceptual categories, drawing in particular on Lacanian psychoanalysis and on Antonio Gramsci's notion of 'hegemony'.

Gramsci was an Italian Marxist writing in the early twentieth century and he similarly sought to understand the role of political struggles in producing particular configurations of power at certain key historical conjunctures, such as the rise of fascism in Italy in the 1920s. Gramsci described the operation of hegemony as the construction of a 'collective will', whereby a particular class is able to win over other classes by tactically presenting its own interests as part of a more 'universal expansion'. This idea is also central to Laclau's approach. He rejected the Marxist idea that it is only 'fundamental classes' that can play this leading or hegemonic role. Indeed, Laclau was inspired by the politics of the new social movements. In his post-Marxist account, any group can, in principle, temporarily represent the universal, and the identities of the various groups do not precede their engagement in political struggles but are essentially forged in and through political struggle. Nevertheless, in much the same mode as Gramsci, Laclau conceived of politics as competition between different groups to 'temporarily give to their particularisms a function of universal representation' (Laclau, 2000: 35) (see Box 8.1).

The ontological and epistemological assumptions of poststructuralism

In this section I examine the way poststructuralists approach the philosophical questions underpinning politics and international relations. I take it that many critics misunderstand poststructuralism, when it comes to questions of ontology and epistemology. The widespread assumption is that poststructuralists avoid making claims about philosophical foundations, or they cannot get beyond a critique of the ontological and epistemological assumptions of alternate approaches, for example of behaviouralists, rational choice theorists and Marxists, all of which poststructuralists dismiss as various forms of 'essentialism' and 'foundationalism'. It is true that much poststructuralist theory has taken the form of exposing and debunking attempts to provide (supposedly) indisputable grounds for work in the social and political sciences. However, it does not follow that poststructuralists imagine they can – for example – carry out empirical work without invoking any prior assumptions of their own. Poststructuralists are not empiricists. Indeed, if 'ontology' is more or less as Marsh, Ercan and Furlong present it in this book (Chapter 10), that is, a set of prior assumptions about the nature of the world, or of the basic coordinates of 'reality', then poststructuralists are firmly in agreement that every theoretical viewpoint, including their own, necessarily presupposes some ontology and it is incumbent on the theorist to render those assumptions explicit. In fact, if anything, poststructuralists have been rather preoccupied with questions of ontology (on this point, see Khan, 2017).

Given that poststructuralists do develop an ontological position, what does this look like? Here, there is considerable disagreement between different strands of poststructuralism. However, there is some convergence on the following points. First, there can be no theory independent account of what is really out there. For poststructuralists 'reality' is mediated through concepts and linguistic structures. Second, if we examine our core assumptions about the nature of 'reality', the characteristics that stand out most are the same points we examined above, that is, the 'world' is only ever manifest – for example, to the gaze of the social and political researcher – in the form of *relations* and *differences*. Indeed, a great deal of dispute among poststructuralists has been about how best to give expression to this irreducible *difference*. Nevertheless, it is these categories that provide ontological conditions for our engagement with the world. However, as we saw in the discussion of Saussure and Derrida, these same categories also prevent us from ever fully capturing the 'object' as it really is, that is, in its 'essence'. In other words, these same ontological conditions of possibility for engaging with the world of objects, also at the same time, paradoxically, represent conditions of impossibility for perceiving the world as it 'really is'. This sense of limit, ambiguity and paradox is characteristic of poststructuralist reflections on ontology, and this stance has been described as an example of 'weak ontology' (White, 2000), that is, in contrast to those approaches such as rational choice theory and Marxism that make strong claims about the fully foundational status of their ontological assumptions. As 'post-foundationalists' (rather than strictly 'anti-foundationalists') poststructuralists *do* recognise the need for philosophical foundations, but they also attribute them with an inherently ambiguous, shifting and essentially contestable status (Marchart, 2007).

This same sense of ambiguity is characteristic of poststructuralist reflections on epistemology. If there is one thinker above all whose work on the status of 'truth' stands behind poststructuralism, it is the late nineteenth-century German philosopher Nietzsche. The late twentieth-century American pragmatist philosopher Richard Rorty summarised Nietzsche's position well when he said Nietzsche's insight was that 'truth is made and not found' (Rorty, 1989). On Nietzsche's view, this same sentiment applies (uncompromisingly) to *all* types of truth claim. Different truth claims are essentially stories we tell ourselves about how the world is, and this narrative form applies as much to the 'truths' of the natural sciences as it does to say poetry or religion. This implies we can never arrive at the truth with a Capital T, because there is a basic disjuncture between the world and the stories we tell ourselves about 'it'. Moreover, this fissure does not follow from present limitations in our methodology. This will not be corrected at some future date, for example as the behaviouralists would have it by developing more accurate forms of measurement and observation. Instead, this disconnection is constitutive. As Rorty says, 'there is no sense in which any of [our] descriptions [including those developed in the natural sciences] is [or ever can be] an accurate representation of the way the world is in itself' (Rorty, 1989: 4). Or, as Nietzsche put it, our concepts relate to the world rather like a person 'playing blind man's bluff on the back of things' (Nietzsche, 1976).

It does follow from this that poststructuralists are sceptical of all those theories that imagine we can identify some narrow epistemological criteria – rules or methods – to arrive at objective 'Truth'. However, poststructuralist reflections on the status of truth do not *only* take the form of a critique of other epistemological viewpoints. With Nietzsche, poststructuralists are committed to a set of affirmative assumptions about the circumstances under which truth claims can be asserted. Poststructuralists do not deny that there is a world out there to be known and talked about (although they are often mischaracterised in this way). They simply maintain that none of our various forms of knowledge will ever map onto or correspond with the world. And in the absence of any pursuit after truth with a Capital T, poststructuralists focus instead on analysing the material 'effects of truth' generated by various historically contingent forms of knowledge, for example as we saw above in Foucault's genealogies.

This stance positions the poststructuralists against those positivists who think that political science should be modelled on a rather outmoded understanding of the hard sciences. Poststructuralists do not think that human behaviour is subject to law-like regularity that can be predicated, either through hypotheses drawn from value-free observations or on the basis of a priori assumptions about human psychology or abstract models of 'rational' behaviour. However, we should note that it does not follow from this that poststructuralism is entirely hostile to the notion of 'science'. In fact, these poststructuralist insights actually resonate with some of the most up-to-date theories within the philosophy of the natural sciences. Indeed, since the intervention of Thomas Kuhn, philosophers of natural science have gravitated towards a position which is very close to poststructuralism. This entails acknowledgement that there is never any access to the 'bare facts'. The 'facts' are always already mediated by a set of theoretical assumptions, that is, by a broad framework of meaning, what Kuhn (1970) called a 'paradigm'. Moreover, as Paul Feyerabend (2010) stressed, the most interesting innovations in science (what Kuhn calls 'revolutionary science') often take place when strict methodological and epistemological rules are either intentionally or unintentionally ignored. From the poststructuralist perspective, the mainstream discipline of political science, especially in the USA, suffers from a stifling myopia and a lack of creativity, and political scientists would do well to catch up with these insights drawn from the most current philosophies of the natural sciences.

We have considered the contrast between poststructuralism and the predominant forms of positivism. However, we should also note the interface between poststructuralism and constructivism. Indeed, one theme that runs throughout this chapter is the overriding concern in poststructuralism with the production of *meaning*. Here, poststructuralists share conjoint assumptions with the traditions of social constructivism examined by Craig Parsons in Chapter 5. As Parsons explains, all forms of constructivism depart to some degree from the positivist claim that human behaviour is subject to law like regularity. This is because human action is inherently meaningful, people do and say things for a reason, and the task of the social or political—is therefore to interpret and understand those reasons, rather than simply explaining behaviour in a causal fashion. With this the poststructuralists are in agreement. However, for many constructivists it remains possible (1) to give a complete reconstruction of the frameworks of significance behind a particular action, and (2) to establish methodological criteria – what Parsons calls 'careful research designs' and principles of 'open debate' – that enable the political science community to establish the relative veracity of one set of interpretations over another. Needless to say, poststructuralists reject both these assumptions. Indeed, we can think of poststructuralism as a radical mode of constructivism. From this viewpoint, work in the social and political sciences is best understood in terms of a range of competing interpretations, but where there simply are no epistemological criteria to distinguish the validity of one set of interpretations over another. Opponents think this inevitably leads to a dangerous form of 'ethical relativism', and it is to this and other criticisms of poststructuralism that we now turn.

Criticism and evaluation

Given the extent of its impact across the social sciences, it is not surprising that poststructuralism has come under considerable and sometimes intense criticism. The list is many and variegated, and here I focus on just a few of the most prominent lines of critique.

Some have challenged poststructuralism with respect to the question of structure and agency. This refers, in part, to the extent to which we can understand political agents to retain a capacity for action. Or, conversely, whether or to what extent those actions are always already predetermined by background structures? For example, in classical Marxist theory the identity of political actors (that is, social classes and their representatives) and the moves available to them are more or less seen to be determined by the underlying structures of exploitation characteristic of capitalism. Perhaps unsurprisingly, some read poststructuralism in similarly deterministic ways. Because meaning is derived from a system of differences that exists prior to individual acts of speaking, so the claim goes, poststructuralists more or less reduce any would-be capacity for agency to an effect of linguistic structure (for example, Bevir and Rhodes, 2003). Perhaps ironically, others see the obverse, and claim instead that poststructuralism is characterised by an excessive voluntarism which gives too much space for agency (for example Morton, 2005). The reality is that the first of these criticisms is understandable, for reasons I go into in a moment, but neither of them is correct. In fact, poststructuralists have offered a range of nuanced reflections on the dynamic between structure and agency.

In much poststructuralist literature, the question of structure and agency is approached via discussions about 'the subject'. When poststructuralists talk about philosophies of 'the subject', they have in mind the foundational assumptions about human nature characteristic of modern philosophers, for example from Descartes to Hegel and the young Marx. One strong impulse in poststructuralism is to 'displace' and 'decentre' these essentialist theories of 'the subject', that is, to challenge the philosophical depiction of 'Man' as something like the source and foundation of knowledge and as the potential author of his (*sic*) own destiny. This critique of humanist philosophy is epitomised in Althusser's call for a vigorous 'theoretical anti-humanism', Barthes' assertion of the 'death of the author', and Foucault's famous image of the erasure of Man (that is, as a potentially autonomous subject) 'like a face drawn in the sand at the edge of the sea' (Barthes, 1977; Althusser, 2005: 229; Foucault, 2008: 422). Given these strong assertions, it is understandable that some read poststructuralism in terms of a complete reduction of agency to the decentring effects of linguistic structure. However, this is not the entire picture, because a lot of poststructuralist theory has actually been about how to reconfigure 'the subject' and 'its' capacity for agency in light of poststructuralism.

This reconfigured subject manifests in a variety of forms. For example, Laclau associates 'the subject' with the inability of any structure to establish closure, and so agency manifests in periodic moments of 'dislocation' of the existing structures (Laclau, 1990). On a different register, Butler associates agency with our capacity to repeatedly reconfigure the dominant norms, through practices of parody and reiteration (Butler, 1990). This is close to Foucault's claim that wherever there is power we also find resistance. As he put it:

> Power is exercised only over free subjects, and only in so far as they are 'free'. By this we mean individual or collective subjects who are faced with a field of possibilities in which several kinds of conduct, several ways of reacting and modes of behaviour are available. (Foucault, 2002: 342)

These various poststructuralist accounts differ from each other, but they share some common ground. Here, 'the subject' is neither unified nor fully (or potentially) autonomous. Her agency does not 'originate', for example, from some intentions in the author. Her identity is always relational and determined to a large extent by established structures and the dominant norms, but she also always retains a certain room for manoeuvre and a capacity to reconfigure those norms to some degree. In other words, this is not an account of the total reduction of human agency to structural determination. In fact, this poststructuralist account of 'the subject' is close to that found in forms of new institutionalist literature, as set out by Vivien Lowndes in Chapter 4; institutions are presented by discursive or constructivist institutionalists as 'sedimented discourses', which shape political actors, while those same institutions are also inevitably contested by the actors who thereby further shape them in turn.

Hopefully, this chapter will have gone some way to dispelling the idea that poststructuralism is a kind of *anti*-theory, concerned exclusively with knocking holes in other people's arguments. However, for those who acknowledge its affirmative qualities, many hastily add that poststructuralism nonetheless ends up in a set of internal inconsistencies. Take, for example, the poststructuralist claim that there is no such thing as truth with a Capital T. Here, the response sometime comes that 'there must be at least one truth, that is, the claim that there is no Truth', and so the poststructuralists are caught in logical inconsistency. This is an example of what Jurgen Habermas has called a 'performative contradiction'. In response, I think poststructuralists should accept the charge, but also contest the idea that this represents any kind of an offence. Of course, one major impulse behind poststructuralism has been to draw into question the high status attributed to the court of 'Reason' in the Western tradition. This does not mean we should abandon any effort to establish consistency, but it does mean that all arguments – and especially those about philosophical foundations or first principles – tend to reach a point of internal inconsistency, and this is because reason and logic cannot provide a transparent account of itself. From the poststructuralist perspective, logical inconsistencies therefore point to the circumstances of our encounter with the world which is characterised by a high degree of contingency. Best to develop theories that give expression to these qualities, rather than to try and iron them out and deny them through recourse to supposedly fully 'rational' arguments.

Yet another line of critique draws attention to the often irritating style of a lot of poststructuralist writing (for example, Nussbaum, 2000). Here, the critics have a point. It is true that a great deal of poststructuralist theory is written in ways that seem unnecessarily difficult, jargon-laden, pretentious and sometimes wilfully obscure. There are probably several reasons for this. In part this is a reaction against the preoccupation with clarity characteristic of French Enlightenment thought, and many poststructuralists would also most likely follow Bathes in his denunciation of 'clarity' as a 'bourgeois value'. This is further exacerbated by an aspiration to demonstrate the principles of poststructuralism not only in the substance of the argument but also in the writing style, and so in Derrida there is an endless fascination with the multiple play of the text, and Lacan's arguments are said to mirror the abstruse movement of the unconscious drives. For somebody like me who likes a good clear argument, most of this stylist play is just an unnecessary irritation. However, it does not follow from this, as Noam Chomsky would have it, that the leading poststructuralists are simply 'charlatans' who engage in nothing more than meaningless 'posturing'. As I hope we have seen in this chapter, the poststructuralists actually have some very important things to say, and so students would do well to persevere with the seemingly difficult terminology in order to dig out the underlying insights and observations.

Finally, poststructuralism has come under a lot of criticism for exhibiting a 'normative deficit'. This assertion comes in different forms. For some, poststructuralism is overly pessimistic, and does away with the possibility of a good society and associated notions of progress and so on. Foucault's account of the pervasiveness of power relationships is often read in these gloomy terms. However, this is a misreading. Poststructuralists do not think we will ever reach a society without power relations, and on this there is an obvious counterpoint with Marxism which anticipates a future reconciled society in the form of Communism. However, this does not lead to an acquiescent pessimism, because, as we have seen, it does not follow that our actions are entirely predetermined by the existing configurations of power. Instead, 'subjects' can always draw the *existing* power relationship into question to some degree, because they retain certain room for manoeuvre.

Habermas recognises this (would-be) critical dimension of poststructuralism. However, on his account the poststructuralists lack the normative recourses to develop an effective critique of established institutions, because of what he calls their 'totalising critique of reason' (Habermas, 1994: 284). The implication is, once again, that the poststructuralists find themselves in a 'performative contradiction'. Poststructuralists typically respond that we don't need rational norms and philosophical foundations in order to establish critical judgements! However, in turn this leads to an additional critique, which is the idea that poststructuralism then opens the door to a dangerous 'ethical relativism' where 'anything goes'.

These arguments have moved back and forth over many pages of contemporary political theory and we won't bring an end to them here. Nevertheless, in my view these various criticisms do not hit the mark. In fact, poststructuralists have developed a range of sophisticated 'post-foundational' approaches to 'normative' questions. For several poststructuralists, the best way to approach these issues is through a turn to ethics (Derrida, 2000; Butler, 2006; Critchley, 2007). Others have recently developed theories of 'agonistic democracy', where the emphasis is not on overcoming power relationships but rather on artfully channelling and sublimating them in ways that are more conducive to a spirit of contestation, creativity and interruption (Norval, 2007; Wenman, 2013). There is no scope here to further elaborate on these 'normative' approaches, but only to acknowledge that this is another area where poststructuralists are often presumed to have little to say but in fact they have made valuable contributions.

Conclusion

In line with other critical approaches such as Marxism and feminism, we have seen that poststructuralism aims to extend the scope of politics and of the political. This has been resisted by those positivist approaches that continue to preside over mainstream political science, and in part this explains the apparently limited impact of poststructuralism on the discipline. At the same time, however, we have seen that poststructuralists have developed sophisticated analyses of 'the political' and, in particular, they have generated novel insights into the operations of power. We have also seen that these poststructuralist analyses have had a significant impact on adjacent perspectives, including Marxism, feminism, constructivism and the new institutionalism. Indeed, there has been a creative synergy between poststructuralism and these various sub-disciplines, and each of them has absorbed themes and vocabulary from poststructuralism, sometimes consciously and other times not.

In fact, even the most resolute forms of positivism have, to some extent, been worn down by the persistent capacity of poststructuralism to draw into question all forms of 'essentialism'. Those who remain committed to the idea that we can identify rational criteria to distinguish genuinely 'scientific' forms of knowledge, and that political behaviour is subject to law-like regularity are certainty less confident in these assertions than their forebears in the 1950s and 1960s. Again, this reflects a more general climate of scepticism in the realm of epistemology which is, in part, a consequence of the impact of poststructuralism. A more positive outlook to emerge from these circumstances – of generalised incredulity – might resemble the position defended by Peters, Pierre and Stoker in the final chapter of this book. There, the emphasis is placed on disciplinary boundary crossing, and the importance of adopting a variety of methods and perspectives in order to capture the diversity of experience. To some extent, this strategy resonates with the general orientation of poststructuralism. On this, however, we should nonetheless close with a note of caution, which is that poststructuralists additionally stress the incommensurability between different viewpoints, and so there are always likely to be significant limits to the range of perspectives that can be credibly brought together in this kind of integrated and pragmatic approach.

Further reading

- On the movement from structuralism to poststructuralism, see Sturrock (1979).
- For a range of critical overviews and introductions to poststructuralism, some sympathetic and others less so, see Belsey (2002), Culler (1983), Dews (1987), Howarth (2013), Sarup (1993) and Williams (2005).
- For texts on some of the leading figures associated with poststructuralism, especially the political implications of their thought, see the Routledge series 'Thinking the Political'.
- For recent collections of essays and critical debates on poststructuralism see Dillet, MacKenzie and Porter (2013); Khan and Wenman (2017).
- For a detailed evaluation of different conceptions of 'discourse', for example in Foucault and Laclau and Mouffe, see Howarth (2000).
- For critical introductions to Laclau and the contributions of the Essex School, see Smith (1998) and Torfing (1999).

Chapter 9

Political Psychology

FRANK MOLS AND PAUL 'T HART

An interdisciplinary enterprise

Spanning systematic research, teaching and policy advice for the best part of a century, the interdisciplinary subfield of political psychology has become a firmly footed part of political science. Political psychologists have contributed significantly to our understanding of the attitudes and behaviours of political *elites*, dissecting their personalities, political stances, policy choices, crisis responses, and the connections between their private and public lives. They have also provided new insights into the sources of political behaviour of ordinary *citizens* in countless studies of mass political beliefs, attitudes, socialisation and participation, as well as into political conflict and cooperation within and between members of different social groups.

Political psychologists also examine the *nexus between* elite and mass political behaviour: electioneering; leader–follower relations; political rhetoric, persuasion and communication; collective mobilisation; behavior change strategies; and political representation and legitimacy. The fruits of many decades of research have been laid down in specialised journals (most notably *Political Psychology,* which by 2016 had become a top journal at ISI 8/120 in Political Science and 12/62 in Social Psychology), a series of major handbooks (Sears et al., 2013), anthologies (Lavine, 2010) and textbooks (Jost and Sidanius, 2004; Houghton, 2009; Cottam et al., 2015).

The case for importing psychological concepts and theories into political science rests on two key assertions. The first is that *political processes and outcomes are shaped at least in part by the preferences, choices and actions of individuals and groups*. To be sure, political psychologists do not deny the relevance of (formal and informal) institutions and political structures – parties, governments, bureaucracies, courts, unions, international institutions, laws, policies, programmes, culture, traditions, norms, discourses – typically studied by mainstream political scientists. However, they reject accounts of political life that implicitly or explicitly assert that these macro- and meso-level factors largely determine what goes on in politics.

Why are small states sometimes able to defy big powers? Why do democratic politicians sometimes make deeply unpopular (and thus politically lethal) policy choices (Vis, 2010; Linde and Vis, 2016)? Why are some countries torn apart by protracted and debilitating religious, ethnic and class conflict, whereas in others such categories have lost relevance? Political psychologists have demonstrated that in each of these situations we need to drill down to the psychology of the actors and relationships between them if we want to explain what macro-level, institutional, rational choice approaches cannot.

As Hermann (2002: 47) argues:

> True, in much of politics, people are embedded in groups, institutions, cultures and governments, and it is the decisions of those entities that we seek to understand. However, it is individuals who identify and frame the problems that face such entities, who have disagreements and jockey for position, who generate compromises and build consensus, and who originate and implement change.

At first glance this may seem to make perfect sense. After all politics involves groups and groups are indeed made up of individuals. However, what should not be forgotten is a large body of social psychological research which has shown that group membership alters people's sense of who they are and what they stand for, and this is why aggregated individual level findings (for example, surveys and opinion polls) typically prove poor predictors of actual political behaviour. Political psychologists are increasingly aware of this problem, which can be described as 'pernicious methodological individualism' (Mols and Weber, 2013).

The second fundamental assertion of political psychology is that to explain the political preferences, choices and actions of individuals and groups, we need to study their characteristics and relationships empirically, with due attention for context-specific group dynamics. This is the crucial difference between political psychology and other perspectives, such as rational choice or bureaucratic politics. The latter impute goals and strategies to actors on the basis of theoretical assumptions in order to predict their behaviour, or to rationalise it post hoc. Political psychologists in contrast are often particularly interested in explaining behaviours and choices that surprise, startle or dismay – and are therefore difficult to explain with models assuming self-interested utility-maximising behaviour.

Political psychology comprises different approaches. For example, social cognition scholars focus on the way in which people view the world and the situations they are in, thereby regarding such perceptions as the products of their core beliefs, prior experiences, and information-processing capacities and styles, which in turn are believed to be rooted in both neurobiological processes (Jost et al., 2014; McDermott and Hatemi, 2014) and childhood and political socialisation (Farnen et al., 2008). Personality scholars study the nature, origins and effects of people's drives, values and styles (Duckitt and Sibley, 2010;

Box 9.1 The field of political psychology

Political psychology is a burgeoning field of social science research, seeking to explain (1) the attitudes and behaviours of influential political leaders, (2) the attitudes and behaviours of ordinary citizens and voters, and (3) the way in which political elites and mass publics influence each other. What gave rise to this field of research were seemingly irrational behaviours (for example, why do the poor often support ideologies that justify status and wealth inequality?), behaviours that could not be explained using traditional 'rational actor models' that conceive of humans as rational, selfish, atomistic utility maximisers. The discipline derives its strength from its openness and its ambition to synthesise insights from different social science disciplines to yield a more complex and integrated understanding of political phenomena.

Jost, 2011; Winter, 2013). And, in an outlook that takes issue with 'individual differences perspectives' and places more emphasis on the context-dependence of leadership, followership and group behaviour, social psychologists concentrate on inter- and intragroup relations of the collectivities in which individual political actors operate and identify with (Huddy et al., 2013).

Combined, these different strands of psychology offer an indispensable body of knowledge for political science (see Box 9.1). At the same time, political psychology is at its best when it fuses (rather than merely applies) the analytical tools of psychologists to political life, but actually combines concepts, theories and methods from *both* disciplines. In this chapter we provide an introduction to the field, and will highlight best-practice studies that do exactly that.

Political conflict and contention

Political psychology began in earnest in 1930s Europe, when Frankfurt School social scientists became interested in explaining the remarkable popular appeal of authoritarian leaders such as Adolf Hitler in Weimar Germany and Benito Mussolini in Italy. Freudian psychology featured prominently in their work, and the appeal of authoritarian leaders, so they argued, was the result of a generation of Germans exposed to a harsh parenting style (due to the Great Depression), and of suppressed anger towards the father figure, which later in life manifested in adoration for authoritarian leaders. In the USA, pioneering scholars such as Harold Lasswell (1986 [1930]) likewise turned to Freud's work to explain the seemingly aberrant traits and behaviours of political leaders. The title of his 1930 classic says it all: *Psychopathology and Politics*.

In the aftermath of the Second World War, there was growing interest in studying political behaviour with help of more rigorous empirical methods (rather than grand Freudian interpretive assertions). One of the ways in which this was attempted was by developing personality tests to measure individuals' propensity to endorse authoritarian leaders. The most famous ones are the Fascism Scale (or F-Scale) developed by Theodor Adorno and colleagues in 1950, and the Right-Wing Authoritarianism Scale (RWA-Scale) developed by Robert Altemeyer in 1981, which continues to inspire researchers interested in the appeal of radical right-wing movements.

The Second World War and the Holocaust would also form the catalyst for systematic empirical research into the origins of intergroup conflict and mass atrocities. The first studies relied heavily on rational actor models developed in economics, and sought to provide empirical evidence that intergroup hostility is the result of conflict over scarce resources. For example, Hovland and Sears (1940) examined the relationship between cotton prices and lynchings of African Americans in the USA, and argued on the basis of their findings that lynchings became more common when cotton prices fell and hardship increased. Another attempt to demonstrate that intergroup hostility boils down to conflict over scarce resources was Sherif and colleagues' famous Robbers Cave experiment (1961), in which two randomly selected teams of boy scouts were asked to compete in games and to collaborate in team tasks. The experiment had to be abandoned prematurely due to rising intergroup conflict, and this was attributed to growing conflict over scarce resources.

These studies would form the basis for Realistic Conflict Theory (RCT) (Campbell, 1965), a paradigm that would leave a lasting imprint, and consolidate rather than challenge widespread belief that intergroup hostility is ultimately a matter of competition over scarce resources. This was to change in the 1970s when Tajfel and Billig (1974) set out to demonstrate that intergroup conflict can erupt without conflict over scarce resources. They demonstrated this using so-called minimal group experiments, in which techniques were used to instil a sense of group belonging among participants, after which participants were asked to allocate reward points to the ingroup and an imagined outgroup. The results of these experiments were startling and showed that members of groups can display ingroup favouritism in the absence of conflict for scarce resources, and that, under certain circumstances, mere self-categorisation can suffice to engender ingroup bias.

Although research into intergroup conflict would become more sophisticated over time, with peace and conflict researchers focusing on violent confrontations and political scientists focusing on frustration, aggression, far-right voting and third-party 'scapegoating', the idea of conflict over scarce resources would continue to underpin the vast majority of this research. As Rydgren (2007: 247) observed of research into the rise of populist right-wing parties, 'the explanations on offer in this literature are almost all based on grievance theory [focusing on] objective – mostly

Box 9.2 Research into the origins of group conflict

Why do countries go to war with each other? Why do some conflicts end in atrocities and genocide? These were the questions political psychologists sought to answer in the aftermath of the Second World War and the Holocaust. The most popular theory at that time was 'Realistic Conflict Theory' (RCT), a theory proposing that conflict ultimately 'boils down' to competition over scarce resources. This theory started to lose appeal in the 1970s, when research revealed that conflict can erupt in the absence of competition over material resources – as a result of differences norms, values and social identification (so-called Symbolic Threat). More recent research suggests that 'Realistic Conflict' and 'Symbolic Threat' perceptions tend to go hand in hand (Riek et al., 2010).

macro-structurally shaped – conditions that have increased grievances and discontent among the people'.

Although no one will deny that perceived increased competition for scarce resources (for example, jobs, housing, welfare) can engender frustration, discontent and perceived Relative Deprivation (RD), and that this, in turn, can enhance the appeal of far-right parties among working-class voters, this focus on material deprivation has prevented research exploring additional factors fuelling support for such movements. For example, there is growing evidence that populist far-right parties thrive in times of economic prosperity, and among wealthier sections of the population (Mols and Jetten, 2016, 2017), a phenomenon that has been attributed to so-called 'Relative Gratification' (RG).

Research into intergroup conflict has become rather fragmented (see Box 9.2). Peace and conflict researchers focus on postcolonial societies and pernicious ideological influences. Social psychologists examine ingroup bias and stereotyping across groups of different gender, race, ethnicity, religion and sexual orientation. Contemporary political scientists have become interested in the appeal of white supremacy groups, militant right-wing movements and 'radicalisation'. This specialisation is positive insofar as it has enabled different strands within political psychology to gain unique insights in all these domains. However, the downside is that there has been limited cross-fertilisation across these strands, and, in our view, the new challenge for political psychologists is to step up efforts to integrate insights across these domains.

Political leadership and followership

Understanding political leadership involves grasping the 'dynamic interplay of wants, needs, motives, values and capacities of both would-be leaders and their potential followers' (Burns, 2003: 16).

Who leads matters

Not all of us are driven to lead, and very few of us come to occupy political offices. Political psychologists have a long-standing interest in the psychological make-up of those that do, and demonstrate that this matters greatly for how and to what effect political leadership gets exercised. Psychoanalytic studies have explored the character, psychological development and psychological disorders – such as excessive narcissism or paranoia – of individual leaders (Post, 2014; Renshon, 2014; Krasno and LaPides, 2015). Others focus on specific personality traits, including the so-called 'big five' in populations of leaders: extraversion; agreeableness; conscientiousness; emotional stability, neuroticism; and openness to experience (Gerber et al., 2011). The link between personality traits, electoral success and 'historical greatness' of leaders has also been studied (Simonton, 1993).

A more specific personality trait that has been extensively studied in politicians is 'need for power'. Leaders with a high need for power, so it is argued, strive for dominance in collegial settings such as advisory groups and cabinets and seek to exercise a high degree of control over subordinates and policy decisions. For example, in a study examining the characteristics and leadership styles of US presidents in foreign policy decision-making, Preston (2001) found that leaders with a high need for power preferred formal, hierarchical advisory system structures, centralised decision-making within tight inner circles of trusted advisers, and insisted on direct personal control over policy formulation. They had assertive interpersonal styles, actively challenging or seeking to influence the positions taken by their advisers, and overriding or ignoring advisers with opposing policy views. In contrast, leaders low in need for power preferred more open and collegial advisory arrangements, were happy to delegate decision-making to subordinates, and were more likely to defer to senior advisers. Each type of leadership style comes with distinctive potential strengths, but also with pivotal risks, such as cognitive arrogance, excessive (sometimes Machiavellian) single-mindedness, complacency and contempt for advisers.

How groups create leaders, and leaders gain followers

In democratic polities, followers are institutionally empowered to select and indeed 'deselect' leaders periodically – thus determining their leaders' fates as much as these leaders are shaping theirs (Keohane, 2010). So, when and why *do* people follow and repudiate political leaders? What is the nature of the 'psychological contract' between them? Virtually all forms of leadership have a transactional quality, with leaders performing a service that the group desires, in exchange for which the group empowers them. Little (1985), for example, surmises that the public at different times and to differing degrees seek either visionary inspiration, safety from danger or collective solidarity from their political leaders. Leaders that effectively appeal to these largely subconscious public moods and emotions, so the argument goes, will be followed.

But why do people so often and for such a long time tolerate leaders who pursue morally abhorrent objectives or proceed in damaging or self-defeating ways to get others to achieve their goals?[1] If we accept that followers are indeed to be understood as more than mere subjects or sheep with a 'herd mentality', why don't they rebel when they find themselves confronted by bad leadership? These questions have intrigued social scientists ever since the publication of Stanley Milgram's experiments on obedience to authority, published around the time of Adolf Eichmann's trial in Israel for Nazi war crimes, in which Eichmann justified his role arguing he was only following orders.

Milgram (1974) found that 65 per cent of subjects (26 out of 40) in a laboratory experiment continued to administer what they believed to be painful, dangerous and ultimately lethal shocks to a peer when instructed to do so by a researcher as part of an alleged scientific study into the effects of punishment on learning performance. Ethically controversial, the experiments generated worldwide debate, and above all pessimistic conclusions about human abilities to differentiate between legitimate and illegitimate commands given to them by authority figures, and to act accordingly (see Haslam and Reicher, 2012).

Milgram concluded that the results showed a human tendency to slip into a passive 'agentic state' when faced with authority, and this appeared to fit well with Hannah Arendt's perspective on the banality of evil (Arendt, 1961). Their combined work would become the new orthodoxy in thinking about genocide, and the view that such atrocities are committed not by exceptionally pathological 'evil' individuals, but by ordinary people in extraordinary (overpowering) situations. Here, too, we see a rift between popular understandings of the roots of evil (the so-called Milgram–Arendt view) and more recent work (published in a special issue of the *Journal of Social Issues* on the subject in 2014) which sheds new light on the Milgram's experiments and challenges the conclusions that are typically drawn from them.

This was not the first time that Milgram's work came under closer scrutiny. For example, in the late 1980s, psychologists Herbert Kelman and Valerie Hamilton were interested in why some of the people in the various permutations of Milgram's experiments *dis*obeyed. Why did they, and only they, rebel against a malevolent authority figure? According to Kelman and Hamilton (1989), people follow (1) because they fear the consequences of not doing so (*compliance*); (2) because they feel a strong personal bond with the authority figure who is giving them orders (*identification*); or (3) because they substantively agree with what they are being asked to do (*internalisation*). They then surmised that only the latter type of follower retains the moral autonomy and psychological

[1]The next few paragraphs are adapted from 't Hart (2014), chapter 4.

strength to stand up to malicious leadership. They will only do what they are told when and insofar as they themselves reach an autonomous judgement that the request is sensible and justifiable. The other two categories tend to externalise the moral judgement, relying either on the prevailing institutional hierarchy in which they are embedded or on the personal judgement of those they have accepted as their leaders.

Kelman and Hamilton further argued that these propensities towards authority are part and parcel of our personality structure, and that the proportion of people with an internalisation-based followership ethos was likely to be comparatively small, though not insignificant. The above-mentioned special issue of the *Journal of Social Issues* on Milgram's experiments raises yet other concerns, such as the fact that Milgram conducted five trials before he conducted what he would later report as the 'baseline study', and that obedience levels in these trials had been rather low and unremarkable. According to these researchers, Milgram paid little attention to the many ways in which participants resisted and disobeyed. One of the conclusions to emerge from this more recent work is that obedience may well have been a matter not of passive and unthinking obedience to authority, but of shared identity and willingness to help 'the researcher' conduct his experiment (Reicher and Haslam, 2011).

That being said, it is unlikely that follower psychology alone can explain the persistence of bad leadership (Kellerman, 2004; Lipman-Blumen, 2006; Helms, 2012). Leadership – good and bad – is produced, sustained and destroyed in a triangular interaction between leaders, constituents and (situational, sociocultural, institutional) environments (Padilla et al., 2007). As can be seen from the predominant slant of the many popular 'self-help' books on leadership, this insight continues to be ignored. Rather, such books tend to focus on famous persons, often men (for example, Martin Luther King, Mahatma Gandhi, Richard Branson, Steve Jobs, Barack Obama), who became regarded as charismatic leaders, and followership is typically assumed to be the by-product of the person's natural charisma.

Thanks to advances in social psychology, we now know that such accounts are problematic. For example, the term 'charisma' is notoriously fuzzy, and thus hardly helpful for predictions about whether a particular leader will become regarded as successful and charismatic. Indeed, instead we seem to always apply the term with the benefit of hindsight, retrospectively projecting the label onto a leader knowing they had great impact. Popular leadership books thus tend to use 'charisma' where they actually mean 'perceived leadership success'.

Fortunately there are several lines of research that do pay attention to the interplay between leaders and followers. For example, research into 'transformational leadership' examines the way(s) in which leaders persuade prospective followers to embrace a new vision for the future (Bass et al., 1987). An oft-used example in this literature is Martin Luther King and his successful campaign to persuade a large proportion of Americans that it was time for social change (McGuire and Hutchings, 2007). One of the key ingredients of transformational leadership is leadership authenticity, and, as several studies have shown, followers who perceive their leader to be authentic do indeed display greater organisational commitment and so-called organisational citizenship behaviour. Although such studies have helped to raise awareness about the importance of an emotional leader–follower relationship and perceived authenticity (Avolio and Gardner, 2005), the explanations on offer in this literature tend to be individualistic in that they rest on the assumption that transformative and authentic leaders are able to 'win over' individuals, who will subsequently become a group by virtue of being inspired by (and following) the same leader. More recent research has addressed this shortcoming (i.e., pernicious methodological individualism), showing perceived authenticity is mediated by shared social identity (Steffens et al., 2016).

As those analysing political speeches will know, politicians seek to mobilise *groups*, and the way this is typically achieved is by persuading groups that their interests and/or identities are not adequately represented, and that under their leadership the group will receive a better hearing. As social identity theorists have shown, to achieve followership a politician will have to craft a sense of 'us', and become perceived by followers as prototypical for the group in question and championing group goals (Haslam et al., 2011; Reicher and Haslam, 2011; Steffens et al., 2014). In other words, according to these researchers, leaders are crafty identity entrepreneurs (Reicher and Hopkins, 2001), and, according to this perspective the key to gaining followership is effective identity leadership (Reicher et al., 2014; Steffens et al., 2014) (see Box 9.3).

Box 9.3 Charismatic leadership: nature, nurture, or both?

Why do some leaders become remembered as 'charismatic'? Is it in their nature, or are they a product of unusual social circumstances? Some may argue from a 'nature' perspective that charismatic leaders must have had the right personality traits and personal resources. They were thus destined to become great leaders. Others will argue from a 'nurture' perspective that leadership success is a largely matter of learning, socialization and particular circumstances: a match between a crisis-stricken group of people looking for a saviour and an ambitious, talented individual seizing the opportunity to fulfil that need. Political psychologists have come to accept that nature and nurture explanations can complement each other. This has led them to focus their attention on the dynamics of leader–follower relationships that underpin the authority leaders can wield. That authority is nearly boundless in the case of charismatic leadership, where leaders become admired by their followers as all-encompassing moral exemplars and towers of wisdom. But in most instances there are definite limits to the 'political capital' that leaders are granted by followers (see Bennister et al., 2017).

Political beliefs and voter attitudes

When we think of political psychology we often immediately think of elections and voter preferences. Although, as this chapter shows, this is by no means the only area of political psychology, it is an area (known as psephology) that has been burgeoning for many decades. The outlook in this debate is very much the product of the behavioural revolution of the 1950s, when there was a push to render social science research (including political research) more scientific. The field would become, and remain, the realm of quantitative methods, with researchers analysing opinion-poll results and conducting large-N studies to 'gauge' voter preferences and voting intentions.

The fact that statistical analyses became the method of choice is both a strength and a weakness. A clear advantage is that commonly heard causal claims can be tested rigorously and, if falsified, be dismissed as myths. Another advantage is that it is possible to accrue robust evidence for the existence of certain correlations. For example, thanks to quantitative opinion-poll research we now know male voters and voters with low levels of education are more likely to vote for far-right parties than female voters and those with higher levels of education. This is one of the few quantitative findings that hold remarkably well across time and jurisdiction. However, many others do not, and this raises the fundamental question of what individual-level responses (obtained in one-on-one settings) can tell us about voting behaviour in real-life settings, where behaviour is influenced by the norms of the groups to which we belong. Indeed, this brings us back to the above-mentioned problem of 'pernicious methodological individualism', which can be said to haunt this line of research, and the question of what preferences disclosed in private (individual) settings can tell us about real-life social and political (collective) phenomena.

Perceiving the political world

Politicians are of course well aware that voters can be mobilised by appeals to meaningful social identities, and that their proposal have a far better chance of being supported if these can be framed as epitomising what the group stands for. To appreciate the true potential of identity-based issue framing, one only needs to consider the way in which populist right-wing leaders have managed to gain support by framing relatively mundane policy issues as signalling 'the nation's downfall' or 'the end of society as we know it' (Mols and Jetten, 2014, 2016).

What is more, our political attitudes and policy preferences as recorded in survey research are in large measure determined by the language in which the question is framed. For example, we know from Prospect Theory (Kahneman and Tversky, 1979) that humans have a tendency to be risk-averse, and that when faced with a choice between two alternatives with the exact same outcome, that we tend to choose the option that is framed as a chance to win, rather than as a risk to lose. These framing effects are equally powerful in real-life settings, and politicians often hire speechwriters to assist them in framing their messages in the most persuasive way.

One way in which a message can be (re)framed is by changing the reference group and/or issue. For example, the average voter's response to the proposition 'wealth inequality is a necessary evil' is likely to differ depending on whether they are reminded of youth unemployment or offshore tax havens. In one instance the voter may feel inequality is useful and morally justified on the grounds that unemployed youths need a financial incentive to look for employment, while in the other instance the voter may feel inequality is morally wrong so long as wealthy people are able to avoid paying taxes using off-shore tax havens.

Causes and consequences of political attitudes

Political attitudes can change quite dramatically. For example, not long ago 'multiculturalism' was a badge of honour that cities and countries with ethnically diverse populations could carry with pride. Now, it is not uncommon for politicians and other observers to assert that multiculturalism has been a categorical failure. This change in attitude can in part be explained by real-world events such as the rise in Islamist terrorist attacks. However, our views about the best response to these events also depends on (1) the group(s) we belong to; (2) the leader(s) we choose to follow; and (3) the interpretation of events advanced by 'our' leader(s).

This brings us to the question of 'who cues whom'? Are influential parties and party leaders good at *reading* public sentiments and good at translating their findings into messages that resonate with public sentiment 'out there'? Or are influential parties and party leaders good at *shaping* public sentiment, through the use of narratives that politicise current affairs? Researchers examining the rise of social movements have described these as demand- and supply-side factors, and emphasise that both matter (Koopmans, 1996; Rydgren, 2005). However, it is not uncommon, especially during election times, to hear journalists praise a winning candidate for having read the public mood more accurately than his/her opponents. And the winning candidate will of course not object to that interpretation, or even use the 'don't shoot the messenger' argument in case their political project is deemed controversial. However, a growing body of research into creative framing demonstrates that politicians can influence followers' views by behaving like rhetorical chameleons who tailor their message to their audience (Reicher and Hopkins, 2001).

Radicalisation and extremism: pathology or politics?

As we saw, there was lively debate in the 1960s and 1970s about whether Holocaust perpetrators like Adolf Eichmann were exceptionally evil individuals with sadistic personality traits, or whether they were 'ordinary men/women who had ended up in extra-ordinary overpowering situations'. In academic circles the latter became regarded as the best explanation, and the message it sent out to the public at large was a stark warning not to be complacent, since anyone could have done what the perpetrators had carried out.

This nature/nurture question also runs through more recent debate about radicalisation and extremism. Are suicide bombers deviant individuals born with particular personality traits, traits that would manifest sooner or later in the person's life, or are they normal people who became disgruntled after experiencing injustices and losing faith in conventional interest representation channels? And what about voters voting extreme right or extreme left? Political psychologists agree in principle that nature and nurture explanations are not mutually exclusive, and that we need to look at both when trying to explain why certain individuals radicalise while others do not. However, in practice there appears to be a nature/nurture split between researchers who conceive of radicalisation as the product of deviant individual-level personality traits (*pathology*) and researchers who conceive of radicalisation as an instrument at the disposal of disenfranchised groups drawn to contentious *politics* (Victoroff and Kruglanski, 2009) (see Box 9.4).

In our view it would be good to avoid either/or thinking, and to look for ways in which we can integrate insights into personality traits, cognition and shared grievances as the basis for identity politicisation, collective action and contentious politics. What would also be helpful in political psychology research is more explicit statements about epistemology and ontology, especially in research into 'individual differences' and 'personality traits', where evolutionary biology insights are often inserted to explain findings, without making this explicit, and, more importantly, without reflecting about possible gender- and/or status quo-bias creeping into our conclusions (for example, the oft heard conclusion that women are underrepresented in executive boards because they evolved differently and value different things).

Box 9.4 Research into elections and voter attitudes

Why have people started to join so-called 'new social movements', movements that take up the plight of a third party (for example, animal rights, human rights for refugees, the environment), even though they do not stand to gain personally? And how can we explain the simultaneous rise of nativist anti-immigration parties? Political psychologists now face the daunting task of explaining the growing rift in Western countries between voters who think of themselves as humans with a (cosmopolitan) duty of care towards all fellow humans, and voters who think of themselves as nationals whose primary (communitarian) duty is to protect fellow nationals.

Understanding political decision-making

A final area of study in political psychology that we focus on in this chapter concerns decision-making. Behavioural decision theory has taught us a lot about how humans choose, both in their everyday lives and as political actors. Thanks to this body of research we now know that these choices are far less 'rational' than model-building economists and sociologists have long thought.

From homo economicus to homo psychologicus

According to neo-classical economics humans are 'rational utility maximisers' whose preferences can be predicted with mathematical precision. The now booming subfield of behavioural economics (BE) shows that humans in fact resort to cognitive shortcuts ('heuristics') when faced with complex decisions and suffering from 'cognitive overload' (Kahneman, 2011). According to behavioural economics, people have two thinking modes. The first one, so-called 'System 1 thinking', is fast, automatic and subconscious. The second one, described as 'System 2 thinking', is slow, conscious and deliberative.

Behavioural economists have gone to great lengths to show that System 1 thinking produces bad decisions, thereby (implicitly) relying on mathematical probability calculations as benchmark of what should be considered a good decision. According to these researchers our challenge is to resist the temptation of System 1 thinking, to avoid flying on automatic pilot, and to make more efforts to activate System 2. Other scholars, however, argue that 'snap decisions' often are as good as slow deliberative decisions (Gladwell, 2007). An oft-cited real-life example is that of a firefighter in a burning building ordering his crew to leave the building instantly, seconds before the building collapsed, and not being able to articulate what it was that motivated his snap decision. As Gladwell explains, in these instances, repeated experience produces an ability to recognise patterns and cues unthinkingly (see also Klein, 1997).

Behavioural economics appears to have taken the world by storm, with policymakers in many countries now taking a keen interest in smart 'choice architectures' with which citizens can be 'nudged' to make better choices (Thaler and Sunstein, 2008). For example, it is clear from randomised control trials that governments can increase organ donations by making it the default option on a driving licence application form, increase timely payment of fines by sending out a reminder text message, and promote water and energy savings by sending utility bills with additional information about average consumption levels in one's neighbourhood. The UK government was the first to establish a Behavioural Insights Team (BIT), and many other governments now have a BIT or behavioural insights unit. Although the nudge approach has been criticised as elitist and unethical (Hausman and Welch, 2010), and for offering limited scope for achieving *lasting* behavioural change (Mols et al., 2015), the approach has many devotees.

Groups as asset or problem in policy decision-making?

A Yale psychologist interested in human decision-making, Irving Janis, turned to foreign policy analysis after reading his daughter's high school essay on the Kennedy administration's Bay of Pigs fiasco. The powerful, Orwellian concept of 'groupthink', which he developed to account for this and other instances of foreign policy failure, drew attention to the role of group dynamics in political decision-making (Janis, 1972). The essence of groupthink is the risk of a lack of rigour and the prevalence of bias resulting from subtle but powerful pressures for conformity in the modus operandi of high-level policy-making groups. Its presence increases the probability of policy failure; its absence increases the probability of success, as Janis's 'counter' case study on the Kennedy administration's handling of the Cuban missile crisis suggested. Symptoms of groupthink have since been detected in a wide range of corporate and governmental fiascos, including the US invasion of Iraq (Badie, 2010).

Groups that are affected by groupthink are likely to display a series of decision-making defects such as an incomplete survey of alternatives, failure to re-examine the preferred choice as well as initially rejected alternatives, and a poor scrutiny of information. Combined, such decision defects set the group up for choosing, and rigorously sticking with, decisions that are unrealistic and often morally questionable. Three types of antecedents are likely to trigger groupthink: the group is highly cohesive; there are structural faults in the organisation in which the group is embedded, serving to neutralise potential checks and balances on and within the group (such as group insulation from the rest of the organisation, a lack of norms requiring methodical procedures for group deliberation and a lack of a tradition of impartial leadership); and the group is acting in a provocative situational context generating a high degree of stress in the members of the group.

Despite ongoing discussions about the status of groupthink theory (Rose, 2011), its practical implications have been underwritten by robust empirical evidence. The main lesson to emerge from this evidence is that governmental structures, processes and leadership practices should harness rather than (wittingly or unwittingly) suppress diversity, disagreement and rigorous information-processing in the committees, teams and cabinets in which public policy is conceived and decided upon, and where crises are managed (see Box 9.5).

Methods and prospects of the field

Political psychology covers a broad terrain, but the underlying methodological challenges encountered in its various subfields are remarkably similar if not identical. First, we continue to use approaches and models that have intuitive appeal, but cannot be falsified. As we saw, 'charismatic

Box 9.5 Are politicians good decision-makers?

We tend to think of managers and government officials as rational decision-makers, who consider all available evidence, and evaluate the pros and cons of available alternatives. Likewise, we are inclined to think of ourselves as rational consumers, or as rational voters. But how rational are we? Researchers studying 'groupthink' have shown that political groups for whom a desire for or the appearance of cohesion and consensus becomes a driving force can take catastrophic policy decisions, such as the 2003 US invasion of Iraq (Badie, 2010).

The most sophisticated recent extension of this research tradition, developed by Schafer and Crichlow (2010), combines the kind of small-N, qualitative, narrative approach to case study analysis that made Janis's book such a gripping read with the kind of large(r)-N, quantitative regression modelling that has thus far been largely absent from non-experimental research on groupthink. The small-N part neatly contrasts four cases of policy failure with three cases of prudent and well-regarded policy choices. The large-N part covers thirty-nine cases covering nine governments in three different countries. Each case was coded for a large number of contextual, group structural, decision process and policy outcome variables. Examining the effects of leaders' traits and behaviours on the quality of group deliberations, Schafer and Chrislow's multimethod research shows that leader traits are not immutable but rather situation-contingent states of mind. Influenced by on-the-job learning, leaders can adapt their beliefs and styles. This helps explain why essentially the same foreign policy elite groups around particular presidents and prime ministers could have produced both conspicuous policy failures and notable successes.

leadership' continues to have appeal, even though we tend to use the term retrospectively to describe individuals who we know became remembered as remarkably successful. As politicians who fell from grace know all too well, leadership success is not exclusively a matter of 'being a born leader' or 'having the right (for example, charismatic) personality traits', but also a matter of contextual conditions, leader–follower relations, and even a degree of luck.

Second, we tend to rely on individual-level responses/data, and are subsequently faced with the question of what individual-level data tell us about collective social and political phenomena. The main challenge here is to avoid aggregating individual-level findings unthinkingly and avoid jumping to conclusions about society at large without considering the risk of unintentional 'pernicious methodological individualism'. Those working from a constructivist perspective will typically pay considerable attention to meso-level contextual factors (for example, social identities and intergroup processes) and thus be in a better position to avoid this pitfall. However, political psychologists seeking to explain political phenomena as reflecting the prevalence of certain 'personality traits' ('individual differences') will run greater risk, and have to think more carefully about what individual-level data can tell us about social and political phenomena.

Political psychologists have been methodological pragmatists who believe that research should be question-driven and not methods-driven. Although many political psychology articles use either qualitative or quantitative methods, there are also contributions that exemplify the strengths of multi-method research in which findings are triangulated using a combination of qualitative and quantitative methods. That said, the methodological trappings of positivist behavioural social science – a preference for experimental designs, behavioural data and large-N datasets – have come to dominate (particularly North American contributions to) the field's more recent output, though still punctuated by strands of small/medium-N, comparative, qualitative (Houghton, 2009) and sometimes explicitly interpretive research (Haste et al., 2015). The theoretical and methodological pluralism that once was its key strength has now become somewhat endangered, and will need to be actively preserved if political psychology is to retain its vitality and relevance, as its popularity among both political science students and scholars continues to grow.

Further reading

- There are several solid political psychology textbooks and handbooks for readers new to political psychology. These include Cottam et al. (2015), Houghton (2014), Huddy et al. (2013), and the anthology by Lavine (2010). Sears et al. (2013) also provides an excellent concise thematic overview of the field.
- Key approaches to studying political leaders using psychological lenses can be found in Preston (2001) and Rhodes and 't Hart (2014).
- Those interested in the alleged dark side of human behaviour as it plays out in public life may want to read Kelman and Hamilton (1989) and Zimbardo (2007), as well as more recent studies by Haslam and Reicher (2007, 2012) and Reicher and Haslam (2006) questioning the lessons typically drawn from Zimbardo's famous Stanford Prison Experiment.

Chapter 10

Normative Political Theory

CHRIS ARMSTRONG

Introduction

Citizens, and politicians, frequently argue about how resources should be distributed within society, how political power should be allocated, what the rights and duties of citizens are, and much else besides. When we argue in this way we make use of normative concepts such as justice, equality, freedom, rights, democracy and authority. They are 'normative' in the sense that they seek to specify what we *ought* to do, rather than simply describing how political life works. Such concepts are in a very real sense the fundamental building blocks of political debate, and the precise meaning we attribute to them can turn out to be enormously consequential. While most of us profess to believe in community, and social justice, and equality of opportunity, say, this superficial agreement masks considerable disagreement about how best to understand those concepts, and this dissensus is inevitably reflected in further disagreement about their political implications.

As a result, you may well find yourself voting for a politician who *claims* to believe in social justice and equality of opportunity only to discover that his understanding of what those words mean is entirely different to yours. If so, you might throw up your hands and announce that the meaning of these concepts is simply a matter of opinion, that they can be made to mean whatever we want them to mean, and that you are not going to listen to politicians any longer. While the conclusion about politicians might be understandable, the conclusion about the meaning of the concepts themselves would be resisted by many political theorists. For many of them are united in the belief that, just as progress is possible in science or (on a good day) in economics, so too might we make progress in sorting good normative arguments from bad, in revealing the inconsistencies and weak points of political arguments, and in building better and more coherent political theories. People engaged in what is usually called the 'analytical tradition' of political theory, in particular, share a commitment to presenting arguments deploying those concepts with clarity, precision and economy (Cohen, 2011), and to carefully demonstrating why we ought to favour one interpretation of the meaning and implications of given political concepts over those defended by other scholars (or indeed politicians). They share, as Wolff (2013: 814) puts it, an ambition to develop theories of political life 'with the precision and economy one finds among scientists or economists, with the fewest possible concepts, all as clear as they can be made' (for more on the comparison between theorising in science and in political theory, see McDermott, 2008; List and Valentini, 2016). In so doing, they demonstrate a belief that progress in grappling with some of the key normative challenges we face together (How can we have majority rule and yet protect the rights of minorities? What is the proper place of religion in public life? What, if anything, can be said to justify the authority of the state?) is within our reach.

Though it has been most often associated with liberalism, analytical work is not by any means confined to the study of liberal ideas. Influential work has been carried out within the analytical tradition from a Marxist standpoint, for instance. Moreover, many feminist scholars have turned analytical tools to productive use. There is, however, a certain degree of mutual scepticism between analytic and 'postmodern' scholars – each of whom often claim to find the contributions of the other arcane and impenetrable – and something of a divide (though its precise contours are contested) between analytical and 'continental' approaches to political theory more broadly. Though my focus here will be on normative theory of an analytical bent, this in no way exhausts the terrain within contemporary political theory.

This chapter begins by sketching two of the most influential contemporary models of how to 'do' political theory from an analytical point of view, which we can associate with John Rawls and G.A. Cohen, respectively (in the section titled 'Methods in normative political theory'). It then illustrates some of the ways in which these methods have been applied within recent debates on global justice (in the section on 'Normative theory and global justice'). We then move on to address a key issue of contention within recent debates in political theory: the relationship between political ideals and feasibility. Must political ideals be somehow 'realistic' or achievable? Must they be capable of 'guiding' political action in the here and now? Are they somehow disqualified as ideals if they do not? This discussion provides a good example of the evolving debate about the terms of normative political theory, which continue to be the subject of lively disagreement (in the section titled 'Political ideals and feasibility'). Finally, the chapter offers some suggestions for further reading.

Methods in normative political theory

Rawls on reflective equilibrium

John Rawls' *A Theory of Justice* (Rawls, 1971) provided not only a hugely detailed and influential account of the demands of justice in a liberal democratic society – including a set of principles of justice which have been the subject of much argument since – but also a *methodology* for political theorists which has also proven to be highly influential. Rawls' faith in our ability to make progress in arguing about politics was particularly welcome given that, in the UK at least, confidence in the health of political theory as a professional pursuit was then at a very low ebb. Schools of thought such as logical positivism had often claimed that the arguments of political theorists or philosophers would tend to boil down to either 'disagreement about facts, to be resolved by the social sciences, or subjective expressions of emotion, about which there can be no rational debate' (Wolff, 2013: 796). If so, the distinctive contribution of political theory was in doubt. In the middle of the twentieth century political theory was considered to be, in Brian Barry's phrase, at least 'on the margins' of academic study, if not 'completely out in the cold' (Barry, 1990: xxxiv).

Political theory has undergone a considerable revival in recent decades, and is now seen as a much more respectable pursuit (though not universally so). Barry himself certainly made an important contribution to the revival of normative political theory; his mode of political argument (which he termed 'analytical') focused, as does much political theory today, on careful conceptual clarification, the drawing of fine distinctions and the presentation of detailed objections to the work of others. The work of the legal scholar H.L.A. Hart has also continued to resonate, not least through its influence on Rawls' own thought. But Rawls' work is particularly noteworthy because he reflected in such detail on the question of *how* to make sound political arguments. His methodological proposals did much to revive faith in theorists' ability to make genuine progress in addressing the normative challenges arising from social and political life. So too did the substantive proposals he produced (including a famous list of principles of justice for a liberal democratic society). By way of evidence, much of the very terminology we now use to capture the work of the political theorist ultimately derives from Rawls' famous work. In terms of substantive conclusions, too, a very great proportion of political theorists today are working in some sense in Rawls' shadow.

The general (and formidable) question which Rawls pursued in his book *A Theory of Justice* is how citizens might live together on terms which are fair to each of us, and therefore ensure that the exercise of the state's coercive power is justified. More specifically, he sought to investigate how the terms of social cooperation in society might be so arranged as to deliver on a key ideal we apparently share, at least in liberal democratic societies: the ideal of free and equal citizenship. (He also assumes that any principles of justice we come up with must be compatible with the deep pluralism and diversity of modern societies, and be amenable to the stability of a just society. I will return to the question of stability later.) How might we ensure that the ideal of free and equal citizenship is made a concrete reality in our day-to-day lives, as opposed to an ideal which we supposedly cherish but consistently fail to deliver on? Clearly, the ideal must imply both a set of freedoms for all citizens, and some constraint on socioeconomic inequalities. But Rawls notes that, while we all agree on the salience of concepts such as freedom and equality, we often have different understandings of quite what they mean. In Rawls' useful terminology, while we may agree on the salience of a general *concept* of, say, equality, we disagree on which is the best *conception* of that ideal (Rawls, 1971: 5–6).

How, then, might we make theoretical progress? How might we be confident that our eventual preferred account of equality, or freedom, say – or indeed our theory of justice as a whole – represents a real advance in our understanding? Rawls suggested two tests for a theory of justice. Passing either, he believed, would give us greater grounds for confidence about any theory's credentials. The first test asks whether a given theory is capable of generating what Rawls called 'reflective equilibrium' (Rawls, 1971: 20). When thinking about the nature of justice, we may begin with some reasonably confident views about particular cases of justice and injustice (or what Rawls called 'considered moral judgements'). We can then test rival political or moral theories according to whether they square with those judgements, and if necessary reject them if they fail. But the process can also work the other way, as theories which appear illuminating in general persuade us to abandon or revise some of our considered judgements about particular cases. In this process of mutual adjustment, our theories of justice, and our considered judgements, increasingly come to square with each other. A theory which is fully compatible with our considered judgements – which appears to deliver the right judgements in the right cases – might be said to have attained a state of 'reflective equilibrium'. If so, this gives us one reason for confidence about it *as* a compelling theory of justice.

But even if a theory is more or less coherent, we might still have reasons for doubting it. One of the most familiar criticisms made of the political arguments presented in public life is that they are self-serving. When one citizen (or politician) suggests a political principle, her opponent will sometimes object that – because she is wealthy, or poor, or a woman, or white – she *would* say that, wouldn't she? Rawls' second test for a theory of justice assesses whether it can avoid this criticism. Rather than simply asking us which principles of justice we are prepared to defend, he asks us to imagine ourselves choosing between principles behind a 'Veil of Ignorance' – that is, in a situation in which we did not even *know* basic facts about ourselves, such as our social class or the nature of our talents. Thinking about justice within such an 'Original Position', as Rawls (1971: 17–22) called it, might have dramatic effects on our reasoning. A rational person would probably select principles which would insulate citizens from excessive economic inequality; after all, if he condoned too much inequality, he might turn out to be on the receiving end of it in 'real life' (if he came from a working-class family, say, or if he had few marketable talents). Likewise, not knowing whether she might in fact have deeply held religious commitments, a rational person would opt for principles ensuring freedom of worship. Although we cannot literally put ourselves into the Original Position, Rawls claims that we can nevertheless see, broadly speaking, that some theories would fail to be agreed upon in such a hypothetical choice situation, and that others would survive his test. Those that would survive such a test cannot be criticised for being merely self-serving (for we do not know, in the Original Position, quite how given principles will turn out to affect us). Rather our conclusions are, in an important sense, impartial between the interests of those whose collective life they are meant to govern.

Rawls provided us, then, with two ways of responding to the claim that any argument about justice is bound to be merely subjective or self-serving. A sound argument should, first, be capable of fitting together into a broader theory of justice, and of illuminating our considered judgements (that is, it should be capable of attaining a state of 'reflective equilibrium'). And it should, second, be capable of emerging under a hypothetical decision procedure which models a kind of impartiality. Unsurprisingly, Rawls believed that his own theory of justice, with principles guaranteeing all citizens a bundle of equal basic liberties, and rejecting inequalities which were not compatible with fair equality of opportunity, and which were not in the interests of the worst-off, was capable of passing such tests. That fact, he thought, counted heavily in its favour.

Cohen on facts and values

Though it has been very widely taken up within political theory – so that there are many 'Rawlsians' out there – Rawls' methodology is not uncontroversial. One of Rawls' sternest critics was the philosopher G.A. Cohen. As we have seen, Rawls' method of reflective equilibrium placed a high premium on the internal coherence of a theory of justice. Norman Daniels (2011) has claimed that, for Rawls, a theory of justice is to be considered *justifiable* if it is *coherent*. But, for some critics, pointing to a theory's coherence is not enough. A theory might be perfectly coherent – in the sense that its individual elements fail to contradict each other – but still be false. More deeply, Cohen suggested that when we assess rival normative theories, 'justifiability' is not necessarily what we should be after. Rather, what we should be seeking – and what Rawls often appeared to be determined to avoid making claims about, especially in his later work (Rawls, 1993, 1999) – is philosophical *truth* (Cohen, 2008). Some theories, and some conceptions of important political ideas, are to be preferred to others because they are *right* and others *wrong*. For Cohen, 'justice is a philosophical ideal truths about which can be identified by careful reflection' (Stemplowska and Swift, 2012: 384). And the special task of the political theorist is to engage in that reflection, and to advance, step by step, our search for the truth about political concepts. For the same reason, the claim that a given principle would have been chosen by someone ignorant of their circumstances (in an Original Position) is far from a decisive argument in its favour. Principles of justice are to be defended because they are true, and not because of the conditions in which we might or might not choose them.

The methodological opposition between Rawls and Cohen can be illustrated by sketching one of the key substantive issues on which they disagreed. As I noted above, Rawls argued that in a just society inequalities would have to be constrained in some way. But this does not mean that no inequality at all would be permitted. In fact, Rawls argued that we should tolerate inequality whenever this improves the position of the worst-off. In case that sounds a little paradoxical, it is worth recalling that an argument of roughly that sort is in fact quite common. It is often alleged within political debate that insisting on perfect equality – of income, say – would lead to a very unproductive society. By contrast, introducing incentives so as to reward the more productive could lead to much greater wealth in society overall. Conceivably, this might lead not only those who attract the incentives themselves to become better off, but also those at the bottom who do not. Even if the proportion of income going to the poor does not increase, an increase in the size of the economy may see them becoming better off in absolute terms than they would have been in a society where the incentives were not present. In Rawls' opinion this is much as it should be. We *should* endorse inequalities which improve the position of the worst-off. In fact, if we really care about the worst-off, we should select whichever society, or economic system, would make them best off – even if the effect was to introduce considerable inequality.

But the interesting question is *why* we have to pay incentives to the talented, in order to get them to work (or work harder, or work in more productive jobs). If the answer is that they simply cannot work harder without such incentives, so that these incentives truly suffice only to compensate them for the extra hard work they are putting in, then perhaps all is as it should be. But often people demand incentives which are not strictly *necessary* in that sense. Rather, they *make* them necessary by refusing to do what they could in fact do: which is to work harder without demanding more. If that is the case, then paying them incentives which are not in fact necessary in order to improve the position of the worst-off, in Cohen's view, is to *compromise* on what justice requires. The talented person holding out on using his socially useful talents until he gets the reward he wants is not entirely dissimilar to a hostage-taker refusing to give up his hostages until a ransom is paid. Certainly demanding such payments looks to be incompatible with a personal investment in making an egalitarian society a reality (Cohen, 2008: 27–86). And perhaps, therefore, Rawls is wrong to give in to such demands – at least when it comes to defining what justice means. Cohen's suspicion, in short, is that in appearing to condone incentives which are only necessary because of human selfishness, Rawls is no longer producing an argument about what justice *is*. He is, instead, answering the entirely different question of what we should do when selfishness means that we can no longer achieve perfect justice.

This example clearly illustrates at least part of the opposition between Cohen and Rawls, then. For Rawls, the right principles to govern a society might make some concession to empirical facts. Indeed, I mentioned earlier that Rawls believes that a defensible theory of justice must be capable of engendering 'stability' – that is, it must be the case that, over time, people could learn to live up to its precepts. A theory of justice which asked more of people than they are likely to accept would fail such a test. For Cohen, by contrast, reflection on justice is simply reflection about what justice, taken by itself, requires, and not about what people are *likely to do*. And that reflection is an essentially fact-insensitive exercise. This does not mean that the kind of exercise Rawls was engaged in is without value. It might be very important. It is perfectly conceivable that, having come up with our fact-insensitive 'fundamental principles' of justice (Cohen, 2008: 245), we could find that we cannot perfectly put them into practice. It might turn out, in fact, that quite a bit of compromise was necessary in order to even approximate them in practice. If so, we should choose rough-and-ready rules which take us as close as possible to what justice in the abstract requires (Cohen calls these more practical rules 'rules of regulation'). But we should be clear about what we are doing when we argue for rules of regulation: we are compromising on the pursuit of justice, in light of the intractability of facts about the real world. The pursuit of the *truth* about principles of justice itself does not, however, admit of that kind of compromise. Even if Rawls is right to say that we should, in practice, pay the talented more simply because they will refuse to work otherwise, we should not pay this situation the compliment of calling it justice.

Normative theory and global justice

One of the major growth areas within normative political theory in recent decades has been the study of global justice. Moving away from a more or less exclusive focus on individual nation states, scholars have turned their attention to the principles which ought to regulate the benefits flowing from international trade, or the burdens flowing from climate change, and much else besides. In so doing, they have often drawn the conclusion that the self-same principles of justice and equality which are held to be appropriate to *national* politics are also relevant to global politics. Global inequalities, they have sometimes argued, look to be equally as objectionable as inequalities within any individual country.

But insofar as they have done so, they appear to depart from the methodological commitments which Rawls, at least, held dear. For Rawls, recall, participants in the Original Position are meant to reflect on how a *society* can achieve fair terms of social cooperation. There was no reason, Rawls insisted, to believe that the same principles should also apply to the global case. To the contrary, when he finally published his own account of global justice (Rawls, 1999), its demands were much more modest than many of his erstwhile supporters had hoped. Contrary to the many 'global egalitarians', who argued that cross-national inequalities were objectionable in the same way as domestic ones (see, for example, Beitz, 1979; Caney, 2005), Rawls claimed that gulfs in living standards between rich and poor countries did not stand in need of justification. Insofar as the citizens of wealthy states have duties of justice towards outsiders, our focus should be on helping other societies to build moderately effective institutions capable of respecting the basic human rights of their own citizens. But, in all likelihood, this would not demand that we actually sent significant amounts of money their way (Rawls, 1999: 110).

Why did Rawls come to this conclusion? I have already suggested that he believed his famous theory of justice was one custom-made for individual societies and not for the world at large. But what is special about individual states, such that their citizens owe it to each other to limit inequalities, whereas they do not owe outsiders the same thing? Rawls seemed to supply several possible reasons, each of which has been taken up and argued over ever since. For one thing, we might think that what is distinctive about the institutions of the state is that they are coercive: that they impose rules on us and that they therefore owe it to us that those coercive rules treat each of us fairly. Or we might think that what is special about the institutions of the state is that they have a pervasive impact on the life chances of the people subject to them. Or, finally, we might think that the state is special insofar as it embodies, or enables, relations of reciprocity between citizens. In each case, the challenge would be to argue that the salient facts apply at the level of individual states but do not 'bleed over' to the international level. In light of economic globalisation, or the coercive nature of state borders, or the emergence of global collective problems such as climate change, making that case might seem to be a tall order. Perhaps the world is fast becoming more like an individual society in the features Rawls thought triggered concerns of justice in the first place (Beitz, 1979; Abizadeh, 2007).

Rawls' claim that certain principles of justice (including egalitarian ones) only apply once certain social conditions are in place marks his theory out as a relational one, as opposed to non-relational views which hold that principles can hold between human beings regardless of such empirical facts (see Sangiovanni, 2007). The debate between relationists and non-relationists rages on, with non-relational egalitarians determined to argue that global inequalities ought to be reduced as a matter of justice (Caney, 2005), and some relational sceptics claiming that whereas *national* justice may demand that, the demands of *global* justice are much more modest (see, for example, Miller, 2000). In this sense, interestingly, scholars are not such much arguing about the meaning of concepts such as equality (though they sometimes do that too), so much as arguing about the conditions that make such concepts *applicable* to social and political life.

Political ideals and feasibility

Let us now turn to contemporary debates about the relationship between political *ideals* and political *feasibility*. Another important distinction which Rawls did much to popularise was that between 'ideal' and 'non-ideal' theory. Although we live in a very unjust world, Rawls proposed that in order to work out what justice is, we should first work out what the right principles would be to regulate a society which is in some sense idealised. For instance, we might ask what the right rules would be to govern a society in which people could be relied upon to follow them. Answering that question gives us our 'ideal theory' of justice (Rawls, 1971). Once we have that theory clear, we can investigate what we should do once we drop the idealising assumption about behaviour, and assume instead that people will comply with our chosen rules only imperfectly. This is the task of 'non-ideal theory', and it is here that we find the most immediate guidance when it comes to what we should actually *do* in the here and now. Crucially, the division of labour between ideal and non-ideal theory does not assume that the former is more important. Indeed, Rawls suggests that working out what to do now, in our unjust societies, is a much more pressing concern. But he also maintained that we cannot make progress in understanding what we should do here and now without working up an ideal theory of justice beforehand. Ideal theory in that sense comes first, although it certainly cannot be the end of the story.

On this issue, Rawls has been assailed from both sides. On the one hand it is apparent that, for Cohen, Rawls' theory is not ideal enough – because it makes concessions to human selfishness even at the level of ideal theory. For Cohen there must be a space for theorising about justice which is *truly* ideal, even if our ability to put the resulting principles into practice turns out to be distinctly limited. Political theory can perform a useful function in telling us what to *believe* about justice even if those beliefs make no practical difference (Cohen, 2008).

On the other hand, ideal theory in the Rawlsian mode (never mind the Cohenian one) has been criticised for its irrelevance. For one thing, ideal theory might turn out to be unnecessary. Amartya Sen (2009) claims that we can make useful comparative judgements about states of affairs in society or the economy without invoking any 'transcendental' ideals, such as visions of the ideal society, at all. Isn't it obvious when we confront a serious injustice? Do we need to know, when we confront one, what a *perfect* society would look like? At the end of the day, isn't the pursuit of perfect, ideal principles ultimately a distraction in the fight against concrete injustice? For another thing, it might be thought that ideal theory can actually lead us astray, obfuscating or masking the decisions we have to make when we seek to tackle injustice. Laura Valentini (2009), for instance, has argued that while idealisations are not in themselves objectionable, some theories are hamstrung by 'bad idealisations', which prevent them from generating concrete recommendations for any of the situations we are actually likely to face. Alternatively, it might be thought that the attempt to do whatever we can to put our first-best principles into practice can serve to blind us to second-best options that actually offer more promise given where we are now (Goodin, 1995).

While this discussion of the salience of ideal theory might sound quite recondite, the question it hinges on – the salience of 'facts' to political theorising – will have great consequences for the way in which political theorists engage with fellow scholars in the social sciences. Put simply, if facts matter when we engage in reflection upon political ideals, then political theorists will probably have to work fairly closely with political scientists, economists or sociologists in working out which political principles we should adhere to. If facts can be placed to one side when we engage in our reflection on principles, by contrast, then, the engagement with empirical scholars will come some way down the line, when we have determined which principles we ought to defend and must now grapple with the question of how those principles might be implemented. On the latter picture, we might even envisage a division of labour according to which theorists engage in the pursuit of the meaning of ideals, and colleagues engaged in empirical study determine how these ideals can best be implemented. There would be, strictly speaking, no necessity for ideal theorists to 'get their hands dirty' themselves.

Whether that is so continues to be the topic of much controversy. In recent years, debates about the role that facts should play in political theory, if any, has often revolved around the concept of *feasibility*. Should concerns about feasibility operate as a brake upon normative theorising? What would it mean for them to do so? Should we reject a political principle if it cannot generate recommendations which are politically feasible? Should we restrict our attention to the pursuit of principles which we already know we have a reasonable chance of translating into practice?

To date, much of the debate on feasibility has assumed a quite specific focus. If a principle is infeasible, this presumably means that there is some serious obstacle to putting it into practice. But there might be any number of obstacles to implementing a given principle. Some of them might be practical or technological, for instance. But the greatest attention, within recent political theorising, has been paid to alleged feasibility constraints relating to people's *willingness* to act in compliance with particular principles. What if people simply won't go along with particular principles? What if they reject the demands they place on them as too great a price to pay for living in a just society? This raises a question which is familiar from the Rawls/Cohen debate: to what extent should people's unwillingness to adhere to a principle disqualify it from being *viewed as* a principle of justice? Rawls, as we have seen, assumes that 'stability' is a desideratum for a principle of justice – and this assumption introduces a concern with what people are in fact likely to abide by. A principle which we are unlikely to abide by over time must, for Rawls, be rejected even at the level of ideal theory.

But for some contemporary scholars this is a mistake. Rejecting a principle because it would be technologically impossible to implement might be one thing. But rejecting a principle *of justice* because people were not likely to make the sacrifices it demands of us is a different matter (Cohen, 2008). When it comes to feasibility, David Estlund has argued that, when theorising politically, we must be careful to distinguish between considerations of what people *will* do, and what people *can* do. The first tells us what is likely, and the latter what is possible. For Estlund, though, whereas principles of justice cannot sensibly ask us to do what we are incapable of doing, they can certainly ask us to do what we currently lack the inclination to do. For it would be unduly timid to rule a principle out of court on the basis that its successful implementation was possible but unlikely. As he puts it, 'the truth about justice is not constrained by considerations of the likelihood of success in realising it' (Estlund, 2014: 115). Our normative ideals should stretch towards what we can achieve. To restrict our theorising to what is likely would exert a chilling effect, which he associates with a position he calls 'utopophobia' (ibid).

There is considerable division, then, on the relationship between the pursuit of compelling political principles on the one hand, and reflection about what people are likely to do on the other. To get a sense of the concrete implications of the dispute, we might look once more to contemporary debates about global justice. Ever since Rawls published his theory of justice, it has been a subject of controversy whether we should, along with Rawls, see his theory as a theory for single societies, or whether we should also subject global inequalities to the same critical attention. One argument in that debate questions whether it is 'realistic' to ask people to make sacrifices for distant others, living in other countries. David Miller (2000) has claimed that a shared national identity usually turns out to be crucial in persuading people to make sacrifices in the common interest, and that absent a shared national identity people are unlikely to tolerate much in the way of redistribution. If so, so much for the more ambitious visions of global justice which would shift resources in the direction of poor countries. But we need to be clear about exactly what kind of claim Miller is making here. Is he making a merely descriptive claim ('people are unlikely to tolerate global redistribution') or a normative one ('people are right to reject global redistribution')? The general implication of Miller's work appears to be that we should in fact *reject* political theories that demand such sacrifices of us – and if so, the claim is a normative one.

But recall that for Estlund (2014: 122), 'The likelihood that a person will not behave in a certain (entirely possible) way simply does not bear on whether they morally should. It is not a fact that has that kind of moral significance.' If Estlund is right, Miller might be thought to be confusing questions about what people will do with claims about what they should do. He might be right about the former, but wrong about the latter. In fact, he might even be wrong about the former, descriptive, claim. For it is not certain that people *cannot* be motivated to accept global redistribution. A number of theorists believe that we *can* encourage people, over time, to feel more 'cosmopolitan' concern for the fates of quite distant people. If so, global redistribution would presumably come to seem more politically feasible. If that seems unlikely, we might usefully remember that the fact that citizens within a country are prepared to tolerate at least a degree of redistribution is itself a kind of political achievement (and, on the flip side, we might suspect that antipathy towards citizens of different countries is at least sometimes engendered by politics, or by ideologies such as nationalism). The willingness to make sacrifices for one's poorer fellow nationals (though often fragile in practice) is not a 'natural' political fact, but to some degree a result of political projects of nation- and state-building. If so, it might be thought that there is no intrinsic political reason why more cross-national forms of solidarity might not be fostered over time. If it is true that states are themselves involved in manufacturing national sentiment (Axelsen, 2013), it might be thought that they have the ability to act otherwise, by fostering cosmopolitan sentiment instead (Ypi, 2012). Given that our fates are increasingly bound up together – in a time when we face global challenges including climate change, pollution, terrorism, financial instability and global public health emergencies of increasing frequency – that result would be politically very helpful.

Debates on the role of concerns about feasibility within political theorising continue to rumble on, and no clear resolution has been reached. In recent years several things have, nevertheless, become more clear. One is that, rather than some ideals being simply 'infeasible' (and others, presumably, 'feasible'), feasibility and infeasibility are best seen as ranged on a continuum (Gilabert and Lawford-Smith, 2012). We should not, in all likelihood, reject some principles for being simply impossible to deliver on. Even the most ambitious principles might be delivered *to a degree* (though this does not establish that we should always aim to do so; it remains possible that there might be even more promising second-best options out there which we should advance instead). A second conclusion is that we often do not *know* in advance what is feasible (Gheaus, 2013). Our understanding of which political proposals, for instance, are likely to garner public support can be quite uncertain, and surprises do happen (consider, for instance, the recent rapid progress towards marriage equality for same-sex partners in many countries, which would have been far beyond the expectations of many of its keenest advocates). A third and final conclusion is that what is politically 'possible' is probably not fixed in advance in any case, but rather is a moving target. What is to be considered feasible can come on in leaps and bounds in response to changing circumstances, and to a considerable extent *beliefs* about what is possible are themselves an influence on what is possible (Gheaus, 2013). After all, people are often unwilling to uphold a rule if they believe that others will not uphold it too. On the other hand, if some can be persuaded to act first, others will often follow suit. All of this suggests that – though debates about the relationship between ideals and feasibility continue to rage – concerns about feasibility should not operate as a hard constraint on political theorising. The implications either way will be hugely consequential for a variety of political debates, including debates on the demands of global justice and on the acceptability of domestic inequality.

Further reading

- On the relationship between analytical political philosophy and analytic philosophy more broadly, see Wolff (2013).
- For an account of how to 'do' analytical political theory, see Cohen (2011). For more on the role of concepts, principles and theories within analytical political theory, see List and Valentini (2016).
- For further discussion of the role of ideal theory, see Stemplowska (2008), Gilabert (2012) and Simmons (2010).
- For more on feasibility as a constraint on normative theorising, see Gilabert (2012) and Southwood (2016).
- For a discussion of how the arguments of political theorists might inform, and be informed by, empirical social science, see Swift and White (2008).
- For discussions of the relationship between political theory and public opinion, see Miller (2013) and Baderin (2016).

PART 2

Methods and Research Design

Introduction to Part 2

VIVIEN LOWNDES, DAVID MARSH AND GERRY STOKER

There is a considerable variety of methods available to political science researchers. The chapters in Part 2 demonstrate ongoing processes of methodological development as researchers try to refine and improve their ways of discovering the political world. We do not regard the diversity of methods that emerges from this process as something to be alarmed about; rather, it is illustrative of the challenge involved in understanding the human condition. Debates about different ways of knowing the political world, and associated choices over methods and techniques, make for a lively and thought-provoking discipline. Deep questions about how we understand our world are never out of the frame.

Some of the most thought-provoking issues are presented in Chapters 11 and 12. David Marsh, Selen Ercan and Paul Furlong argue in Chapter 11 that clarity over ontological and epistemological positions is crucial because they shape what it is we think we are doing as political scientists, and also how we do it, and what we think we can claim from our results. There are clear, if not always acknowledged, links between the researcher's ontological position, epistemological position, conception of theory, research design and methodology. An ontological position, and the related epistemological stance, is not something that is merely on the surface of an approach. It is ingrained. The discussion of epistemological and ontological issues is itself an area of dispute and controversy within political science. Not all of our authors, let alone the wider world of political science, would share the arguments presented in Chapter 11, but the chapter raises some fundamental issues that account for diversity among approaches and methods in political science.

In Chapter 12 David Marsh reviews a range of meta-theoretical issues relevant to the way that researchers approach their understanding of politics. He explores how researchers try to understand the relationship between structure and agency. How actors behave involves active choice and agency, but, at the same time, these choices are structured by the wider context and the environment, and even constrained by deep-seated ways of thinking. The chapter also examines the balance between material factors and ideas within the different approaches that researchers take to explaining the driving forces in politics. Finally, the chapter looks at understandings of change embedded within different ways of doing political science. Is the political world seen as relatively stable or always in a process of change? Marsh argues that different ontological and epistemological positions tend to conceive in a different way the relative role of structure and agency, material factors and ideas, and the nature of change.

Alongside major questions about how to understand the world, researchers also face a series of other challenges of a practical nature. The process of developing a research design may be more like trying to resolve a puzzle than undertaking a set of clearly sequenced and preordained steps. How to think through the puzzles of research design is the focus of the discussion by Dimiter Toshkov in Chapter 13. The chapter will have easier application to some of the approaches reviewed in Part 1 than others. The dynamic of research is obviously rather different when using a behaviouralist frame, a constructivist or poststructuralist approach. Yet, for all researchers, the shared and crucial challenge is to be able to explain the logic of the research design that you have followed and what makes it fit for purpose. To some extent this is a matter of learning, but it is also a matter of practice. There is a craft element to doing research. It is not about the rigid application of rules, but an exploratory journey of discovery that you can become better equipped to undertake over time.

On that journey of research, you are likely to need to master both qualitative and quantitative skills. There is broad distinction that can be drawn between qualitative and quantitative methods. The former stretches from observation to interviews and focus group discussion as ways to find out about politics. The latter involves the collection of data on a repeated incidence of a political phenomenon and using statistical techniques to analyse that data. Chapters 14 and 15 on qualitative and quantitative methods, respectively, introduce the debates and current best practice in political science in each of these areas. Both authors – Ariadne Vromen and Peter John – are at pains to point out the range and subtlety of the methods available under their broad categories. Both, too, are supportive of the idea of mixed methods, that is, research designs that use an element of quantitative alongside qualitative data.

Chapter 16 addresses another key methodological issue, namely the role of comparative work. The comparative method takes advantage of the fact that the world includes a rich mix of political systems, institutions and actors. Comparing these different arrangements provides the opportunity to test ideas about the way that politics works. Research can move forward by looking at political issues in the context of the 'natural laboratory' of the mixed systems of the world. There are many difficult issues to be addressed when using the comparative method, as Matt Ryan points out in Chapter 16, but it is hard to think of a political science that could do without it. The chapter examines the emergence of qualitative comparative analysis (QCA) as a way of developing research across multiple cases, alongside more conventional 'within case' methods such as process-tracing.

Chapter 17 offers insights into a growing area of interest in political science, the use of experiments to investigate political phenomena. The logic of the experimental enables powerful claims to be made about establishing causality (which, of course, will be disputed by some of the approaches discussed in this book), but at the same time raises significant problems of practicality when applied to the political world. The chapter by Helen Margetts and Gerry Stoker shows how political scientists have increasingly been using laboratory-based work, internet experiments and full-blown field experiments. The experimental method as a way of doing political science will increase in importance they argue and, in any case, all students of politics will benefit from thinking about political situations (like voting, for instance) through the perspective of experimental design.

Chapter 18 introduces another relatively new method that is rising to prominence with political science – the use of 'big data'. Michael Jensen argues that there is a dual revolution that provides new opportunities for political science. First, our lives are marked by digital traces which are archived in various databases creating new data resources for social scientists to study social and political life. Second, innovations in computational tools are making these data accessible to researchers to facilitate the collection and analysis of these data. This new chapter for the fourth edition of *Theories and Methods* provides a great beginners' guide to the possibilities of using big data in political science research. Big data as an approach could play a complementary part in the practice of the research of those who use comparative methods and experimental approaches, with implications for both quantitative and qualitative research.

There are some that hold the view that the job of political scientists begins and ends with their description and analysis of politics. It is probably true to say that much political science is written in such a way that it would be difficult for those involved in politics (whether politicians, citizens or pressure groups) to relate to, or gain much from in terms of the explanations presented. Does that matter? Some may feel there is no issue to be addressed. Why should political science care if its work is useful or used? Others might take the view that a discipline that studied politics, but had nothing to say to those involved in politics (or who might be involved if politics was constructed in a different way), was somehow failing. The question of the relevance and purpose of political science is the focus of the final chapter of the book. B. Guy Peters, Jon Pierre and Gerry Stoker argue in Chapter 19 that here, as elsewhere in political studies, there should be an expectation of plurality. Political science is approaching the issue of relevance in a variety of different ways. The challenge is to demonstrate relevance as part of the everyday practice of political science.

Chapter 11

A Skin Not a Sweater: Ontology and Epistemology in Political Science

DAVID MARSH, SELEN A. ERCAN AND PAUL FURLONG

Several chapters in this book contain references to ontology and epistemology, some of them relatively lengthy. Perhaps more often, positions on these issues are implicit, but no less significant. Each social scientist's orientation to his/her subject is shaped by his/her ontological and epistemological position. Even if these positions are unacknowledged, they shape the approach to theory and the methods which the social scientist uses. At first the questions raised may seem difficult, but they are not issues that can be avoided. Because they shape our approach, they are like a skin not a sweater; they cannot be put on and taken off whenever the researcher sees fit. In our view, all students of political science should recognise their own ontological and epistemological positions and be able to defend them. This means they need to understand the alternative positions on these fundamental questions and be able explain why they have chosen certain positions and methods over others. This chapter aims to introduce these ontological and epistemological questions in a comparative and accessible way for readers who are new to these issues.

The chapter is divided into three major sections. In the first section, we introduce the concepts of 'ontology' and 'epistemology' and consider why they matter in social science research and how they relate to each other. The second section then outlines different positions on ontology and epistemology and presents the arguments, which have been put forward for, and against, these positions. In doing so, this section also considers how these different positions shape the approaches that researchers take to their research and the different role that theory plays in each of them. In the final section, we illustrate some of these points by focusing on empirical studies of deliberative democracy. Here, our aim is to show how researchers adopting different ontological/epistemological positions study this topic, and discuss the way different positions shape the overall empirical research design as well as the researcher's expectations from his/her empirical research.

Ontology and epistemology introduced

Ontology and epistemology are contested issues. While there is general agreement about what the terms mean, there is much less agreement about either the ontological and epistemological positions that researchers adopt or the relationship between ontology and epistemology. We begin this section by outlining the meaning of these two terms, before discussing the relationship between the two, which, as we shall see, is a particularly contested issue.

The meaning of ontology and epistemology (and methodology)

Ontological questions focus on the nature of 'being'; literally, an ontology is a theory of 'being' (the word derives from the Greek for 'existence'). This sounds difficult, but it really isn't. The key ontological question is: what are the form and nature of reality and, consequently, what is there that can be known about it? To put it another way, as we will see below, the main issue is whether there is a 'real' world 'out there' that is, in an important sense, independent of our knowledge of it. Here, we distinguish between two broad ontological positions: foundationalism, more commonly seen as objectivism or realism, which posits a 'real' world, 'out there', independent of our knowledge of it; and anti-foundationalism, more commonly seen as constructivism or relativism, which treats the world as always socially constructed. We discuss the difference in nomenclature below.

If an ontological position reflects the researcher's view about the nature of the world, her epistemological position reflects her view of what we can know about the world; literally, an epistemology is a theory of knowledge. As researchers, our central interest in epistemology focuses upon the question: how do we know about the world? Again, this sounds difficult, but, as we will see below, this question relates directly to important and familiar issues about certainty, logic and evidence.

There are two key questions in relation to epistemology. Can an observer identify 'real' or 'objective' relations between social phenomena? If so, how?

The first question itself subsumes two issues. Initially, it takes us back to ontology; an anti-foundationalist argues that there is not a 'real' world that exists independently of the meaning which actors attach to their action. This entails an interpretivist theory of knowledge; it would be illogical to argue for our capacity for independent knowledge of an external world we do not believe exists. At the same time, such an anti-foundationalist would also suggest that no observer can be 'objective' because s/he lives in the social world and participates in the social constructions of 'reality'. This evokes what is sometimes called the double hermeneutic (Giddens, 1984); the world is interpreted by the actors (one hermeneutic level), and their interpretation is interpreted by the observer (a second hermeneutic level).

Figure 11.1 *Connecting ontology, epistemology and methodology*

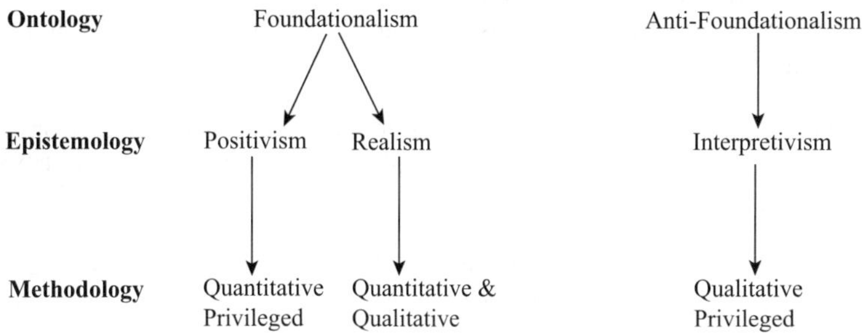

The second question raises another important, and clearly related, issue. To the extent that we can establish 'real' relationships between social phenomena, can we do this simply through direct observation, or are there some relationships which 'exist', but are not directly observable? The answers that one gives to these questions shapes one's epistemological position and, in particular, how one understands the concepts of causality and explanation (see Chapter 5).

As such, our argument here is that ontology and epistemology are related. So, as Figure 11.1 indicates, a foundationalist ontology leads to either a positivist or a realist epistemology, while an anti-foundationalist ontology leads to an interpretivist epistemology. However, we acknowledge that this is a contested position, which would not be accepted by some poststructuralists, and this is an issue discussed in the next section. In addition, it also needs emphasising that one's epistemological position has clear methodological implications, an issue to which we return throughout this chapter. So, positivists tend to privilege quantitative methods, while interpretivists privilege qualitative methods.

The relationship between ontology and epistemology

Ontological and epistemological issues are inevitably related, given that epistemology is concerned with how human agents can enquire about, and make sense of, ontology. However, the relationship between ontology and epistemology is a contested issue. Colin Hay (2006a) argues that we cannot prove an ontological position, or indeed the relationship between ontology and epistemology. We should therefore adopt a position that makes sense to us and use it consistently, while acknowledging that it is contested.

Hay contends that ontology precedes epistemology:

> Ontology 'relates to the nature of the social and political world' and epistemology 'to what we can know about it', (so) ontology is

> logically prior in the sense that the 'it' in the second term (the definition of epistemology) is, and can only be, specified by the first (the definition of ontology). This, I contend, is a point of logic, not of meta-theory. (Hay, 2007a: 117)

However, poststructuralists do not agree with this positioning of ontology and epistemology. As Deborah Dixon and Jean Paul Jones III (1998: 250) assert:

> ontological assumptions put the cart before the horse, for ontology is itself grounded in epistemology about how we *know* 'what the world is like'; in other words, the analysis of ontology invariably shows it to rest upon epistemological priors that enable claims about the structure of the real world.

Spencer (2000) argues that this poststructuralist line of argument reduces questions of ontology to questions of epistemology (what is usually termed the 'epistemic fallacy'). He continues:

> There is no escaping having a theory of ontology, it is only a question of whether or not it is consciously acknowledged and studied or whether it is left as an implicit presupposition of one's theory of epistemology. [...] While (post-modernists) deny that there is such a thing as truth (clinging to the realm of epistemology and denying that ontology is even a legitimate subject) any argument they make must surely be making an assertion about the way things are (hence having a theory, albeit implicit and contradictory, of ontology).

For Spencer, ontology cannot, and should not, be reduced to epistemology, because, if it is, everything becomes thought and discourse and social structures/the material world have no causal power. As Spencer puts it (2000: 15):

> [Poststructuralists refuse] to countenance the idea that knowledge stands in a causal relationship to both society and to the entities of which it is knowledge. Knowledge is influenced, and indeed is dependent upon, society through received ideas and through the provision of the very apparatus of thought, in particular through language. [...] But knowledge is also knowledge *of* something – of nature or society. [...] Hence, it is possible that knowledge is a social phenomenon but that the entities that it studies are not, that is, that they exist independently of society.

Here, Spencer is not claiming that ideas or discourses do not affect how the 'real world' impacts agents/groups, but only that these are ideas/discourses about 'real', that is extra-discursive, social phenomena.

It should be clear from these claims that the relationship between ontology and epistemology is strongly contested. Poststructuralists see the two as co-constitutive; they 'consciously conflate ontology and epistemology' (Bates and Jenkins, 2007: 60; for a detailed discussion of poststructuralism, see Chapter 8). In contrast, Spencer (2000: 2) poses an important question: how can we have a theory about what knowledge is, without some presupposition about the nature of the world? There is no uncontentious way to resolve this issue. However, it is crucial as researchers that we recognise the logical and practical consequence of the different ontological and epistemological positions we adopt, and the different views on their relationship.

In the next section, we outline various positions on ontology and epistemology, which help clarify some of the issues discussed so far.

Distinguishing ontological and epistemological positions

We begin by distinguishing between broad ontological and epistemological positions, before considering the various epistemological positions, and the contestations between them, in more depth. In doing so, we also identify why such debates, and the positions researchers adopt, are important. Here, our broad argument is that they are important as they shape what we study as social scientists, how we study it, what role we think theory plays in our empirical study and what we think we can claim as a result of that study. While distinguishing between broad positions, we acknowledge that not everyone, indeed not even all contributors to this volume, would accept our classification; to emphasise the point again, this is a very contested area.

One contestation is particularly important and that concerns how we should categorise poststructuralist approaches. As we saw, they deny the utility, or possibility, of a distinction between ontology and epistemology and are strongly idealist in Spencer's (2000) terms. Consequently, we could locate them in our anti-foundationalist ontological category and our interpretivist epistemological category. However, as Craig Parsons (Chapter 5) emphasises, if poststructuralism is a variant of constructivism, it is a particular one and he sees modern constructivism (discussed briefly below), in epistemological terms, as interested in explanation and engaging with more mainstream political science approaches.

In this context, it is important to acknowledge that, even if we establish broad categories to classify ontological and epistemological positions, there will be different strands within each of these broad positions and the boundaries between them may be blurred. Two examples will suffice here. First, to return to Parsons' point above (see Chapter 5), there are significant epistemological differences between different strands of constructivism. Second, increasingly the boundary between realism, more specifically critical realism, and interpretivism as epistemological positions are being blurred, as is clear in the work of Colin Hay discussed below and in Chapter 12.

Distinguishing broad ontological positions

As already emphasised, we distinguish between two broad ontological positions, foundationalism and anti-foundationalism. However, as we have already emphasised, poststructuralists deny any separation between ontology and epistemology. Such researchers would clearly deny that they have an ontological position and, as such, many would put them into a separate category and the reader needs to recognise that qualification when considering what follows. However, we classify them as anti-foundationalists, because they deny the existence of any extra-discursive 'reality'.

Foundationalism/objectivism/realism

We termed the first position foundationalism in a previous edition of this book, although it is more commonly termed either objectivism or realism. The key point here, however, is that the different terminology refers to the same position. From this perspective, the world is viewed as composed of discreet objects which possess properties that are independent of the observer/researcher. All researchers should view and understand these objects in the same way, if they have the necessary skills and good judgement. So, to put it another way, there is a real world which exists independently of our knowledge of it. As such, Lakoff and Johnson (1980: 159) argue that those adopting this position, whom they term objectivists, posit the existence of objective, absolute and unconditional truths. However, this view is not uncontested, with many foundationalists contending that their understanding of ontology entails a probabilistic, rather than an absolutist, account of causality.

There are significant differences within this position, notably between epistemological positivists and epistemological realists as we elaborate further below. In this vein, epistemological realists emphasise the role that theory plays in any interpretation of the causal power of any structure/institution in that real world; so, the real-world effect on actions is mediated by ideas. Similarly, realists would recognise the partialities of researchers who interpret the world and, therefore, they have a more limited conception of 'truth' than positivists. However, they share the crucial feature of a foundationalist position – causality operates independently of the observer and can be established objectively (essentially the position defended by Spencer above).

Anti-foundationalism/constructivism/relativism

In contrast, anti-foundationalism/constructivism/relativism, the other broad ontological perspective, is less easy to classify; there is more variety, as one would expect given the constructivist position. However, the position has some common features. Guba and Lincoln identify three (1994: 110):

1. In this perspective, realities are local and specific; they vary between individuals/groups. As such, constructions are ontological elements of reality. They are not true, but rather more informed or more consistent. Consequently, although all constructions are meaningful, some are flawed because they are inconsistent or incomplete.
2. At the same time, reality is not discovered, as it is from the other ontological position, rather it is actively constructed. As we saw above, this means that the distinction between ontology and epistemology is blurred. To put it another way, it is the actor (and the values he holds) who decides what is rational. Given this perspective no actor can be objective or value-free.
3. Overall, reality is socially constructed, but, while it is individuals who construct that world and reflect on it, their views are shaped by social, political and cultural processes.

It is important to emphasise one point here. Our claim that anti-foundationalists argue that there is not a real world out there, independent of our knowledge of it, is a limited one. We are not claiming that such researchers do not acknowledge that there are institutions and other social entities. Rather, they contend that this 'reality' has no social role or causal power independent of the agent's/group's/society's understanding of it.

Distinguishing broad epistemological positions

With regard to epistemological positions, there are different ways of classifying them and little agreement as to the best way of doing so. Probably the most common classification (which is used in Chapter 1) distinguishes between scientific (sometimes positivist) and hermeneutic (or interpretivist) positions. We begin with a brief review of that distinction, before proposing an alternative, which distinguishes between positivist, realist and interpretivist positions.

Scientific versus hermeneutic approaches

The development of social science, as the name implies, was influenced by ideas about the nature of scientific understanding. In particular, the *empiricist* tradition played a crucial role in the development of social science. David Hume famously argued that knowledge starts from our senses. On the basis of such direct experience, we could develop generalisations about the relationship between physical phenomena. The aim was to develop causal statements which specified that, under a given set of conditions, there would be regular and predictable outcomes (on this see Hollis and Smith, 1991: chapter 3). The adherents of the scientific tradition saw social science as analogous to natural science. In ontological terms they were foundationalists/realists; they thought there was a real world 'out there' which was external to agents. Their focus was on identifying the *causes* of social behaviour and their emphasis upon statistical *explanation*. Initially, many felt that the use of rigorous 'scientific' methods would allow social scientists to develop laws, similar in status to scientific laws, which would hold across time and space.

In methodological terms, the scientific tradition was very influenced by logical positivism, which utilised a very straightforward characterisation of the form of scientific investigation (Sanders, 2002). As Hollis and Smith put it (1990: 50), the purpose of such investigation is:

> to detect the regularities in nature, propose a generalisation, deduce what it implies for the next case and observe whether the prediction succeeds. If it does, no consequent action is needed; if it does not, then either discard the generalisation or amend it and (test the) fresh (predictions).

In contrast, there is an alternative, hermeneutic (the word derives from the Greek for 'to interpret') or interpretivist tradition. The adherents of this position are anti-foundationalists, believing that the world is socially constructed. They focus upon the *meaning* of behaviour. The emphasis is on *understanding*, rather than *explanation* (see Chapter 5 for a critical discussion of this important distinction). Understanding relates to human reasoning and intentions as grounds for social action. In this tradition, it is not possible to establish causal relationships between phenomena that hold across time and space, since social phenomena are not subject to the same kind of observation as natural science phenomena (Schwartz-Shea and Yanow, 2012).

Positivist, interpretivist and critical realist positions

We suggest distinguishing between positivist, critical realist and interpretivist positions, rather than conflating positivism and critical realism, as some scholars do (see, for example, Hollis and Smith, 1991). Positivists adhere to a foundationalist ontology and are concerned to establish causal relationships between social phenomena, thus developing explanatory, and indeed predictive, models. The critical realist shares the same broad ontological position, although with differences identified above. However, critical realist, unlike positivists, do not privilege direct observation. The realist believes that there are deep structural relationships between social phenomena which can't be directly observed, but which are crucial for any explanation of behaviour. So, as an example, a critical realist might argue that patriarchy as a structure cannot be directly observed, although we can see many of the consequences of it. We will examine the distinction between positivist, critical realist and interpretivist approaches in more depth in the next section. In what follows, we discuss briefly why such distinctions are important.

Why are such distinctions important?

In our view, ontological and epistemological concerns cannot, and shouldn't, be ignored or downgraded. Two points are important here. First, ontological and epistemological positions shouldn't be treated like a sweater which can be 'put on' when we are addressing such philosophical issues and 'taken off' when we are doing research. In our view, the dominance of a fairly crude positivist epistemology throughout much of the postwar period encouraged many social scientists to dismiss ontological questions and regard epistemological issues as more or less resolved, with only the details left to be decided by those interested in such matters. Such social scientists have tended to acknowledge the importance of epistemology without considering it necessary to deal with it in detail; positivism has been regarded as a comforting sweater that can be put on where necessary. In contrast, for us epistemology, to say nothing of ontology, is far from being a closed debate.

Second, researchers cannot adopt one position at one time for one project and another on another occasion for a different project. These positions reflect radically different approaches to what social science is and how we do it, and are therefore not interchangeable. A researcher's epistemological position is reflected in what is studied, how it is studied and the status the researcher gives to his/her findings. So, a positivist looks for causal relationships, tends to prefer quantitative analysis and wants to produce 'objective' and generalisable findings. A researcher from within the interpretivist tradition is concerned with understanding, not with predictive explanation, focuses on the meaning that actions have for agents, tends to use qualitative evidence and offers his/her results as one interpretation of the relationship between the social phenomena studied. Critical realism is less easy to classify in this way. The realists are looking for causal relationships, but argue that many important relationships between social phenomena can't be observed. This means that they may use quantitative and qualitative data. The quantitative data will only be appropriate for those relationships that are directly observable. In contrast, the unobservable relationships can only be established indirectly; we can observe other relationships which, our theory tells us, are the result of those unobservable pre-relationships. We return to these issues in the next section.

Interrogating different approaches to ontology and epistemology

Here we outline the positivist, the interpretivist and the critical realist positions in more detail. We focus on the major criticisms of the positions; the variations within these positions; and the way the positions have changed over time.

Positivism

The core of positivism, the position strongly associated with behaviouralism (see Chapter 2), rational choice theory (Chapter 3) and certain strands of institutionalism (Chapter 4), is fairly straightforward, although of course there are variants within it (as discussed by David Sanders in Chapter 2):

1. Positivism is based upon a foundationalist/realist ontology. So, to the positivist, like the realist, but, unlike interpretivists, the world exists independently of our knowledge of it.
2. To the positivist, natural science and social science are broadly analogous. We can establish regular relationship between social phenomenon – using theory to generate hypotheses, which can be tested by direct observation. In this view, and in clear contrast to the critical realist, it is meaningless to talk of deep structures if they cannot be directly observed. Traditionally, positivism contended that there is no appearance/reality dichotomy and that the world is real, and not socially constructed. So, direct observation can serve as an independent test of the validity of a theory. Crucially, an observer can be objective in the way s/he undertakes such observations.
3. To positivists the aim of social science is to make causal statements; in their view, it is possible to, and we should attempt to, establish causal relationships between social phenomena. They share this aim with realists, while interpretivists deny the possibility of such statements.
4. Positivists also argue that it is possible to separate completely empirical questions (questions about what is) from normative questions (questions about what should be). Traditionally, positivists thought that the goal of social science was to pursue empirical questions, while philosophy, meta-physics or religion pursued the normative questions. In this approach, the proper role of modern philosophy in dealing with normative questions would be purely analytical, clarifying meaning and identifying and resolving contradictions and inconsistencies, not developing normative solutions. If we can separate empirical and normative research questions, with the aid of analytical philosophy, then it is possible for social science to be objective and value-free.

Many social scientists are positivists, although much of the positivism is implicit, rather than explicit. The behavioural revolution in the social sciences in the 1960s, dealt with in Chapter 2, was an attempt to introduce scientific method into the study of society. It was an explicit reaction to political theory, which it saw as concerned with normative questions (see Chapter 10), and the 'old institutionalism' (explained in Chapter 4), which it saw as lacking theoretical and methodological rigour. In contrast, it was based upon an objectivist/realist/foundationalist ontology and, most often, a quantitative methodology. The view was that a social 'science' was possible if we followed the scientific method – deriving hypotheses from theory and then testing them in an attempt to falsify them. We needed 'objective' measures of our social phenomena, our variables; so, we would focus upon 'hard' data – from government statistics, election results and so on – rather than soft data – from interviews or participant observation. So, for example, if a positivist was studying political participation, s/he would be interested in measuring the level of voting, party or pressure group membership, direct action and so on, and relating it to demographic variables such as class, gender, race and education. The aim would be to establish the precise nature of the relationship between these variables and participation in order to produce causal models. We shall return to this example later. As is now widely acknowledged, the ontological and epistemological position adopted had clear methodological implications that the scientific aspirations and confidence of the behavioural revolution tended to mask.

The criticism of positivism takes two broad forms. The first line of criticism broadly argues that, in following the methods of science, positivists misinterpret how science really proceeds. Two lines of argument have been particularly important here.

First, there is the pragmatist position of Quine (1961), who develops two crucial critiques of positivism.

1. Quine argues that any knowledge we derive from the five senses is mediated by the concepts we use to analyse it, so there is no way of classifying, or even describing, experience, without interpreting it.
2. This means that theory and empirical research are not simply separable, rather theory affects both the facts we focus on and how we interpret them. This, in turn, may affect the conclusions we draw if the facts appear to falsify the theory. If we observe 'facts' that are inconsistent with the theory, we might decide the facts are wrong, rather than the theory. Of course, this undermines the notion that observation alone can serve to falsify a theory.

Second, there is Kuhn's view (1970) that, at any given time, science tends to be dominated by a particular paradigm that is more or less unquestioned, which affects the questions scientists ask and how they interpret what they observe. Consequently, scientific investigation is not 'open', as positivism implies, rather particular arguments are excluded in advance. There is a paradigm shift when a lot of empirical observation leads certain, brave, scientists to question the dominant paradigm, but, until that time, and for the most part, scientists discard observations which don't fit (obviously, this fits well with the second of Quine's criticisms above) and embrace the results which confirm the paradigm.

The second main line of criticism of positivism is more particular to social science. It argues that there are obvious differences between social and physical or natural phenomena that make social 'science' impossible. Three differences are particularly important. First, social structures, unlike natural structures, don't exist independently of the activities they shape. So, for example, marriage is a social institution or structure, but it is also a lived-experience, particularly, although not exclusively, for those who are married. This lived-experience affects agents' understanding of the institution and also helps change it. Second, and relatedly, social structures, unlike natural structures, don't exist independently of agents' views of what they are doing in the activity. People are reflexive; they reflect on what they are doing and often change their actions in the light of that reflection. This leads us to the third difference. Social structures, unlike natural structures, change as a result of the actions of agents; in most senses the social world varies across time and space. Some positivist social scientists minimise these differences, but, to the extent that they are accepted, they point towards a more interpretivist epistemological position.

Many positivists avoid these critiques, regarding them as either unresolvable or irrelevant; they merely get on with their empirical work, solving puzzles from within a positive paradigm, relatively successfully in their view When they do acknowledge other perspectives that acknowledgement can be perfunctory, an assertion easily demonstrated by a brief consideration of King, Keohane and Verba's (1994) treatment of interpretive (for them this appears to subsume critical realist) approaches.

King, Keohane and Verba argue that interpretivist approaches, by which they actually mean interpretivist methods, have utility as long as they are integrated into a positivist, or scientific as they term it, position. In this vein, they assert:

> In our view, however, science [...] and interpretation are *not* fundamentally different endeavours aimed at divergent goals. Both rely on preparing careful descriptions, gaining deep understanding of the world, asking good questions, formulating falsifiable hypothesis on the basis of more general theories, and collecting the evidence needed to evaluated those hypotheses. (King et al., 1994: 37)

They continue:

> Yet once hypotheses have been formulated, demonstrating their correctness [...] requires valid scientific inferences. [These] must incorporate the same standards as those followed by other qualitative and quantitative researchers. (King et al., 1994: 38)

King, Keohane and Verba see interpretivism as a methodological orientation, which may have utility, rather than as an epistemological position. They view interpretivism as a means of generating better questions to be utilised within a positivist framework. Indeed, it almost seems that they are advocating a major/minor methodological mix (see Marsh and Read, 2002), in which qualitative, interpretivist, methods are used to generate better questions for survey research designed to test, and attempt to falsify, hypotheses.

It also bears repetition that King, Keohane and Verba seem to conflate critical realism and interpretivism. So, in their section on interpretivism, they assert the usual positivist critique of epistemological realism: 'social scientists who focus on only overt, *observable*, behaviors are missing a lot, but how are we to know if we cannot see?' (King et al., 1994: 41).

However, although King, Keohane and Verba are among the foremost US political scientists, there are much more sophisticated positivists, among them David Sanders and Peter John who write in this volume (Chapters 2 and 15 respectively), who are more willing to acknowledge and respond to criticisms of the position. It is particularly worth examining David Sanders' view in a little more detail because it represents an excellent example of the modern, more sophisticated, positivist position. Sanders (2002) accepts he has been strongly influenced by the positivist position, but acknowledges the 'ferocious philosophical criticism' to which it was subjected. He argues that 'post-behaviouralists', who might also be called 'post-positivists', acknowledge the interdependence of theory and observation; recognise that normative questions are important and not always easy to separate from empirical questions; and accept that other traditions have a key role to play in political and social analysis. As such, this post-positivism has moved a significant way from more traditional positivism, largely as a result of the type of criticisms outlined here.

One other aspect of Sanders' position is important here (see also Chapter 2). He accepts that interpretation and meaning are important, which might suggest that the differences between positivist and interpretivist traditions are beginning to dissolve. So, Sanders argues (2002: 53) in criticising prior studies of voting behaviour: 'There are other areas – relating to the way in which individuals reflect, to a greater or lesser degree, upon themselves – where behavioural research has simply not dared to tread.' He recognises that such factors might, or might not, be important, but emphasises that they would be difficult to study empirically. However, the crucial point is that Sanders wants to treat interpretation and meaning as intervening variables. In this view, how a voter understands the parties and his/her position may affect his/her voting behaviour. At best, this acknowledges only one aspect of the double hermeneutic; the interpretivist tradition would argue that we also need to acknowledge the dependence of the observer on socially constructed filters affecting frameworks of knowledge.

So, positivism has changed in response to criticism. However, it still privileges explanation, rather than understanding, and the primacy of direct observation. In our terms, it is still objectivist/realist/foundationalist, and firmly located in the scientific tradition.

Interpretivism

The interpretivist tradition is the obvious 'other' of positivism. It is particular associated with some strands of institutionalism (Chapter 4) and feminism (Chapter 6). However, it is a much broader church than positivism, as Parsons (Chapter 5) clearly demonstrates. Nevertheless, it is useful to begin with an outline of the core of the position.

1. In the interpretivist tradition, researchers contend that the world is socially or discursively constructed; a distinctive feature of all interpretivist approaches therefore is that that they are based on to a greater, or lesser, extent on an anti-foundationalist ontology.
2. This means that, for researchers working within this tradition, social phenomenon cannot be understood independently of our interpretation of them; rather, it is these interpretations/understandings of social phenomena that directly affect outcomes. It is the interpretations/meanings of social phenomena that are crucial; interpretations/meanings that can only be established and understood within discourses, contexts or traditions. Consequently, we should focus on identifying those discourses or traditions and establishing the interpretations and meanings they attach to social phenomena.
3. This approach acknowledges that 'objective' analysis of the kind aspired to in the natural sciences is unattainable. Social 'scientists' (interpretivists would not use this term) are not privileged, but themselves operate within discourses or traditions. Knowledge is theoretically or discursively laden. As such, this position acknowledges the double hermeneutic.

This position has clear methodological implications. It argues that there is no objective truth, that the world is socially constructed and that the role of Social 'Scientists' (sic) is to study those social constructions. Quantitative methods can be blunt instruments and may produce misleading data. In contrast, we need to utilise qualitative methods, interviews, focus groups, ethnography, vignettes etc., to help us establish how people understand their world (for an overview of such methods, see Ercan and Marsh, 2016). So, for example, someone operating from within this tradition studying political participation would start by trying to establish how people understand 'the political' and 'political' participation.

In addition, the position puts a premium on the reflexivity of the researcher. She must be as aware as possible of her partialities and, as far as possible, take those into account when interpreting her respondents' interpretation of their experiences/actions.

Given this, some, maybe an increasing number, of interpretivists would want to explain, not merely understand. Parsons is an excellent case in point. He argues in Chapter 5 that:

> 'Modern' constructivists, on the other hand, tend to think that we can posit social construction among actors but still manage to make some acceptable (if modestly tentative) claims about how the socially constructed world 'really' works. The core of their position is usually quite simple (and is also a standard position in non-constructivist scholarship): just being aware of our inclination to interpretive bias

> helps us to solve the problem. If we set up careful research designs, and submit our arguments to open debate among many people with different views, then we can arrive at pragmatically acceptable claims about how the world really works. In short, for modern constructivists – like for other 'modern' scholars – how much the world is socially constructed is something we can show.

Here, the emphasis is upon a systematic study of the respondents' social constructions and clear and effective reflexivity on the part of the researcher. Even so, the claims that could be made for explanation on the basis of such research would not satisfy many behaviouralists, as Parsons himself acknowledges.

The major criticism of the interpretivist tradition comes, unsurprisingly, from positivists, though some critical realists would agree with elements of that critique. To positivists, the interpretivist tradition merely offers opinions or subjective judgements about the world (that, of course, is the core of King and colleagues' (1994) implicit critique of interpretivism). As such, to a positivist, there is no basis on which to judge the validity of interpretivists' knowledge claims. One person's view of the world, and of the relationship between social phenomena within it, is as good as another's view. To the positivist this means that such research is akin to history, or even fiction, whereas they aspire to something more akin to a science of society. It is difficult for someone in the interpretivist tradition to answer this accusation, because it is based on a totally different ontological view, and reflects a different epistemology and thus a different view of what social science is about. However, as we shall see, most researchers do believe that it is possible to generalise, if only in a limited sense. Perhaps more interestingly, even Bevir and Rhodes (2002, 2003), whom Parsons might not see as modern constructivists, attempt to defend their approach against this positivist critique by establishing a basis on which they can make knowledge claims; on which they can claim that one interpretation, or narrative, is superior to another.

Bevir and Rhodes (2002) distinguish between the hermeneutic and postmodern, or poststructuralist, strands in the interpretivist position (on this distinction, see also Spencer, 2000). In essence, the hermeneutic tradition is idealist; it argues that we need to understand the meanings people attach to social behaviour. So, hermeneutics is concerned with the interpretation of texts and actions. This involves the use of ethnographic techniques (participant observation, transcribing texts, keeping diaries and so on) to produce what Geertz (1973) calls 'thick description'. As Bevir and Rhodes put it (2003: 22), quoting Geertz, the aim is to establish: 'our own constructions of other people's constructions of what they and their compatriots are up to.' However, ethnographers do generalise. They develop a narrative about the past based upon the meanings which the actions had for social actors. Then, on the basis of this 'thick description', they offer an interpretation of what this tells us about the society. The point is that these interpretations are always partial, in both senses of the world, and provisional; they are not 'true', in any unconditional sense.

Broadly, Bevir and Rhodes are within the hermeneutic, rather than the postmodern, or poststructuralist, stream of the interpretivist tradition. As such, they follow Geertz and others in arguing that it is possible to produce explanations within the interpretivist tradition. However, their understanding of explanation is very different from that of a positivist. In their view, the researcher can produce an explanation of an event, or of the relationship between social phenomena. But, this explanation is built upon their interpretation of the meanings the actors involved gave to their actions. What is produced is a narrative which is particular, to that time and space, and partial, being based on a subjective interpretation of the views of, most likely, only some of the actors involved. Consequently, any such narrative must be provisional; there are no absolute truth claims.

However, Bevir and Rhodes do wish to make some, more limited, knowledge claims. They contend: 'Although, we do not have access to pure facts that we can use to declare particular interpretations to be true or false, we can still hang on to the idea of objectivity.' They follow Reed (1993) and argue that a field of study: 'is a co-operative intellectual *practice*, with a *tradition* of historically produced norms, rules, conventions and standards of excellence that remain subject to critical debate, and with a *narrative* content that gives meaning to it' (Bevir and Rhodes, 2003: 38).

As we can see, Bevir and Rhodes develop their own take on the interpretivist tradition. It is particularly interesting because it directly addresses the key issue raised in the positivist critique of this tradition. They argue that social science is about the development of narratives, not theories. As such, they stress the importance of understanding and the impossibility of absolute knowledge claims, but they want to explain and they defend a limited notion of objectivity.

There are a number of other variants within the interpretivist tradition, as Parsons (Chapter 5) makes clear. However, they are all anti-foundationalist and critical of positivism. These approaches have become much more common in political science over the last few decades for a number of reasons. First, philosophical critiques have increasingly led to the questioning of positivism, in particular its claims to an absolutist notion of certainty that is increasingly questioned even within the natural sciences, from which it is held to originate. Second, the poststructuralist turn in social science has had an effect on political science, although much less so than in sociology. Third, normative political theory has changed fundamentally. Historically, it was foundationalist; the aim was to establish some absolute notion of the good or of justice, but that is no longer the case (see Armstrong, Chapter 10). Some normative political theorists have been influenced by postmodernism, again variously defined, and more by the work of Quine and others. Today, most political theorists are anti-foundationalists or, at the very least, have a very limited conception of any universal foundations. Fourth, as Kenny and Mackay show in Chapter 7, much, but by no means all, feminist thought has been strongly influenced by poststructuralism; it is anti-foundationalist and operates within the interpretivist tradition. As such, we can see the influence of this interpretivist tradition very broadly across political science.

Critical realism

Critical realism shares an ontological position with positivism, but, in epistemological terms, modern realism has a great deal more in common with interpretivism. The core views of classical realism are again fairly clear and owe much to Marx's work (for a broader discussion on Marx's work, see Chapter 7), although this broad approach also underpins historical institutionalism (as explained in Chapter 4):

1. To realists, the world exists independently of our knowledge of it. In ontological terms, they, like positivists, are foundationalists.
2. Again, like positivists, realists contend that social phenomena/structures do have causal powers, so we can make causal statements.
3. However, unlike positivists, realists contend that not all social phenomena, and the relationships between them, are directly observable. There are deep structures that cannot be observed and what can be observed may offer a false picture of those phenomena/structures and their effects (for an excellent exposition of this position, see Smith, in Hollis and Smith, 1991: 205–208; see also Sayer, 2000; Elder-Vass, 2007).

As Smith puts it, although we cannot observe those structures: 'positing their existence gives us the best explanation of social action. To use a phrase familiar to the Philosophy of Science, we are involved in "inference to the best explanation"' (Hollis and Smith, 1990: 207). As such, in the realist approach, there is often a dichotomy between reality and appearance. Realists do not accept that what appears to be so, or what actors say is so, is necessarily an active version of how reality is structured. As an example, Marxism is the archetypal realism, and classical Marxism argued that there was a difference between "real" interests, which reflect material reality, and perceived interests, which may be manipulated by the powerful forces in society. Given this view, we cannot only ask people what their interests are, because we would merely be identifying their manipulated interests, not their "real" interests.

The criticisms of classical realism were of two sorts, which reflect different epistemological positions. The positivists denied the existence of unobservable structures (for example, see the above-cited quote from King, Keohane and Verba). More importantly, positing such structures makes the knowledge claims of realism untestable and thus un-falsifiable. Realist claims that rely on the effect of unobservable structures have the same status to positivists as the claims of scholars from within the interpretivist tradition. In contrast, authors from the interpretivist tradition criticise the ontological claims of realism. In their view, there are no structures that are independent of social action and no 'objective' basis on which to observe the actions, or infer the deep structures. So, realist claims that structures 'cause' social action are rejected on both ontological and epistemological grounds.

Beginning with the Italian Marxist Antonio Gramsci, who is particularly associated with the concept of hegemony, critical realism has been significantly influenced by the interpretivist critique. For Gramsci, it is the deep structures that shape/manipulate consent – that establish hegemony. Modern critical realism acknowledges two points. First, while social phenomena exist independently of our interpretation of them, our interpretation and understanding of them affects outcomes. So, structures do not determine; rather, they constrain and facilitate. Social science involves the study of reflexive agents who interpret and change structures. Second, our knowledge of the world is fallible; it is theory-laden. We need to identify and understand both the external 'reality' and the social construction of that 'reality' if we are to explain the relationship between social phenomena.

Critical realism also has clear methodological implications. It suggests that there is a real world 'out there', but emphasises that outcomes are shaped by the way in which that world is socially constructed. As such, it would acknowledge the utility of both quantitative and qualitative data. So, for example, they might use quantitative methods to identify the extent to which financial markets are 'globalised'. However, they would also want to analyse qualitatively how globalisation is perceived, or discursively constructed, by governments, because the critical realist argument would be that both the 'reality' and the discursive construction affects what government does in response to global pressures.

Modern critical realism then attempts to acknowledge much of the interpretivist critique, while retaining a commitment to causal explanation and, specifically, the causal powers of unobservable structures. The key problem here, of course, it that it is not easy, indeed many would see it as impossible, to combine scientific and interpretivist positions because they have such fundamentally different ontological and epistemological underpinnings, one focusing on explanation and the other on understanding (on this point, see Hollis and Smith, 1991: 212).

Having considered how these categories relate to some important issues in the social sciences, we can now move on to apply the arguments to the case of deliberative democracy research in order to illustrate their use and their limits.

Ontology and epistemology in empirical research

The aim in this section is to examine how a researcher's ontological and epistemological position affects the way she approaches empirical questions in political science. In the last edition of this volume we used the example of globalisation; here, we examine the field of deliberative democracy, but, in our view, similar arguments could be made in relation to other substantive areas. Our purpose here is not to defend one particular research approach over others; rather, through this example, we seek to show how researchers' ontological and epistemological decisions matter because they: (1) determine the role of theory in empirical research; (2) shape the way the researcher conceives the relationship between theory and practice; and (3) affect what the researcher expects to achieve thorough her empirical research (for example, generalisability, specification, contextualisation and so on).

Empirical research on deliberative democracy – positivism versus interpretivism

Our example comes from the area of deliberative democracy, a growing branch of democratic theory that is also very influential in contemporary political practice. Deliberative democrats define democracy as a communication process, in which participants exchange reasons for their preferences, rather than solely voting on them. The core idea here is that individual preferences are not (pre-politically) fixed and might change as a result of collective deliberation, which also promises greater democratic legitimacy (for an overview, see Ercan, 2014). Deliberative democracy was first developed as a normative project about how political decisions ought to be made, and the initial research in this area was mainly theoretical. However, in recent years, especially with the 'practical turn' in this field (Dryzek, 2010), there has been a significant increase in, and diversification of, empirical studies of deliberation. This has also led to the emergence of methodological discussions about how to translate normative theory into the terminology of empirical social research, how to 'operationalise' deliberation, and which methods are better suited to analyse deliberation (see, for example, Mutz, 2008; Ercan et al., 2015, Bevir and Bowman, forthcoming).

At the core of the empirical research on deliberation lie questions about how individuals deliberate, how when and under what conditions deliberation leads to preference transformation and how the success of deliberation can be measured. Researchers from different ontological and epistemological positions approach these questions differently.

Diane Mutz's work offers an example of a positivist position. According to Mutz (2008: 524), what makes a social theory good/productive is its falsifiability: 'it must be the case that if a study were set up in a particular way, its result could conceivably contradict the predictions of the theory.' She continues, 'a steady accumulation of such negative evidence would build a convincing case against it' and help specify the logical relationships among concepts within the theory. Mutz (2008) proposes breaking down deliberative theory into specifiable parts that can be formulated as hypothesis to be tested in experiments, so determining which parts of the theory are falsifiable. These experiments require control groups, which, according to Mutz (2008: 536), constitute the baseline for comparing deliberation with other models of decision-making. Mutz suggests using these experiments to test individual factors involved in deliberation, such as 'reason-giving', 'face-to-face', 'reflection', 'civility' and a 'link to political action', to see whether or not they bring about desired outcomes. The desirable outcomes linked to deliberative processes include 'awareness of oppositional arguments'; 'opinion change toward more "public-spirited" views'; and 'social trust'.

Once these different factors and possible outcomes are identified, the next step involves establishing hypotheses to be tested in experiments and, ultimately, identifying which individual factors produce which kinds of desirable outcomes. This may include, for instance, finding out whether 'offering rational arguments' in a deliberative setting increases the parties' 'willingness to compromise'. The overall aim of the research underpinned by positivist ontology is to establish precise associations between different variables, and ultimately develop generalisable laws to explain past events, or predict future ones. Deliberative theory plays a straightforward role in this kind of research; it serves as a basis to build hypotheses for empirical testing.

Some scholars have criticised the use of a positivist approach to deliberative democracy research (see, for example, Bevir and Ansari, 2012) and argued that interpretivism is better suited to studying deliberative democracy, because it can capture the perspectives of participants in the deliberative process; and is sensitive to the contextual and contingent nature of such processes. Empirical studies underpinned by interpretivist ontology pay particular attention to the way actors themselves make sense of their experiences with deliberative practices (Ercan et al., 2015). They seek to capture the lived experience of deliberators (Talpin, 2012), or understand how a particular phenomenon is enacted in context; for example, how deliberative forums generate legitimacy (Parkinson, 2006); interest advocacy works alongside citizen deliberation (Hendriks, 2011); discourses travel from one deliberative site to another (Boswell, 2015); or deliberation is enacted and experienced in the context of social movements (Della Porta, 2005). These studies use data from interviews, focus groups, documents and participant observation to examine the deliberative democratic qualities in particular contexts.

As noted before, the purpose of empirical research in the interpretive tradition is not to achieve generalisability. Neither does an interpretive researcher seek to determine causality in a mechanistic sense. This is not to say that an interpretive researcher disregards causality; rather, she seeks 'to explain events [or phenomena] in terms of actors' understandings of their own contexts' (Schwartz-Shea and Yanow, 2012: 52). The goal is not to test hypotheses drawn from theory or previous studies, but to draw on theory and experience in a way that is iterative and recursive. An interpretivist may still emphasise causality, but she understands it in discursive, rather than mechanistic, terms.

In this context, deliberative democracy research that is underpinned by an interpretivist research tradition focuses more on agency, and how agents make sense of deliberative norms and practices, rather than on testing the predefined factors identified by the researcher at the outset of the research. For example, adopting an interpretive approach, Hendriks (2011) studies how advocacy groups and policy elites make sense of mini-publics in Germany and Australia. Through a combination of interpretive methods, including interviews and documentary analysis (of media articles and public and parliamentary debates), her comparative study finds that the discursive context of a mini-public greatly affects the attention it receives from interest advocates and elites. The interpretive insights gained by talking directly to policy elites and studying their reports and debates suggests that citizens' forums are most likely to influence policy elites when there is enough discursive activity to attract public and political interest, but not so much that the citizens' forum loses its capacity to be heard.

Similarly, although not framed in deliberative terms, Poletta's (2002) study of deliberative practices in the context of social movements offers another example of studying deliberation from an interpretivist perspective. Poletta inductively explores deliberative practices among several diverse social movements in the USA and identifies key cultural norms and practices that have been typical of these movements – especially friendship, tutelage and religious fellowship – and develops a nuanced account of how these characteristics work both to enable democratic capacity and also to constrain it. In studying the dynamics of small-scale deliberation in specific contexts, interpretive studies demonstrate that deliberation requires more than adopting predefined conditions; it also matters how actors involved in such practices make sense of their involvement and how their input interfaces with, and has an impact on, conventional policy actors and existing political institutions (Hendriks, 2011).

Considering these examples of interpretivist research on deliberative democracy, we can see that theory plays a different role than it does in the positivist research tradition. Rather than serving as a basis for developing hypotheses, theory in interpretivist research offers a lens (or a heuristic) for making sense of the practice. It is through the theory that the researcher defines the analytical problem and gives direction to her empirical analysis. As such, it is impossible to think of an interpretivist research without theory. As Wagenaar (2011: 9) rightly puts it: 'interpretive inquiry without theory is like an airplane without lift. It never gets off the ground.' In an interpretivist enquiry, theory informs both the generation and the analysis of the data; it offers a perspective to make sense of the practice in its specific context.

Conclusion

It is not possible to resolve ontological and epistemological disputes in a way that all would accept. Rather, we have sought to introduce the reader to these complex issues in a way designed to make them intelligible to a non-philosopher. In our view, a number of points are crucial. First, to reiterate, ontological and epistemological positions are better viewed as a skin, not a sweater. It may be tempting to attempt to find a synthesis of all the available positions, in the hope that, at some level of analysis, agreement is possible over these fundamental issues. Experience and logic combine to warn against this temptation. They continue because they reflect disagreements not just about logic or technicalities, but about the proper scope of human action in society.

Second, in the face of methodological difficulties, another strategy, alluring at least to risk-averse researchers, is to avoid the issue. Far from being safe, this position is actually the opposite, since it does not enable one to distinguish between good and bad research and between good and bad arguments. The least one can say about these issues is that they are of sufficient importance to warrant a genuine commitment to come to terms with them. Coming to terms with the issues requires one to think through the different arguments separately, to compare them and to evaluate them. As we emphasised, this means that all researchers should identify and acknowledge their epistemological and ontological underpinnings and how these affect their research design and research method and, most importantly, the claims the make on the basis of what their research reveals.

The purpose of this chapter has been to provide an introduction to some of the main ideas and methods involved. Like everyone, we have an ontological and epistemological position, and a position on the relationship between ontology and epistemology, which we acknowledge. However, our aim has not been to defend the superiority of one position over others, but to introduce readers to the variety of positions; it is up to you to decide where you stand.

Further reading

- On the relationship between ontology and epistemology and the corresponding debates, see Spencer (2000), Bates and Jenkins (2007) and Hay (2007).
- On the difference between positivism and interpretivism, and how they shape the research design, see Schwartz-Shea and Yanow (2012).

Chapter 12

Meta-Theoretical Issues

DAVID MARSH

If we think about why Donald Trump was elected, or why the UK voted to leave the European Union in 2016, we inevitably evoke the relationship between structure and agency. How important were structural factors in these votes? For example, how far were votes for Trump and Brexit shaped by structural factors such as class, gender and age? In contrast, what effect did the personal attributes and actions of Donald Trump, or in the UK Boris Johnson or Nigel Farage, have on these votes? At the same time, these voting patterns also focus attention on the role of material and ideational factors. For example, how far did voting patterns reflect the fact that some areas of both the USA and the UK are hardly integrated into the increasingly globalised world economy, and thus voted against the political elite? In contrast again, how important was the role of ideas, about, for example, sovereignty/nationalism or immigration.

These, here termed meta-theoretical issues, are two of the crucial issues in social science, and they are clearly related. In addition, positions on structure/agency and the material and the ideational are invariably invoked to explain stability and change, another meta-theoretical issue, and surely the most fundamental one in social science. So, for example, if we ask questions about the likely future of democracy, we might consider the possible effect of growing inequalities, the increased importance of religious or nationalist views and/or the role of individual political leaders. At the same time, it is important to recognise that an author's position on these meta-theoretical issues is influenced by her ontological and epistemological starting point. As such, this chapter illustrates many of the issues raised in the previous one. In addition, when addressing the relationship between stability and change, I also briefly consider how, in approaching these issues, authors think about/conceptualise time and space, which is also crucial in any discussion of stability and change. Consequently, the chapter is divided into three sections: initially, I examine how structure, agency and the material realm are conceptualised, in part using recent literature on the power of business as an illustrative case; then I examine the dialectical approaches to these issues in more detail; and finally, I focus on the relationship between stability and change.

Conceptualising structure, agency and the ideational realm

I argued in the previous edition of this volume that there are five broad positions in the literature on these two issues: structuralism/materialism; intentionalism/idealism; a dialectical position; an additive position; and a post-structuralist position. In both cases, historically at least, these issues have been treated as dualisms, with analysts privileging one or other element/side of the *dualism*; so, they have been structuralists *or* intentionalists and materialists *or* idealists. However, more recently many, if not most, analysts view them as *dualities*, arguing that the relationships between them should be viewed as dialectical, that is interactive and iterative. Here, the argument would proceed along the following lines:

- Structures provide the context within which agents act, but agents interpret structures, and, in acting, change them, with these 'new' structures becoming the context within which agents subsequently act.
- Similarly, material relations provide the context within which ideas develop and operate, but ideas are used to interpret those material relations and these interpretations help change those material relations. These 'new' material relations then become the context within which ideas develop.

This dialectical position provides the focus of most of this chapter, because, in my view, it is where the cutting edge of these debates is at present. For many authors, like Archer and myself, the position is underpinned by a critical realist epistemology (see Chapter 10), but to others who adopt a discursive institutionalist, rather than a historical institutionalist (see Chapter 3), view, it is underpinned by a constructivist epistemology.

We also need to recognise two other approaches which have received much less attention in discussions of these issues: an additive approach; and a poststructuralist approach. The additive approach is common in political science and probably most associated with positivist and empiricist positions. For example, the literature on voting behaviour evokes both structural/material variables, like class, gender or education, and agential/ideational variables, like the policy preference of voters and how far they correspond to the parties' policies, to explain voting outcomes. In essence, the argument is that both structural (or material) *and* intentional (or ideational) factors shape voting decisions. From this perspective, the relative causal power of each of these sets of factors in a particular case is an empirical question. Of course, that does not mean that voting behaviour researchers do not want to explain voting behaviour (indeed, that is what regression analysis entails), or generalise their results (provided their samples are representative), but there is no attempt to theorise the way in which structural and intentional variables interact iteratively. To put it another way, this approach can see the relationship between structure and agency and between the material and the ideational as interactive, but it doesn't view it as iterative.

The poststructuralist position (on poststructuralism, see Chapter 7) is also common, but barely integrated into the discussions about these meta-theoretical issues in political science. It is of course a fundamental critique of the way in which most social science is conducted, rooted as it is in a broadly constructivist position (see Chapter 4). From this position, structures do not exist independently of agents; rather, they are co-constitutive in, and through, discourse. So, the distinction between structure and agency is not an ontological one (an issue discussed at more length below), neither does it have much, if any, analytical utility.

Two points are worth emphasising here about the poststructuralist position. The first follows obviously from the previous paragraph. From this position, any focus on the two meta-theoretical issues considered here is of limited utility at best, because there is no extra-discursive realm. Rather, the role of structures, material relations, agents and ideas exist within, are shaped by, and understood in terms of discursive formations. As such, from this perspective, we need to focus on discursive formations, how they develop, interact and change. This position is reflected in the Foucauldian-inspired work of Johal, Moran and Williams (2015) referred to below.

Second, with the increased focus on ideas in the comparative politics and international political economy literature, several authors have taken a clear constructivist turn. So, for example, as we shall see at some length below, Hay adopts a constructivist institutionalist position and argues that the distinctions between structure and agency and the material and the ideational are analytical, not ontological. As such, he is clearly closer to the poststructuralist position than authors like Archer (1995, 2000), McAnulla (2006) or myself, a point I return to below.

In the next section I focus on dialectical approaches to the relationships between structure/agency and the material/ideational. However, before doing so, it is important to address another important, but neglected, issue. It is crucial to define terms; what is meant by structure, agency and ideas/the ideational realm. I illustrate these issues through a consideration of recent work on the power of business.

Structure

In his classic work *Politics and Markets* Lindblom (1977) argued that in capitalist societies, businessmen, rather than ministers or public servants, control the key decisions about production and distribution, which affect the well-being of citizens and the re-election chances of governments. For him, this was the root of the structural power of business. However, subsequently, others have suggested that our understanding of the structural factors that affect policy outcomes needs to be expanded.

As just one example, in explaining the outcome of the Australian mining tax case, Bell and Hindmoor (2014) see the role of the broader economic, political and institutional context of the time as constraining the government, emphasising: the global financial crisis, which clearly gave ammunition to the miners; the troubles that Prime Minister Rudd was experiencing in the Australian Labor Party; and two institutional factors, the three-year electoral-cycle in Australia, which accentuated the electoral slump, and the Australian Labor Party rules, which mean it is relatively easy to overturn a leader in caucus.

At the same time, Bell and Hindmoor (2014) treat ideas, or ideology, as resources which can be used by business to constrain or facilitate government, thus treating them as, in effect, a structure. In my view, that is a mistake, because it neglects the question of the relationship between those ideas and material relations, when it is important to emphasise that the relationship between ideas and structures remains important.

Agency

Discussion of how we can conceptualise agency are few and far between, which is surprising given that, as Moran and Payne (2014) suggest, the dominant traditions in political science have been agency-centred. The most cited piece on agency in social science is by Emirbayer and Mische (1998), who focus exclusively on reflexivity, as does Archer (2000) in her later work. She sees reflexivity, or 'the internal conversation', as a process in which agents 'deliberate upon a precise course of action in view of their concerns and in light of the circumstances they confront'. This raises two important points.

First, Archer's approach neglects two other aspects of agency. She prioritises the rational, reflexive aspects of agency, which leaves no space for emotions; yet, as Sayer (2005) shows, emotions are crucially important in shaping actions. Perhaps more important for discussions of the power of business, she also ignores the work on agency in social-psychology (for a good review, see Bandura, 2006). This literature focuses not just on reflexivity, but also upon the intentionality of agents, that is the action plans of agents and the strategies they have for realizing them, and upon their self-reactiveness, that is their 'ability to construct appropriate courses of action and to motivate and regulate their execution'. At the same time, the psychology literature also distinguishes between three different modes of agency (Bandura, 2006, 166–167): personal agency, which is the focus of the sociological literature and involves individuals bringing influence to bear on their actions and the context within which they operate; proxy agency, which involves influencing others with resources to act on your behalf; and collective agency, which involves working together with others through interdependent effort.

Bell, although he uses Archer's work, avoids conflating agency and reflexivity. Indeed, he focuses on the capacities which agents must use the resources at their disposal, to utilise their agency. As such, he and

Hindmoor argue that governments face major problems in negotiating with financial interests because of large inequities in capacity. They contend: 'Both the City and Wall Street have historically been one jump ahead of regulators in the game of regulatory arbitrage'. Similarly, in examining the Australian mining tax, Marsh, Lewis and Chesters (2014) argue that the Australian Government had significant resources with which to bargain with the Australian miners, but failed to use them, partly because of lack of capacity and partly because of ineptitude.

Second, neither Archer, nor Bell, discusses how agency (for them reflexivity) is affected, or 'structured', by one's access to resources. With more resources, an individual may be more reflexive, or reflexive in different ways. In this way, business is likely to have more opportunity to be reflexive, and therefore strategic, while citizens have less, and so be more likely to have their ideas shaped.

Third, and this is a common critique of rational choice theory, where do agents' concerns (preferences) come from: are they manipulated? This brings us to the contested issue of whether, or not, an agent's preferences can be manipulated in ways of which s/he is unaware.

In this vein, Johal, Moran and Williams (2014) identify a 'fourth face of power', they term it 'capillary power', rooted in a Foucauldian approach: 'It entails the internalisation of values in such a way as to ensure that discipline becomes something not imposed externally but the product of restraints learnt and then followed voluntarily'. Their argument is that the City of London increasingly used this form of power, although the Government was unaware that this was occurring (the section on Bourdieu's concept of habitus below explores another, similar, way of conceptualising this form of power). Here, agents' actions are shaped by a dominant, if unacknowledged, narrative; so, ideas are crucially shaping agents' actions. Interestingly, Johal, Moran and Williams argue that the use of this face of power was increasingly unsuccessful and that the City moved back towards more direct attempts to influence government policy.

Two other, related, points are important here. First, we always need to be clear about what or who is the 'agent'. So, for example, neither 'business', nor 'government' is an undifferentiated whole. Some authors write about the power of business in general, while others focus on the power of the banks (or the mining industry) Similarly, none of these authors discussing the power of business make any systematic distinctions between the power of the government, the power of certain government departments and the power of government agencies.

Second, when discussing agency we need to be clear whether we are talking about collective or individual agents. We might talk about the power of business, of interest groups which represent business sectors or of individual firms; all are collective agents. However, the literature is also full of references to individual agents, whether politicians, regulators or businessmen, with no consistent discussion of the relationship between the individual and the collective agents.

The ideational realm

As argued, there has been a growing focus on the role of ideas in social science over recent years, and particularly in fields of comparative politics and international political economy, where much of the literature on the power of business is located. However, this literature is not good at specifying what is meant by 'ideas'. Indeed, in analysing the global financial crisis (GFC) from 2008, various analyses highlight the role of different ideas/sets of ideas, including: neo-liberalism or a general commitment to free-market economics; the idea that what is good for the financial sector is good for the country's economy; interventions, written or oral, by particular actors; politicians ideas about the GFC; bank leaders' ideas; and a hegemonic regulatory narrative which stressed the capacity of financial markets to function as self-regulating entities (Johal, Moran and Williams, 2014, 409). Of course, all these elements of the ideational realm may affect policy outcomes, but the key point here is that we need more precision about our treatment of ideas and about the inter-relation between these different elements, particularly in analyses which stress the role of ideas.

Dialectical approaches to the relationships between structure and agency and the material and the ideational

In this section I use the work of Hay as a starting point for four main reasons. First, he is concerned to look systematically at the relationship between these two meta-theoretical issues in a way which is uncommon in the literature. Second, he relates the different positions back to the ontological and epistemological issues which underpin them, another important issue here. Third, his work reflects a major trend in political science, the move to treat ideas more seriously, which has become very important in recent years. Fourth, in my view, if one does not adopt a poststructuralist position, then the most important issues in the literature on these meta-theoretical issues revolve around the debates within the dialectical position and particular between those who, to use Hay's phrase discussed below, adopt a thin constructivist or a thick constructivist position.

Structure and agency: the dialectical approaches

It is common to distinguish between three dialectical approaches: Giddens' structuration theory; Archer's morphogenetic approach; and Jessop and Hay's structural relational approach. Here, I look at each in turn, but also examine the position of Bourdieu, which has rarely been utilised in discussions of structure/agency in political science, because his concept of habitus is useful for thinking about the way in which structures can affect agents in ways of which they are unaware.

Structuration theory

Giddens' argument is that structure/agency is a duality, not a dualism; they are interdependent and internally-related. Giddens uses a coin as an analogy to evoke the relationship between the two, arguing that one cannot see the effect of both structure and agency at one time, just like one cannot see both sides of the coin at once. So, methodologically, at any given time one can only study either structure or agency, while holding the other constant, or 'bracketing it off' (Giddens 1984: 289). Hay (1995: 193–195; 2002, 118–121) criticises Giddens in broadly the same way, emphasising that the approach is not dialectical because it does not allow us to study the interaction between the two and, in empirical terms, tends to privilege agency, because, in his empirical work, Giddens 'brackets off' structure. I return to Giddens' treatment of agency below.

The Morphogenetic approach

This is the approach developed by Archer (1995; see also McAnulla, 2002). Archer, argues that there is an ontological and an analytical distinction between structure and agency, while Giddens, and particularly Jessop and Hay, see the distinction as only analytical. To Archer, structure and agency operate in different ways; in her analogy they are two strands that entwine with one another. As such, the temporal dimension is crucial for Archer and she identifies what she terms a morphogenetic cycle, a three-phase cycle of change over time (see Figure 12. 1). At T1 there is structural conditioning from a pre-existing context within which action occurs and which affects agents' interests. Social interaction

Figure 12.1 *Archer's three-phase cycle of change*

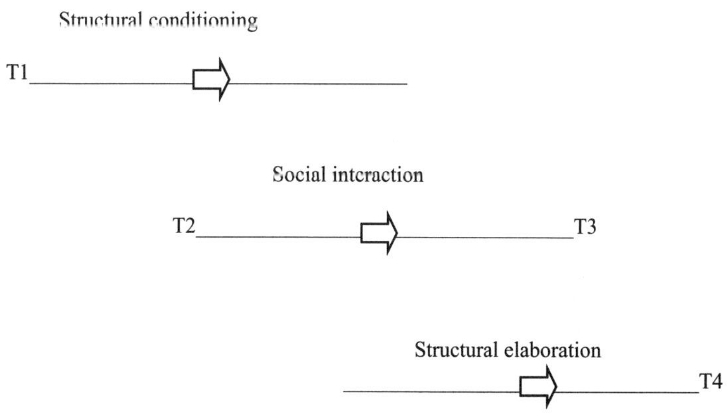

Source: Adapted from Archer (1995).

occurs at T2 and T3. Here, agents are influenced by the structural conditions at T1, but can also affect outcomes using their abilities and so on to forward their interests, often through a process of negotiation with other agents. At T4, as a result of the actions at T2 and T3, the structural conditions are either changed (this is morphogenisis) or, much less likely, not changed (morphostasis). T4 then provides the starting point of the next cycle.

Hay is highly critical of Archer (Hay, 2002: 122–126), arguing that structure and agents are only analytically, not ontologically, separate, an issue I return to below. More specifically, he takes issue with what he sees as a temporal separation of structure and agency in Archer and, particularly, her view that structure pre-dates agency. As such, he argues (2002, 125) that, in the end, Archer, like Giddens, presents an: 'agent-centred and individualistic view of morphogenisis'.

The strategic-relational approach

Hay (2002: 89–134) adopts a strategic-relational approach. I spend more time on this position because it raises the questions that, in my view, are at the forefront of the contemporary structure/agency debate. Here, the distinction between structure and agency is seen merely as an analytical one and, as such, structure and agency co-exist, and indeed are co-constitutive; they are not, and cannot be temporally separated, as Figure 12.2 indicates. As Hay puts it (2002: 127): 'Stated most simply, then, neither

Figure 12.2 *Structure, strategy and agency in the strategic-relational approach*

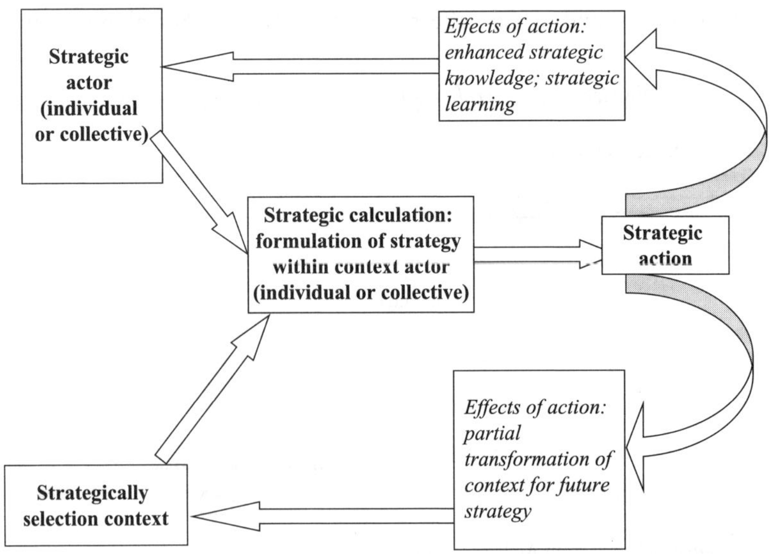

Source: Adapted from Hay (1995: 202).

agents nor structures are real, since neither has an existence in isolation from the other – their existence is relational (structure and agency are mutually constituted).' This approach is reflected in Hay's development of Giddens' coin analogy. To Hay, structure and agency are better seen not as two sides of the same coin, but rather as 'two metals in the alloy from which the coin is moulded' (Hay, 1995: 200).

As such, the core of the strategic-relational approach is 'the interaction between strategic actors and the strategic context within which they find themselves' (Hay, 2002, 128). Agents are viewed as 'conscious, reflexive and strategic', and in reflecting on their behaviour and preferences can change them. The agent's strategic action both change the structured context and contributes to the agent's strategic learning which changes her preferences and her view of her interests. Crucially, in this position structure has no independent causal power.

There are two crucial issues about the strategic relational approach. First, if structure (or indeed agency) has no independent causal power, then it is hard to see how the relationship between structure and agency can be dialectical. In fact, in my view, in this position there is an inevitable privileging of agents, and indeed ideas, which has clear methodological consequences. It is agent's choices which are important, and structures, which don't exist independently anyway, only affect agents to the extent that they recognise them and purposefully *choose* to be influenced by them. As such, in order to identify the agent's preferences, their perceptions of the strategic context, the reasons for their strategic choices and their reflections on the outcomes of their actions, we need to ask them.

For Hay, the other key element in any explanation of outcomes is the strategic context. He defines strategy as 'intentional conduct orientated to the environment within which it is to occur. It is the intention to realise certain outcomes and objectives which motivates action. Yet, for that action to have any chance of realising such intentions, it must be informed by a strategic assessment of the relevant context in which strategy occurs and upon which it subsequently impinges' (Hay, 2002:129). Here, it is clear that the explanatory power lies with the consciousness of agents and the relevant strategic, largely discursive, context. As such, we need to identify the contesting, and particularly the dominant, discourse(s), which shape, but of course don't determine, the context, and therefore the outcome.

In contrast, if one conceptualises structure and agency as ontologically, not just analytically, separable, then the relationship between structure and agency would be viewed as dialectical in the following sense.

- Structures provide the context within which agents act; these structures are both material and ideational.
- Agents have preferences/objectives which they attempt to forward.
- Agents interpret the context within which they act, a context which is both structural and strategic.
- However, structures, both material and ideational, can have an effect on agents of which they are not necessarily conscious.

- In acting agents change the structures.
- These structures then provide the context within which agents act in the next iteration.

This formulation differs from that of Hay in three main ways. First, because it's rooted in an ontological, not merely an analytical, separation between structure and agency, it sees both as having causal powers, although not independently of one another, given that there is a dialectical relationship between the two. Second, this formulation, unlike Hay's, emphasises that the relationship is dialectical, in the sense that it is both interactive and iterative, so structure constrains or facilitates agents, who in acting change structures, which, in turn, constrain or facilitate agents and so on. Third, and this is by far the most important point, it suggests that structures can have an effect on agents of which the agents are not conscious; a position that Hay does not explore. In fact, this latter point is so important that it needs developing. Here, the work of Bourdieu, and particularly his concept of habitus, offers a way of conceptualising how structures can affect agents without their being conscious of that influence.

Bourdieu and habitus

Pierre Bourdieu was one of the major social theorists of the last few decades, but his work is largely neglected in Political Science, while it has been very influential in Sociology. One of his key concepts, and the one which is important here, is habitus, which offers a potentially useful way of conceptualising an understanding of the way in which structure affects agents in a pre-reflexive, or pre-conscious, way (for an extended treatment of this issue, see Akram, 2009). Habitus refers to socially acquired and culturally embodied systems of predispositions, tendencies or inclinations. These are 'deep structural' propensities, involving both classification and assessment and they are embodied in all aspects of our life – including the way we walk, talk, sit and eat. To Bourdieu, the social construction of reality is structured, because all our cognitive structures have social origins which are inscribed in the habitus.

So, Bourdieu (1977) uses habitus as a conceptual mechanism to explain the way in which social norms become embedded in agents as 'durable dispositions', with a disposition seen as 'a pre-disposition, a tendency, propensity or inclination' (1977: 214), of which the agent is not conscious (1977: 72). An individual's habitus develops in response to the social sphere in which s/he lives and acts: a space that Bourdieu (1977) terms a 'field'. Bourdieu defines a field as 'a system of objective relations that is constituted by various species of capital' (Bourdieu: 1977: 201). Thus, we might speak of the 'education field' or the 'family field'. The positions in a field are related to one another, not directly through interactions or connections, but in terms of exterior relations of difference, especially in regards to forms of power [capital] (Bourdieu, 1977). The habitus is thus both a 'structured structure,' as it is affected by external structures, and a 'structuring structure', given that it impacts directly on agents. This leads Bourdieu to suggest that 'habitus is generative' (1977: 73).

Two points are important here before we move on. First, Bourdieu's work provides an example of how positions on the two meta-theoretical issues can be linked. So, habitus, a set of durable dispositions/ideas, can be seen as structured, by for example class and gender, and structuring, affecting the behaviour of agents. Second, any notion of the habitus raises crucial methodological issues. If habitus operates on a pre-conscious or unconscious level, then, by definition, it is difficult to access. So, if we ask people about their class and how it influences them, they may, usually do, deny they think or act in class terms, but, in Bourdieu's terms, they may be influenced in ways of which they are unaware; so, the effect of class may be pre-reflexive. Social class to Bourdieu is a relational concept, so individuals are located in social space, a position shaped by their access to economic, social and cultural capital. There is no space here to explore these issues (see Akram, 2012), but, the issue of whether structure is ontologically separate from agency and whether and how we can develop a concept of the sub-conscious/pre-conscious, perhaps rooted in Bourdieu's concept of habitus, to show how structures can have independent causal power is at the core of the contemporary structure/agency debate. This is a debate which will continue to generate a lot of interest, and it is a crucial one for explaining stability and change.

The material and the ideational: thin and thick constructivism

Colin Hay (2002: 206, table 6.1) argues that both thick and thin constructivism see the relationship between the material and the ideational as dialectical, but the former prioritises ideational factors and constitutive logics, while the latter prioritises material factors and causal logics. This issue lies at the core of the contemporary debate about the relationship between the material and the ideational and deserves further consideration. It also clearly relates to the structure/agency debate. Hay adopts what he terms a constructivist institutionalist position as a response to the limitations of historical institutionalism (see Chapter 4). As such, he argues that historical institutionalism has major problems with explaining change and that in the hands of many historical institutionalists, the concept of path dependency becomes an almost determinist one (see Hay, 2006[a] and 2006[b]). Once again, Hay argues that the distinction between the material and the ideational is an analytical, not an ontological, one.

The core features of constructivist institutionalism are (Hay, 2006a and 2006b):

- Actors are strategic.
- They seek to realise certain complex, contingent and changing goals.
- They act within contexts that favour some strategies over others.

- Ideas matter because they provide the guide for action.
- Interests are social constructs; they are not rooted in material differences.
- The functionality/dysfunctionality of institutions/structures is an open question in both empirical and historical terms.
- There is a focus on ideational, as well as institutional, path dependence.
- The aim is to 'identify, detail and interrogate the extent to which – through processes of normalisation and institutional-embedding – established ideas become codified, serving as cognitive filters through which actors come to interpret environmental signals' (Hay, 2006a: 65).

Hay (2006a: 65) acknowledges that, for constructive institutionalism, change occurs:

> in the context which is structured (not least by institutions and ideas about institutions) in constantly changing ways which facilitate certain forms of intervention whilst militating against others. Moreover, access to strategic resources, and indeed to knowledge of the institutional environment is unevenly distributed. This in turn affects the ability of actors to transform the contexts (institutional and otherwise) in which they find themselves.

He notes that 'it is important to emphasise the crucial space granted to ideas' within such a formulation (Hay, 2006a: 65).

This passage reveals clearly where Hay is positioned. First, he emphasises the role that ideas play in shaping the structural and discursive context within which agents act. Second, he recognises that the context is strategically selective – that it favours some strategies over others. These positions would be shared by both thin and thick constructivists. However, what is missing here is any idea that there are material, as well as ideational, constraints on the actions of agents. This is an important issue which is clear if we briefly consider the case of globalisation.

The literature on globalisation is voluminous, but there are major contestations about the extent to which it is a structural constraint on the actions of states, as actors; and whether such constraints are largely material or ideational. Initially, hyperglobalists saw globalisation as a very strong material structure which significantly constrained the policy autonomy of states – an extreme structuralist and materialist position (Reich, 1991; Ohmae, 1996). In contrast, authors such as Hirst and Thompson (1999) took a sceptical view, downplaying both the extent of globalisation and, particularly, its effect on state autonomy, so the state as an agent could resist the structural pressures of globalisation (for other critical responses, see Held et.al., 1999, who develop what is usually termed the complex globalisation thesis; and Hall and Soskice, 2001 who focus almost exclusively on the role of institutions in mediating the effects of globalisation).

All these contributions see the debate largely in terms of the relationship between the structure (the process of globalisation) and agents (the state and business). In contrast, Hay focuses upon globalisation as an ideational, rather than a material, process. He argues that, if policymakers believe in globalisation, then this is likely to shape their approach, whether or not globalisation actually exists. In other words, neoliberal ideas are creating neoliberal policies. In turn, this process undermines the nation state, with governments adopting policies that, in turn, affect their power and sovereignty.

For Hay, by behaving as if it were a reality, policymakers may actually be making it a reality. Consequently, Hay suggests that globalisation is best understood as a (political) consequence, rather than as an (economic) cause. This 'ideational' approach to globalisation is clearly important because it recognises that discourses have real effects in two ways. First, if policymakers believe, wrongly in Hay's view, that globalisation gives them no alternative but to pursue neoliberal economic policies, and perhaps especially active labour market policies, then they will adopt these policies; this is the logic of no alternative. Second, if states and other actors believe that there are high levels of globalisation, then they will act as if that was so and, in doing so, by increasingly competing in that global marketplace, bring about more globalisation.

A thin constructivist would have no problems accepting that discourses about globalisation have had real effects (see, for example, Marsh et al., 2006). However, they would contend that is only part of the picture. From their perspective, the relationship between the material and the ideational is dialectical and this means that the material reality has an effect on the discourse; in other words, a dialectical relationship cannot be unidirectional. One way to think about this is to invoke a concept of resonance, which Hay eludes to, but does not develop (see also Marsh et al., 2006). Here, the argument would be that, while any narration of the processes of globalisation is possible, the real economic processes associated with globalisation will constrain the effectiveness and longevity of that discourse.

Stability and change

As Hay argues (2002: 138): 'For any *normative* and *critical political* analyst, the question of change is far from a complicating distraction – it is, in essence, the very *raison d'être* of political enquiry' (his emphasis). In addition, as Hay emphasises: 'political analysts have increasingly turned to the question of structure and agency derives in no small part from concerns about the capacity of existing approaches to deal with the complex issues of social and political change'. Of course, positions on the relationship between stability and change are rooted in different conceptualisations of time (for a more thorough discussion of the role of time in politics, from an historical institutionalist position, see Pierson, 2004; from a constructivist position see Shapiro, 2010). Here, I identify three conceptualisations of time: the linear position adopted by Hay (2002);

the non-linear approach favoured by Tonkiss (1998; see also Bevir and Rhodes, 2003, 2006b), which, of course, problematises the whole idea of a distinction between stability and change; and what I term a flexi-time model. Subsequently, I look critically at Hay's punctuated evolution model of change, particularly his analysis of postwar British politics, because it highlights many of the main issues involved in conceptualising stability and change.

Hay: a linear conception of time

Hay concentrates upon diachronic, linear conceptualisations of time, and thus of change. He begins by acknowledging (Hay, 2002: 150) that: 'even among those who engage in [diachronic analysis] there is little agreement as to the temporality and resulting shape or pattern of social and political change over time'. He initially criticises revolutionary and evolutionary theories of change, before focusing on the idea of punctuated equilibrium (later punctuated evolution) model. He sees this model as associated with two ideas: (1) that a significant amount of institutional change occurs in short bursts of time; but (2) there are extended periods of relative stasis after bursts. So, as Hay puts it (2002: 161): 'As the term would itself suggest, punctuated equilibrium [evolution] refers to a discontinuous conception of time in which periods of comparative modest institutional change are interrupted by more rapid and intense moments of transformation.'

He illustrates the argument with reference to the contemporary state (2002: 161): '(the model) points to the ability of the liberal democratic state to respond successfully to societal demands and to disarm opposition, but also to its proneness to periodic moments of crisis in which the ability is compromised and in which the pace of change accelerates significantly'. As such, he suggests (2002: 161) that, taking the UK as an example, the dual crises of Fordism and the Keynesian welfare state, after a long period of postwar consensus, led to the triumph of the monetarist and neoliberal paradigm in the 1980s. However, Hay argues (2002: 163) that the concept of punctuated equilibrium does not afford enough attention to the periods of stability. As such, he prefers the concept of punctuated evolution to that of punctuated equilibrium.

Tonkiss: a non-linear conception of time

In contrast, Tonkiss (1998: 34–5), a poststructuralist, advocates a non-linear conception of time. He draws on Foucault's work which highlights the discontinuity of social change, emphasising (1998: 45) that it represents a serious challenge to the notion of historical explanation in social science. Indeed, Tonkiss argues (1998: 45) that, to Foucault, change is: 'arbitrary, accidental or unpredictable'. So, Tonkiss contends (1998: 46) that a non-linear approach is superior because: 'An interest in the local effects of social change, in the diverse connection between different factors, places and agents, offers a descriptive richness which can be missed by broad-brush theories of change.' For Tonkiss, change is both ubiquitous and untheorisable, at least in any way a positivist or critical realist might understand. As such, his position is based on an ontological and epistemological claim, which I, like Hay and Bates, would reject.

A flexi-time model: a circadian conception of time

Bates (2006) advocates a circadian conception, strongly associated with the work of Adam (1990, 1995, 1998). He argues (2006: 154–156) that to transcend the dualism between structure and agency and stability and change, we need to adopt a circadian conception of time; here time is not linear or cyclical, it is both. Adam (1990: 74) emphasises that a 'circadian' conceptualisation indicates an openness to variation, rather than sameness, invariant repetition and fixed accuracy. We might term this a flexi-time model. There is no simple progression, as in the linear model, rather change is context-based, multidimensional and capable of different interpretations.

For Adam (1990: 87), natural time is characterised in terms of a series: 'of many intersecting spirals, where linear, irreversible, processes fold back on themselves in multiple feedback cycles'. As such, change is ubiquitous, in the sense that these processes never merely reproduce (for similar views of time see systems theorists such as Easton, or Luhmann and from an interpretivist position, Wagener 2011). However, the degree of change varies depending on the context, and indeed, as Shapiro (2016) emphasises, on whose 'time' it is; so we need a much more nuanced study of the relationship between the two. As such, in my view, change occurs in the context of stability – a point I return to in the next section.

More on punctuated evolution

Here, I focus on two issues around the punctuated evolution model: the argument that long periods of relative stasis are followed by a period of rapid change as a response to crisis; and the absence of any spatial dimension in the analysis.

Relative stasis and rapid change

Given Hay's position, the key question almost inevitably becomes: what causes the rapid change? Hay's response is clear, it is crisis, and particularly how that crisis is narrated, that leads to radical change. As such, Hay distinguishes (2002: 201) between normal periods of policy-making and radical or exceptional institutional innovation that results from a successful crisis narrative. So, in the normal periods, the response to a policy problem occurs largely among elite policymakers who operate with a given set of values and a particular definition of the problem, although there is always strategic learning involved. In this context, and given those perceptions/values, the outcome will be policy evolution within existing parameters. In contrast, in a period of crisis the elite cannot retain control of the definition of the problems, and indeed their perceptions of the problem may change; rather, the problem is clearly visible and broadly aired. In that context, if a successful crisis narrative is developed and 'believed', then there will be a paradigm shift – the idea of a paradigm shift used by Hay was adapted from Kuhn (1962) by Hall (1993) – and significant policy change.

The argument is particularly clear in Hay's analysis of postwar British politics, which builds upon the work of Hall (1993). Hay suggests that a new paradigm was established or emerged after 1945: the postwar consensus, rooted in social democracy, a mixed economy and a Keynesian welfare state. However, this consensus was increasingly questioned in the 1970s, as a result of a crisis of Fordism and the Keynesian welfare state. What Hay adds to Hall's analysis is the idea that a transformation occurred because this crisis was successfully narrated by the Conservatives and their allies in the 'Winter of Discontent'. The Winter of Discontent in the UK in 1978/79 involved a series of public sector strikes which had a major effect on most of the population; to take two perhaps especially important examples, a strike among local authority workers meant that the 'dead were not buried'; and a strike among petrol-tanker drivers meant that there was little petrol and long queues at the pumps. Hay is particularly interested in the media narratives of this crisis. To Hay, the result of this crisis was another paradigm shift and the emergence of neoliberalism as a new consensus which, while it evolved, remained dominant and shaped policy options.

In my view, the punctuated evolution model has two main problems. First, Hay treats stability and change as a dualism and focuses too heavily on change. According to Hay, in the UK from 1945 to the time of his writing there were extended periods of relative stasis, followed by rapid change, resulting from the successful narration of crisis by 'change-agents'. It almost inevitably follows that the focus is much more on change, which may be regarded as more interesting, than on stability. Second, and this is perhaps unsurprising given our previous discussion, his empirical analyses appear to privilege agency over structure and the ideational over the material. In my view, both these problems can be addressed if we develop a more adequate temporal and a spatial understanding of the relationship between stability and change, and it is to that issue I now turn.

On the spatial dimension

Bates and Smith (2006: 2) argue that even when there is some consideration of the spatial in political science, usually in the form of a comparison between polities, there is 'little accompanying ontological reflection on the nature of space and spatial relations'. More specifically, they are critical of Hay's conceptualisation of change, arguing: 'it seems odd that Hay explicitly argues that we should treat change as an open and empirical question and yet (on the very same page) goes on to provide a rather neat theoretical model' (Bates and Smith, 2006: 3–4). Consequently, they advocate empirical mapping, rather than theoretical modelling – in effect emphasising the complexity of the relationship between stability and change and suggesting, particularly, that change has a spatial dimension. In their view, Hay's punctuated evolutionary model is unidimensional and seems to imply that there is either continuity or change in different ideological, cultural and discursive areas, in all jurisdictions within the UK, and in all policy areas. So, Hay's work has a major flaw because it is cast in terms of a dualism; there is either gradual evolution or rapid change. In my view, the relationship is much more complex and much better viewed as a duality. Let us return to the empirical case which informs much of Hay's work: contemporary politics in the UK.

The first point to emphasise is that change and stability often co-exist in different spheres/policy areas; there is an important spatial dimension here. Of course, it might be possible to argue that change occurs, as a response to crisis, in the more fundamental areas, while elsewhere there is stasis. However, if we return to the case of the 1970s in the UK, which both Hay and Hall use as an example, then, while there may have been major changes in economic policy and a move to monetarism, there was much less change in other areas. Indeed, Marsh and Tant argue (1989; see also Marsh and Hall, 2007) that Mrs Thatcher, far from being a break with the past, was a perfect embodiment of crucial aspects of the British political system, and especially what they term the British Political Tradition (BPT), a conception of democracy which stressed a limited liberal notion of representation and a conservative notion of responsibility, emphasising that 'government knows best' (Hall, 2011).

Second, and more importantly, the relationship between stability and change is better seen as interactive and iterative, given that stability inevitably provides the context within which change occurs. In particular, the balance between stability and change may affect outcomes in several ways. As such, it seems plausible to argue that the persistence of the BPT and its discourse of limited democracy (Marsh and Hall, 2007) made it easier for the Conservatives under Mrs Thatcher, as a strong leader, to introduce radical legislative change.

However, there can also be areas in which an old paradigm/narrative – underpinning stability – and a new paradigm/narrative – advocating change – conflict, with the outcome being open. Here, Brexit provides another instructive UK example. So, Hall and colleagues (2017) argue that, in recent years, the BPT has been under increasing threat from a combination of the growth of anti-politics (which clearly questions the idea that government knows best), growing economic inequality, the situation in Scotland (where the devolved system is underpinned by a different conception of democracy) and conflict over Europe (culminating in the Brexit vote) (see Marsh, 2017).

One way to look at these developments, which has become increasingly common, is through the lens of populism. Of course, populism is a contested concept, but here I want to utilise a distinction made by Mudde between 'explicitly populist' groups and those within the Establishment who simply use populist discourse to respond to pressure from an external populist movement. For Mudde (2004: 551), in the UK, Blair's New Labour was an example of centrist populism, in which a politician adopted an opportunistic 'populist *style*, rather than populist *politics*'. The New Labour period saw an increase in socioeconomic inequality; fierce protection of centralised power, despite devolution; and a failure to fully implement its constitutional reform agenda. As such, Blair's populist style fitted very happily with the BPT (on how the BPT fits with the economic interests of the socioeconomic and political elites, see Marsh and Hall, 2014).

However, the rise of anti-politics (on anti-politics, see Vines and Marsh, 2017), linked in part to rising economic inequality (as well as immigration in the context particularly of the Europe question), led to the development of 'explicitly populist groups', and particularly of the United Kingdom Independence Party (UKIP), which campaigned for Brexit. This was certainly a challenge to the BPT, but, in part at least, the Brexit campaign was marked by a not-always-easy alliance between UKIP populism and disaffected members of the political elite who wanted to use populist sentiment for their own purposes. It is impossible to predict what will happen, but the reaction of the political elite, led by new Conservative Prime Minister Theresa May, has been to try to control the process as much as possible: to reassert crucial elements of the BPT in the light of populist pressures. In a sense, May has also been opportunistic politically (she did after all oppose Brexit). More importantly, however, if she fails to respond to, and satisfy, the populist pressures, especially around immigration, then she may be increasingly seen as a political opportunist, which would deepen distrust in politicians and democracy. I don't have a crystal ball, but the key point here is that, while Brexit challenges the existing stability of the British political system (for example, what is happening to the party system), and the dominance of the BPT, any change will occur within the context of that system and that previously dominant view of democracy.

Of course, there are other spatial dimensions, notably geographic space. Again, using the UK as an example, the Scottish case shows how this spatial dimension can affect stability and change. Scottish devolution was one area in which New Labour introduced a radical constitutional reform with speed and without any attempt to de-radicalise the original proposal, to a large extent for electoral reasons (see Marsh and Hall, 2007). As such, the Scottish political system differs from the UK one in a number of important ways, which reflect the perceived limitations of the

UK system and a critical response to the BPT which underpins it. In particular, Scotland has an Additional Member electoral system, a proportional system in which the composition of the legislature roughly reflects the votes cast for the parties; so, the system is more representative, at least in terms of votes cast. In addition, the Scottish Parliament has a powerful committee system designed to act as a check on the power of the executive, making it more responsive. In this context, Scotland developed different policies from the UK in several areas in which it had legislative competence. This, in part, explains the much higher levels of trust Scots had in their Scottish politicians (73 per cent), as distinct from their UK (23 per cent) counterparts in the 2015 Scottish Social Attitudes survey (http://natcen.ac.uk/our-research/research/scottish-social-attitudes/). It also goes a long way to explaining the overwhelming support there is for substantially more devolution up to, and including, DevolutionMax, in which the Scottish Parliament would have legislative competence in all areas except defence and foreign affairs (http://whatscotlandthinks.org/questions). The point here is that a Scottish political system with more autonomy would most likely pursue different policy options, which, if successfully, might lead to changes in the UK in both policy and, more broadly, the political system.

Conclusion

Meta-theoretical issues examined here are crucial ones for any social scientist. The key issue addressed in much – maybe most – social science revolves around the question of stability and change, and it is the other meta-theoretical issues considered here which are usually evoked to explain the extent of stability and/or change. I have outlined the major positions on these issues and showed how they relate to one another. As regards the relationship between structure and agency and the material and the ideational, I have argued that we need to treat these as dualities, not dualisms. The key focus should be upon how the two sides of what are too often seen as dualisms interact, in an iterative way; I thus adopt a dialectical approach. In advocating this position, I am arguing that both structure and agency, and the material and ideational realm, have independent causal power, thus taking issue with a poststructuralist approach which would, at most, see both distinctions of only analytical utility.

On the issue of stability and change the problems are different, if related. Here, the poststructuralist would see change as ubiquitous and un-theorisable and suggest that any distinction between stability and change can only exist within a particular discourse or narrative. If we move beyond that position, then, in my view, the debate revolves around a key issue. Should we embrace the punctuated evolution model, which sees stability and change as cyclical and thus in essence as a dualism? Or, is it better to accept that stability and change, like the other meta-theoretical issues discussed here, is best seen as a duality? In this latter case, the relationship between stability and change is also viewed as dialectical, so that stability provides the context within which change occurs.

Further reading

- On meta-theoretical questions, see Hay, C. (2002) and Marsh (2010).
- On time, see Pierson (2004) and Wagener, (2011).

Chapter 13

Research Design

DIMITER TOSHKOV

What is research design?

Research design is about getting valid answers to research questions in a reliable and efficient way. It is about maximising the validity and scope of application (generalisability) of scientific inferences, given the goals of the researcher and the practical and ethical constraints. From one perspective, research design can be considered applied epistemology as it deals with the big question 'How do we know?' at a more operational level than philosophy. From another perspective, it is a branch of the decision sciences as it is about making optimal choices under constraints.

Research design choices are made at three levels of generality (see Figure 13.1). At the first, most general, level research design is about the adoption of certain general ontological and epistemological positions and a broad theoretical outlook. For example, it is about whether one approaches the problem of political inequality from an interpretivist or positivist, Marxist or feminist vantage point. The ontological, epistemological and theoretical vantage points also *direct* the researcher's attention towards some research questions at the expense of others. Consider that gender-based political inequality is a much more central problem for feminist theory than it is for classic Marxism, for instance.

At the second, less abstract and more operational, level of research design we choose a research goal, formulate a precise research question, clarify the role of theory in the project, conceptualise and operationalise the concepts, and select the class of research methodology to be used. For example, we might: (1) choose to research the question 'What is the impact of the electoral system on the political representation of women?', which implies an explanatory goal of identifying a causal effect; (2) specify that the research interest is in *testing* this existing hypothesis derived from institutional theory; (3) settle for an observational (non-experimental) design based on a large number of cases to be analysed using quantitative (statistical) methods; and (4) identify observable variables that capture the conceptually relevant dimensions of electoral systems and representation, such as the level of

Figure 13.1 *Three levels of generality of research design considerations*

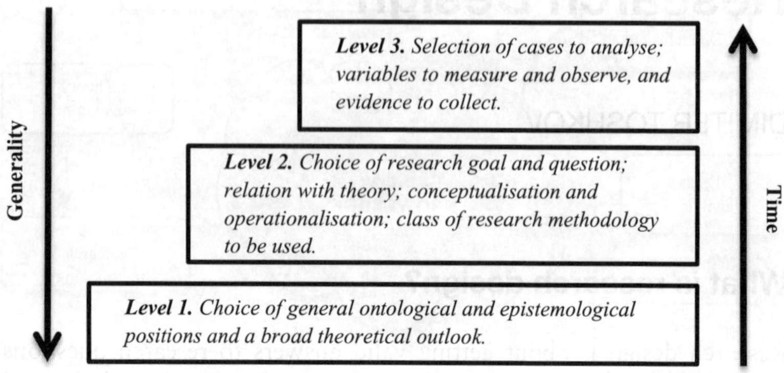

proportionality of the electoral system and the share of women elected in the national parliament.

Once these choices are made, at the third level research design concerns even more concrete and specific issues, such as the selection of cases to analyse, variables to measure and observe, and evidence to collect. To continue our example, we may decide to study sixty countries, sampled randomly from the list of all sovereign countries in the world, and collect data for each of these countries about the level of proportionality of their electoral system, the share of women in their parliaments and several additional variables, such as the type of political system and predominant religion, which might be needed in order to answer our original research question. This chapter focuses on research design at the second and third levels of generality. Within the context of this volume, however, it should be noted that Figure 13.1 has limited applicability for research using a poststructuralist or normative theory approach.

The research process

Before we are ready to discuss the design principles of individual stages of the research process, it will be helpful to get an overview of the process in its totality. Inevitably, such a view must remain rather abstract in order to fit the multitude of research projects political scientists engage with. So, think about the scheme represented in Figure 13.2 as an organising device rather than a faithful description of how political science works. And bear in mind that individual research projects, especially the relatively small-scale projects that students are expected to deliver, need not cover all stages of this research process at once.

Figure 13.2 *A schematic representation of the research process*

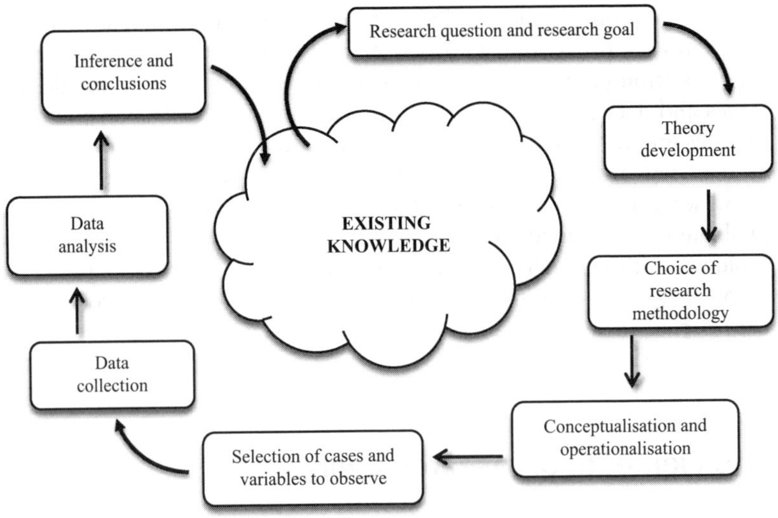

In the beginning, there is the research question. Of course, research questions do not pop up into being straight from the void, but are conceived in relation to existing knowledge. In fact, the whole point of research is to expand the boundaries of existing knowledge. The research question already sets the research goal. Once the question and the goal are relatively clear, it is usually time to settle on the broad type of research methodology that is going to be employed. What typically follows is the stage of theory development.

The output of this stage is often a set of hypotheses, but it could also be a more unstructured elaboration of the theoretical context of the research question, or even the realisation that there is not much theory available to guide the project at all. In any case, theory points to the most important concepts to study, and the next stage engages with the conceptualisation and operationalisation of these concepts into observable variables.

What follows is the selection of cases to observe, the variables on which to collect data and the types of evidence to search for. As explained above, all stages up to this point can be considered part of research design. Afterwards, the stage of data collection ensues, and once it is completed, data analysis can begin. The final outputs of this stage are the inferences and conclusions of the research process that feed back into the body of existing knowledge.

The stages shown in Figure 13.2 represent both logical and temporal relationships. While some projects travel the full cycle from research question to inferences through every stage, other projects might focus exclusively on one stage, such as theory development or conceptualisation or data collection. But even when they do, individual projects contribute to the collective scientific enterprise that moves along the stages represented in the figure.

The figure omits a host of links of secondary importance, such as the contributions of existing knowledge to theory development and conceptualisation (and vice versa) or the iterative loops between the design stages and data collection on the one hand, and data collection and data analysis on the other. Nevertheless, it will do for our purpose of providing an overview of the research process. The figure is general enough so that it can serve a variety of research goals, like description of populations or explanation of individual cases, and is consistent with different epistemologies (although derived from a broadly defined positivist outlook).

Now that we have the general overview of the research process, we can discuss in more detail each stage in the context of more specific research design considerations.

The elements of research design

Research questions and research goals

It is easy to say that research starts with a question. It is more difficult to answer where good research questions come from (for some solid general advice, see King et al., 1994: 14–19; Lehnert et al., 2007: 21–40; Gerring, 2012a: 37–57; Toshkov, 2016: 44–54). Inevitably, to select a research question that can advance the state of existing knowledge, one needs to figure out what we already know about the topic of interest. To push the boundaries of knowledge, we need to know where these boundaries lie.

Interest in a topic can come from a wide variety of sources, including personal dispositions, values, and experiences; academic scholarship and literary fiction; current events; and, lest we forget, direct assignment from someone who commissions the research. Whatever the source of interest in a topic, only a diligent review of the relevant scientific literature would reveal what the current stage of knowledge is (the fabled 'state of the art'). Fortunately, these days it is easier than ever to explore the state of the art in political science using free online bibliographical databases and encyclopaedia, comprehensive literature reviews published in academic journals, or blog posts by researchers active in a field. (At the same time, the amount of research being done on any topic is also growing at an unprecedented rate, which makes staying on top of the existing literature harder.)

Despite the enormous varieties of ways in which a research question can be encountered and phrased, there are several typical constructions. First, it is now popular to frame research questions as puzzles to be solved (Grofman, 2001). A puzzle is a pattern of empirical observations that does not make sense in light of existing theory and knowledge; for example, human cooperation in light of (a simple version of) rational choice theory (see Chapter 3). Puzzles are relevant, but so are substantively important problems, which cannot always be construed as real puzzles. In short, research questions can be motivated by a pattern of empirical observations that cannot be accounted for *or* by theoretical and real-world concerns that have not yet been addressed empirically in a satisfactory way.

Second, when it comes to explanatory research, researchers use three typical forms. They ask about the causes of an effect, about the effects of a cause, and about a particular relationship between a pair of concepts. Examples of the three types would be, respectively: 'What caused the UK to vote for leaving the European Union in 2016?'; 'What are the effects of globalisation?'; and 'What is the effect of changing income inequality on support for European integration?'.

The research question is intrinsically connected to the research goal. In its turn, the research goal is one of the major considerations when choosing a research design and methodology. Even when we exclude purely normative and theoretical research, scientific projects can still set a variety of different goals (including predictive, exploratory, interpretive and problem-solving ones). For the purposes of this chapter we discuss two of the most prominent: description and (causal) explanation.

Description

Etymologically, the word 'description' comes from the Latin *describere* with the meaning 'to write down, sketch, represent'. Scientific description also deals with writing down (listing) features of units (cases) and representing these units in a narrative, a survey, a collection of categories or a set of numbers. Description can be about a comprehensive (yet never complete) representation of a single unit or event, but it can also be about classifying many cases along a single or small set of variables. If the classification is into a large number of equally spaced categories, the process is also called 'measurement'.

What separates casual observation from scientific description? First, scientists strive to use reliable and precise, public and well-documented descriptive procedures and measurement instruments. Second, the value of scientific description is in selecting a set of important analytical dimensions on which to project the empirical world (Toshkov, 2016: 123). These analytical dimensions should offer insight into the essential nature of a case and its relationships with other cases. Third, scientific description is attentive to the representativity of the cases being described to larger populations of interest. In fact, one of the major purposes of research design for descriptive projects is to make sure that the cases that will be studied will deliver valid inferences about a population from which they have been drawn.

Contrary to what some political scientists believe, description is a worthy scientific goal in its own right (Gerring, 2012b). It involves inference, it is linked with theory (which suggests the important case features to be measured and described), and it can also have important normative implications (for example, when we classify a state as a democracy, or a conflict as a civil war).

There are many, widely different, methods to carry out (collect and analyse data for) scientific description: participant observation, (semi-) structured interviews, document analysis, archival research, and also various statistical techniques for surveying, data reduction and the compact representation of systems of associations. Public opinion surveys (such as the World Values Survey or the European Election Studies), which are perhaps the most recognisable products of political science research, are in essence descriptive projects. (Of course, scholars later use data from these surveys to build and test explanatory models as well.) Examples of other important recent descriptive work in political science includes the mapping of interest group populations across countries (for example, Gray and Lowery, 2000), the collection and classification of public policy outputs related to agenda-setting (Baumgartner et al., 2009), the measurement of political party positions based on a variety of data sources (such as party manifestos, voting records and/or expert surveys) (for example, Budge et al., 2001; Bakker et al., 2012), the classification of the institutional features of political regimes across the world (see the Polity IV and V-DEM projects), the collection of data on international conflicts (for example, the international UCDP/PRIO Armed Conflict Dataset), and many more. Dense histories of political events and the evolution of public policies provide research in radically different modes, but ones that still remain descriptive in nature.

Explanation

Explanation is the second major research goal we will present in some detail. Explanation is a subject of long-standing and sophisticated debates in philosophy and the sciences, including statistics (see, among others, Lewis, 1986; Salmon, 1998; Woodward, 2003; Pearl, 2009). Reviewing these debates is beyond the scope of this chapter. Suffice it to note that in contemporary political science the focus is on *causal* explanation (Elster, 2007), which is often understood in *counterfactual* terms (Lewis, 1986). Causality is taken to be *probabilistic* rather than deterministic (so there are no real laws in social science) (Glymour, 1998), but it is still based on causal *mechanisms* (Little, 1991). A cause is a 'difference maker' (Lewis, 1973) so that if the cause would have been different, a different outcome would have occurred (in probability). Such a view of causal explanation is compatible with various research methodologies, from within-case analysis to experiments, but is by no means consensual even within the domain of political science. Constructivists, for example, altogether prefer to focus on constitutive rather than causal arguments (Chapter 5), and radical subjectivists question the very existence of causality in the social realm. Other scientists (including many statisticians) are uncomfortable with the idea of causes that cannot be directly manipulated (Holland, 1986).

Even within the parameters of our broad definition of causal explanation given above, there is room for different explanatory research goals. We might want to explain a single event (for example, 'What led to the Cultural Revolution in China in the late 1960s?') or test for a systematic causal relationship ('What is the effect of economic prosperity on democratisation?'). We can focus on causal mechanisms ('*How* does international mediation help solve military conflicts between states?') or on estimating causal effects ('What is the average effect of facial attractiveness on the electoral success of political candidates?'). We can ask, 'What would be the effect of lowering the voting age on turnout in Ukraine?', which would be a *prospective* causal question; and 'What was the impact of social policy on the integration of demobilised paramilitary and guerrilla fighters in Colombia?', which would be a *retrospective* causal question. Further distinctions are possible, such as the ones between questions about the causes of effect versus effects of causes (Gelman, 2011) that we introduced earlier in the chapter.

Interpretation

It is difficult to position interpretation (in the narrow sense of the type of work interpretivist political scientists engage in) between description and explanation. Clifford Geertz (1973: 20) notes that (ethnographic) description is interpretive, but that still leaves open the question whether all interpretation is descriptive. Bevir and Rhodes (2016) insist that interpretivists reject a 'scientific concept of causation', but suggest that we can explain actions as products of subjective reasons, meanings and beliefs. In addition, intentionalist explanations are to be supported by 'narrative explanations'. In my view, however, a 'narrative' that 'explains' by relating actions to beliefs situated in a historical context is conceptually and observationally indistinguishable from a 'thick description', and better regarded as such.

It is important to be aware of the different types of descriptive, causal and interpretive questions because they allow freedom in honing your research question to your actual research interests. But also because different goals call for, and tend to go together with, different research designs and methodologies.

Theory and empirical research

After we choose the research question and clarify the research goal, we must examine how the proposed research project relates to existing theory. Theory in political science serves many purposes. It collects and integrates what we have learned about the world; it provides the major concepts and ideas that we use to discuss and analyse politics and governance; it specifies the causal mechanisms that we assume to hold; it identifies empirical puzzles, gaps in our knowledge and open questions that need more research; and it provides hypotheses and predictions about the world.

Research projects engage with theory in different ways (see Box 13.1; and Toshkov, 2016: chapter 3, on which this section draws heavily).

Box 13.1 Types of engagement of research projects with theory in political science

- Theory development (purely deductive from premises to propositions; no input from empirical data during the process, only at start)
- Theory generation (inductive, summarising patterns in empirical data in order to provide theoretical ideas and starting points)
- Theory testing (probing theoretically derived hypotheses against empirical data to examine the veracity and scope of the theory)
- Hypothesis testing (matching a substantively important hypothesis embedded in a theoretical causal model against empirical data)
- Theory application (routine application of existing theory to new empirical cases)
- Abductive explanation of individual cases/events (iterative testing of competing hypothesis against empirical evidence about a case/event with the aim of identifying the most plausible explanation; theory provides source of hypotheses and knowledge of general causal mechanisms)

(1) Some projects are interested entirely in theory development without any recourse to the empirical world. One can use a variety of tools, such as game theory, agent-based modelling, simulations, mathematical analysis, formal logic, thought experiments, and more to conduct such deductive theory analysis and development. (2) In projects where theory meets empirics, we are sometimes interested in testing a theoretically derived proposition about the observable world in order to see whether it is corroborated by the empirical facts or not. Such a proposition is called a hypothesis. (3) Other projects might be interested in testing a hypothesis not because it is derived from theory, but because it is substantively important. Such projects would still need to elaborate the theoretical context of this hypothesis. (In other words, they would need to reconstruct the causal model of the phenomenon of interest in which the hypothesis is embedded.) (4) Yet other projects might be interested in producing theoretical ideas through inductive empirical analysis: studying patterns of empirical observations with the aim to generate theoretical ideas that can be later analysed further and eventually tested. (5) Some projects of more modest goals might want only to *apply* an existing theory to a particular, previously unstudied case, without necessarily testing old or generating new theories. (6) When we are interested in explaining the outcome of a single case, theory provides the initial competing hypotheses and the knowledge of causal mechanisms that we investigate in a process called logical abduction (Peirce, 1955). Abduction involves the iterative examination of competing hypotheses against empirical evidence about a case or event until only one hypothesis remains as the most plausible explanation, because it is not contradicted by any of the evidence we have assembled. Box 13.1 summarises the ways in which research projects engage with theory in political science.

Whatever the exact terms of engagement between a research project and theory, theoretical reflection is always necessary, even if the goals and ambitions of the project are predominantly empirical and exploratory. This is because theory not only provides hypotheses and elaborates the assumed causal mechanisms, but it also supplies the main concepts of research.

Conceptualisation and operationalisation

Concepts are the building blocks of scientific arguments and ideas. As they are by definition abstract (and it is their generality that makes them useful), they are not directly observable. It is one of the tasks of research design in empirical political science to translate these concepts into variables that can be measured, indicators that can be detected and evidence that can be encountered in the real world.

Concepts are typically defined in terms of a set of necessary and sufficient conditions (Braumoeller and Goertz, 2000). For example, a *limited access social order* (North et al., 2009) can be defined as a social order in which participation in politics is limited, access to economic resources is severely constrained and political power is concentrated into a small elite. These three conditions then would be individually necessary and jointly sufficient for an empirical case of a social order to fall into the concept's definition, or not.

Concepts in political science are often complex and hotly contested – think about power, democracy, equality or ideology, for example. This makes it even more pressing that their intended meaning, attributes (intension), empirical scope (extension) and classification structure (how the various objects that fall under the concept's definition are grouped together) are clarified in a process called conceptualisation. Conceptualisation prepares the ground for the subsequent step of operationalisation, in which the now clearly defined attributes of concepts are connected with observable variables and indicators (Sartori et al., 1975; Adcock and Collier, 2001; Goertz, 2006). In the process of actual research, during the data collection phase, the cases will be assigned values on these variables and classed into categories according to the indicators.

Operationalisation is also relevant for research that eschews the language of variables and measurement, such as in-depth single-case studies and interpretive work. In these research modes it is more appropriate to think of operationalisation linking concepts with pieces of empirical *evidence* that would be searched for and collected in the process of research.

In the process of research design, all concepts relevant to the project must be conceptualised and operationalised. Ideally, already in the design stage the researcher should also specify how the necessary data would be discovered and collected.

To recap, so far we have discussed the following elements of research design: the choice of research goal and question; the clarification of the relationship with theory; and the double process of conceptualisation and operationalisation. What remains is a discussion of the type of research methodology that the project will employ and the third-level issues of case and variable selection (see Figure 13.1).

Types of research methodologies

The choice of the broad type, or class, of research methodology that a project will use is already more or less clear once its precise question is formulated, its goal is set and its theoretical ambition is explicated. In principle, there is no logical reason why the choice of methodology must precede conceptualisation and operationalisation (see Figure 13.1), but in practice the way we operationalise the concepts is closely linked with the type of data collection that would follow and, by implication, with the type of research methodology. And, to repeat, researchers go back and forth between the design stages to make sure the elements fit together. So let's just say that the choice of research methodology is made during the design phase of a project and is completed before data collection begins.

This book contains in-depth chapters on the most common research methodology classes in political science, so this chapter will only explain how they relate to each other and highlight the features that are important for the purposes of research design.

Experimental methods (see Chapter 17; see also Morton and Williams, 2010; Druckman et al., 2011; Kittel et al., 2012) are in a class of their own owing to the control researchers have over some aspects of the environment during the study. To qualify as a true experiment, or a randomised controlled trial, the researchers must be able to control one crucial design aspect, namely the assignment of experimental units (the cases) to different groups according to their status in the experiment – typically, 'treatment', which receives the experimental manipulation of interest, and 'control', which does not. Assignment is carried out randomly in order to ensure the comparability of the groups with respect to any possibly relevant attribute other than the experimental manipulation.

When researchers do not control the assignment of the experimental manipulation, the experiment technically does not qualify as such, even if other aspects of the environment are controlled. Conversely, sometimes nature provides (almost) random assignment of units into different conditions, and in that case we speak of natural experiments (Dunning, 2012). From a design perspective, natural experiments are similar to real ones, even though researchers have no control over any aspect of the situation.

Research that is not experimental is called observational because the researchers are left to collect observations that the world provides in the course of its undisturbed operation. In observational research, which is a vast category with many different types, what the researchers do control is what to *observe* in a particular project.[1] Hence, the major decisions they make relate to the issues of which and how many cases to observe, which attributes of these cases to observe, and what evidence from the cases to collect.

When many cases are observed and analysed, we speak of large-N designs (the 'N' stands for the number of observations) and quantitative methodology. Data gathered in the context of large-N projects is usually analysed using statistical techniques derived from probability theory. While large-N designs have many cases (the units), they usually have data about only a small number of aspects of these cases (the variables).

Although large-N projects can have millions of observations and use sophisticated statistical methods for data analysis, in essence they rely on comparisons across the cases to derive causal inferences. In that sense, they are not fundamentally different from comparative studies that use a smaller amount of cases (sometimes even as few as two, as in paired comparison designs) and undergo no statistical analysis. With a greater number of observations, large-N designs are better at filtering random unsystematic noise out of the empirical data to detect the systematic 'signal' of interest, for example a descriptive association, a predictive effect or a causal relationship. But their ability to provide causal inference, in particular, comes from design, and not from the number of cases.

This also holds true for big data methodologies (see Chapter 18), although currently big data projects are usually deployed for purposes other than causal analysis and explanation: classification, measurement, prediction and other applied goals such as process control.

Comparative research projects (Chapter 16) with a smaller number of cases are similarly dependent on their design to derive valid inferences. Their leverage comes from the careful selection of the set of cases to study, so that the similarities and differences across the cases can support or contradict causal hypotheses about suspected causal effects. Small-N comparative designs typically use a combination of quantitative measures and qualitative information to describe the cases they study. The data they collect for every case is much richer than in large-N studies, not only in terms of scope (more variables per case), but also in terms of depth.

When the number of cases we study goes down to one, we speak of single-case design, which is affiliated with qualitative methodology (Chapter 14). Qualitative methodology is a fuzzy label that covers various modes of research, such as interpretivist and constructivist work, small-N comparisons, broadly positivist but descriptive case studies, and more. The commonality is that they all avoid quantification. But from a design perspective, whether cases are described and compared with numbers or with qualitative categories does not matter too much.

[1]Note that by observation we do not mean passive reception but the active, purposeful and often laborious measurement, classification and collection of empirical facts.

What matters is whether or not inferences are based on comparisons across cases.

By definition single-case designs cannot rely on comparisons across cases for inference. Instead, they rely on within-case evidence only. Within-case evidence can be used to examine competing theoretical hypotheses. It is also useful to trace the process through which a causal effect obtains and the mechanisms behind, a causal relationship (Weller and Barnes, 2014). Via theory, single-case studies can also contribute to the study of general relationships and their contribution need not be restricted to the understanding of the particular case being observed (Blatter and Haverland, 2012).

Research projects in political science also can, and do, *mix* designs and methodologies (Lieberman, 2005; Rohlfing, 2008; Small, 2011). The combination can be carried out sequentially, for example when a smaller number of people are interviewed in-depth after a large standardised public opinion survey or when a pilot qualitative study identifies appropriate measures that are later collected in a large-N dataset, or in parallel. There are other interesting ways to mix methods and designs to combine their respective strengths and alleviate some of their weaknesses. But it should be noted that mixing only works for methodologies part of the same epistemological paradigm.

Case and variable selection for different types of research

So far we have covered issues of research design at the second level of generality (Figure 13.1). The next step is to discuss even more operational issues such as case and variable/evidence selection. Because these issues are rather specific, there is little that can be said about them outside the context of particular research goals and methodologies; that is, case and variable selection strategies depend crucially on the goal of the research project and on the methodological design. Accordingly, we will proceed to discuss the issues of case and variable/evidence selection in the context of the major types of research methodologies introduced above and with reference to the different research goals outlined earlier in this chapter. To recap, the purpose of case and variable selection, as elements of research design, is to support the reliable and efficient discovery of valid inferences.

Experimental research

In experimental research (see Chapter 17) case selection occurs at two moments. The first moment is when the cases (units, most often individuals) that are going to take part in the study are selected from some wider population. This is the sample selection stage. To make sure that the sample is going to be representative of the population, ideally the sample case should be selected *randomly* from the population, so that each unit in the population has exactly the same chance of ending up in the sample. This is done to ensure that the results of the experiment conducted on the sample will be generalisable to the broader population.

Despite its methodological attractiveness, random selection is not always feasible or available to the researchers. Experiments are often run on 'convenience' samples, such as students or panels of online volunteers. This opens the door to potential bias, so that any results from the experiment would not be relevant for the broader population, unless we are willing to assume that all people would react in the same ways to the experimental manipulation as have the students or online volunteers in our samples.

The second moment when case selection issues come into play in experimental research is when the sample is divided into 'treatment' and 'control' groups. As explained above, the assignment of units to experimental conditions (treatment/control) must be done randomly so that every unit has exactly the same chance of ending up in any of the groups. Random assignment is crucial for valid causal inference because it helps to rule out all alternative explanations of any difference between the groups we might observe after we apply the experimental manipulation.

In principle, in the presence of random assignment, researchers need not collect additional data on any variables other than the status of the sample units (treatment or control) and their response to the experimental manipulation. In practice, however, researchers would gather additional data on variables that possibly confound the relationship between the treatment and the response, that can shed light on the mechanisms through which the treatment works (if it does), and that can account for any differences (heterogeneity) in the way the treatment works across subgroups. Some of these variables can be used to 'assist' random assignment by forming homogeneous groups in which randomisation is applied and/or to adjust the results during the analysis stage (Cox and Reid, 2000; Imbens, 2011).

In the design phase, researchers should also decide on the number of cases that will be recruited to participate in the experiment. This issue is related to the power and sensitivity of the experiment to detect the hypothesised relationships in the data. The required number of cases needed depends on the likely strength of the hypothesised relationship (the stronger the hypothesised effect, the fewer cases needed), the within-group variability of the population (the greater the variability, the more cases needed) and some other factors of lesser importance. Once the researcher can estimate these factors, the numbers can be plugged into a statistical power calculator that would suggest the required number of cases for the experiment (Duflo et al., 2006). Underpowered studies, no matter whether experimental or observational, can produce very biased and misleading inferences (Gelman, 2011).

Large-N observational research

When random assignment is not available, political scientists have to use other strategies to derive valid inferences from data. As with the generalisability of experimental research results, in the context of large-N descriptive inference, random selection of the cases to observe is still crucial for the validity of the inferences to a broader population of interest. Even in professional large-scale surveys, however, sample selection is never that simple. Because of practical considerations, such as the need to reach respondents efficiently or the requirement to include a sufficiently large number of respondents from small subgroups within the populations, sample selection is typically done with a mixture of purposeful and random sampling (Lohr, 2009; Valliant et al., 2013). While the details of these procedures are too involved for this chapter, it is important to realise that when sampling is not random and some groups are systematically over- or under-represented in the sample, the results from the research on the sample would not be generalisable to the target population.

Selection bias can also mar causal inferences with observational data. But it is but one possible source of bias and but one manifestation of the general difficulties of deriving causal inferences from observational data. In general, the problem arises from the fact that causality is not directly observable. Associations between variables X and Y that we can observe can arise under several different scenarios, including (1) X causes Y, (2) Y causes X, (3) Z causes both X and Y (so Z is a *confounding* variable), (4) conditioning on a variable caused by both X and Y, and (5) chance (see Glymour, 2006); that is, all five scenarios would produce observationally equivalent data even when the underlying data-generating mechanisms are very different.

Research design comes to the rescue. There are three different logical strategies one can use to try to solve the general problem of causal inference as outlined above (Pearl, 2009). First, we can try to measure all confounding variables during the data collection stage, which would allow for estimating the residual 'true' causal effect of X and Y during the data analysis stage. Second, even if we cannot measure all suspected confounders, we can try to identify the effect of X and Y via the mechanisms through which it works (for example, X leads to M which leads to Y). This is called mediation analysis. Third, if we can find a variable I that strongly influences X, but is not affected by the confounder Z and does not directly affect Y, we can also identify the effect of X on Y by including measures of I in the analysis. In this case I would be called an 'instrumental variable', and the causal identification strategy is one based on instrumental variables.

In the practice of large-N research in political science, researchers most often rely on the first strategy, and implement it in a number of different designs: time series (where a single unit is observed over time), cross-sectional (where a set of units is observed at the same point of time), pooled (which combines variation over time and across units) and more complex multilevel ones.

To recap, depending on the causal identification strategy, large-N projects need to plan to observe different sets of variables in addition to the hypothesised cause and effect of interest. For conditioning strategies, these include all confounders; for mediation analysis – the mediating variables; and, rather obviously, for instrumental variables – the instrumental variable itself. Note that the status of variables as confounders, mediators or instruments cannot always be verified against empirical data and has to remain to some extent based on theoretical assumptions (Pearl, 2009).

Coming back to case selection, when random selection is not available, it is advisable to ensure that the sample of cases has ample variation on both the outcome variable of interest and on the main explanatory variable (King et al., 1994). This advice presumes that the values of the outcome variable are known in advance, before the actual data collection has taken place, which is often not the case. In such situations, cases that exhibit variation on the explanatory variable should be selected. Selecting on the values of the outcome (dependent variable), so that all cases exhibit a single outcome, is not advisable outside the context of preliminary, exploratory studies, because it can lead to biased causal inferences.

When it comes to the number of cases to be observed, the same considerations about design sensitivity and power that we introduced earlier apply. Increasing the sample size, however, often comes at the price of increasing its heterogeneity (how different the units in the sample are). Heterogeneity is bad news for estimating causal effects, and the problems it introduces may not be worth the increased statistical power that comes with a larger number of observations (Rosenbaum, 2005).

Comparative research

In small-N comparative research the selection of cases can be approached differently depending on the goal. For theory-testing projects, the most straightforward strategy is to keep the cases similar across all theoretically relevant variables and let only one variable – the one related to the hypothesis of interest – vary. In this way alternative explanations are controlled for by being kept constant across the set of comparison cases. For theory-generation projects, one can adjust this strategy so that a set of similar cases that exhibit *different* outcomes of interest are compared (Przeworski and Teune, 1970). (Confusingly, both of these strategies can be referred to as most-similar system designs, but they serve quite different research goals.) One can also find a set of different cases that happen to share an outcome and use them with the intention of identifying a crucial similarity across the cases that can account for the shared outcomes. This is called 'most-different system design', and is also a strategy better suited for exploration and theory generation rather than theory- and hypothesis-testing.

Single-case studies and within-case analysis

Experimental and large-N observational projects rarely care about the individual cases part of their samples as such. The cases are valuable only to the extent that they can serve to support descriptive or causal inferences that are about a general relationship and/or a broader population of interest. But in political science we are often interested in particular cases because of their substantive, real-world importance. For example, we want to know not only about democratic survival in general, but about the chances of India remaining a democracy; not only about government formation in general, but about the record-breaking duration of the government formation process in Belgium in 2010–11; not only about the appeal of populism, but about the astonishing campaign of Donald Trump in the 2016 presidential elections in the USA. When we are interested in a case because of its substantive importance, the research design concern about case selection seems misplaced. We select the case to study, because it is, well, the case we want to study. And that is fine, so long as we do not intend to generalise the findings based on that one case to others.

When we are interested in explaining, rather than just describing, a single case, we must do that with recourse to more general theories. When such general theories exist, they provide hypotheses about possible explanations of the case. The task of research design is then to anticipate what kinds of empirical evidence will support or contradict these hypotheses, and to devise plans to search for such evidence. For example, if the two main competing hypotheses we have formed, based on prior research, about the onset of the 2011 Jasmine Revolution in Tunisia are that it resulted from (1) the deteriorating economic conditions, or (2) increasing political repression, we would want to collect evidence about the evolution of the economic situation and the state of political freedoms in the country and seek to connect these pieces of evidence to the timing of the revolution process. The methodology behind this work is often called 'process tracing' (Bennett and Checkel, 2015; see also Chapter 4 of this volume on institutionalism).

Not all pieces of empirical evidence would carry the same inferential weight. Some evidence would be expected to occur under both hypotheses (for example, increased political polarisation), while other evidence would be present only if one of these actually holds (for example, protesters citing economic rather than political grievances as a motivation for their discontent). This idea has been extended and formalised as a typology of the kinds of empirical evidence in terms of their uniqueness and certitude in light of competing theories (see Van Evera, 1997; Collier, 2011; Mahoney, 2012; Rohlfing, 2014).

Things get more complicated when we *do* want to generalise based on a single-case study. For descriptive inference, we would normally want to select a case that is typical of a population. But under some circumstances, the description of a truly aberrant case might actually be more valuable. Descriptive case studies can also be used to check whether measures capture the empirical aspects they should (for example, whether people interpret survey questions in the way the researchers intended or whether people discuss a political theme in the terms researchers assume). Process-tracing methodology can also help to establish and illustrate the mechanisms behind known or suspected causal relationships.

For causal inference, the way single-case studies can contribute to general knowledge is via theory (Blatter and Haverland, 2012). If there is very little prior theory on a research question, an in-depth single-case study can be deployed to generate initial theoretical insight, which can be later developed deductively and tested. When a novel theory is proposed, it might be worth testing the theory in a so-called plausibility probe (Eckstein, 1992), a pilot case for which the theory is most likely to hold. Conversely, when the theory is strong and well established, we would be more interested in testing it on a least likely case in order to probe the limits of its applicability (see Gerring, 2007). Sometimes, even single-case studies can deal fatal blows to existing theories (an often-cited example is Lijphart, 1968), but there are not many such examples, because political science theories are typically flexible enough to accommodate a small number of disagreeing observations or predictive failures. Altogether, for the design of single-case projects, the relationship with theory is even more important than for projects based on other types of research methodologies.

Conclusion: the power and promise of research design

This chapter presented an integrative perspective on research design in political science. Instead of arguing that some research design or methodology is inherently better than others, the chapter argued for a pluralistic and pragmatic approach. Political scientists can use a variety of designs and methodologies that are all legitimate, but some are more appropriate for particular research goals than others. Instead of exaggerating the differences between interpretivist and positivist, or quantitative and qualitative research (see Goertz and Mahoney, 2012), we showed that they can all be used to answer different research questions and address different research goals.

Attention to research design can unleash the power of political science research by supporting the discovery and testing of valid inferences in a reliable and efficient way. But it also protects against the long list of biases of human cognition (Kahneman and Tversky, 2000; Sloman, 2005). Many of these biases are troublesome for scientific reasoning in general. But some, in particular the ones related to the covert influence of political ideologies on information-processing and other aspects of cognition and decision-making (for example, Nyhan and Reifler, 2010; Kahan et al., 2013), are especially pertinent to political science research.

For all their special training, researchers remain human and could benefit from the disciplining role of research design to avoid cognitive and ideological biases.

The empirical social and behavioural sciences, political science very much included, face significant challenges in the form of increased scrutiny to research ethics and integrity. Research design can help address these concerns as it enhances transparency, supports replicability and encourages reproduction.

In a recent development, some academic journals in the social sciences, and political science in particular (see the winter 2013 issue of the journal *Political Analysis*), encourage the public registration and publication of research designs before data collection and analysis have been conducted. Such pre-registration is supposed to ensure that researchers do not misrepresent the goals of their research projects (for example, selling inductive theory-generating studies as theory-testing ones) or 'game' their data analysis to produce 'significant' but unwarranted results. While pre-registration is most directly relevant for theory- and hypothesis-testing designs, it holds a broader promise to improve the research process in the social sciences.

At the same time, research design should not be considered a straitjacket, constraining creativity and the discovery spirit of scientific research. It should enhance rather than limit the potential of research projects and give wings to, rather than weigh down, original research ideas.

Further reading

- The themes introduced in this chapter are discussed more comprehensively in the chapters of my book *Research Design in Political Science* (Toshkov, 2016).
- Other recommended general books on research design and methodology include Gerring (2012a) and Gschwend and Schimmelfennig (2007). King et al. (1994) remains a standard reference, read preferably in conjunction with Brady and Collier (2004) and the 2010 special issue of the journal *Political Analysis*.
- On theory in the social sciences, Elster (2007) is recommended, and on concepts and conceptualisation, Goertz (2006).
- On causal inference in large-N research, see Morgan and Winship (2015) and Imbens and Rubin (2015).
- On case study designs, see the books by Rohlfing (2012) and Blatter and Haverland (2012), and on the related subject of process-tracing methodology, Bennett and Checkel (2015).

Chapter 14

Qualitative Methods

ARIADNE VROMEN

When we seek to understand or explain *how* and *why* a political institution, event, issue or process came about, we are asking questions that can be answered using qualitative methods. The focus of qualitative methods in political science is on detailed, text-based answers that are often historical and/or include personal observations and reflection from participants in political institutions, events, issues or processes. This is often characterised as the use of 'thick' description and analysis. This chapter shows that, while there has been a recent emphasis on the use of mixed methods in political science research design, there are still some essential features of qualitative methods that need to be understood. Qualitative methods tend to be used within particular sub-disciplines of political science (for example, by researchers who study political institutions, rather than those who study political behaviour and use quantitative methods), by those committed to a particular approach (such as feminists) and by those coming from a non-positivist epistemological position (such as interpretivists and critical realists). Yet these divides are far from straightforward and qualitative methods are used by those with both a positivist and a non-positivist epistemological position, and differences are based on claims made about explanation and the purpose and goals of research itself.

The chapter is structured around two main themes, providing an overview of the debates about qualitative and quantitative methods in political science; and an introduction to the main types of qualitative research techniques, with research examples that focus on both design and analysis.

Debates on qualitative methods: the rediscovery of qualitative analysis

Historically, political science was built on a descriptive qualitative approach, because, until the 1950s, the discipline predominantly studied political theory and the development of legal and political institutions (see Chapter 4). It was then that advocates of the study of the role of individuals in the political world, that is behaviouralists (see Chapter 2), challenged the dominant, qualitative, institutionalist tradition. Political science has always been shaped by its relationship to other disciplines within the social sciences, such as sociology, history and economics, as well as law, psychology and geography. This openness to other disciplinary perspectives can enrich the discipline, but also leaves it open to the accusation that political science lacks a distinctive theoretical and methodological core. Indeed, at times, the differences between political scientists in any given department can be quite stark. We often have different influences, read different books, publish in very different journals and seem to speak a different conceptual language. As such, there is an increasing tendency for political scientists to specialise in their subfields of the discipline, and it is here that either a qualitative or a quantitative approach has become dominant.

This sub-disciplinary bifurcation on methods was reflected in a survey of the methods used by political scientists publishing in high-impact scholarly journals (Bennett et al., 2003). The study coded 1,000 articles published over twenty-five years in ten political science journals that claim to be multi-method, and differentiated between three main types of methods:

1. Quantitative methods: included statistics, survey research and content analysis
2. Qualitative methods: including case studies, in-depth interviews, text/discourse analysis, historical analysis
3. Formal modelling: including game theory and complex mathematical/economic models

Overall, the results showed that 49 per cent of all articles used quantitative methods; 46 per cent used qualitative methods; and 23 per cent used formal modelling (this adds up to more than 100 per cent as some articles were multi-method). This demonstrates that, while quantitative and formal approaches (which both rely on statistics or econometrics) make up a sizeable proportion of articles published in top journals, qualitative methods are being broadly used by many political scientists. (The journals were *American Journal of Political Science*, *American Political Science Review*, *Comparative Political Studies*, *Comparative Politics*, *International Organization*, *International Studies Quarterly*, *Journal of Conflict Resolution*, *Journal of Politics*, *Political Science Quarterly* and *World Politics*.)

The methods used in three major sub-disciplines of political science, international relations, comparative politics and US domestic politics, were also compared. Statistical approaches were dominant in all three (shown here as the percentage ratio of quantitative; qualitative; formal modelling): international relations (48:46:20); comparative politics (65:40:18); and US politics (90:1:28) (Bennett et al., 2003: 375). This alerts us to two factors: international relations as a sub-discipline is the most pluralist in its methodological practices, domestic-oriented US politics is by far the least, with only 1 per cent of articles published using qualitative, case study-oriented approaches. The role of high-impact journals in fostering this bifurcation between methodological approaches is important and Yanow and Schwartz-Shea argued (2010: 743) that there has been a 'poor record of methodological inclusivity, diversity or pluralism' in these journals.

Another more pointed analysis found that of ninety-two articles in *American Political Science Review* only four used qualitative data; though another twenty-two were political philosophy or theory with no data. Similarly, of sixty-four articles published in *American Journal of Political Science* none were qualitative and three were theory-based (Kasza, 2010). This tendency for positivist, quantitative political science to dominate publications in the highest impact journals is asserted regularly (see Pierson, 2007) and, while some believe the quantitative/qualitative divide is no longer important, owing to an emerging focus on mixed method research design (see Chapter 13), others assert that there remain 'two traditions' of doing political science research (Mahoney and Goertz, 2006).

This chapter subscribes to the 'two traditions' paradigm, but also shows that both geographically distinct political science traditions matter, as does the epistemological position of the researcher. For example, Marsh and Savigny (2004) compared the approaches taken within two US-based journals and two UK-based journals, and showed that, while positivist quantitative research was dominant in the USA, UK political science is more pluralist through having a strong tradition of normative theory, as well as non-positivist, qualitative research.

Similarly, it has long been acknowledged that the study of politics in Australia has been underpinned by a humanities-oriented qualitative tradition, largely inherited from the UK (Rhodes, 2009). Indeed, a recent categorisation of the main methods used by ninety-five professors at Australian universities found that only eight use mainly quantitative methods, all of whom are in politics, rather than international relations, with six of the eight being men. The authors acknowledge that this imbalance will change, as there has been more recruitment of US-trained political scientists at junior levels in some universities in recent years (Sawer and Curtin, 2016).

There has been a similar change in the methodological backgrounds of staff in UK and European universities, as well as increased discussion about political science research methods teaching. In the UK this has led to the introduction of compulsory methods courses within postgraduate research degrees (Marsh and Savigny, 2004: 156). At the same time, the European Consortium for Political Research runs methods training courses for postgraduate students that are deliberately broad-ranging and pluralist, and inclusive of both interpretive and more positivist, comparative approaches to qualitative research design and analysis (Blanchard et al., 2016).

The emergence of feminist approaches in political science in the 1970s and early 1980s (see Chapter 6) pioneered the use of qualitative methods. Qualitative methods were important for emerging feminist methodologies as they prioritised women's voices and experiences which otherwise may have been ignored through the use of quantitative methods (see Ezzy, 2002: 46; Reinharz, 1992). More recently, scholars within feminist international relations have focused on the question of method and shown how the use of qualitative approaches, such as oral history, ethnography, interviews, archival research, participant observation and discourse analysis, can further feminists' overall challenge to the research agenda of conventional security studies (see Ackerly et al., 2006). While not all feminists use qualitative methods, the importance of feminism's early challenge to mainstream political science through the use of qualitative methods is now little recognised. Most books which advocate a resurgence of qualitative or pluralistic political science (for example, Schram and Caterino, 2006; della Porta and Keating, 2008) pay little attention to the influence of feminism on the shift towards individual case-based interpretation and meaning in social research.

Bennett and colleagues (2003) attribute the minimal presence of qualitative methods in political science in the USA to the way research methods are taught, given there are very few opportunities for graduate students to be properly trained in the use of qualitative methods. Bennett and colleagues' (2003) survey of thirty political science departments (covering 236 methodology courses) found only 16 per cent focused on qualitative methods.

There has also been an ongoing debate about the extent to which political science research methods textbooks promote the ongoing dominance of quantitative methods (Schwartz-Shea and Yanow, 2002). This has included a critique of the dominance of textbooks such as King and colleagues' (1994) *Designing Social Inquiry* which is charged with assessing the qualitative approach solely in terms of positivist and 'scientific' indicators of rigorous research (Brady and Collier, 2004; della Porta and Keating, 2008: 20; Mearsheimer and Walt, 2013). There is little recognition in many texts of both the distinctiveness of qualitative methods and the way in which they are used by researchers from a range of non-positivist epistemological positions.

Overall, qualitative methods are still more likely to be used and taught outside US-based political science, and within sub-disciplines such as international relations or public policy, although there is growing concern that both these sub-disciplines are now also more heavily using quantitative methods, neglecting theory building and rigorous, detailed explanation (see Mearsheimer and Walt, 2013; Baumgartner, 2016).

Of course, qualitative methods continue to be used, but, due to epistemological differences and assumptions, they tend to be marginalised in some sub-disciplines. In the early twenty-first century, there was a renewed focus on the use and role of qualitative methods in political science as a result of the 'Perestroika' debates. A debate started within the powerful American Political Science Association (APSA) that signalled dissatisfaction with the mainstream and dominant quantitative approaches. The 'Perestroika' movement started in 2000 with an email writer, Mr Perestroika, questioning the continuing dominance of positivist, quantitative methods within the most powerful journals, editorial boards and associations in the discipline. The aims of the movement converged around the need for methodological pluralism and political science research that was relevant to the real world (Schram, 2006: 18–19).

Two of the main Perestroika protagonists, Sanford Schram and Brian Caterino, edited a collection *Making Political Science Matter: Debating Knowledge, Research and Method* that adopted a political science specific position, based upon the arguments of a Danish scholar Bent Flyvbjerg in his book *Making Social Science Matter: Why Social Inquiry Fails and How It Can Succeed Again.* Flyvbjerg argued that social science never has been, and probably never will be, able to develop the type of explanatory and predictive theories that are at the base of the natural sciences. Instead, the social sciences ought to reorient the focus of enquiry and play to its strengths. This, in Flyvbjerg's view, would 'restore social and political science to its classical position as a practical, intellectual activity aimed at clarifying the problems, risks, and possibilities we face as humans and societies, and at contributing to social and political praxis' (Flyvbjerg, 2006: 68). He calls his approach a social science, derived from Aristotle, based on 'phronesis'. What this means is that political science should not be merely a technical exercise in positing and answering research questions through scientific and technical expertise (see also Mearsheimer and Walt, 2013), but rather should take into account what we know from everyday practices of politics and ethics. As such, the 'real-world' of politics needs to feature more in political analysis and these analyses need to more readily connect with the 'real-world' of politics (see also Donovan and Larkin, 2006: 12).

The broader implications of developing a relevant political science are considered in Chapter 19, but what does this manifesto mean for the use of qualitative methods in political science? A core dimension of Flyvbjerg's vision is to foster a new political science that does not rely on sophisticated quantitative modelling, but uses qualitative approaches found in the study of historical context, interviews based on people's experiences of politics and the attention to political and social meaning of text-based discourse analysis.

In 2015, *Perspectives on Politics*, the well-regarded APSA journal, which started in the wake of Perestroika to open up political science to new epistemologies, methods and questions (Hochschild, 2005), published a retrospective on the medium-term effects of these debates. While there was some agreement that some change occurred (Gunnell, 2015; see also Tarrow, 2008), including a broader acceptance of methodological pluralism, there was still doubt about whether a new respect and/or better publication outcomes were being achieved by qualitative political science. If anything, there is increasing evidence that the effects of the Perestroika movement, and the ideas of Schram, Caterino and Flyvbjerg, were short-lived and have not changed the orientation of political science research.

The short-lived effects of Perestroika are further demonstrated through the increased focus on both sharing data, and transparency in data collection and analysis within quantitative political science. This has led to initiatives such as the Evidence in Governance and Politics Network (EGAP) (www.egap.org); the Berkeley Initiative for Transparency in the Social Sciences (BITSS) (www. bitss.org); a symposium on the increased need for transparency in qualitative methods (Elman and Kapiszewski, 2014); and the recent Data Access and Research Transparency (DA-RT) statement (www.dartstatement.org/).

Yanow and Schwartz-Shea (2010) highlighted the increased requirement from many high-impact journals to make research data available for future replication. Sharing primary data sources is more challenging in qualitative research, for ethical reasons and the need to preserve the anonymity of research subjects, than it is if we are dealing with a de-identified quantitative dataset. Yet, by 2015, twenty-seven journals had signed on to DA-RT and made a commitment to increasing data access and research transparency as a social science standard. One of the few vocal opponents to DA-RT is Jeffery Isaac, the editor of *Perspectives on Politics*, on the grounds that it unnecessarily narrows the mission of political enquiry (Isaac, 2015; though for a counter view emphasising the need for transparency in qualitative methods, see Elman and Kapiszewski, 2014).

The next step in increased transparency is pre-registration, where researchers are asked to pre-submit their theory, hypotheses and intended empirical analysis before they submit an article for review. Where does the inductive, thick description of qualitative analysis fit with this model of carrying out social science research? A pilot study of pre-registration and 'results-free review' was published in *Comparative Political Studies*. Unsurprisingly, no qualitative researchers volunteered to participate in this pilot and the authors suggested that:

> ...qualitative case studies, comparative historical analyses, and other similar types of research *cannot be preregistered*... and *results cannot be removed from case studies*. These are types of research in which scholars generally accept that theories and arguments are informed by the interaction between a researcher's initial hypotheses – in some cases little more than hunches – and the specifics of a case. (Findley et al., 2016: 1690)

They continued:

> It is hard to escape the conclusion, though, that any requirement that research manuscripts have been preregistered will almost certainly affect the types of submissions that a journal receives. One possible consequence is a bifurcation of publication outlets, and as a result, of researchers. One set of researchers adheres strictly to a normal science template to produce manuscripts that are eligible for journals that insist on results-free review, while others adhere to and are assessed on

> a very different set of standards in a different set of journals. For the discipline as a whole, this would almost certainly generate divisions and inequalities. (Findley et al., 2016: 1692)

It is clear that new post-Perestroika initiatives like DA-RT and pre-registration will further bifurcate political science into 'two traditions', and marginalise qualitative analysis, if it does not subscribe to a more positivist orientation. We have moved further away from the hopeful call of political theorist John Dryzek (2002), who suggested that methodological pluralism in political science has been an insufficient goal, and instead the discipline needs to reorient around critical pluralism which:

> necessitates engagement across research traditions, not just more tolerance of different approaches, not just communication of findings. It is only in their engagement with one another that the shortcomings or indeed strengths of particular approaches and styles of inquiry can be explored. (Dryzek, 2002: 13; see also Isaac, 2010; Bleiker, 2015)

His argument that researchers with different epistemologies and different method choices need to, and can, deliberately engage with one another in creating a more nuanced and useful political science, is far from being heeded.

What is distinctive about qualitative methods and analysis?

The debate above demonstrates that much of the challenge of qualitative methods to dominant, non-qualitative, strands of political science lies in the centrality of meaning, context and history. For example, Paul Pierson writes of 'periphery' research specialisations, such as the American Political Development (focused on historical understandings) and public policy subfields, that pay in-depth and substantive qualitative attention to both historical context and long-term dynamic processes in explaining political institutions (Pierson, 2007).

Qualitative researchers focus on a single or very few cases/examples to be able to gain an in-depth understanding of their research subject; thus generalisation, or inference from and/or to many cases, is rarely a goal of qualitative analysis. Mahoney and Goertz (2006: 230) argue that qualitative research primarily seeks to explain the outcomes in individual cases. For example, analysis of a major event (such as a revolution) works backwards to *explain* how and why that event, in that place, at that particular time, occurred. They call this the 'causes-of-effects' form of explanation and contrast it with the 'effects-of-causes' approach taken by quantitative researchers, where an explanation of causality seeks to estimate the average effect of one or more causes across a population of cases.

Mahoney and Goertz (2006) further contrast these approaches to explanation by highlighting the vastly different initial research questions posed by qualitative and quantitative researchers. They suggest that quantitative researchers formulate questions such as: 'What is the effect of economic development on democracy?' In contrast, a qualitative researcher might ask: 'Was economic crisis necessary for democratisation in the Southern Cone of Latin America?' The key difference is whether a researcher is 'interested in finding some general law-like statements *or* in explaining a particular event' (Mahoney and Goertz, 2006: 231, emphasis added). Correspondingly, Blatter and Haveland (2012) argue that case study research can take a broad set of theoretical approaches into account, collect finely grained empirical evidence and understand the complexities involved in change over time by taking both individual agents and socio-political structures into account.

In focusing on just a few cases, qualitative researchers clearly do not view all possible cases as equal, rather suggesting that a chosen case is 'substantively important' (Mahoney and Goertz, 2006: 242) and worth examining in detail. Case studies involve in-depth, qualitative study of lived human experiences by means of on-site fieldwork and some combination of observation, interviews and/or document analysis. But, even if it is classified as a single-site case study, the qualitative researcher is not only studying a single phenomenon as the case study generates many qualitative-interpretive, within-case 'observations' that demonstrate patterns of interaction, practices, relationships, routines and actions (Yanow et al., 2010).

However, not all qualitative researchers prioritise causality in their research, even if it is understood as process-tracing, 'involving the mechanisms and capacities that lead from cause to an effect' (or outcome or event), rather than a quantitative focus on measuring causal effects (Bennett and Elman, 2006: 457–458). Instead, some interpretivist qualitative researchers reject causal analysis based on observation and process-tracing as a positivist exercise, seeing the main goal of research as interpretation of meaning, in order to provide understanding, rather than explanation (Schwartz-Shea and Yanow, 2002: 461; Caterino and Schram, 2006: 5).

This means that not all qualitative methods share the same epistemological position. Some researchers who use qualitative methods are committed to 'small-N' research, but also to standards of observation, objectivity and causality more central to positivism. In contrast, others focus on the interpretive dimension of using qualitative methods. Further differentiation can be made between qualitative approaches in design (accessing data) and analysis (analysing data), and this distinction also reveals a positivist and non-positivist divide in the use of qualitative methods.

Qualitative research techniques

For most qualitative researchers, explanation and understanding of human social and political behaviour cannot be independent of context. Therefore, the qualitative researcher tries to convey the full picture, often referred to as 'thick' description. There are four core attributes of qualitative political science research:

1. Inductive analysis that is premised on discovering categories and being exploratory with open questions, rather than *only* testing theoretically derived hypotheses.
2. A holistic perspective that seeks to understand all the phenomenon, and the complex interdependence in issues of interest, rather than reducing analysis to a few discrete variables. This also demonstrates a sensitivity to context, as analysis is located in the social, historical and temporal context from which data has been gathered.
3. Qualitative and adaptive data collection based on detailed, thick description and depth. For example, analysis uses direct quotation to capture unique perspectives and experiences. Further, the research design process is adaptable to changing situations and allows the researcher to pursue new paths of discovery as they emerge.
4. Empathetic neutrality in doing research is important as most qualitative researchers believe complete objectivity is impossible. The researcher's agenda is to understand the complex social world with empathy, while also attempting to be non-judgemental (adapted from Pierce, 2008: 43).

All four of these points suggest the importance of the processes and practices of reflexivity in undertaking qualitative research. Qualitative political scientists are expected to be transparent and reflective on their choices as researchers about: subject matter; research questions; how and what data is collected; and the analysis and interpretations of that data. Reflexivity entails explicit acknowledgement of the existing value positions of the researcher, and how their research design choices and interaction with the research field are shaped by their own values.

Reflexivity in research is an iterative process, shaped by contact with research subjects and with data itself. Analysis and data collection often changes via the process and experience of being in the field for those who undertake primary research, or for those engaged in uncovering and analysing large volumes of qualitative text. Undertaking research is also embedded in the political, cultural and social context, and in relationships of power. Some argue that what makes qualitative research distinctive is this self-reflexivity of the researcher: studying political phenomena within its natural setting, from the point of view of the research subjects. This is contrasted with quantitative researchers' application of rigid, preformulated concepts and variables onto observations and data collection (Alvesson and Sköldberg, 2009: 7–10).

Table 14.1 summarises research techniques that qualitative researchers commonly use and contrasts them with quantitative research techniques widely used within political science. The list is not exhaustive of all research techniques used by qualitative researchers, but deliberately contrasts a small-N approach with an equivalent large-N approach used

Table 14.1 *Contrasting qualitative and quantitative methods and techniques*

Techniques more oriented to producing qualitative data	*Techniques more oriented to producing quantitative data*
1. Case study, narrative approach, historiography 2. Interview, focus groups, life history, ethnographic observation 3. Textual and discourse analysis	1. Database construction or comparative statistical analysis 2. Questionnaire 3. Content analysis

in quantitative methods. Focusing on qualitative approaches, it is helpful to contrast those that involve the collection of new data with those that study existing documents or texts.

Primary research: interviews, group discussion and ethnography

Primary research involves the collection of new data, usually through interaction with human research subjects. One of the most commonly used qualitative research techniques is semi-structured or in-depth interviews. Interviews tend to be exploratory and qualitative, concentrating on the distinctive features of situations and events, and upon the beliefs and personal experiences of individuals. Interviews provide information on understandings, opinions, what people remember doing, attitudes, feelings and the like. They are used by political scientists to study political behaviour inside and outside political institutions, and are associated particularly with institutionalism, post-positivist behaviouralism, constructivism, interpretivism and feminism. Each of these approaches utilise interview data in different ways. For example, institutionalists may use interviews with political elites, in combination with other case study data such as documentary evidence, to reconstruct a narrative of an event; while post-positivist behaviouralists may focus on a select sample of interviewees to compare and contrast their subjective experiences, such as in the study with Green Party parliamentarians described below.

There is an extensive political science literature on the practice of 'elite' interviewing, that is, interviews with individuals prominent in politics, public service or business, who are activists or commentators in the public sphere (see Burnham et al., 2008; Mosley, 2013). These individuals are often willing to participate in research, although this may be dependent on guaranteed anonymity, and are relatively easy to identify, purposively sample and locate. In contrast, a researcher may be interested in interviewing non-publicly identifiable small populations of people who have specific characteristics of interest to her (perhaps they vote for a new party, are unemployed or engage in protests). In this case, other methods for interview recruitment will be needed, such as advertising, or accessing client or member lists of organisations. Qualitative researchers who interview rarely attempt to make generalisations to a broader population based on the small sub-section or sample they study. Instead, there is an emphasis on the distinctive nature of their sample populations and a detailed criteria-based explanation of purposive (rather than random) sampling used for selecting interviewees.

For a study of the Australian Green Party, I conducted semi-structured, elite interviews with all sixteen sitting Federal and State Green Party parliamentarians (see Vromen and Gauja, 2009). All interviewees were asked similar questions about the internal and democratic processes of their party, and their views on their own legislative roles. The interviews were audio-taped and subsequently transcribed. The transcriptions were coded and analysed using the NVivo qualitative software programme. The theme-based coding in NVivo was based on paragraphs of the transcript and was used to identify where the interviewee spoke about their experiences within Parliament and society and how this related to their approach to representation.

MPs were not assigned to predefined categories based on theoretical conceptions of representation. Rather, they were broadly asked about their political roles and experiences and, on the basis of their responses, their diverse attitudes to representation and parliamentary activity were analysed. In our analysis we attempted to be as transparent as possible in our categorisation of MPs within tables that summarise their approach to representation. As is common with a qualitative approach, we also used many quotes from the interviews to illustrate the thematic categorisations, and to incorporate the voice of the interview subjects (Vromen and Gauja, 2009: 91). This use of theme analysis is based on the idea that codes or themes emerge from studying the interview transcript data holistically, and make it possible to explore the resonance of themes between different interviews. This type of qualitative analysis, in which theoretical ideas (such as 'representation') are explored in data, coded and then further developed based on the data, thus involving a 'to and fro' process between data and theory, is commonly labelled 'grounded theory' and is associated with the theorist Anselm Strauss (see Ezzy, 2002: 86–95). This is not an interpretivist approach to qualitative data analysis, as it tends to focus on looking for patterns and causal links within interview data, something it shares with a positivist approach. Yet a preference for grounded, inductive (rather than deductive) analysis is often now shared by interpretivists (see Grbich, 2007: 80–81).

Political scientists also increasingly use focus groups or group-based discussion as a specialised form of interviewing. Common in the professional worlds of market research and political opinion polling, where qualitative group discussion is used to understand the 'mood' of the electorate, they are a regular feature of background research for election campaigns. The key feature of focus groups is 'explicit use of the group interaction to produce data and insights that would be less accessible without the interaction found in a group' (Van Willigen, 2002: 148). The size and composition of the group are both very important, and about 8–10 participants is most common. Composition particularly needs to be thought of in terms of the research questions and practicalities involved in using this method. So, researchers do not necessarily need a homogeneous group, if what they want to study is debate, but, if they want to understand the formation of shared attitudes and ensure an environment conducive for participants' discussion, they need a group with some commonalities, or a pre-existing affinity group of some kind (see Waller et al., 2016: 97–105). This research technique has also been used to study group processes. In sum, focus groups are useful for providing interactive discussion on a topic that cannot be found through other qualitative information collection approaches such as in-depth interviews or observation.

For example, Marco Antonsich (2008) used focus groups to understand the construction of European identity, as a way of capturing the meanings associated with this particular form of territorial attachment. He identified 'EUropean' attachment in relation to three different notions of Europe: cultural-national; cultural-transnational; and functional-utilitarian (2008: 706). The qualitative information used to explore these meanings was collected in four European regions: Lombardia (Italy); Pirkanmaa (Finland); North-East England (UK); and Languedoc-Roussillon (France). These places were chosen because they reflected different socio-economic, political and geographical conditions. The study used in-depth interviews with both political elites and four focus groups, with 4–5 participants in each, men and women aged between 18 and 26.

Antonsich (2008) explains that his qualitative data was coded utilising an inductive approach, whereby codes were not generated on the basis of an a priori theory, but based upon the observation of recurring patterns. Data analysis, however, was not based on a quantitative, positivist, approach, but 'on (an) "analytic induction" approach which, echoing the grounded theory method, relies on the iterative process of going back and forth between original data and theoretical concepts in order to reach successively more abstract categorizations' (2008: 697).

Antonsich uses quotes from interviews and focus group participants to demonstrate his categorisations. One Italian focus group participant is quoted to demonstrate the cultural-national interpretation of identity:

> Language still remains something which differentiates, in terms of belonging, those who speak your language from those who don't. Then, if a person is able to speak English and to communicate with others, it's ok. However, your language. I mean there is a greater belonging with those who speak your language. (2008: 699)

A sense of identification based upon the idea of a Europe narrated as a functional-utilitarian space, was evident in a response from an English focus group participant:

> Europe to me is it's a bit like the GB, UK thing to me, they're kind of, not so much to do with culture and identity, they're political things, they're to do with money and economy and managing people and

> Europe has recently just incorporated a whole lot of new countries[.] I don't actually feel European, I just want to reap the benefits from being a European citizen. (2008: 704)

By using in-depth qualitative methods and inductive analysis, Antonsich *interprets* his focus groups discussions to show how we can better *understand* the variation in identification with the *idea* of the European Union, rather than seeing it as either a static or a universally experienced concept.

One other primary research technique is worth mentioning here. Ethnography that uses both participant and non-participant observation within 'natural' political and social contexts has, unfortunately, had limited use in political science. Zoe Bray (2008) suggests that this particular imbalance ought to be redressed if we are to understand both macrostructures and stratification processes, such as race and gender, and micro-level processes, such as interactions within organisations and socialisation processes. Ethnographic methods provide an approach to recording and analysing data 'in a flexible fashion' and, importantly, can be used to explore the dynamics and power relationships between people (Bray, 2008: 298).

For example, Rod Rhodes (2002) argued for the usefulness of ethnographic methods in understanding policy networks by making sure all voices are heard, not just those of elites, such as departmental secretaries, but also other actors, such as social workers and service consumers. He suggests that the 'thick description' of ethnographic observation demonstrates how different individuals within the network give it meaning and understand it in quite different ways, through both their actions and what they say in interviews (Rhodes, 2002: 412–413).

Secondary research: using text/document-based techniques

Many political scientists undertake secondary research, rather than primary research, and analyse existing texts as part of their analysis. Most texts are primary source documents produced by political actors, including the executive, parliamentary or judicial arms of governments, policy-making agencies and non-government organisations. Primary sources can also be archival material, such as photos, diaries, meeting notes and memoirs. Strictly speaking, documents that reflect a position of an actor and do not have analysis in them (such as a secondary source like a scholarly journal article) are generally considered to be primary sources. However, there are clear exceptions to this, such as newspaper articles and organisational research reports (for example, a World Bank report), which contain analysis, but can also become the object of text analysis, involving studying the discursive meaning they give to the political context from which they originated.

The qualitative analysis of texts and documentary primary sources involves interpreting social and political meaning from them, that is, using them to 'tell the story' or recreate a historical sequencing of events. This is substantively different from the systematic study of primary texts via quantitative content analysis which looks for patterns and seeks to make generalisations. Consequently, two main traditions of analysing documents and texts within political science are introduced here: the historiography approach; and interpretivist discourse analysis. These approaches are predominantly used within the sub-disciplines of public policy, comparative politics and international relations.

The use of historiography in political science has a substantial lineage through the study of political institutions. It involves the 'writing of history based on a selective, critical reading of sources that synthesises particular bits of information into a narrative description or analysis of a subject' (Thies, 2002: 351). Selecting primary source materials for a historiography is not straightforward as the process tends to prioritise some sources over others, for reasons of accessibility (for example, many government documents are not available for 20–30 years after the event they record) or the researcher's awareness of their existence (for example, researchers may know that a political actor has lodged their personal documents with an archive). This form of 'selection bias' is somewhat inevitable and, instead, Thies suggests that researchers' historical research will be more reputable if they provide more reflective *justification* of their selection of research materials (2002: 356). Certainly, the capacity to identify and analyse primary sources created by official institutions has increased since the creation of online data archives.

Much of the use of historiography within political science is found within the historical institutionalism school, defined as scholars 'specifically interested in explaining real-world outcomes, using history as an analytic tool, and they are strongly interested in the ways in which institutions shaped political outcomes' (Steinmo, 2008: 122). Historical institutionalists locate their explanation of political events, issues and processes in context through their use of historiography. They are less interested in making predictions, but are still committed to positivist (or critical realist) concerns with process-tracing and causality (Steinmo, 2008: 134).

Charles Tilly (2006: 420) wrote that any 'sound explanation of political processes' necessarily involves history as an essential element. However, he also argued that a focus on explanation within historical analyses does not mean a commitment to a teleological (that is, a predetermined) view, but instead encompasses a recognition that all political processes occur within history and thus need knowledge of the historical context, and 'also where and when political processes occur influence *how* they occur'. For example, in his detailed history of social movements, Tilly points out that the means of claim-making, or repertoires of action, available to social movements depend on what has gone before in history. His examples of actions used by 'ordinary people' in Great Britain in the 1750s includes attacks on coercive authorities (for example, resisting police); attacks on popularly designated offenders (for example, collective invasion of land and destroying fences); celebration at both popular or official gatherings (for example, marches using partisan symbols); and workers' sanctions (for example, trade unions marches). These historical antecedents help us to reflect on the means available for movements to make claims on the state in contemporary politics (2006: 426–427). Historical explanations and understandings rely on context, but can also be contingent, developing over time with the collection of more evidence and the advancement of theoretical ideas.

One of the influences of interpretivism on political science, outlined in Chapters 5 and 6, has been in terms of methodology, given the growing use of discourse analysis. Ezzy (2002: 101–109) describes how an interpretive approach locates the interpretation of texts within an analysis of broader social, political and cultural processes. Discourse analysis does not focus on texts alone, but interprets how the data relates to, or is emblematic of, broader social, political and cultural frameworks. Researcher reflexivity helps to 'problematise the politics of the interpretive process, asking from whose perspective, and for whose benefit, the interpretation has been conducted' (Ezzy, 2002: 107). Discourse analysis is concerned with the analysis of language, and offers a qualitative method for 'uncovering some of the ways in which people or groups (or actors or agents as they are often termed in discourse analysis) seek to represent their actions in texts and language' (Jacobs, 2006: 138).

Norman Fairclough is an influential proponent of discourse analysis and his analytical framework is based on:

- The micro concern evident in linguistics. Analysis is centred on vocabulary and structure of texts to look at how alternative usage of words is developed over time. For example, looking for the political meanings and symbolism attached to words such as refugee, asylum seeker, boat people, illegals or migrants. Analysts also focus on discursive practices used in the text, such as rhetoric or irony, to reinforce arguments.
- The meso interpretation of the social production of texts. Social practices are examined in terms of hegemony and power, and how language reflects a broader ideological or political context.
- And, macro analysis associated with social theory (Fairclough and Fairclough, 2012).

Other discourse analysts use social theorist Michel Foucault's framework. He posited that power was developed and exercised though the *control* of knowledge and that powerful interests created, and maintained, particular discourses to minimise any challenge from others also interested in these forms of knowledge (Grbich, 2007: 147). Discourse analysts using this approach start from a similar place to Fairclough's approach, but also look for disunity, discontinuity and limits to discourse, especially in terms of locating and following challenges to dominant discourses (Grbich, 2007: 149).

Lastly, text is not the only data source available for discourse analysts. Increasingly, images, photographs, cartoons and videos are also important sources for understanding the construction of political ideologies and discourses. In a time when photo or meme sharing is common on popular social media platforms, such as Facebook, Twitter and Instagram, there has been a corresponding development of 'small data' analysis of visual images to accompany largely automated big data analysis (see Chapter 18). Visual images need to be understood and interpreted for meaning within the political context in which they are produced. Roland Bleiker (2015) analyses visual images in international relations and argues that they 'frame what can be seen, thought and said. In doing so, they delineate what is and is not politically possible' (2015: 874). Bleiker advocates multilevel analysis of images that includes the production of an image, the image itself and how it is seen by various audiences. He acknowledges that these will often entail different kinds of methods and analysis, often both quantitative, such as content analysis or audience surveys, and qualitative, including semiotic, policy process-tracing and discourse analysis.

Conclusion: the use and future use of qualitative methods in political science

This chapter has introduced some of the major debates on contemporary use and development of qualitative methods in political science. It has suggested that, while qualitative methods remain marginalised by the dominance of quantitative methods within many sub-disciplines, such as comparative politics, there are notable exception such as in the core fields of international relations and public policy, where historical institutionalism and interpretive analyses remain important.

A critical approach to methodological pluralism asks us to consider more deeply the contribution qualitative methods can make to understanding the social and political world, and move beyond the silos associated with the 'two traditions'. It is likely that debate will continue as acceptance of reflexivity processes among researchers, and uses for qualitative methods in political science, will emerge and become accepted into the mainstream. Furthermore, some sub-disciplines will undertake a new and self-conscious exploration of epistemology and methodology with an overall increase in rigorous qualitative approaches. This includes both positivist process-tracing and path dependence analyses, as well as interpretive discourse analysis using texts and images. These contemporary methodological debates will also continue to reinvigorate and develop the key qualitative research techniques of interviewing and historiography.

Further reading

- On designing case studies, see Blatter and Haveland (2012).
- On discourse analysis, see Fairclough and Fairclough (2012).
- For an introduction to qualitative data analysis, see Grbich (2007).
- On interview research, see Layn Mosley (ed) (2013).

Chapter 15

Quantitative Methods

PETER JOHN

The divide between quantitative and qualitative methods remains as wide as ever. Many researchers still tend to use one approach, but not the other. Not only is the divide personal, it often sorts out researchers into topics of study. As a result many academics assume that quantitative investigation only concerns elections, voting systems, party manifestos and political attitudes rather than having a more general application. The division becomes manifest in the descriptors researchers apply to themselves and to others: quantitative researchers are known as political scientists; the rest often have the labels of students of politics, area specialists and public policy scholars. Not only do different topics, skills and networks help create the divide, it is sustained by apparently clashing conceptions of the purpose and practice of social science. Some critics believe that quantitative work is underpinned by a crude version of positivism while qualitative work describes complex realities, acknowledges that researchers cannot separate their values from the political world, engages with and seeks to understand the beliefs and aspirations of those who are being researched and rejects the idea that there are universal laws of human behaviour.

But are the differences really so big? After all, King, Keohane and Verba in their influential book *Designing Social Inquiry* (1994) write that both fields apply a 'unified logic of inference with differences mainly of style and specific technique' (1994: 1) and there are many commentators who say that qualitative and quantitative studies are complementary rather than fundamentally different activities (for example, Box-Steffensmeier et al., 2008). In this chapter, a new tack is tried. Recently, quantitative researchers have rediscovered the field aspect to their studies and have argued that extensive work needs to go into planning research projects and into the collection of data. This aspect of quantitative work has been highlighted by the move to increase research transparency by requiring researchers to register studies, to submit pre-analysis plans, and to ensure the results from the data can be replicated. Such procedures are intended to reduce or make explicit the large amount of discretion researchers have in using quantitative techniques long before the final regression or simulation results have been presented. This attention to detailed planning of the research instruments can be similar to qualitative work in the attention to specification of research questions, the piloting of techniques and the awareness of how the application of research techniques is sensitive to the context of the field. As more quantitative data is now collected by field experiments (see Chapter 17), there is much more emphasis on field techniques and managing relationships with partners, much like a qualitative research project (see John, 2017). In fact, qualitative research has also gone down this path of more detailed recording of the research design and in paying attention to replication (see www.qualtd.net). Both approaches share an interest in getting the details right and in acknowledging that human discretion and the complexity of the social world need to be reported by researchers much more than they have been hitherto.

In this chapter, the basic features of quantitative methods are set out: the characteristics of the data and their measurement; the use of descriptive statistics to review the data; the design of tables to explore relationships; the application of inferential statistics to test those relationships; and the selection of the appropriate multivariate model to understand the complex causes of the phenomena under study. Then recent developments, such as requirements for greater transparency, are reviewed. Overall, the reader will find that quantitative methods do not correspond to the positivist or 'number-crunching' stereotype. As to be expected, quantitative researchers carefully test their hypotheses and make cautious claims in a complex social and political world.

The collection and management of data

Quantitative work rests on the observation and measurement of repeated incidences of a phenomenon, such as voting for a political party, an allocation of resources by a government agency or citizen attitudes towards taxation and public spending. By observing variables over a large number of cases, it is possible to make inferences about a class of behaviour, such as who votes for a political party, which area gets resources from governments and what is the distribution of attitudes to public spending in the adult population. With large numbers, social scientists can confidently make generalisations about the empirical world. Statistical theory shows that the larger the number of cases (or the greater number in proportion to the whole population), the surer data analysts can be that what they observe is not a random occurrence. Moreover, political scientists often want to analyse whole populations, such as the voting record of all Members of Parliament or all electoral systems in the world, which involve large numbers.

Some researchers are suspicious about the way in which quantitative studies generate observations, particularly when measuring attitudes and behaviours, such as opinions drawn from large-scale surveys using standardised questions. These measures appear to ignore social and political contexts (Kirk and Miller, 1986). Even official statistics that government departments produce can reflect political decisions about what kinds of data to collect. In the end, official information is what politicians and bureaucrats wish to make public. Some techniques, such as content analysis (the classification and counting of data drawn from the texts of media or political debates), appear to strip out the context of the language and render it meaningless or sterile. Quantitative researchers appear to be blind to the relationship between the observer and the observed, which makes each act of collecting data unique. Critics claim that quantitative researchers ignore the complexity of the world in their quest to turn politics into a series of repeated and identical experiences or events (Ragin, 2000).

But the practice of quantitative research does not conform to this stereotype. Quantitative researchers are usually fully aware that complex social realities may not always be captured by repeated observations. In certain situations, quantification may not be appropriate, as what is being measured could be made either meaningless or biased. Researchers usually take a lot of care to find out whether measures are valid or not. For example, survey research that depends on standardised questions may not be replicated across countries because of differences in cultures and languages. In the qualitative prelude to most surveys and in pilots, questions are bandied about, interviewers evaluate interviews and respondents fill in an additional questionnaire about their experience of completing questions. Survey researchers have frequent discussions about the effect of question wording and order on the responses to their questions. Quantitative researchers pay a lot of attention to reliability (that data are produced independently of the activity of measurement) and seek to improve it where possible. Content analysis researchers, who seek to extract key terms from documents like newspapers, use intercoder reliability scores to find out whether two different researchers coded an item in the same way (Krippendorff, 1980: 129–154). Such problems do not just occur in surveys and the analysis of texts. Statisticians who use data from government departments frequently investigate how the data are collected. They consider the possible biases in the results and think of ways to correct for them. There is even discussion about the extent to which research instruments, such as survey questions, reflect biases within social science, such as in favour of class-based explanations in voting behaviour (Catt, 1996: 67–69, 92).

Quantitative researchers spend much time and effort thinking about their data. Choosing data or sampling appears an easy task but it contains many hidden pitfalls. The sample must allow the investigator to make inferences, but often it is not clear what constitutes the population. If the topic of study is about change over time, which years should the researcher choose to analyse? Surveys pose many dilemmas, such as how to define a household. Surveys may need to be re-weighted so they are more like a representative sample (Skinner et al., 1989). There are also choices about how to measure variables. No perfect dataset exists; for example, response rates to surveys may be low and archives may contain missing years. Although the electronic storage of data gives the impression of permanence, and has massively improved due to the expansion of the internet, files sometimes become corrupted and data get lost.

The collection and manipulation of data invite errors. Interviewers, research assistants or survey companies sometimes input responses to questionnaires incorrectly; researchers accidentally delete cases and variables; the transfer of files between software packages and across the internet can create dirt in the data; and researchers can even accidentally work on the wrong or old dataset because they did not label it correctly. They may even forget how they created their variables because they did not note what they did at each stage or failed to save the statistical command file correctly. One of the problems is that the speed and efficiency of modern computers encourage researchers to believe that their data are clean. But most political scientists learn to be careful after making silly errors when their concentration lapses. As mistakes are so easy to make, researchers spend a large amount of their time carefully collecting data, checking and rechecking how they or research assistants entered the information. Even with this culture of paranoia, minor mistakes still occur in published work, sometimes in the best quality journals (for example, see the correction by Gerber and Green, 2005).

Data collection and management require attention to practical issues and to theory about what are the best data for the study. No solution is ideal, but researchers pick up practical knowledge about how to solve these problems and learn about the pitfalls of particular choices. A few words typed into an internet search engine can produce all sorts of useful information, much of it posted by political methodologists in helpful pdf summaries.

The power of description

One of the advantages of descriptive measures is that they allow the observer to split the observations and to examine the proportions, such as the percentage of a group who support a political party. Judgements about these proportions form an essential part of the interpretation of data. In journalism and other forms of commentary, there are debates about whether a percentage is too big or too small, and descriptive political science is no exception. Consider an imaginary statistic showing that 5 per cent of the electorate believes in repatriation. Commentators can interpret it as evidence either of alarming racism or of tolerance of the bulk of the population. To resolve this dilemma, social scientists would place the statistic in its proper context, taking into account arguments about what defines a liberal society and existing empirical knowledge. The interpretation of the 5 per cent would differ with the additional information that, for example, 10 per cent of the population believed in it twenty years previously.

Summary statistics are useful to understand the data, such as measures of central points so that researchers can know the average or typical point for a variable. The most common is the mean or average, but there is also the median (middle observation) and mode (the most frequent value). As important are measures of dispersion. Observers find it useful to know whether the observations converge on the average value or are widely distributed. For example, if the interest is in response times of fire brigades in different locations, researchers and residents may be interested in finding out which area has the lowest average response time. But they should also be interested in the dispersion around the average, as residents would like to know how likely the fire engines arrive close to the mean time. As with central points, there are several measures, such as the interquartile range (the distance between the upper and lower quartiles) and the standard deviation (the square root of the variance). When deciding which measure to use, researchers need to think carefully about their data and decide whether it is nominal (with categories that are just different to each other, for example male or female), ordinal (with measures that involve ranking) or ratio/interval (with values that have equal intervals between categories). Investigators may wish to look at the shape of the distribution, such as whether it is unimodal (spread evenly around one point) or bimodal or multimodal (having a number of peaks), which can inform much about what the data reveal. Alternatively, the data may be skewed or symmetrical, leptokurtic (bunched around the mean) or normal. The normal is particularly interesting because it shows the distribution is random.

When technical terms appear, like the ones in the paragraph above, some students start to think that quantitative topics are not for them. But often they merely formalise what people do in everyday life. Imagine a person walking into a room full of people. The person would immediately size up the gathering by asking how many people are there, how many are of a certain type or how many people old or young people there are. When coming to these judgements, people make approximate proportions, averages and distributions. Descriptive statistics standardise these common-sense ideas (or common-sense ideas make sense of the statistics). Moreover, such statistics appear regularly in newspapers and in qualitative research.

Paradoxically, quantitative researchers do not use descriptive statistics enough, often only reporting them as the prelude to applying sophisticated tests and models. But much can be gained by their careful and imaginative use. To obtain the best results, quantitative researchers must first immerse themselves in their data and explore the myriad of possible ways of cutting and representing the information. Familiarity with descriptive measures assists an understanding of the topic and can help researchers interpret output from more complex statistical models. Much can be gained by representing descriptive data visually in the form of bar charts, pies and plots – most software packages easily provide these. In short, quantitative researchers should be as intimate with their research materials as their qualitative colleagues. As Jenkins writes: 'The statistician should fall in love with her data' (cited by Franzosi, 1994: 45).

Tables and inferential statistics

Social scientists often want to infer or deduce models of causation that they wish to test. Such models often hypothesise a strong relationship between two variables (either positive or negative). Social scientists assume that the values of one variable cause or influence variation in another. The explaining terms are called independent variables and what is being explained is known as the dependent variable. For example, consider a project on what causes people to volunteer, which is an important topic in the literature on social capital (see, for example, Verba et al., 1995). Theory – in the form of the social-economic status (SES) model of political behaviour – may suggest that those from wealthy families are more likely to join organisations. This suggests researchers should collect observations of the variables of wealth and social capital for a sample of individuals to see if the former leads to the latter.

One of the simplest ways to find out if one variable determines or is associated with another is a table or cross-tabulation. A table shows how the values or categories of one variable are expressed as the categories of another. Researchers frequently use tables in survey research, tasks that were carried out in the period before modern computing – if in a time-consuming way as records had to be stored manually. With the volunteering project, researchers would have sorted all the records or cards containing the records of the interviews into the piles of wealthy volunteers, non-wealthy volunteers, wealthy non-volunteer and non-wealthy non-volunteers. Then they would have counted the numbers of observations in each category, worked out their percentages as a proportion of each variable and represented the results in a two-by-two table. A table is usually titled as follows: 'Table N: dependent variable by independent variable'; or in the example, 'Table N: Volunteering by Wealth'. If the tables are set up to display column percentages, with totals of 100 per cent at the bottom of the table, the dependent variable (volunteering) is shown in the rows with the columns displaying the independent variable (wealth). The researcher can compare the proportion of the independent variable taken up by the dependent variable, the numbers of wealthy and non-wealthy people who volunteer – the eye can look across the table to compare the proportion of volunteers in the wealthy and non-wealthy groups. But it is just as respectable for the independent variables to be the column and to compare row percentages. In the end, whichever way round are the columns and rows, the analyst learns to read the table by comparing the amount of influence the independent variable has on the response or dependent term. It is best also to include the total number of observations for each row or column so the reader can see whether cases are being lost through missing cases and get a sense of the size of each group.

Now that the records of surveys can be stored as data matrixes in software packages, such as Stata 14.2 (StataCorp, 2015) or in free open-source software, such as R (R Development Core Team, 2014), researchers can create such a table in seconds. But their construction is surprisingly tricky. Often variables need to be re-coded, such as by transforming the individual ages of respondents into bands of age groups. Working out which measure to use requires knowledge of the data and attention to theory to select the appropriate units. There is an art of creating a table that is attractive to look at and is formatted professionally. Researchers should not paste across the output from a software package as the result is terrible to look at and is often hard to understand. Statistical software packages often have the facility to export the table into Microsoft Word or LaTeX in a professionally acceptable format with all notes included in the table output, which can be inserted into the research paper. Even with this level of automation, report or paper writers need to spend time ensuring all the required information is present, such as the totals (Ns) of each column or row. Clear labelling of the labels of the variables helps the reader and shortened computer-generated names should not be used (for example, Labour Party Identifier as opposed to labpartyid). Rounding up the percentages to a number or to one decimal place also helps.

Researchers who use tables from surveys also need to run tests to show that the associations could not have happened just by chance. Statisticians conventionally argue that researchers should have 95 per cent confidence that the association is not random. The 95 per cent confidence level is convenient because it is just under two standard deviations (typical deviations) from the mean or average level. Survey researchers could calculate the probability of the association being non-random by hand, using a formula; but most computer packages routinely produce this figure. If the figure were 0.04, for example, researchers would believe that the association had not occurred by chance. But the ease with which computers can implement these tests makes researchers forget to examine the strength of the associations, which show how much one variable affects another. In large samples, such as those in excess of 4,000 respondents, it is easy to find statistically significant but meaningless or imperceptible relationships. Researchers should also not forget to take note of the sign of the association, whether positive or negative, and whether it corresponds with the expectations of the model or theory.

One common objection to testing hypotheses from using correlations presented in tables is that they do not establish causation but only show associations. They have no way of knowing whether the relationships they observe in their data are accidental, spurious or causal. Theory comes to the aid of the social scientist because a relationship between two variables needs to be logical and consistent as well as following from existing empirical studies. The association between wealth and volunteering is not a correlation found by what is called dredging the data, but derives from sociological theory that argues that as some people have more resources and advantages than others so they are more able to engage with public life. The relationship is logical in the sense that social background can affect volunteering. Logically it would not be possible for volunteering to affect social background (at least in one generation).

Such research can only test whether background affects voluntary activity or not, but not the other way round. It is plausible because investigators compare the SES with other models, such as the rational choice model of participation or models that emphasise contextual factors, such as friendship networks or the neighbourhood. As always, theory should specify the direction of the causal arrow, but as long as the independent variable is genuinely thought to be prior to the dependent variables and where each independent variable is independent from each other, it is possible to make an inference.

When researchers appraise hypotheses they are not satisfied with just observing relationships in the data. To support their case they would look for other relationships to make a set of plausible arguments. They might be interested in change over time; they could run multivariate models as indicated below. Rarely do quantitative researchers claim that an association in the data proves causation (unless it is from an experiment or similar technique), but that correlation has importance only when applied by theory and used alongside other evidence.

Multivariate analysis

The social and political worlds are multi-causal, which makes it hard to identify one specific relationship. For example, there may be no relationship between wealth and volunteering because wealthy volunteers tended to go to schools that encouraged voluntary activity. The causal relationship between schooling and volunteering makes the correlation between wealth and volunteering spurious because wealthy people go to a certain type of school that also produces volunteering as well as good examination results. It may be entirely possible for poor people to have as high a level of volunteering as rich people if they had been to a school that encouraged it. How is it possible to know how much each one influences the response variable? Sometimes it is possible to overcome this problem by using multiple regression to examine all the determinants. This technique allows a test to determine whether other factors than wealth affect voluntary activity. Researchers do not aim to show that X causes Y, but that X causes Y alongside or allowing for or controlling for Z and W. Analysts become more confident of testing hypotheses because they have allowed for all the possible causes of behaviour or attitudes. They can run one model against another and carry out robust tests of each one. However, multivariate analysis carries more risks than descriptive statistics because the regression models that social scientists commonly use make restrictive assumptions about the data.

The most common multivariate model is ordinary least squares (OLS). The intuitive idea is that a plot of the points between two interval variables, X and Y, may contain a relationship. It may be possible to plot a line that minimises the distance between it and the data points. It is then fairly easy to see the relationship in data by moving the eye along the bunch of data points in the scatter plot of X and Y. This line would have a gradient or slope that indicates the constant relationship between the two variables. Rather than eyeballing the data, OLS uses a formula to estimate the slope of the line from the mean or average value of the independent variable and from the data points. In addition, OLS estimates the distances between the regression line and the data points, what are called the residuals or errors. OLS calculates the overall explanatory power of the model offers which is a statistic, the R-square, which falls between 0 and 1. The same mathematics governs models with more than one independent term. This neat extension allows the estimation of the effects of each of the independent terms upon the dependent variable. OLS allows researchers to test hypotheses in the knowledge that they are controlling for all the known hypothesised effects and that these are independent of each other.

Because OLS assumes the data are a sample from the population of possible data points, everything that the model does not explain is random. For each variable there is a standard error or measure of spread that indicates the probability that the relationship between the independent and dependent variable is there by chance or not. Political scientists have been happy to run hypothesis tests based on the 95 per cent confidence level. If the probability is equal or greater than 95 per cent, researchers accept that an independent variable has an effect on the dependent one; if it is less, then they reject the hypothesis that there is a statistically significant relationship. The procedure easily tests models that derive from social science theory.

The other advantage of OLS is that it is standard; it is very comprehensible across political science, indeed most of social science. Most political scientists know how to read an OLS table or output as they can look at a column of coefficients and see if an effect is big or not (either by comparing standardised measures or thinking about the units of measurement). They will also know that they can divide the coefficient by the standard error to create a *t*-statistic, which they remember must equal or exceed 1.96 to meet the standard 5 per cent probability test. Most tables display stars next to the coefficients, which people often glance at when looking for the statistically significant relationships. The eye is naturally drawn to a star and can conclude that one star is good at 0.05 probability, two stars are better at 0.01 and three stars even better at 0.001, though most are satisfied with .05 or just under. They can also look at the R-square statistic to see if it is big or not. This knowledge can allow non-technical researchers to know a little about what is going on rather than skipping the middle sections of quantitative papers.

For the bulk of the second half of the twentieth century the OLS model held sway, particularly as it was taught as the central component of most political science methods courses. In spite of its ease of comprehension, OLS has disadvantages. It is worth recalling that the model depends on ten assumptions that are frequently breached in most contexts. For example, one assumption is that the variables are constant and linear over time and space (Wood, 2000). Also, in many research situations the number of cases is too small, for example with studies that use the developed or OECD countries as the units of analysis.

In recent years, political scientists have moved away from OLS, partly because they know more about the properties of the variables they wish to explain. Some variables may be dichotomous, so requiring a logit or a probit model; other variables may be ordered rather than interval, which would require an ordered logit or ordered probit model; other variables may be censored, with a cut-off point at one or both ends of the distribution, requiring a censored or tobit model; and other data may be count or event data, like wars, requiring a Poisson model. Just as OLS was standard fare for a previous generation of political scientists, these different estimators are now part of a familiar menu of choices for today's, easily implemented by commands in most software packages or in an R package that can be downloaded. Most regression output has the same format to OLS, so it is possible to read them in the same way, transposing the R-coefficient to another measure of fit and searching out for the ubiquitous stars. Another change is that statistical theory and its applications have advanced massively in recent years. This means it is possible to estimate relationships with different statistical assumptions (see Box 15.1 on non-parametric estimation). Simulation-based approaches have now become common, which can manipulate various assumptions behind the data and model.

Along with the increase in the range of models, standards of reporting in political science have improved and most articles in good journals convey at least some of the vast range of diagnostic statistics, rather than just R-squares and probability values. This caution is wise as King (1986) shows that the R-square statistic can be misleading, making 'macho' comparisons of its size rather meaningless. For example, the R-square can increase by including more variables in the model rather

Box 15.1 Non-parametric models

Monte Carlo simulation allows the investigator to estimate a variable and to make inferences to the population. It needs vast amounts of computer memory to generate data from an artificially created population that resembles the process being investigated. Then the researcher estimates a statistical model from this population and assesses its performance. Political scientists use bootstrapping models that are similar to Monte Carlo simulation and relax the restrictive assumptions of the OLS model (Mooney and Duval, 1993; Mooney, 1996; Mooney and Krause, 1997), arguing that the OLS model only developed because of the limitations of computational capacity and now the microchip revolution makes other forms of estimation possible. Bootstrapped estimators are available on statistical packages, such as Stata, and articles in journals now appear with reports of both OLS and bootstrapped estimates.

than because of any real improvement in explanation. Similarly, stepwise regression has now fallen into disuse. Stepwise is a facility available in some of the more popular software programmes, such as SPSS, which allows the researchers to select their variables by automatically discounting non-significant terms or including significant ones in each equation.

The current wave of reforms could go further as there is a range of tests that researchers can apply to the interior of their regression models (Franzosi, 1994). For example, it is common that one case in a model can cause a variable to be significant, and researchers need to find out why this is (sometimes it is caused by a data entry error). There are tests of the contribution each case makes to the final model, which help the researcher to understand what is going on inside the model. Moreover, political scientists could consider abandoning some long-held conventions that do not have a scientific justification. The most sacred is the 0.05 and 0.01 significance tests (respectively 95 and 99 per cent confidence levels) that can lead researchers to reject or accept a hypothesis because the probability exceeds or does not reach the required level only by small margin. But there is no theoretical reason why these rules should exist. Tanenbaum and Scarbrough (1998: 15) remind us they derived from the period before computers automatically calculated the probability values and researchers had to look up the values in printed tables, which had limited space so they summarised cut-off points. Now that no one uses tables researchers should be forbidden from adding asterisks to the variables in models they publish to indicate that a variable has passed a significance test. They should only report the standard errors and the probability levels and discuss them in the text. Such a practice would not be so satisfying for the researcher, but it would lessen the file drawer problem and lead to a more balanced and nuanced discussion of the research. Psychologists have already conceived of life beyond significance tests (Harlow and Mulaik, 1997), with one journal *Basic and Applied Social Psychology* banning *p*-values from its submissions. And a discussion has begun in political science (Gill, 1999). Along with analysis plans and the replication standard, such a practice would reduce the incentive for researchers to massage their results; but at the same time it would not interfere with the inspirational and creative aspects of quantitative work.

Finally, the leading political methodologists argue that researchers should make efforts to present their data more effectively so the ordinary reader can understand how the research shows the relationships between the variables of interest (King et al., 2000). There is a danger that too much output and reporting of statistics can be off-putting to the reader and even obscure results. As a result, the graphing of predicted values or probabilities from a regression show in a simple and attractive way the influence of a variable on another controlling for other factors in the regression model. Although they were always possible to implement, software routines make this much easier, such as Gary King's 'Clarify' programme, which uses simulation (http://gking.harvard.edu/clarify/docs/clarify.html).

Although the multiple regression model is still the workhorse of empirical political science, it is worth knowing that the structure of causal relationships may be more complex than it often implies. For example, the existence of marginal Westminster seats causes governments to direct public resources to them (Ward and John, 1999), but the receipt of those resources will affect which areas are going to be marginal seats in the following election. Over time, how can a researcher know what level of resources it takes to win marginal seats? This is the problem of endogeneity or selection. It can be partly overcome by more sophisticated use of statistics, such as two-stage models or selection models (Heckman, 1979). These models depend on restrictive assumptions, such as finding a perfect variable with which to instrument the data, something that rarely occurs. Structural equation models (SEMs) (Schumacker and Lomax, 1996; Maruyama, 1998) available in software packages, such as LISREL, MPLUS and AMOS, can estimate more complicated sets of relationships when there are many measures of the same underlying concept. But the analyst should be careful; more complex statistics cannot cover up the difficulty of specifying a causal relationship. Sometimes it is better to be modest in describing the data rather than make too many claims about the direction of causation.

In recent years there has a greater interest in using experiments to make causal claims (see Chapter 17). With randomisation and the allocation of subjects to treatment and control arms researchers can safely make a causal inference that the intervention variable caused the variation in the outcome variable. This procedure relies on a set of assumptions being met and researchers use the language of potential outcomes to examine if the assumptions have been met or breached (see Gerber and Green, 2012). This is called causal inference, taking inspiration from classic studies in statistics. In observational research, it has become important to see how far the research design departs from the experimental ideal and whether the model is capable of making a causal inference (identification).

Testing and reporting models

When non-specialists read quantitative articles they may come away with the impression that political scientists only tested a single model that derived from theory. But even with a small number of independent variables, there are many choices about which ones to exclude or include in the final equation. These choices should be driven by theory, but sometimes theory provides arguments and counterarguments for a number of models. For example, researchers could include all or some of the independent variables in the final model irrespective of whether they reach the 95 per cent confidence level or not. Alternatively, they could include only those variables that reach the required significance level. Moreover, the number of choices increases if researchers include interactions.

These are terms created by multiplying two variables to indicate a joint impact on the dependent variable and they may be included along with the original independent terms (Friedrich, 1982). In many situations, it does not matter which model is used as all of them show broadly the same strength of relationships and levels of probability. But competing models can show the hypothesised variables to be statistically significant and sometimes not. Moreover, the profusion of new techniques of estimation means that researchers face many choices over the estimator. Then there are different ways in which the data may be estimated, such as whether to have clustered or robust standard errors, which can affect the statistical significance of a variable. Or it can be a multilevel model to take account of the different levels in the data, so the individual's behaviour or values is affected by his or her individual characteristics, but also by the community or other spatial context in which he or she is located or nested.

Researchers may be tempted to present the model that shows the hypothesised variable to be outside the 95 per cent confidence level. With the speed of current computers and the easy manipulation of software packages, modellers can engage in the much-despised practice of significance hunting or fishing, which can involve running many hundreds of equations until the preferred one emerges. Because journal editors cannot require researchers to report every model they run, it is hard to detect this practice. Gerber and Malhotra (2006) show that reported papers in political science journals cluster just over the 0.05 probability level at the same time as they show a gap on the non-significant side of this cut, something that should not be expected in the real world. Basically, political scientists select and present results that meet the arbitrary cut-off point and reject models that do not.

The incentive to present the most favourable model exists because until recently few journals publish papers containing negative results. Most journal editors and reviewers find these papers to be less interesting and less publishable than those that reach positive conclusions; alternatively, there is self-selection at work whereby researchers only send off papers to journals when they have positive results. The alternative explanation is that political scientists choose to carry out, and research councils usually fund, research projects that are likely to yield new findings. In the natural sciences the bias has been studied and is called the file drawer problem (Rosenthal, 1979; Rotton et al., 1995; Csada et al., 1996; Bradley and Gupta, 1997).

To deal with the problem of model specification, King (1995) campaigned for a standard of replication, whereby any person may repeat other scholars' work using the same dataset and coding of the variables. Such a standard has now been adopted by the main US journals. The ability to replicate not only guards against the false presentation of data, which is anyways rare, but it ensures that researchers carefully check their data for mistakes. Replication encourages researchers to consider the steps towards the presentations of their final results and to check the health of their models, such as for breaches of the assumptions of OLS. Many journals require authors of accepted papers to deposit their replication files on the journal's website or a recognised repository, such as Dataverse (http://dataverse.org).

Recently, there has been a statement on Data Access and Research Transparency (DA-RT) which has been signed by leading journal editors (see Elman and Lupia, 2015, www.dartstatement.org) that calls for a common standard of replication and reporting. It aims to: 'Require authors to ensure that cited data are available at the time of publication through a trusted digital repository.' The agreement sets a standard for the release of data, normally one year after it has been collected, to allow researchers to analyse their own data before other researchers have a chance to look at it too. DA-RT has been backed up and approved by the world's largest political science association, the American Political Science Association. Controversially, the statement extends such considerations to qualitative researchers. Twenty-seven political science journals editors have signed the agreement.

A further development to deal with researcher discretion has been to call for greater transparency and accountability in the research process (see Humphreys et al., 2013). Transparency may be aided by the advance publication of a pre-analysis plan, which is a document where the researcher commits to a scheme of data analysis in advance of getting the data. This is designed as a self-denying ordinance to incentivise researchers to keep to what they promised rather than to select good results from their data. Even though it can be hard to keep to these plans, because of new issues with the data and an occasional opportunity emerges which was not there at the start, they are a record about what the researchers intended to do and then readers of the final article can see how they have departed from their original plans. This information could be posted on the researcher's website, along with the original data and the programme code or Stata 'do' file, so that those who are interested can see how the researchers got their results and allow them to analyse the data to generate their own, which would be much less cumbersome than downloading it from a data archive. When authors submit their papers to academic journals, they might in future also send their original analysis plans, data and command files for the reviewers to see. They could also compose a note of how they implemented their plans so the journal's reviewers may re-run the data to see if minor changes to the commands change the results or whether there are alternative specifications.

The other recent trend, which comes from the experimental community, is for registering the data in an online repository. These facilities are becoming increasingly common, so political science experimenters, especially within the developing country context, use the Evidence in Governance and Politics (EGAP) registry http://egap.org/content/registration. In economics, there is the American Economics Association registry www.aeaweb.org/journals/policies/rct-registry focused on trials. What the researcher has to do is to fill out an online form, which summarises the study, the sample size and group, and says what is going to happen during the research and what estimator is to be used. Key is the specification of hypotheses, which is about which variable is expected to cause the change in the response variable and at what level of statistical significance. Very important is the listing of the hypotheses from the interaction terms as these can be large in number and this forces the research to pre-commit to a few key ones (rather than dredge all possible combination of variables). Researchers can also upload the pre-analysis plan which sets out the study design in more detail, which may specify the equations to be used and what sample size calculations or power analysis have been carried out. In some cases, researchers may wish to set out their code to analyse the data with the expectation that once the data arrive all the researcher has to do is press a button in the software or enter one command and the data are analysed and output created (it is rarely that easy).

For a while now, it has been thought that registration and pre-analysis plans are only for randomised experiments, which replicate practice in the medical and health fields; but advocates of registration point out that the case is just as strong for observational research (Humphreys et al., 2013). In fact, it is possible to say that the case is more compelling for observational research as it is usually very clear in experiments that the hypotheses follow from the treatment design, whereas observational research can take many courses that follow from the structure and extent of the data, such as data from official sources which can be added to, or survey responses with many questions, which also has the ability to match observational data to.

Recent developments

Political methodology is a fast-moving field, which is responding to new statistical work, recent applications (as illustrated by new R packages) and developments in econometrics. It is not possible to do justice to these in the space here. Some are simply listed with some references or web links for interested readers to follow up:

- *New forms of content analysis*: Software and analytic developments have produced a cottage industry of different programmes and methods to collect text-based data. Particularly influential has been Wordscores, developed by Ken Benoit, which is suitable for coding left–right scores (http://wordscores.com/). One that does not have so many assumptions built in is Yoshikoder (www.yoshikoder.org/). Another approach to content analysis is to code crowdsourced data (Benoit et al., 2016).
- *Advances in panel data analysis*: Panel data is where there are repeated observations of a cross-section, which are particularly useful in political science which wishes to compare changes across countries and other large units. The main impetus and source of innovation is from

economics (for example, Arellano, 2003). The main use is in the study of comparative politics (Plümper et al., 2005).

- *Increasing use of Bayesian statistics*: Bayesian models use an updating model of human behaviour, which generates a more flexible approach to estimation, which acknowledges the bounded nature of human behaviour (Gill, 2007).
- *Field experimental methods*: There is a growing band of political scientists who have been carrying out the real-world experiments on topics such as voting behaviour, deliberation, political participation, collective action and media impacts (see Chapter 17, Gerber and Green, 2012; John, 2017). Field experiments have necessitated a new range of techniques to correct estimates when there is attrition and non-compliance with the treatment.
- *Natural experiments*: This is where a feature of the political world resembles an experiment, such as an accidental division of the population in two differently treated groups, such from a cut-off point or boundary (Dunning, 2012).
- *Renewed interest in quasi-experiments*, which seek to look at different features of the data to gain leverage or use a technique called matching to select cases that are very similar to each other bar that one has the causal variable of interest (see review by Sekhon, 2008).
- *More sophisticated design of survey experiments*: Using surveys to test for framing, for example, have become more sophisticated, such as by using conjoint experiments that can test how respondents choose between many alternatives (see Hainmueller et al., 2015).
- *Spatial models:* Politics varies across space and what happens in one place may affect what happens elsewhere. Spatial econometrics seeks to model these processes. Their application to political science has been modest, but important in international political economy (Ward and Gleditsch, 2008; Darmofal, 2009).
- *Big data*: The recent explosion of big data creates large opportunities for political science (Grimmer, 2015), but there are challenges in applying statistical techniques on large samples. For quantitative analysis there is the problem of collecting, storing and analysing such large tranches of data which need advanced computers; and conventional statistical theory relies on samples rather than large populations which requires new techniques (see Chapter 18).

Conclusion

As is to be expected in an introduction of this kind, a lot of ground must be covered fairly rapidly. The interested reader should now look at longer treatments as indicated in the Bibliography and 'Further reading' section. However, the hope is that enough of the basics have been conveyed so as to give a good impression of the characteristics of quantitative analysis, such as the nature of the data and how it is collected, the use of descriptive statistics, and to examining and testing relationships in the data. Then, through examining recent estimators and new sources of data, the reader can get an impression of the vitality and diversity of the field, whose techniques can be used to study almost any phenomenon, not the parties and voting outcomes of yesteryear's choice of topics. Today's quantitative researchers cover subjects as diverse as civil wars, environmental outcomes, legislative speeches over a hundred years, spending decisions and lobbying. They use a variety of techniques to resolve problems they face. The reader should get an idea of the cautious and problem-solving way in which quantitative researchers carry out their studies.

Most quantitative researchers resist the labels that some attach to them, such as positivist or being methods-centred rather than problem-centred or just mindless number crunchers. Key is the importance of the theory, and then to find the right context to evaluate the research question, with sensitivity to questions of internal and external validity. Such concerns are growing these days, with much more focus on research planning and detailing the precise instruments and forms of measures to be deployed. Quantitative researchers have the skills and resources needed to answer the key questions of contemporary politics.

Further reading

- A textbook for beginners in statistics is Wonnacott and Wonnacott (1990).
- *How to Lie With Statistics* (Huff, 1991).
- For introductions to quantitative methods in political science, see Miller's (1995) chapter in the first edition of *Theory and Methods in Political Science*; the classic book by Tufte (1974).
- More advanced readers could *The Oxford Handbook on Political Methodology* (2008), edited by Janet Box-Steffensmeier, Henry Brady, and David Collier.
- Econometrics books are essential for going beyond the basics: e.g. Gujarati (2003), then Greene (2007).

Chapter 16

The Comparative Method

MATT RYAN

Introduction

Plenty of political scientists will say that one of the ways – or perhaps *the* way they study politics is by using the comparative method. You may hear some distinguish their work by saying that that they are 'comparativists', or that they work in the subfield of 'comparative politics'. What do they mean? There is no such thing as a research method that is not comparative. As Swanson nicely puts it, 'thinking without comparison is unthinkable' (cited in Ragin, 1987: 1). Every thought or action we come across is understood with reference to previously acquired information, thoughts and experiences. Why then do political scientists talk about a distinctive comparative method?

This chapter answers that question by first explaining the historical development of comparison in the study of politics. I then present 'Mill's methods' and update them by drawing a lineage to current developments in case-based/set-theoretic methods, providing examples along the way. The chapter focuses on important debates about how cases are chosen for comparison and discusses critiques of comparativists' research strategies. I discuss how recent evolutions in methods and approaches in the discipline pose difficulties for proponents of a distinctly valuable comparative method. I argue, nevertheless, that the strategic expertise of a good comparativist is witnessed in their sensitivity to the implications of trade-offs among different sampling strategies for explaining and predicting politics. Good comparativists know how to identify and exploit opportunities for reasoning from the comparison of attributes in particular cases. Understanding the logic and purpose of comparison is paramount for those who engage in political science because comparison is not just a method, but it is the fundamental process by which any branch of academic scholarship develops and consolidates itself.

Comparative politics and comparative method – politics beyond the armchair?

The comparative method is as much about what political scientists study as it is about how they study it. Impulsive parents have been known to give their children unfortunate names and this might well be true of the founders of 'comparative politics'. The moniker of comparative politics emerged in the discipline of political science to designate that category of research that was not primarily concerned with either normative political theory or international relations. The legacy of this move is one source of confusion. Both conceptual and normative analysis imply comparison and often employ comparison explicitly, for example in the form of considering counterfactuals in thought experiments. Nevertheless, early proponents of a distinctive comparative method saw themselves to be moving the discipline beyond armchair theorising by deliberately observing the world outside their own narrow experiences; strategically collecting information; and describing empirical realities in different political contexts (Blondel, 1999).

Almost without exception, the principal approach to political analysis in the early twentieth century involved understanding and describing politics, political institutions and administrative laws in one's own polity (usually a Western nation state). Such descriptions might be interrupted by cross-national comparisons in the form of analogical cameos or the consideration of a state or state institutions in relation to an ideal type thereof, but that was about as good as it seemed to get. Moving beyond this default approach meant gathering more comprehensive evidence on polities outside that of one's own in a more comprehensive and systematic way. Comparison in the context of political science then became associated with aiming to understand what meaningfully marks different political systems and their devices of governance apart. Early comparativists concerned themselves with identifying the key institutions, and later key actors and groups, which affected political outcomes in other countries. This meant that in-depth case studies of one or a handful of underdescribed countries became a staple of the comparative method. Comparativist is to this day synonymous in some parts of the discipline with country-expert, or is used to describe those engaged in area studies which focus on comparisons of a relatively small number of cases in a particular geographic region. There are many established and respected area studies journals, and case studies are still a staple of leading comparative politics journals. Some accounts of the comparative method draw sharp distinctions between comparative and case study research, but this distinction while sometimes useful can be another source of confusion which I hope to overcome in this chapter.

Comparative method and the scientific method – why small-N research strategies?

The 1950s and 1960s saw an increasing number of studies which set out to systematically compare two, a handful, or even more states, regions or individuals. Examples include Lipset's *Political Man* (1963

[1960]) employing aspects of cross-case comparison to understand the relationship between economic development and democratic stability, as well as Almond and Verba's *The Civic Culture* (1963), which asked how democracy is related to differences in political and social attitudes across countries. Many of these works were to be considered classics and their contributions to theories of politics endure. These studies took advantage of what became known as the behavioural revolution. As described in other chapters, the discovery of mass survey techniques had a profound impact on the discipline, allowing the study of large amounts of individual-level data in particular – that is, measuring citizen's attitudes, beliefs and behaviours. Advances in statistical analysis allowed for ever more sophisticated controlled comparison and inference from relatively large samples of cases to the population level, allowing better judgements on the evidence for alternate explanations of political behaviour.

For some the behavioural revolution marks the coming of age of a political *science*. We study politics so that we can better understand and explain political outcomes. One important way of explaining an outcome is to identify causation. But we cannot observe causal effects directly. If we wanted to directly observe causation of one condition by another we would have to somehow step outside our current world, rewind time and run the world again with the condition removed, or find a parallel universe without the condition and be able to watch both universes at the same time, to see whether the outcome still occurred or not in both cases. Ambitious students of politics are welcome to try this procedure and if they manage to succeed they may be invited to write a chapter in any subsequent edition of this book. Until then, this inability to directly observe each potential outcome in common presents the fundamental problem of causal inference (Holland, 1986). So what is a political scientist to do?

As explained in Chapter 17 experiments in the form of randomised control trials provide an imperfect but enabling substitute for the procedure for observing causes outlined above. Similarly, discoveries in statistical theory allowed the manipulation of data covering a large number of individual records to mimic the experimental method favoured by many natural scientists. First published in 1970, Arendt Lijphart's 'Comparative Politics and the Comparative Method' has become a seminal article describing the place of the comparative method within modern political science after the behavioural revolution. It is within this context that Lijphart distinguishes 'the comparative method' from experimental and statistical methods. The comparative method he wrote 'is not the equivalent of the experimental method but only a very imperfect substitute … awareness of the limitations of the comparative method is necessary but need not be disabling … [Researchers] … should also recognize and take advantage of its possibilities' (Lijphart, 1971: 685).

The experimental method at the time Lijphart wrote was thought even more so than now to be a mostly impractical method for answering questions concerning political science and international relations. A modern understanding of the comparative method thus emerged to signify comparisons aimed at generalisation, where the number of cases in the sample is too low for meaningful statistical research in the form of partial correlations to be carried out on the units of analysis. In short, the comparative method became synonymous with small-N research (where N stands for number of cases). The argument goes that when we cannot perform an experiment because we cannot control an intervention, and we cannot make use of inferential statistics because we do not have a sufficient sample of cases, the comparative method is the best tool we are left with. Many comparative studies therefore justify their approach by arguing that the kinds of things political scientists are interested in do not lend themselves to randomised control trials or inferential statistics. For example, for both ethical and practical reasons we cannot start multiple wars in order to understand the effects of war – and if only we could stop them so easily to understand what causes peace! We cannot readily create more welfare states in order to better understand existing welfare states.

Some of the most interesting objects of investigation in politics are naturally small in number. It might seem then that political researchers are faced with a stark choice; either ask questions which can be meaningfully answered using these state-of-the-art large-N comparative research methods, or, ask perhaps interesting small-N questions but answer them in inferior ways. These stark distinctions between large- and small-N research strategies are problematic because they mischaracterise the role of data sampling/case selection in research strategy and I will return to debates about Ns. These introductory sections aimed only to provide a brief overview of the historical development of a distinct comparative method in political science – how do you actually compare cases to help explain stuff?

Mill's methods of experimental inquiry and their influence on comparative political science

This section first introduces some of John Stuart Mill's inductive methods of what he called experimental inquiry (1843 [1950]) before explaining why these methods have become so synonymous with small-N comparative research in the social sciences. Mill's contribution to the philosophy of scientific method was not really to invent a novel set of methods – the basis for these procedures can be traced in some shape or form far back before Mill's time – but his capacity to clearly consolidate and communicate approaches to test for causes have meant that his association with these methods has endured.

Method of agreement

Suppose I started out on a new research project and wanted to provide an explanation for the puzzle of why certain countries are affected by horrific acts of terrorism while others are not. This is certainly an important question for scholars of politics and security if we want to understand terrorism and consider prevention strategies. The question of what causes terrorism is not one for which I might claim any real expertise initially, but an interesting one for which I am aware from my reading of public media of many folk theories that abound. The first thing to think about when answering any research puzzle is what explanations might be good ones (this is called theorising and a literature review helps). The next is to find evidence to allow a judgement as to which of those theories might be more or less correct. In the case of the latter, we might at least know of some countries that have been relatively unharmed by terrorism in recent times. Therefore it makes good sense to compare and study those cases to begin with. The method of agreement works by identifying only cases where an outcome is observed (or only cases where it is not) and then identifying the one condition (or the set of conditions) that agrees in presence (or agrees in absence) among *all* cases of a phenomenon. Table 16.1 provides a snapshot of how the method of agreement might be used to answer this question.

Table 16.1 uses hypothetical data to compare three different countries that have not suffered from acts of terrorism and asks whether they also had low net immigration, whether their societies were religiously fragmented and whether their security services share intelligence internationally. With the evidence here we might want to conclude that intelligence sharing explains (or at least partly explains) avoidance of terrorism. But more importantly, we might want to reject the other proposed causes as being necessary conditions for terrorism – the outcome occurs in our cases with or without those other conditions. Removing irrelevant determinants of outcomes (reducing overdetermination) is an underappreciated skill in political science, as many of us get busy in providing 'new' explanations rather than repairing other ones. However, we might then want to subject our findings to further tests – a problem that arises here is the issue of a potentially trivial condition. We have no information in these cases on what happens when countries do not share intelligence – would that alone be sufficient to cause terrorism? Almost certainly not – in fact Interpol has

Table 16.1 *Method of agreement – a basic example*

Case	*Net immigration low?*	*Religious fragmentation low?*	*Member of shared international intelligence organisation, e.g. Interpol?*	*Terrorism?*
Country A	X	X	✓	X
Country B	X	✓	✓	X
Country C	✓	✓	✓	X

✓ Signifies Yes/Condition Present; X Signifies No/Condition Absent

190 members; non-members are either pariah states, failed states, or very remote small states. If a potential cause is ubiquitous it may be a necessary condition for the outcome but a trivial, uninformative one. As a researcher I might then go back and continue my review of the literature and theory to see if my intuitions about intelligence sharing require more refinement and recoding to consider some particular type of intelligence. This iteration and refinement among evidence, tests and theory is a hallmark of the comparative method. Of course, the example above is a highly stylised, made-up and simplistic account, but the next time someone suggests to you that any particular condition like those above is responsible for causing or avoiding terrorism you might want to help them out in their sincere quest for the truth with a bit of the method of agreement.

Are there other limitations of the method of agreement? The method of agreement is perhaps the most egregious example of the problem of biased sampling due to 'selecting on the dependent variable' (see for example King et al., 1994; Geddes, 2003). The example above contains no evidence of cases of countries that have suffered from terrorism. It may be that quite a lot of countries share quite a lot of intelligence for strategic reasons but are still unable to prevent terrorism; however, in this example we have not included those outcomes in our test. And should we simply dismiss the role of religion in terrorism because in just one case of non-terrorism religious fragmentation was high? Perhaps whoever coded the cases made an error. And then what about other explanations I have not included such as absence of political leadership, individual characteristics of the terrorist and so on? We have many variables but few cases to test them against, and many questions remain unanswered. The method of agreement in small-N research, then, is one good way of systematically comparing data, but no method is error-free.

Method of difference

Mill's method of difference works by comparing instances where a phenomenon does occur with ones where it does not. The method of difference seeks to identify the variable that is present in the positive case and absent from the negative. We could equally say absent in the positive case and present in the negative. Note that the absence of a condition logically signifies the presence of its negation. So when we say democracy is absent, it is the same as saying non-democracy is present. So to take a different example for variety, if we wanted to try to answer the classic question of what causes democratisation we might consider a comparison of two cases such as countries D and E in Table 16.2.

Using the method of difference in this simplified two-case example, economic development and British colonial heritage do not explain democratisation in these cases, but an inability to rely on wealth generated by natural resources to maintain support for the regime can. Our small sample is again problematic – we have only studied a couple of economically developed former British colonies – and despite the reach of the British colonial

Table 16.2 *Method of difference – a basic example*

Case	*Economic development*	*British colonial heritage*	*Abundant natural resource exports*	*Democracy*
Country D	✓	✓	X	✓
Country E	✓	✓	✓	X

project, a full sample of all those cases could not cover even half the world. Indeed, this observation exposes one important strategy for interacting with small-N data, that is, considering whether causal conditions can be considered scope conditions (see Walker and Cohen, 1985). For example, we may want to make the more moderate but perhaps no less interesting claim based on the cases we selected and evidence presented, that within the scope of economically developed British colonies democratisation is prevented by regimes having access to abundant natural resources.

Joint method

The *joint method of agreement and difference* combines the logic of comparing across cases that agree in order to then indirectly apply the method of comparing cases that disagree on the outcome. In Mill's version, the joint method first identifies common factors across cases where the outcome was present and then checks whether those factors were not also present in negative cases. If both tests are passed explanatory value is enhanced with regard to other potential explanations. For Table 16.3 let us consider another classic question for comparative politics – what explains high or low voter turnout across countries. In this example the researcher has collected data on sets of both positive and negative cases, allowing more variation across the dependent and independent variable than we have seen in previous examples.

In Table 16.3 we have variation in our outcome across cases but we cannot directly apply the method of difference. There are no two cases that differ on the outcome and differ on only one potential explanatory

Table 16.3 *The joint method*

Case	*High campaign spending*	*Proportional representation*	*Compulsory voting*	*High voter turnout*
Country F	✓	✓	✓	✓
Country G	X	X	✓	✓
Country H	✓	X	X	X
Country I	X	✓	X	X

condition. But by applying the method of agreement to the two pairs that agree on the outcome of cases [F and G] and [H and I], we are able to eliminate irrelevant variance for the outcome and its negation, leaving us with the presence/absence of compulsory voting as the remaining potential explanatory variable for the presence or absence of the outcome. The difference in the outcome is reflected and corroborated in the difference across the pairs of cases for compulsory voting; thereby we arrive at the method of difference indirectly.

As Mill and others since have pointed out, these methods are methods of elimination (Mill, 1843 [1950]: 216). They effectively ask what conditions co-vary in line with the outcome, serving to reduce the relevance of other conditions in explaining the outcome. Mill also introduces some other methods in his volume including most notably the *method of concomitant variation* which states that when any two phenomena co-vary in a systematic and consistent manner it signals some causation. The method of concomitant variation preludes the correlations that have become the workhorse of large-N quantitative analysis aided by the emergence of statistics based on probability theorems (see Chapter 15). It is the methods of agreement and difference outlined in depth here that provide the foundation for reasoning in small-N comparative politics.

Readers may have gathered from the examples above that small-N comparisons are limited by their sensitivity to the way an investigation is specified and cases selected. Looking at Tables 16.1, 16.2 and 16.3, it is not hard to imagine how the addition of another case or condition with varying characteristics could completely change the weight of evidence for a theory. Mill (2002 [1843]) himself was quite sceptical about whether the methods outlined above could be used to identify causes in complex social sciences owing both to the indeterminacy of interacting causes and the unsatisfactory weight of evidence provided by a small number of experiments/cases (see, in particular, his book III, chapter X). Debates on whether this dismissal of the use of these methods in social science was an appropriate one have not gone away (see, for example, contributions by Savolainen and Lieberson, 1994).

Much of the confusion among competing methodological arguments seems to emanate from perverse incentives to give very different accounts of the limits of different methods and approaches, as well as the inherent limits presented by the messy social world we are trying to make sense of. As has been outlined above, the units of analysis we want to analyse (welfare states, revolutions and so on) often present themselves in small numbers and we must use theory to try to reduce indeterminacy. The reality is that social scientists have continued to employ Mill's methods in ways that have helped us better understand social phenomena. Perhaps a most famous example is Skocpol's *States and Social Revolutions* (1979), which explained the role played by the conjunction of administrative collapse in the face of war losses and peasant revolts in bringing about successful social revolutions. Skocpol applies the method of agreement and difference with no shortage of iteration between evidence and theory to show that these conditions were more or less present in France, Russia and China but not in cases where revolution was negated including rebellions in areas of modern-day Germany and in Japan.

The moral of the discussion is that comparativists working with a small-N need to provide clear justifications that they are not merely selecting cases to suit a priori arguments, but selecting cases that allow important gains in understanding of explanatory theory, by exploiting the opportunities of the logical tests outlined above. The advantage for small-N research is that with a smaller number of cases the researcher can take the time to engage in a number of ancillary investigations to try and answer the questions of potential error. This can be done by iterating recurrently between theory and evidence, adding a particularly useful further case, mixing methods or gathering more in-depth information on what is going on within cases. It should become clear that comparison or the comparative method is inextricably linked with good practices and knowledge in sampling as well as conceptual delineation and description. This does not mean that small-N researchers can respond to criticism by simply saying, 'leave me alone I know my cases', but they should be able to make arguments about the scope of their generalisations with reference to other relevant cases in the population and an awareness of important background conditions and theories that apply more indirectly to their models of the world.

Most different and most similar strategies

Rather than confining all studies that require purposive small-N sampling to the dustbin as untenably indeterminate, one way of addressing the problem of selecting on the dependent variable in small-N research is to simply select on the dependent variable better. This requires what Flyvbjerg calls information-oriented sampling (2006). That is selecting cases to compare because you know something about them already, and crucially, that you know quite a bit about the applicable universe of cases and theory. Good case selection allows for relatively controlled or simply more useful investigation of your theories. Small-N researchers necessarily need to spend more of their time figuring out what information can and cannot be garnered and then inferred from their cases as they conduct their research.

In the first example above it might be difficult to think initially of what a more or less informative case of terrorism is for comparison. Are cases where terrorism is a dormant but significant threat, or cases which have suffered significantly in their recent history from terrorism, more useful for understanding causes? Here understanding strategies of most different systems designs (MDSD) and most similar systems designs (MSSD) can be helpful (Przeworski and Teune, 1970). If we deliberately select cases that are most different in as many important respects as possible for explaining an outcome, yet agree on one factor as well as the outcome (MDSD), then we may have more grounds for claiming that that factor is causal than if we applied the same procedure to more similar cases. We can argue that a condition that appears along with an outcome in more diverse contexts has more explanatory value than one that is context-dependent. In fact, there are even good arguments for testing the received wisdom about what is 'comparable' with our comparisons. By comparing two phenomena that appear to be of an entirely different class we may be able to uncover 'eclectic affinities' that reveal insights otherwise bound to disciplinary silos (cf. Boswell and Corbett, 2017).

Alternatively in a MSSD we select cases that are as similar as possible in important factors thought to predict the outcome, but that differ on the outcome, in an attempt to mimic experimental control and reduce extraneous variance. We can then explore the cases to see if there is an important factor or a set of factors which is different among them and may explain the outcome under these controlled conditions. De Meur and collaborators have laterally expanded and developed MDSO–MSDO (most different cases, similar outcome–most similar cases, different outcome) selection methods for systematically identifying cases from a population and dataset where the comparative logic outlined above could be most feasibly employed (De Meur and Berg-Schlosser, 1994; De Meur and Gottcheiner, 2009).

The logic of most similar designs is reached for often by comparativists because of its ability to use purposive sampling of cases to mimic the experimental method. In fact, all comparisons within the various area studies literatures benefit from this ability to control for extraneous cultural and historic variance. For example, if we want to understand democratisation in a comparison of Latin American countries, we can obviously control at least for the direct effect of British colonialism. But some of my area studies friends can become quite frustrating when they deny the 'comparability' of countries or other units of analysis far across the globe. By comparing very disparate cases we can understand commonalities as well as understand whether variables such as geographic area are themselves redundant in explanations of phenomena (at least at that level of abstraction). Of course, the best studies often can combine both strategies of enquiry and build arguments by looking for appropriate cases to plug gaps in knowledge. We now turn to look at more recent development of sophisticated methods of first cross-case and then within-case analysis.

The changing nature of comparative research strategies – qualitative comparative analysis

In 1987 Ragin published *The Comparative Method*, a book that has had a significant influence on methodological developments and debates in small-N and mixed method research in the last thirty years. Roughly speaking Ragin argues that there are at least two broad approaches to social science; one that is variable-oriented where the variables are the star of the show and one that is case-oriented or case-based where the cases are the stars. Variable-oriented research is characterised by a focus on identifying correlations between independent and dependent variables. Large-N statistical analysis of this sort applies tests across cases in order to assess the probability with which the data reflects the hypothesised relationship in which independent variables of interest predict a given response in the dependent variable, controlling for other variables. Case-based research on the other hand is said to treat cases more holistically as conjunctions of conditions or attributes. Case-based researchers tack back and forth between theory and evidence to try to understand and describe important invariant relationships in a smaller set of carefully selected cases. Ragin is not out to run down either approach, but argues that distinctions that make a value judgement, in particular on which is the greater between quantitative and qualitative approaches (see Box 16.1), are unhelpful (2000: 22).

Most interesting and most enduring of Ragin's contributions is his introduction of the use of Boolean algebra to help compare conjunctions of conditions across cases, in particular where researchers want to employ case-based research strategies with more cases than they can compare effectively in their head. Developing this argument more strongly in *Fuzzy-Set Social Science* (2000), Ragin maintains that many of the research puzzles that social researchers present themselves with are set-theoretic in nature. That is, rather than ask whether 'more or less of x leads to more or less of y', we ask things like 'is x required for y' or does a combination of 'x and y always produce z'. In other words there is a fundamental difference between asking whether economic development increases the likelihood of democratisation and asking if economic development is necessary or sufficient for democratisation. Thiem and colleagues (2016) explain that the former increases/decreases question assumes a symmetrical relationship of covariation across all cases. It can be tested by regressing proxy variables and basing inference on linear

Box 16.1 Qualitative, quantitative and comparative

Readers may have noticed that I have up to now not made much of an effort to use the terms qualitative and quantitative. As explained in Chapters 14 and 15, the discipline has been marked in the past by a methodological divide of sorts between the two and it is important to be aware of what the terms connote. Though I think we are probably stuck with these terms for the time being, they become less useful as our methodological toolboxes become much more sophisticated in their ability to integrate what were previously seen as incompatible types of data. At a basic level quantitative research is concerned with counting stuff and qualitative research is concerned with describing stuff using language. If I was writing this chapter thirty years ago I am sure I would have been equating small-N comparative research with qualitative and non-quantitative research. But we have become much better at counting words (e.g. quantitative text analysis) as well as operationalising (coding) conceptual states using numbers (e.g. fuzzy sets). As 'mixed methods' strategies increase in popularity it will be interesting to watch how the disciplines' epistemic vocabulary adapts.

algebraic expressions. The latter sufficiency/necessity question allows asymmetry in relationships among conditions and proposes that cases will and will not be found in particular subset/superset relationships. Inference is then drawn from Boolean algebra.

Qualitative Comparative Analysis (QCA) as developed by Ragin (2000) and later Schneider and Wagemann (2012) among others provides an integrated method for causal interpretation of these set-theoretic relationships (Schneider and Wagemann, 2012: 8). QCA provides an advance on Mill's methods through its core analytic tool – the truth table. The truth table visualises the combinations of properties that observed cases take, mapped on to those combinations they could logically take. The advantage of this is that it allows for systematic comparison of empirical cases as well as transparent evaluation of counterfactuals.

As an example, suppose we wanted to investigate again what conditions are required for high voter turnout and we are interested in conjunctions of the three conditions – high campaign spending, proportional representation, and compulsory voting. We want to compare nine countries. For ease of explication, and despite the changing examples, we will assume the countries have the same combinations of presence and absence for these conditions across cases as was found for countries A–I in Tables 16.1, 16.2 and 16.3. We have three explanatory conditions and therefore we have 2^3 possible combinations of their presence and absence represented by the eight rows in Table 16.4. The final column on the right-hand side tells us which cases share these logical combinations of presence and absence of the three explanatory conditions. In the outcome column (high voter turnout) we can evaluate what the outcome is for the cases that share the logical properties in their row.

Table 16.4 *Truth table example*

Row #	*High campaign spending*	*Proportional representation*	*Compulsory voting*	*High voter turnout*	*Cases (countries)*
1	1	1	1	Contradiction	C, E, F
2	1	0	1	?	None
3	0	1	1	No	B
4	1	1	0	Yes	D
5	0	0	1	Contradiction	A, G
6	0	1	0	No	I
7	1	0	0	No	H
8	0	0	0	?	None

Following Boolean notation 1 denotes presence/membership of the set; 0 denotes absence/non-membership of the set.

The truth table allows us to analyse what kinds of cases we have no examples of in our sample (here type 2 and type 8). This is useful information and should prompt us to think about why our sample is void of such cases and whether we need to add representative examples. The table also shows us in its 'crisp' form (with dichotomised presence or absence) the cases for which we have logical contradictions. These are cases that have the same logical properties but lead to different outcomes (rows 1 and 5). Such a finding can suggest that another condition that has not been analysed explains the difference in the outcome, or that some error has been made in coding. We would want to resolve these contradictions using theory or by revisiting classifications in cases. Most QCA analyses nowadays use fuzzy sets (see Ragin, 2000) which allow for partial membership between 1 and 0 in a set. Allowing cases partial membership in multiple truth table rows can reduce the problem of contradictory truth table rows to an extent, and also can allow for a richer analysis of variation in presence/absence of conditions across cases.

Once such an analysis is undertaken we can finally engage in Boolean reduction (elimination) to provide parsimonious explanations of outcomes. Here for example rows 3 and 6 agree on the outcome and only differ on one condition. Therefore we can assume that the conjunction of proportional representation and the absence of high campaign spending is sufficient for the absence of high voter turnout (eliminating the role of compulsory voting). Note, though, that the alternate explanation for the absence of high voter turnout represented by row 7 is not affected by this finding. A QCA approach assumes that outcomes display equifinality (that they can be equally explained by a number of different alternative conjunctions of conditions).

Although QCA originated as a case-based strategy for comparing a small-to-medium-N of cases, because its use is effectively dictated by the nature of the research question, it has increasingly been applied for comparisons across large-Ns of cases. A number of excellent packages in the free R statistical computing programme have been developed to enable researchers to quickly compute reductions across multiple rows, and also to compute measures of fit for subset/superset relations across cases.

The number of articles employing QCA in mainstream political science journals continues to grow year on year but its critics have also been many and vocal, and as QCA has enjoyed more publicity it has enjoyed more scrutiny. In particular QCA has been shown in simulations to be unreliable and particularly sensitive to case selection and specification (Hug, 2013; Lucas and Szatrowski, 2014; Krogslund et al., 2015). However, other scholars have suggested that these simulations are inaccurate and do not provide a fair test of the QCA procedure (Rohlfing, 2015; Thiem et al., 2016). Another major limitation of QCA is the static nature of the analysis. Up to now researchers who have tried to introduce a temporal or sequential dimension to QCA have only been able to use fairly blunt instruments. They cannot compete with the within-case research that is prioritised by other small-N researchers. More recently QCA scholars have argued for a mix of cross-case and within-case analysis (Schneider and Rohlfing, 2013) and it is to the latter of those which we now turn.

Case studies, within-case comparison and process-tracing

Case studies describe research projects that are designed to focus their investigation on a single instance of a phenomenon. But, as outlined in the introduction to this chapter, case studies, like all other methods, are inherently comparative. Comparison is important for case studies in at least two respects. First, case studies and the concepts used to describe them exist in a wider universe of cases and concepts. As for all methods, any explanation drawn from a single case will need to be very aware of, and clear as to how, that case relates to its wider universe. Like other small-N researchers, throughout their research those engaged in case studies must think about what their case is a case of (Ragin and Becker, 1992). Second, case studies are often interested in within-case analyses aimed at identifying intervening variables and establishing causal mechanisms. As we shall see this invokes an increasingly sophisticated set of methodological tools that resemble those introduced above.

Case selection

In media debates in the UK prior to the European Union (EU) referendum in June 2016 it became commonplace for different politicians, commentators and journalists to explain the future of the UK following a 'Brexit' by claiming that the UK outside the EU would look just like any number of countries – from Canada to Norway, Kosovo and Greenland. These are simple claims that those countries are good cases for explaining the nature of political life outside the EU. But which of those cases would have been the best case to select for an explanation of the UK outside the EU? Case selection is the art of answering this kind of question. Political scientists may choose to focus their research on a single case for a number of reasons. These can include contributions to general theories (Lijphart, 1971; Flyvbjerg, 2006) and exemplars for learning (Flyvbjerg, 2006), as well as providing psychologically satisfying narrations of established causal mechanisms (Dowding, 2016). Box 16.2 outlines at least four different case selection strategies.

Diagnostic case studies are chosen with an interest in explaining a particular case in light of existing theories in mind. As Dowding points out, case narratives aid understanding by providing more

Box 16.2 Case study selection strategies

Combining and abridging Lijphart (1971: 692) and Flyvbjerg (2006: 230)*

- Interpretative/Diagnostic case studies
- Hypothesis-generating case studies
- Deviant/Extreme/Outlier case studies
- Critical/Crucial/Limiting/Sinatra/Most or Least Likely cases

* I have added some extra synonymic descriptions not used in those articles but used elsewhere in the literature for what are effectively the same case selection strategies.

psychologically satisfying explanations of phenomena than explanations based on general models (2016: 147–152).

Hypothesis-generating case studies are often associated with grounded theory and ethnographic methods and aim at establishing new general theories to be tested in other cases. These kinds of case studies are extremely important, but most susceptible to problems of overdetermination which can be a limitation of all small-N research. Where hypotheses are generated with a small-N, in particular a single case, it is often tempting to consider many events important to the explanation of the outcome when in fact some are superfluous. In any case, hypothesis-generating case studies should be seen in a context where future testing of general propositions is anticipated.

Deviant cases are often seen as the most useful of case selection strategies. Here a researcher deliberately selects an outlier case that is known to contradict the typical cases which otherwise provide evidence for the veracity of a theory. The logic is that these deviant cases can tell us a lot about how we might need to modify general theories.

Finally, the *crucial* case study is the most controversial of case selection strategies. 'Least likely' cases work on the logic that if we can find a case where a theory is least likely to be confirmed and observe that it is confirmed in that case, we can provide significant evidence for the confirmation of a theory. Similarly, if a theory fails in a 'most likely' case it can provide critical evidence for disconfirmation. The language of 'crucial' or 'critical' cases is usually associated with a strong version of this logic where a case is envisaged as an essential test for a theory. Many scholars are sceptical that a crucial case that can on its own serve to undermine a theory entirely can actually exist (e.g. Dowding, 2016: 116). It is particularly difficult to argue in the social sciences that a single case could ever really be used to reject a theory in perpetuity.

Case studies like other forms of research are necessarily descriptive, but description is a form of comparison. By reading a good description of a parliament we are better aware of what parliaments are in relation to presidents, courts and so on. Even the act of describing a case in itself improves our knowledge of the class of cases. Good comparativists should be sensitive to understanding what their cases are cases of, and how they can be interpreted differently. Often the research process will reveal that a case is in fact a different kind of case study, in relation to the general population of cases, than imagined before the researchers entered the field (cf. Flyvbjerg, 2006). The key lesson is that case study research is a comparative, iterative process. Comparativists are well-served when they discuss case selection strategies more openly, and should not be ashamed of the theory-laden construction of their samples.

Within-case analysis

Often we will be interested in understanding the sequence of events, processes or mechanisms that led to an outcome in a particular case. To take our example of the case of EU withdrawal by the UK, we are seeking to explain a relatively unique event, potentially made up of a sequence of key decisions, reactions and ideational changes. Any explanation which we proffer might involve reference to emerging social processes, actions of key decision-makers and changing ideas about the UK's role in Europe over time. There may be many theories that seek to explain Brexit by invoking renewed support and desire for a democratic mandate for EU membership among elites, or reactions to growth in support for the UK Independence Party, or actions resulting from the ambitions of various individual politicians to lead the Conservative Party and so on. But which actions and ideas influence other ideas and actions, and what observations are necessary to provide a valid answer?

The information needed to answer these questions requires within-case analysis of observations which we would not normally consider comparable in cross-case research. Collier, Brady and Seawright (2004) call these 'causal process observations'. These observations are often collected through painstaking fieldwork, via interviews, archival research and direct observation of action. How can we know which evidence is important in explaining the outcome in a case and what the key links are in a causal chain? Process-tracing methods (George and Bennett, 2005; Bennett and Checkel, 2015) are an attempt to provide a framework for identifying causal mechanisms within cases (see Chapter 14). Process-tracing aims to provide standard tests to eliminate bias when assessing the odds that alternative hypotheses are true using within-case observations. In effect, process-tracing considers a set of alternative explanations of an event or sequence of events and asks of each explanation: if this particular explanation were true, what evidence would we expect to see? The appearance of a particular piece of evidence can have a different weight on the odds that a theory is a true reflection of events depending on prior expectations about whether such evidence could be found.

Van Evera (1997: 30–32) elucidates four different tests for the value of evidence with regard to theory confirmation in case study research which depend on two dimensions: whether evidence can be uniquely predicted by a particular hypothesis, and the certitude with which observed evidence is necessary for a hypothesis to be true. *Straw-in-the-wind tests* are low in uniqueness and uncertainty, evidence that passes this test for a hypothesis does not really distinguish its credentials from other hypothesis, nor would it be completely necessary to confirm a hypothesis. *Hoop tests* concern evidence that is necessary for a hypothesis to be true, that is, if this hypothesis were true it would need to pass through a given hoop. We can more or less eliminate theories that do not pass a hoop test. *Smoking gun tests* have high uniqueness; just like a smoking gun in the hands of a suspect at the scene of a crime, a piece of evidence that passes a smoking gun test provides strong evidence for one hypothesis, and is evidence that is unlikely to be attributable to any other hypothesis. The *doubly decisive test* combines the latter two tests to provide evidence that is necessary and sufficient for the confirmation of a hypothesis.

Bennett (2015) has shown how these tests have important affinities with Bayesian approaches to social science. Bayesian methods aim to predict in a useful and systematic way the probability of an outcome given some new evidence. The formula for Bayesian probability requires the researcher to ask two questions (for each hypothesis) about a new piece of evidence in order to recalculate their beliefs that a causal explanation is true: (1) what was the probability the explanation was true before this new evidence came to light? (called prior probability); and (2) what is the probability of seeing this new evidence were this the true causal explanation? (conditional probability). To that we must also add a third question: what are the prior and conditional probabilities for all alternative explanations? The Bayesian approach effectively takes prior expectations about evidence into account. It provides an important advance for process-tracing in case studies by allowing formal, transparent and comparable expression of assumptions and tests for evidence. Also, outcomes of one investigation can provide the information to update prior probabilities for another, allowing systematic and transparent accumulation of evidence among case studies.

Causal process-tracing will still suffer from accusations levelled at small-N research that the 'researcher is the major independent variable!' (Peters, 2013: 169), or that the process-tracer's emphasis on successive observations can be infinite and therefore not particularly useful. Nevertheless, advances in theory and practice of process-tracing have advanced case study research by providing a common vocabulary and standards for robustness of inferences.

Conclusion: evolving comparison in response to challenges

This chapter introduced the comparative method as an evolving and adaptable approach to political science. Much has changed in political science since Lijphart's classification of a hierarchy of research approaches, not to mention since Mill introduced his methods of induction. Developments in econometrics, rational choice, machine learning and the experimental boom have meant that it is often less easy for proponents of a distinct comparative method to rest their worth on the argument that political science is prone to the problem of many variables and too few cases. Yet many celebrated studies in political science are based on an understanding, or a direct application, of the comparative methods outlined in this chapter.

The difficulty in writing about a distinctive comparative method is that comparison is a thread that links many approaches to political, social and other forms of research. Improvement in the plurality of methodological training has meant that comparative methods often form an important part of a suite of tools and knowledge that political scholars bring to the interesting questions that puzzle them. However, many studies in political science are weakened by their inability to take advantage of opportunities for the use of comparative logic or, conversely, by misunderstanding the limitations of their comparisons.

Most political scientists will agree that all research is small-N research at some level of abstraction. Even the most carefully constructed randomised control trial will engage a specific population frame for units of observation, and any interest beyond that population, even if attempts to generalise findings are modest, requires some knowledge of the arguments of comparative method and case selection strategies. I know many experimentalists who randomly assign units of analysis to treatments, but I have yet to meet one who randomly assigned all their trials. The sites of their trials are chosen for pragmatic as well as theoretical reasons, and they will often use small-N reasoning to justify that choice. Similarly statisticians will need to draw on the logic of comparative method and case selection when asked to justify their decision to study some countries they had previously known very little about. The answer that they realised there was 'good data' available for them to work with does not quite cut it. All researchers must recourse to the value of information-oriented sampling at times.

Finally, I want to return to Mill but this time to his discussion of comparison's role in the classification of phenomena (1843 [1950: 298]). Comparison challenges conceptions and helps us understand what is unique or common to things. The skill of a comparativist is to know and accurately describe the contours of the things they come across and relate them to some other accepted contours of things. Comparing politics with other things is the process by which a branch of science called political science was first discovered and then consolidated. Expertise in comparison is essential for political scholars because it is the comparison of attributes that serves to distinguish a field and subfields of expertise.

Further reading

- Full book-length treatments of comparative method that I have found very useful for both new and more familiar scholars include Ragin (1987), Landman (2000) and Peters (2013).
- Schneider and Wagemann (2012) is authoritative on set-theoretic methods and QCA.
- Rohlfing (2012) is an excellent introduction to issues in case studies and process-tracing.
- For an accessible and entertaining introduction to Bayes and some other basic statistical concepts, see Bram (2012).

Chapter 17

The Experimental Method

HELEN MARGETTS AND GERRY STOKER

Experimentation has rapidly become a popular method of choice for today's political scientists (Druckman et al., 2006: 627). For years, researchers underplayed the possibility of experiments, following Lijpart's gloomy assertion in 1971 in the *American Political Science Review* that: 'The experimental method is the most nearly ideal method for scientific explanation, but unfortunately it can only rarely be used in political science because of practical and ethical impediments' (Lijphart, 1971: 684–685). Since then, political scientists have been overcoming these impediments in droves, in the laboratory and the field and in newer online settings. This chapter is devoted to their work and the contribution it can make, as well as a careful analysis of the pitfalls and problems of the experimental method. Our conclusion is that political scientists need to get used to the idea that experimental evidence is increasingly mainstream in theory testing and the enhancement of understanding of how politics works. Just as it becomes essential, experimentation has also become more affordable, with web-based experiments and some natural experiments revealed in large-scale data, with the only cost that of analysis. As experimentation becomes part of the growing toolkit of 'social data science' political scientists will need to develop new expertise to take advantage of these opportunities.

What is the experimental method?

Political scientists are drawn to experiments primarily because of established academic concerns to generate evidence and theory that can establish causal connections. The most obvious reason for adopting the experimental method is that its design features deliver unrivalled claims for the making of causal inferences. An intervention, random allocation between groups and measuring outcomes are the three essential ingredients of the experimental method if it is to be practised in a way that delivers unrivalled claims for causal inference. If the experiment is designed well and conducted effectively with these ingredients in place then we are in a strong position to infer a causal relationship between the intervention and any group differences detected. If the trial is repeated we are in a stronger position again to make causal inferences (Torgerson and Torgerson, 2008). Let us look at the three ingredients of the experimental method – manipulation, control and random assignment – in a little more depth.

The defining characteristic of experimental research is intervention by the researcher in the process of generating data, what Morton and Williams (2008) describe slightingly as 'playing god'. In observational research all variance in data is outside the control of the researcher but in the case of the experimental approach the researcher actively creates variation. The logic of experimentation is driven by a situation where the researcher does not just observe but intervenes to observe the effect of that intervention. As McGraw and colleagues (2001: 13) note:

> Experimentation ... is intervening or manipulating a real environment in which behavior occurs, controlling the environment to test whether hypotheses about the relationships between variables are supported, and randomly assigning subjects ... to control for extraneous factors that can influence the empirical results.

Control is important to experimentation, most usually in terms of dividing subjects into a treatment group, where they receive the intervention, and a control group, where they do not. But as Morton and Williams (2008) note, it is helpful for political scientists to abandon the idea that all experiments must follow some ideal pattern of manipulating a variable by way of intervention, establishing a treatment and control group and randomly assigning the subjects to the treatment. Such a design may be appropriate in some circumstances, but just as in observational research, experiments can and should take different forms according to the research question at hand. Control does not need to come in the form of establishing a group to gather data from that have experienced no intervention. Particularly in laboratory settings control can come through careful management of the variables that are in play. In many respects having a comparison group is the essential element in the experimental method so that different groups are making choices under different controlled circumstances. For example, Escher and colleagues (2006) divided subjects into three groups, each of which looked for information about a different national government with no control group, enabling cross-country comparison. It is of course possible not to have a control group and to make comparisons between two or more interventions, but the same principles apply.

In field but also in laboratory experiments it is the *random* allocation of research subjects (be they people, groups or institutions) to one or other group that is used to ensure that the groups are similar in ways relevant to the research questions. These groups are then treated the same in all ways except those which are the focus of the research. Often observations are made on key variables for each member of the two groups both prior to and after the intervention, though it is possible just to have post-intervention measures. A 'post'-intervention measurement is the minimum required; in practice many field research projects with an experimental design also monitor the implementation of the policy action using a variety of qualitative and quantitative methods. The strength of random allocation to different groups is that it can control for the influence of factors that are known to affect the outcome *and* the influence of factors that may affect the outcome of the trial but are *unknown* to researchers.

The rise of experimentation

So the experimental method appears to offer unique advantages in establishing causality but even while acknowledging such advantages, some of its critics have doubted its practicality for political science in particular. Green and Gerber (2003: 102) comment:

> The most widely cited drawback ... is the inability to manipulate key political variables of interest. It is difficult to imagine how one could randomly assign presidential and parliamentary regimes for the purpose of evaluating their relative strengths and weaknesses. Surely, world leaders cannot be persuaded to allow political scientists to randomise their foreign policies, systems of patronage, or prospects for retaining power?

The response of political scientists such as Green and Gerber to this challenge has been to argue that experiments have a much greater role to play than is commonly understood if the focus is moved to establishing causal connections between particular variables in order to build up a bigger picture answer. As they put it: 'there is more parity than is often realised between big unanswerable research questions and narrow tractable ones' (Gerber and Green, 2003: 103).

Through the twentieth century, experiments in political science were sparse compared with other disciplines, but not absent. One review of experiments published by established political scientists revealed a total of 105 articles between 1926 and 2000 (McDermott, 2002: 43). In the 1990s Kinder and Palfrey (1993) managed to provide some twenty cases of previously published research using, primarily, laboratory-based experimental methods. The next decade saw reports of experimental research or studies appearing in increased numbers in mainstream political science publications (McGraw et al., 2001; Druckman et al., 2006; Morton and Williams, 2008). Bouwman and Grimmelikhuijsen (2016) recount the history of experimentation in public administration.

So, by 2017, experimentation seems to have a firm footing in the methodological firmament of political science, and is becoming progressively professionalised within the discipline. There is an Experimental Research section of the American Political Science Association, established in 2011, which through its Standards Committee has started to produce guidelines for experimental research reports (Gerber et al., 2014). There is a *Journal of Experimental Political Science*, established by Cambridge University Press in 2014, where experiments are reported and standards discussed, and a comprehensive *Cambridge Handbook on Experimental Political Science* (Druckman et al., 2011). Within certain types of experimental research, there are substantial textbooks and monographs; field experiments (Gerber and Green, 2012; Glennerster and Takavarasha, 2013; John, 2017); natural experiments (Dunning, 2012); and laboratory experiments (Morton and Williams, 2010). Once experiments are conducted, they seem to receive greater than average attention; Druckman and colleagues (2006: 633) found that experimental articles are in fact cited with greater frequency than other contemporaneous articles: experimental articles had an expected citation rate approximately 47 per cent higher than their non-experimental counterparts. A huge internet-based experiment (Bond et al., 2012) looking at voter turnout and Facebook was cited over 800 times within four years of publication.

Technological advances in terms of the invention of computer-assisted telephone interviewing (CATI) survey experiments and the availability of relevant computer software have fuelled further the adoption of experimental research methods in political science (Sniderman and Grob, 1996; Druckman et al., 2006). Miller and colleagues (2000), for example, use CATI methods in their survey of citizens to show how alternative wordings produce similar positive responses to the need for both more central control and more local autonomy in the arrangements of British government, suggesting that public opinion on such matters is loosely formed and potentially confused. Morton and Williams (2008) note that some social scientists are beginning to use functional magnetic resonance imaging (fMRI) equipment to measure brain activity as subjects make choices. Internet-based micro-labour platforms such as Crowdflower, Amazon Mechanical Turk and Google Consumer Surveys, combined with digital methods of designing, running, managing and analysing the results of experiments, have made experimental methods affordable for graduate students and researchers without large research grants.

Learning from laboratory experiments

Experiments in political science have been differentiated according to various dimensions. In the discussion below we distinguish between laboratory and field experiments, before discussing the newer development of internet-based experiments (which can exhibit characteristics of both) and so-called natural experiments, where some kind of 'naturally' occurring change may be considered as a random intervention. In laboratory experiments, the researcher recruits subjects to a common location, where the experiment is conducted and all the variables to be investigated in the environment are controlled within that location with the exception of subjects' behaviour. Field experiments, on the other hand, are not conducted in a common location and rely on an intervention into a real situation, with the advantage that a far greater sample size becomes possible. However, the distinction between laboratory and field experiments is becoming blurred as combinations of both types of experimentation are now being carried out via the internet – the virtual laboratory. In sociology but with strong potential application to a political environment, Salganik and colleagues (2006) used dedicated websites to replicate a field experiment online, where citizens' ratings of cultural artefacts were compared against different information environments in an artificial 'music market' in which 14,341 participants downloaded previously unknown songs, finding that citizens were more likely to rate highly songs that other people had also liked. Remote experiments of this kind represent a halfway stage between laboratory and field experiments, where the information environment is controlled during the course of the experiment, yet a far larger pool of subjects becomes available. Finally, in natural experiments some kind of accidental differences between different populations or within the same population at some point in time, brought about by government or a corporation (such as a social media platform), can be thought of 'as if' they were random (Dunning, 2012).

Many laboratory-based experiments into political behaviour use designs and mechanisms borrowed from economics, where there is a well-established methodology to investigate economic behaviour in games and bargaining. The most well-known political science experiments of this kind have centred around collective action problems and the design of institutions in order to overcome such problems in the creation of public goods or the allocation of common pool resources. Early research explored which kind of mechanisms work best to overcome collective action problems – for example, money-back guarantees in case of failure or enforced payments in case of success, with Dawes and colleagues (1986) using experiments to show that only the former affects collective action. He ascribes this difference to motivations from 'greed' rather than 'fear' of one's own loss. Nobel Prize–winning Elinor Ostrom, together with colleagues, has carried out extensive experimental research into trust and reciprocity and the consequences for institutional design (see, for example, Ostrom and Walker, 2003; Ostrom, 2005). Laboratory experiments have also been used to show that many people are willing to contribute to public goods and to punish those who do not contribute, even when these activities are costly and when members of the group are anonymous (Fehr and Gächter, 2002; Fehr and Fischbacher, 2004) and Smirnov and colleagues (2007) used similar experiments to argue that these individuals underlie the capacity of political parties to organise.

The claims made about the value-added of laboratory work are largely about the capacity they deliver to examine the aspects of political processes that could not be explored easily by other means. In his paper on laboratory experiments in political economy, Thomas Palfrey (2005) argues that researchers, particularly those who are theorists or with theoretical interests, turned to laboratory experiments to test the underlying assumptions of theories or hypotheses due to lack of adequate observational field data. Such laboratory experiments are conducted to study participants' behaviour under controlled conditions in order to understand political processes and outcomes – for example, committee decision-making, elections and so on. In the case of committees, for example, laboratory experiments are designed to test and hence provide insights into how the policy choices or preferences (and shifts/changes in such preferences) of participants might influence not only the deliberations and proceedings but also the outcome in terms of the decisions reached on policy issues/areas. Laboratory experiments into committee decision-making help us to understand the dynamics of how committees operate in terms of their focus (often determined by agenda setting), deliberations and bargaining – ultimatums and/or concessions, how coalitions or alliances are formed around certain issues and how such coalitions/alliances may or may not shift their allegiances depending on the ultimatums and/or incentives/concessions that are offered and the issues that ultimately carry the day – that is, the decisions or policy outcomes that are agreed upon (Fiorina and Plott, 1978; Eavey and Miller, 1984a and 1984b; Palfrey, 2005).

The argument for continued use of laboratory experiments, as well as field experiments, is made by Elinor Ostrom (2007), based on their value in developing the work she and colleagues have conducted on the effect of communication (direct and indirect), sanctions, fines and agreements on the behaviour and outcomes of users of common pool resources. She makes a simple distinction between the two types of research: 'To test theory adequately, we need to use methods that together combine external and internal validity. One gains external validity in doing field research, but internal validity in the laboratory' (Ostrom, 2007: 26–27). She goes on to argue that laboratory experiments enable researchers examining a particular social and political phenomenon to isolate and test specific variable(s) of interest – out of the several other factors involved – within repeated controlled settings in order to establish how they influence behaviour (choices and preferences) and the outcomes. The argument is that researchers studying social and political phenomena using only non-experimental field research or settings cannot clearly establish or ascertain causality or causal relationships especially in terms of the extent/magnitude to which the multiple factors involved impact on behaviour and thus contribute to an outcome. However, there is a call for a combination of experimental and non-experimental (field) research methods in order to overcome the limitations of both approaches and fully understand social and political phenomena.

Ostrom (2007: 26–27) concludes:

> solving common-pool resource dilemmas is non-trivial, but feasible for those directly involved if they can communicate with one another and agree on future actions. ... When they cannot change

> each other's expectations, individuals behave as short-term, payoff maximisers.... we have shown that groups that can communicate and design their own appropriation and sanctioning systems achieve substantial improvements—at times very close to optimal results. It is rarely feasible to observe such processes in the field but the findings are very important in regard to the importance of discourse and deliberation in a self-governing setting.

For Ostrom, laboratory experiments helped to highlight what it was in her fieldwork that was, in particular, driving participants towards effective common pool resource solutions.

The most widely cited experimental paper published in the *American Political Science Review* (Druckman et al., 2006: 631) is that of Quattrone and Tversky (1988), who set out to explore whether, as assumed in much formal political theory, actors behave according to the basic axioms of rationality. They showed that actors made choices that reflected their greater sensitivity to loss rather than gain by offering actors in the experiment choices framed in different ways that would have led to the same objective outcome and found that actors choose differently depending on how the choice was framed. Information-processing difficulties, cognitive challenges and heuristics frame actors' decision-making rather than assumed rationality favoured by modellers. This work and other experimental work that shows how behavioural assumptions are violated by 'real' actors have led to increased interest in the underpinning of political behaviour (Druckman et al., 2006: 631). Frey and Meier (2004) explore how assumptions about instrumentality driving behaviour – another common feature of political science theorising – can be violated by constructing experiments that show the conditions under which prosocial behaviour are likely to emerge.

Learning from field experiments

Various reviews identify the range and variety of experiments conducted by political scientists that stretch way beyond the fields of political psychology and policy evaluation (McDermott, 2002; Druckman et al., 2006; Morton and Williams, 2008, 2010; Gerber and Green, 2012; John, 2017). We are only just at the beginning of being able to judge what might be susceptible to field experiments or not. Various rather common political occurrences open up opportunities for field experiments that might not yet be fully exploited. By expressing faith in the value of randomisation, developing imaginative research designs and working in close proximity with policymakers and social actors, opportunities for creating experiments can be forged by political scientists. The implementation of new programmes, the diversity created through decentralised structures and even financial constraints that encourage piloting (rather than full-throttle roll-out) all provide a context in which experimentation can come to the fore. For Green and Gerber (2012), field experiments offer a way forward by focusing research into tractable questions and creating useable and tractable knowledge.

A variety of field experiments have examined the impact of mobilisation techniques such as the use of text messaging, door-to-door canvassing and other information and communication technologies (ICTs) on voter turnout – including, for example, for youth and other population groups like ethnic minorities (Gerber and Green, 2000, 2001a and 2001b; Phillips, 2001; Gerber et al., 2003; Suarez, 2005; Wong, 2005; Michelson, 2006; Dale and Strauss, 2007). Other studies have explored the effect of issues (for example, ballot measures or initiatives) on voter turnout (Barabas et al., 2007); and the effect of political debates on voting decisions and the outcome of elections (Williams, 2007). Experiments using variable survey questions in controlled conditions can cast doubt on established theories by showing how effects central to the theory seem very sensitive to the wording of questions (Clarke et al., 1999). One particular value of the experimental method is the ability it provides, in some instances, to check measurement instruments alongside substantive findings. These and other studies show experiments making a general contribution to study of subjects that are at the core of political science. Experiments appear to offer in particular a penchant for discovering evidence that has the capacity to trip up existing theories.

Field experiments have been increasingly useful in evaluating or predicting the effects of public policy interventions and testing new policy alternatives, and are more amenable to policymakers who fear the artificiality of the laboratory environment. There is a long-established tradition of using field experiments in the USA in particular to test social policy measures (Greenberg, et al., 2003). Burtless (1995) notes the Health Insurance Experiment in the USA, which provided convincing evidence about the price sensitivity of the demand for medical care and unprecedented information about the health consequences of variations in medical care that are caused by consumers facing different prices for medical treatment as a result of differences in their insurance coverage (Brook et al., 1983; Manning et al., 1987). More recently King and colleagues' experiment to evaluate a major new health programme in Mexico, billed as 'what may be the largest randomised health policy experiment ever' (King et al., 2005: 479) will, when completed, be able to make claims about the success or failure of a massively expensive and important policy, in terms of the extent to which it increases the use and availability of universal health services.

Learning from internet-based experiments

Increasingly widespread use of the internet from the early 2000s (and social media from the mid-2000s) has allowed new forms of experimentation, developing lab, field and natural experimental methods. First, it facilitates further possibilities for experimental research design by making it easier to reach subjects remotely and, combined with associated digital technologies, providing new possibilities to control and vary the information provided to large numbers of subjects, observing the effects on political behaviour. These are like laboratory experiments, but on a far larger scale. In an innovative experiment using the internet instrument of the *Time-Sharing Experiments for the Social Sciences* (a virtual laboratory for experimental research), Weaver (2003, 2005) investigated the effect of skin colour on people's willingness to vote for a political candidate, varying the race/ethnicity and skin colour of the candidates across experimental groups. To control for visual candidate differences, this study used a morphing technique, which digitally averaged several faces to produce distinct candidates, equating all relevant characteristics, while altering the race and skin colour of the target candidate, thus allowing realistic variation in race and skin tone while controlling for other sources of variation such as attractiveness and facial expression that might affect the outcome of the experiment. Another more recent experiment investigated the relationship between trust and transparency, by testing the effect of showing subjects the minutes of council meetings on their trust in local government organisations (Grimmelikhuijsen and Meijer, 2012), showing how increased transparency may have a subdued or negative effect on trust.

Internet-based experiments can also be designed as field experiments, where interventions are built into social media or other internet-based platforms and their effect measured through use of the analytics for that particular platform. In an early example, Horiuchi and colleagues (2007) present an internet-based study on the role of information in voting turnout. Perhaps the most famous (and certainly the largest) of such experiments to date was Bond and colleagues (2012) where a team of academic researchers working with Facebook during the 2010 congressional elections used the 'I voted today' button to see whether seeing that their Facebook friends had voted would increase an individual's propensity to vote. For 61 million voters, the platform randomised which voters saw photos of a selection of their friends, with the information that they had 'voted today'. Because Facebook was keen that the experiment could claim to have played a positive role in turnout, the control group was very small (only 1 per cent of the sample). But because of the huge size of the experiment, the results were still significant, and although the effect size was very small, Facebook could claim that around 60,000 people voted who would otherwise not have done so.

Third, the internet makes possible new kinds of natural experiment because online platforms are often changed, leaving the possibility of analysing behaviour on the platform before and after the change. Indeed, a 'build and learn' mentality is built into the design of most large websites, where A/B testing (trying two alternative designs of a page, advertisement or service and seeing which generates the most revenue) is commonplace for corporations, retailers and (to an ever increasing extent) election campaigns. A/B testing is not the same as a randomised control trial, because the collection and measurement of data is not usually rigorous enough to satisfy the more rigorous definition of an experiment given above, but the strategy could easily be extended to a randomised control trial if required. Due to the increasing barrage of evidence that targeted advertising on social media played an important role in the 2015 general election in the UK, the EU referendum of 2016 and the US 2016 presidential election, working out ways of understanding or simulating quasi-experiments of this kind will be an important challenge for political science in the future – see various sources for the UK 2015 general election (www.oii.ox.ac.uk/blog/digital-disconnect-parties-pollsters-and-political-analysis-in-ge2015) and the US 2016 presidential election (www.wired.com/2016/11/facebook-won-trump-election-not-just-fake-news/?mbid=social_twitter).

Learning from natural experiments

In natural experiments, the intervention occurs by chance, which either provides a natural random allocation, or can be analysed 'as if' it had been applied randomly. For example, Erikson and Stoker (2011) looked at the effect of being drafted into the Vietnam War, using the fact that the decision over which young people to draft was based on birth date, a relatively irrelevant characteristic within the year of birth. They used this 'as if' random allocation to explore whether those that were drafted exhibited different political behaviour and attitudes to those who did not, as indeed they did. Natural experiments can occur when policies are rolled out, or when funds are allocated across areas, particularly in education or social policy (see Angrist et al., 2002, 2006; John, 2017).

Natural experiments can be tantalisingly difficult to find; since by definition the intervention cannot be controlled, it means it is unlikely to be based on the variable in which you are interested a priori. Also, as you may not be aware of the change, you may not have collected or be able to collect post hoc the data required for measuring the effect. However, internet-based environments are quite frequently changing, for example when a website is changed or offers some new feature, and such platform changes will create natural experiments where the analytics data from the platform may be analysed before and after the change, in a Regression Discontinuity Design (RDD). Margetts and colleagues (2011) investigated the effect of trending information being introduced onto the UK government's petition platform by analysing hourly data on signatures after the change with the same data gathered before. They found that while the change did not increase the overall number of signatures to petitions, it did concentrate signatures on the most popular ones appearing at the top of the trending list, at the expense of those that were not on the list. Theoretically it should be possible to find some natural experiments like this on social media platforms such as Twitter when a new feature is added, but there are no published examples as yet.

Pitfalls in the experimental method

Although political scientists seem to be surmounting some of the 'insurmountable' challenges to experimental research claimed by earlier researchers, several ethical and practical challenges remain. These pitfalls in the experimental method are explored further as follows.

Ethical challenges

First, one common but misplaced criticism often made of medical experiments in particular is that if we think that an intervention (for example, relating to health or education services) might work, how can a researcher justify providing that benefit to the treatment group but not the control group? For example, the huge randomised and controlled field experiment conducted by King and colleagues (2007) to evaluate the Universal Health Insurance program in Mexico noted above, involved people in treatment areas receiving free services while people in control areas did not, whereas a large education experiment designed to test the effects of class size involved providing some subjects with smaller class sizes (Krueger, 1999). In some experiments, ethical concerns may be answered with the argument that we do not know that a benefit will accrue to the treatment group and hence the need for the experiment. As in other forms of research a variation of the harm principle could be used to judge the conduct of the experimenters in their work so that experiments could be considered ethical unless they knowingly cause harm to others. However, for many experiments to test public policy interventions, there appear to be clear benefits to the treatment (free health services and smaller class sizes in the two noted above) and indeed the evaluation may only be assessing the extent or cost of the benefit. So even where experimental researchers are able to quieten their consciences, there will often be political and popular opposition to such experimental designs, and concerted attempts by participants to switch to the treatment group, which jeopardises attempts to randomise (see King, 2007: 481).

Deception – that is, the misleading of participants – is another key ethical issue in experimental design. There is often a clear rationale for its use, either to save time or to test something that would be otherwise impossible. A seminal psychology experiment carried out by Milgram in 1963 is probably the most famous example of this latter kind of deception (and has done much to damage its ethical reputation). Milgram tested the willingness of participants to harm another person 'while only following orders'. Subjects were told to administer a series of electric shocks via what they believed to be an electronic shock generator to a participant behind a wall, who they were led to believe was another subject in the experiment. The subject was told that an electronic shock of increasing voltage was given each time they pressed a button and they were played various sounds of the other participants: screaming, complaining of a heart condition and eventually, silence. The results showed that 65 per cent of participants administered the full shock of 450 volts and all went to 300 volts, even though all expressed concern. Several other experiments have replicated the results since then (and an experiment carried out by Sheridan and King in 1972 where subjects applied real electric shocks to a puppy, to test the hypothesis that Milgram's subjects had seen through the deception in his experiment, with similar results, cannot have done anything to improve the image of the social science experiment).

University ethics committees or institutional review boards (IRBs) generally impose restrictions on deception in experiments and certainly Milgram's experiment would not pass through an ethics committee today. But even within what will pass through a university ethics committee, there are strong variations in norms for what is possible across disciplines. Economists are categorical in not allowing deception, even where subjects are debriefed afterwards. The objection is not really moral or ethical but more methodological. If a subject pool is 'contaminated', then in future experiments involving the same pool, subjects will be less likely to believe the information with which they are provided, and adjust their behaviour accordingly. Following the psychological tradition demonstrated so clearly by Milgram's experiment described above, social psychologists, on the other hand, argue that deception is vital to many of their experiments, even if not on the scale of Milgram's experiment.

Other experiments involve interventions that do not involve deception but arouse ethical concerns because they involve participants (albeit knowingly) sacrificing some right or benefit in favour of financial reward, which they might later regret. Again, there is a seminal experiment of this kind which was an investigation into how much people valued their voting rights, by giving participants a chance to sell their right to vote in the 1994 German Bundestag election (Guth and Weck Hannermann, 1997). The experiment found that most participants did not want to sell their voting right even for the top price of DM 200, while one quarter were willing to do so at substantial prices, but not at very low prices, which the experimentalist used as evidence that people do not see votes as worthless as rational choice arguments about pivotality might suggest. The experiment involved participants actually destroying their real voting card if they accepted a price. Many political scientists might like to replicate such an experiment which endeavours to answer a question so central to political science, and Guth himself dismisses moral objections to the design on the basis that: 'Our experiment could be repeated with any group of participants where one only should take care to explain the optimality of truthful bidding in an appropriate way' (Guth and Weck-Hannermann, 1997: 40). But as before, it seems inconceivable that such an experiment would pass through a contemporary ethics committee.

Newer types of experiments based on the internet or social media introduce new ethical challenges, particularly where they involve working with corporations. So, for example, when a team of researchers from Cornell University and Facebook (see Kramer et al., 2014) looked at the effect of an increase of negative (or positive) material in people's Facebook feeds on the emotions expressed in what those viewing the material posted themselves, the company was accused of manipulating the emotions of people participating in the experiment. Facebook's algorithms are already selective in what people see in their feeds (less than a sixth of what their friends post), and run A/B tests continually on the platform (their terms of use require users of the platform to agree to be part of experimental research), but the idea that they should be manipulating feeds explicitly to provide more negative or positive information without informing people was viewed as ethically problematic.

Practical problems

Experiments are often 'bedevilled by practical problems of implementation' (Jowell, 2003: 17) – the 'practical impediments' bemoaned by Lijphart at the beginning of the chapter. Lack of training among the staff involved in the intervention may create problems, and for political scientists it can be difficult to seek advice from colleagues who have experience of experiments given the lack of experiments in the mainstream of the discipline. Decisions made in the heat of the research may prove problematic to the experiment. Greenberg and colleagues (2003) review the long history of experimental trials in the USA in the social field and provide examples of where experiments have had to be aborted or modified because of administrative and other problems. Equally, although problems exist they can be overcome in most instances. John (2017) provides an outstanding account based on a decade or more of experience about how the practice of experiments can be undertaken and the challenges overcome.

These logistical problems vary across field and laboratory experiments. For laboratory experiments, running a laboratory requires ongoing management and administration and the maintenance of a subject pool, from which subjects can be rapidly recruited for individual experiments. Privacy of subjects must be protected, which means that an experimentalist may know very little about the subjects recruited for her experiment. Recruiting subjects, particularly non-students, can be a key challenge; economists are usually content to use students, but political scientists may view the distinctive characteristics of a student cohort (for example, young and inexperienced in voting and other types of political activity) unsatisfactory for observing political behaviour. Mintz and colleagues (2006), indeed, use experimental methods to show how students and military decision-makers differ and suggest that students can be assigned to experiments when they represent citizens but not elites. Theoretically the validity of an experiment rests on the difference between the performance of randomly allocated control and treatment groups, rather than the representativeness of the subject group. But policymakers are often uncomfortable with results derived from student subjects – and they may be right, because socially homogeneous subjects may fail to reveal behaviour distinctive to other groups – NAO (2007) revealed distinct differences across control and treatment groups for students and non-students. The same issue may apply to the geographical basis of subjects offered through crowdsourcing platforms such as Amazon Mechanical Turk, where participants are largely based in the USA or India, so may not be appropriate for experiments looking at some aspects of political behaviour in the UK or other European countries. Finally, incentivisation can be a logistical challenge, particularly for some of the remote internet-based experiments discussed above, with much larger numbers of subjects than conventional laboratory experiments – the collective action experiment carried out by Margetts and colleagues (2011) involved paying 700 remote subjects using Amazon vouchers, with the value of each adjusted to account for variable small donations made by individual participants. Although crowdsourcing platforms can minimise the cost of laboratory experiments conducted remotely, the costs can mount up, and such platforms cannot offer the tightly controlled environment that is sometimes required.

For field experiments, estimating the effects of system-wide reform can be particularly problematic using randomised trials because of contamination effects. Feedback mechanisms (networking between people, media coverage), perhaps in part caused by the intervention, may in turn make it difficult to maintain the purity of trial. There can be, for example, particular problems caused by the attrition of participants from programmes. A more significant problem for field experiments is that when it comes to implementing the intervention multiple actors may also be not only involved but central to the effectiveness of any intervention.

For internet experiments that operate like a field experiment, or occur naturally when a platform is changed, the most serious practical problem can come from the difficulty of obtaining data from the platform itself. Although Twitter has an open application programming interface (API) that allows researchers to draw down data, or to pay for data services, Facebook data is not freely available. The only way that experiments can be carried out on the platform are to work with Facebook itself, as in the Bond and colleagues (2012) experiment discussed above, but the furore over the 'emotional manipulation' experiment (Kramer et al., 2014) means that Facebook has pulled out of such collaborations with academic researchers, and the planned follow-up study using the 'I voted today' button in the 2012 US elections has never been published. And with the newer platforms favoured by younger citizens, the problem is even more acute – Instagram is owned by Facebook, WhatsApp is encrypted, while Snapchat feeds are mostly deleted as soon as they are read. This lack of data poses a major barrier to academic researchers wishing to run experiments on these platforms just as they play an ever more important role in political life pushing them towards other methodologies from the toolkit of data science, such as machine learning (see Chapter 18 on Big Data).

Conclusion

The experimental method requires the breaking down of big questions into tractable, manageable questions that can be investigated. In that sense the experimental method can provide a way forward for political science as a whole, and at the very least all political scientists should understand the logic of experimental work and the possibilities it affords. Those political scientists who use observational data need to understand how the logic of the experimental method enhances the application of their own favoured method. Many who use the comparative method or statistical analysis recognise this connection but we go further and argue those that use simple case studies might learn more from the experimental method

Of course the key aim in this chapter is not just to widen the appreciation of the experimental method but to get more researchers thinking about the idea of doing an experiment work. Although experiments as innovative and dramatic as Milgram (1963) and Guth and Weck-Hannemann (1997) remain rare in political science, there is a scattering of ardent experimentalists across the political science domain, who are enthused about and confident of, the experimental method. One point that does not come so clearly out of the literature but is well known to anyone who has been involved in designing or running an experiment is that experiments, in spite of all the logistical and ethical challenges discussed in this chapter, are exciting and fun. It is unclear whether the attraction of experiments comes from the comparative freshness of the approach, the simplicity of the methodology with the clear cut search for significance on the intervention, the sense of excitement in gambling on a particular research design, the potential for rich pay-offs in terms of identifying causality or perhaps the chance to 'play god', but it is immediately evident when experimentalists talk about or present their research.

The experimental method, in its field form in particular, demands a greater interaction between political science and society and in its other forms often lends itself to greater involvement of issues of policy and political practice. Given the subject matter of politics and the challenges that democratic systems in particular face in an era of growing populism and distrust in the institutions of politics, this greater engagement with society would seem both overdue and desirable for the discipline of political science. Achieving relevance in terms of influencing public policy may be more challenging than many experimenters recognise (see Stoker and John, 2009; Stoker, 2010) but as Chapter19 in this book argues it is a laudable objective. And as elections and political mobilization are increasingly played out on social media, overcoming the barriers to running experiments on platforms like Facebook, Twitter and Instagram seems like a challenge we must surmount.

Further reading

- For a comprehensive set of articles by a variety of political science experimentalists see the *Cambridge Handbook of Experimental Political Science* (Druckman et al., 2011), while for updates on standards and guidelines and recent experimental research see the *Journal of Experimental Political Science.*
- Political science experimentalists tend to have their own preferred type of experiment and publications are segregated accordingly. So, for field experiments see Gerber and Green (2012) and John (2017); for laboratory experiments see Morton and Williams (2010); for natural experiments see Dunning, (2012); and for 'nudge' type experiments geared at increasing civic engagement in a UK policy context see John et al. (2011).
- Torgerson and Torgerson (2008) provide a good overview of experimental methods for those beginning their studies
- If you are interested in the use of experiments in public management research, take a look at Blom-Hansen et al. (2015), a special issue on Experiments of the *International Public Management Journal.*
- A special issue of *The Annals of the American Academy of Political and Social Science*, March 2010 is worth examining

Acknowledgements

The authors would like to thank Peter John for his comments and suggestions for the chapter.

Chapter 18

Big Data: Methods for Collection and Analysis

MICHAEL J. JENSEN

Introduction

Today there is a dual revolution going on in the social sciences. First, more and more daily life leaves behind digital traces which are archived in various databases creating new data resources for social scientists to study social and political life. Alphabet's Eric Schmidt once claimed that we produce as much information in two days as we had in all of human history up through 2003 (Siegler, 2010). Whatever the veracity of the claim, the accelerating rate of information production and its utilisation in all aspects of political and social life is undeniable (Crozier, 2010, 2012; Ekbia et al., 2015). Second, innovations in computational tools are increasingly making these data accessible to academic researchers through the creation of various libraries and packages which extend popular data analysis platforms, such as NVivo, and programming languages, such as Python and R, to facilitate the collection and analysis of these data.

'Big data' is a popularised term that has come to refer to the collection and analysis of digital traces. Similar terms to characterise these methods include 'computational social science' (Bankes et al., 2002; Conte et al., 2012; Alvarez, 2016), 'data science' (Loukides, 2011; Baesens, 2014; Grus, 2015) and 'digital methods' (Rogers, 2009). These methods are being used by political scientists (King et al., 2013; Barberá, 2015; Freelon et al., 2015; Jensen, 2016; Jungherr, 2015), sociologists (Ackland, 2013), communication researchers (Lewis, 2015; González-Bailón and Wang, 2016) and literary scholars (Ramsay, 2011; Jockers, 2013). The techniques being developed enable scholars to access large volumes of social media data; scrape and organise information from websites; develop network maps between communication nodes; and code and analyse the content of text, images and video. Phone records, web traffic data, credit card databases, insurance claim records, traffic cameras, shopper loyalty cards and social media posts provide a wealth of data regarding individual and aggregate patterns of communications, interactions and behaviours. In a digital format, these data can be easily accessed and combined with supplementary data sources, providing unparalleled insights into human engagement in society (Kallinikos et al., 2010).

These developments raise serious challenges to researchers in the social sciences; to the extent these data are accessible, they may be rendering other methodologies obsolete. For instance, if the networks and communications of participants in a field of activity are already stored by telecommunications companies, or on web platforms, then surveys and ethnographic fieldwork represent costly – in time and resources – and often inferior alternatives to understanding how people interact and form networks (Savage and Burrows, 2007; Lin, 2015). As social and political life increasingly leaves digital traces, big data methodologies will become an increasingly important approach within the social sciences. The aim of this chapter is not to provide readers with the capacity to write their own data collection and analysis scripts, as that requires a significant investment of time in learning one or more programming languages. Rather, the aim here is to provide an introduction to big data, explaining what it is, the basic concepts that are involved, what one can do with it and its limitations. The examples contained throughout the chapter should provide readers with a good idea of whether to use these techniques in their own work and how they might go about acquiring the skills to competently carry out big data research.

Defining big data

In contrast to other topics discussed in this volume, big data does not constitute a discrete, singular theoretical approach and set of attendant methods. Rather, it denotes a range of methodological approaches to the collection and analysis of digital artefacts. These varied approaches may involve differing claims about the nature and organisation of society and politics which are consequential for the inferences researchers may draw.

Just as big data involves varied approaches to data collection and analysis, the term has been subject to a wide range of definitions by academics and practitioners, and there is generally a lack of consensus on the term (Ekbia et al., 2015). Definitions developed by consulting companies which focus on big data management – managing the volume, variety, variability, velocity and so forth – rather than big data itself (Laney, 2001, 2012; Dumbill, 2012) have become influential even in academic discussions (Kitchin, 2014). These definitions treat the bigness of big data as its defining quality. But this has been a slippery criterion as both changes in computing capacity and conceptual ambiguity over the level at which data is parsed make it difficult to specify thresholds discriminating big data from more conventional kinds of data. Not only is computing power constantly growing, resulting in relatively fast computation of previously impractical quantities of data (Shah et al., 2015), the objects of big data analysis can often be parsed with varying levels of granularity rendering the 'bigness' of data a function of the analytics in use. For instance, one could write a computer programme to identify semantic content photos, but the question arises, if this is applied to only one photo, does that make the analysis outside the realm of big data? What if one were to consider the millions of pixels, the properties of each of these pixels and the operations relating pixels together in the process of discovering semantic content? Even if we consider the relative size of data, our capacities to access and store it has historically outpaced analytical capacities so confronting the relative bigness of data is not a distinguishing characteristic (Yoo, 2015). And, even machine learning techniques which have been developed to classify very large datasets often outperform traditional statistical operations on smaller datasets (Hindman, 2015). Nevertheless, many of the technique used to analyse big data are selected precisely because they can scale from small to very large bodies of data.

How one defines big data depends on its context of application. We define big data here as the collection and analysis of the digital by-products of transactions and communications. As such, big data entities are digital objects with the following attributes:

1. They may be subject to lossless reproduction (Poster, 1990);
2. They are editable, meaning they can be modified either systematically or in part (Kallinikos et al., 2010); and
3. They are interoperable meaning that otherwise heterogeneous data objects such as sound, text and visual data can be combined and related (Crozier, 2012).

Big data is defined with respect to the material of the data object for two reasons. First, it is concerned with the new challenges and opportunities presented by these kinds of data which are ubiquitously generated through everyday activities. Far from being 'indirect evidence' of social and political phenomena (Dalton, 2016: 9), these data are the native objects which directly constitute a field of activity. Second, the focus on digital artefacts differentiates big data from other forms of data with respect to a distinctive set of specialised techniques involved in its collection and analysis. Given this definition, we have denoted a type of object that is worked on and we can point to a range of unique data collection and analytical tools which distinguish big data from other bodies of analytical work on the basis of the nature of the data objects.

The qualities of big data combine aspects of quantitative and qualitative social science, as well as some unique characteristics all its own. Like qualitative social science, big data may involve the extraction of meaning from texts, images or videos. Like quantitative data analysis, operations with big data may involve various forms of regression or scaling based on properties numerically derived from the analysis of those texts, images and videos. However, unstructured data also provides unique opportunities to gain insights into the social and political world, as these data are produced not by a system of expertise, as is the case with qualitative, quantitative and structured big data, but through the productions of individuals, collectivities and networks, for which they have meaning (Constantiou and Kallinikos, 2014). Unlike a survey, interview or observational notes, where the categories of analysis must be determined beforehand or in the moment of analysis, digital objects may be revisited and recoded multiple times, without doing violence to the original object.

The computational interface to collect and manipulate these data often exceeds the capacities of standard statistical packages such as SPSS or Stata which are familiar to many social scientists. Likewise NVivo has limited capacities to collect and process social media data. Instead, much of the work in data science is done using programming languages such as R and Python with their growing libraries which interface with application programming interfaces (APIs) and wide breadth of analytical packages (Theuwissen, 2015). Many kinds of data are more meaningfully related hierarchically and are accessed using a structured query language to extract and analyse subsets of data held in a relational database. For example, one might organise data from a Facebook page in terms of the page, when it was created, data about the user (for example, name, age, gender, friends) and so forth. Below that level are individual posts on those pages and the characteristics of those posts, such as the time and date of creation, or the number of likes, shares and comments. Below that level one can find comments, the data and time the comment was created, comment likes and replies – and all of these items also have metadata.

Big data and data collection

Digital objects pose unique possibilities and difficulties for researchers. The by-products of communications and transactions make take the form of unstructured social media communications, web pages and so forth, as well as administrative data which is collected and ordered in accordance with a system of expertise defining the values relevant for understanding a transaction. Each of these data formats poses different challenges for researchers. Administrative data is perhaps the most straightforward to handle as it is already structured into unique variables. Government departments often produce large volumes of administrative data, such as tax, census and electronic health records. These data are available in many countries, both developed and developing. Aggregate statistics about regions are often easily downloaded enabling the combination of these data with other geospatial information. Individual-level anonymised census data are often more difficult to obtain, being subject to a significant embargo period, with the provision for individual respondents to opt out of public disclosure. Likewise, as more medical records are made electronic, health researchers have access to very large volumes of data to track the effectiveness of treatments and procedures, as well as identify risk factors (Jensen et al., 2012; Bates et al., 2014).

Data formats

Digital data are often housed in online spaces which can be accessed, either openly, by anyone, or once a researcher has received special permission. In addition, the data obtained often comes with restrictions on the terms of service which do not always conform to standard practices of scientific research. For example, although Twitter makes very large volumes of data freely available (up to 1 percent of the entire 'firehose' of tweets at any one time which may amount to over 3,000 tweets per minute), they restrict researchers from making this data available to others seeking to replicate a set of results, as Twitter is also in the business of selling access to its data. There are four common ways in which researchers obtain digital data, whether the data is administrative or relatively unstructured social media. These comprise text formatted with extensible markup language (XML), via an API, web crawling and web scraping. We will deal with each of these methods of data collection in turn.

Extensible markup language (XML)

Extensible markup language, commonly referred to as XML, does not designate a particular language in which data is presented or ordered. Rather, it involves marking documents such that they may be accessed across different computer systems by tagging different parts of a document as units of meaning arrayed along nodes which connect them (Long, 2005). It was developed through the World Wide Web Consortium in 1996 as a means to facilitate the sharing of information across different systems in a way that enables them to be easily parsed, yet still be readable by humans (Bray et al., 1998). Each unit of meaning is administratively determined, making it easy to parse the data into discrete cells within a relational database. XML has been designed with accessibility in mind as these files can be often parsed into a table using import features in word processors such as Microsoft Word or the Calc programme from the free open source office suite, LibreOffice. Box 18.1 provides an example of what XML looks like. Here, we have a snippet of data from the Indian Open Government Data Platform concerning the disbursement of funds used for water sanitation across districts in India (Open Government Data Platform India, n.d.).

Each of the terms inside < > symbols provide instructions regarding the organisation of the data. As the data here is granular down to funds dispersed at a district level, the XML structure enables the data to be ordered hierarchically by state, such that analyses of funds received at the state level may be calculated, or they may be ordered in terms of a 'flat' file, suitable for storage in an ordinary spreadsheet if aggregated at the level of each district. Each value of meaning is demarcated by the category or variable to which it corresponds, bracketed on both sides with that category name. The '/' in the closing brackets indicates to an XML

Box 18.1 Nirmal Bharat Abhiyan under the Ministry of Drinking Water and Sanitation


```
<FinancialProgress>
<row>
<State_Name>ANDHRA PRADESH</State_Name> <District_Name>
ADILABAD</District_Name>
<Center_Release_of_funds>3334.50</Center_Release_of_funds>
<State_Release_of_funds>1026.28</State_Release_of_funds>
<Beneficiary_Release_of_funds>632.57</Beneficiary_Release_of_funds>
<Total_Release_of_funds>4993.35</Total_Release_of_funds>
<Center_Expenditure_Reported>2665.10</Center_Expenditure_Reported>
<State_Expenditure_Reported>1026.28</State_Expenditure_Reported>
<Beneficiary_Expenditure_Reported>619.96</Beneficiary_Expenditure_
Reported>
<Total_Expenditure_Reported>4311.34</Total_Expenditure_Reported>
</row>
<row>
<State_Name>ANDHRAPRADESH</State_Name>
<District_Name>ANANTAPUR</District_Name>
<Center_Release_of_funds>2213.51</Center_Release_of_funds>
<State_Release_of_funds>1456.50</State_Release_of_funds>
<Beneficiary_Release_of_funds>1331.82</Beneficiary_Release_of_funds>
<Total_Release_of_funds>5001.83</Total_Release_of_funds>
<Center_Expenditure_Reported>1242.57</Center_Expenditure_Reported>
<State_Expenditure_Reported>1456.41</State_Expenditure_Reported>
<Beneficiary_Expenditure_Reported>1325.30</Beneficiary_Expenditure_
Reported>
<Total_Expenditure_Reported>4024.28</Total_Expenditure_Reported>
```


parser that it has reached the end of a particular value and it is instructed to place subsequent information in a new cell.

Application programming interfaces (APIs)

APIs have been developed to make interfacing between various computer systems easier, by prescribing rules which stipulate how the systems operate. They standardise the range of activities a user may engage in order to both wall off certain functionalities and create capacities for users to accomplish prescribed tasks (Proffitt, 2013). They may do this by creating capacities for a system operating in one programming language to be accessible to a system operating in another (de Souza et al., 2004). If you have ever posted on Facebook or Twitter from a mobile phone, used Windows on a Macintosh, done online banking, then you have made use of an API. Governments have used APIs to make available parliamentary transcripts (The New South Wales, Australia Parliament http://data.nsw.gov.au/data/dataset/990b71fd-6f1e-456c-a42e-f4e0a4d0c93f). This data based on the transcripts which are professionally taken can be organised into a database enabling researchers to sort data based on party affiliation, each individual member, day or parliamentary session and so forth. APIs often include access limitations to reduce the strain on their systems. For example, Twitter offers free access to its 'streaming API' which provides up to 1 per cent of the total flow of tweets at any given time, allowing researchers to capture tweets in real time. This works well for many low-volume topics, and returns normally a little more than 3,000 tweets per minute. However, during some political or international sporting events, the volume can often be in the hundreds of thousands per minute. To receive access to those tweets, one must pay for access and the costs can sometimes be significant.

Other forms of data have been compiled and archived in a database, and subsequently made available for use by researchers. Scholars have shown a great interest, for example, in aggregating polling data to produce electoral forecasts. For those studying American politics, the Huffington Post Pollster project is a significant resource which archives polling data from the national and state level and makes these data available through the project API. Libraries have been written in many programming languages, such as Python, Ruby, R, Go and Node.js, to make accessing and utilising this data easier. Box 18.2 provides some sample code using the R pollsteR library (Arnold et al., 2016).

Box 18.2 Accessing the Huffington Post Pollster API

```
#Load the necessary libraries
library(pollstR)
library(scales)
library(ggplot2)

#list available poll topics
pollstr_polls()

#Select a polling topic (note: these can be found in the URL on the Pollster website)
polls<-pollster_chart_data(slug="2016-general-election-trump-vs-clinton-vs-johnson")

#calculate the margin in the polls
polls$Clinton_margin<-polls$Clinton-polls$Trump

#Select only polls from the start of June 2016 onward
pollPlot<-polls[polls$end_date>="2016-06-01",]

#Plot the margin over time
ggplot(pollPlot, aes(x=end_date, y=Clinton_margin))+geom_point()+
geom_smooth()+ylab("Clinton Lead")+xlab("Date")+ggtitle("Clinton-Trump Polling Margin (Clinton, Trump, Johnson)")+scale_x_date
(labels=date_format("%B %d"), date_breaks = "1 week")+theme(axis.
text.x = element_text(angle = 90, hjust = 1))
```

Figure 18.1 *Clinton–Trump–Johnson polling margin*

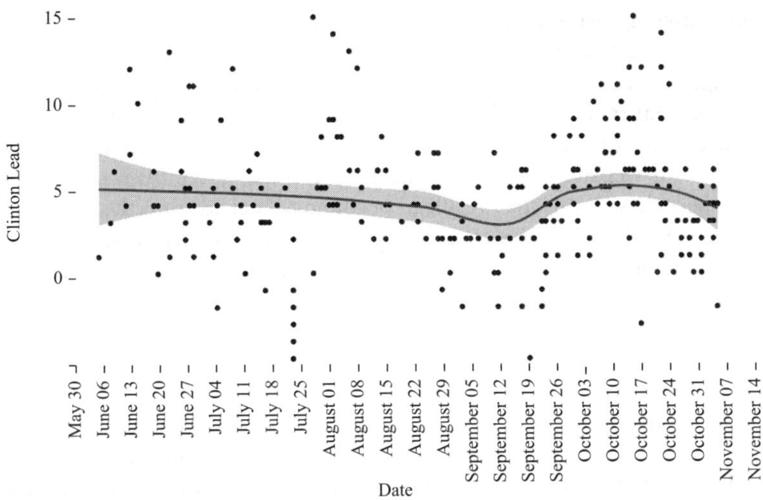

The calculations involved in most polling aggregators draw upon state-level data and involve fairly complex forecasting algorithms which have been developed using historical data. The model created here is very simple for purposes of illustration, it calculates the margin between the two leading candidates for President of the USA. The resulting plot of poll margins is presented in Figure 18.1. A local regression (loess) smoothing line is added to identify trends in the otherwise noisy data. Once one settles on the specific polling data, and a forecasting model, a computer can be set to run automatically, regularly updating the polling data on its own and producing a new forecast. As the polls in the 2016 US election cycle were off by a considerable margin, scholars may wish to study these data to figure out which polling models were most accurate and to identify if there were any factors that should have suggested lower confidence in the topline polling figures.

Web crawling

Web crawling is a process of tracing out connections from one website to a range of sites to which they link. Most web pages have a series of links to sites elsewhere on the web and identifying the range of these connections can help identify networks between actors which otherwise might not be readily apparent. The result of a web crawl is usually a list of hyperlinks indicating the connections between websites which may then be used to construct network maps between websites. Web crawling is not a simple task and there are complicated practical and ethical issues involved in web crawling. There is a variety of commercial and open source software products that enable one to crawl websites, which makes the process easy to execute, but also easy to get into trouble with for several reasons. First, each crawl of a website uses a lot of resources which takes away capacity for providing that web page to other users. It not only involves loading a single page, but searching through its links and loading all of the pages that form layers of a site. For this reason, many websites contain a document called 'robots.txt', which declares the terms on which automated access of a website may be conducted (Ackland, 2013: 90–91). Failure to respect these terms may result in becoming blocked from the website.

Web crawling requires at least one seed URL at which to start. From there, it identifies all entities connected to that starting page or series of pages and follows those links. Ethical web crawling can be achieved by setting limits on the number of links to follow, the time elapsed in collecting links or by limiting the 'recursion depth'. The recursion depth refers to the number of layers beyond the seed level which sets up the crawl; a recursion depth of one would capture all of the links contained within a page and follow those links to other pages without continuing further.

The output of web crawling is often the production of a network map showing which sites are linked to which sites and measures of particular network parameters, such as the centrality of various nodes. Network analysis has informed work such as Bennett and Segerberg's (2013: 79–80) study on the 'logic of connective action'. There are a number of software platforms that can be used to create and visualise this data, such as NodeXL, a plugin for the Microsoft Excel spreadsheet, and Gephi, which is a standalone open source software platform which can be also accessed through platforms such as R. Connections between different nodes can often be quite 'noisy' with all or most nodes having some connection to another, so researchers will often isolate just nodes with connections at a higher end of the distribution scale, or they may seek to isolate nodes at the other extreme with few connections to understand why those nodes connect significantly less than the rest of the network.

Web scraping

Web scraping involves capturing either entire pages or the content of pages from websites. In many cases, websites archive and render information, but do not provide an API which can systematise the delivery of information (Munzert et al., 2014). In those cases, web scraping can be a useful alternative. One may choose to scrape a single page, loop though a list of pages or combine web scraping with web crawling, in order to capture the pages linked to/from an initial page. The tools to conduct web scraping may be as simple as saving a web page in a web browser or using specialised programmes, either produced by others or developed by the researcher, to collect one or more web pages. Web scraping can be limited to a defined set of web sites or it may be combined with a web crawler to collect an undefined series of pages which are linked.

Web scraping can be useful to a variety of lines of research. For political scientists, one may be interested in how political parties or government agencies use their websites. One could scrape several layers of these websites collecting the content of the pages which can be later used to identify their emphasis on policies, the major lines of appeal to an electorate or, in the case of governments, the extent to which they emphasise participation in policy development. Researchers at Slate.com wanted to get a sense of where the US presidential candidates were holding campaign stops in 2012, so they used web scraping to obtain that information from campaign calendars (Kirk, 2012). Subsequent analyses could combine that information with precinct level voting patterns using data available through Google's Civic Information API to determine the effects of campaign stops on voting results. Sociologists may wish to use web scraping to get at the framing or messaging of organisations such as interest groups or to identify cultural positions advanced by advocacy organisations.

Web scraping typically returns the .html content of web pages. This content is often incomplete as many web pages have dynamic information being fed into the page which keeps it up to date. Therefore, web scraping does not always retrieve the entirety of the information in which one may be interested. In addition, once the pages have been captured, some mode of data extraction is often necessary to capture information embedded in the .html, such as the text and links which are presented on pages, and often the coding is not entirely standardised, so data extraction can be difficult. Researchers have developed libraries such as Beautiful Soup in Python (Richardson, 2016a) or rvest for R (Wickham, 2016) which aid in the separation of .html code from text and links, even when the .html code does not follow traditional coding conventions. Scrapes can be automated to capture data over set intervals to observe changes in organisational web pages. The output of web scraping can be then loaded into either a relational database or a flat file spreadsheet depending on the needs of the research.

Big data and data analysis

Once one has collected data, it needs to be analysed. Digital objects require a distinct set of techniques to extract information. We identify two kinds of analytical techniques which are often used on text and image data, natural language processing (NLP) and machine learning. Both of these techniques are used to extract meaning from relatively unstructured data sources. Before applying either of these sets of techniques, it is often imperative that the data is prepared. For simplicity, we will focus on text data here, but similar insights may be applied to graphics and video data. The preparation of text data usually involves normalising the text such that all words are reduced to lower case, since whether or not a word is at the start of a sentence normally does not affect its semantic meaning. Additionally, for functions which treat words as the basic unit of analysis, text undergoes a tokenisation process where the words are separated from punctuation and treated in a list format. In addition, some data collection processes will introduce, or leave, certain systematic errors, so those errors will have to be removed in order to prevent errant results. Depending on the data, one may wish to remove website URLs or mentions of other users, as they may be confused for semantic content.

NLP is a technique to identify the frequency of words, phrases, parts of speech and statistical relationships between words, across texts (Bird et al., 2009). One may classify a text or a genre of texts in relation to the terms most commonly used or the styles of speech most commonly found in these texts. There is a school of rhetoric which holds that meaning is disclosed through the relationships between terms which can be observed as statistical associations (Burke, 1974; Butler, 2011). Texts can be rendered in the form of a term document matrix (Feinerer and Hornik, 2015) which treats each word as a data point, enabling researchers to identify relationships between terms with respect to statistical properties. Text mining may involve searching documents for particular words or text strings.

Examples of this kind of research include analysing the emphasis on, and manner in which, human rights is discussed over time in the state newspapers in China, as an indication on shifting attitudes towards human rights. Scholars have also used natural language processing to categorise the political ideology of Twitter users in Spain and the USA to determine whether Twitter users tend to form online echo chambers or if they interact with persons who are ideologically distinct (Barberá, 2015; Barberá and Rivero, 2014). Scholars have coded strings of text using dictionaries which define emotional content as a means of understanding the role of emotions in social movement mobilisation, such as in the case of demonstrations in the wake of a rape attack in New Delhi, India (Ahmed et al., 2016).

Machine learning is an algorithmic process for classifying patterns (Richert and Coelho, 2013; Burscher et al., 2015). Classification involves predicting content across documents or data objects whereby patterns in the data are taken to be evidence of meaningful content. Machine learning is often applied to organised texts, but other applications have involved extracting semantic content from images, and even facial recognition (Bartlett et al., 2004; LeCun et al., 2015; Uçar et al., 2016). One of the more common applications of machine learning is called topic models. Topic models are useful for identifying the contents of a large body of text or large bodies of texts. There are several different algorithms with varied assumptions that go into topic models and there are a variety of topic model packages across programming languages which can implement topic models. One with the lowest learning curve is the structural topic model package, stm R (Roberts and Tingley, 2016); however, the Gensim package for Python enables a great deal of model specification (Rehurek, 2016) and most other common programming languages used by data scientists have the capacity to implement topic models.

Validation of text classification is critical to all of these procedures. Whether algorithmic text analysis is carried out deductively, through some form of NLP or a supervised form of machine learning, or through unsupervised topic models, there is always a potential error defined in terms of the deviation of a classification from some other mode of classification. Typically, human coding on a subset of the data not previously used to develop or train a classifier is used to check the extent to which the algorithm succeeds, or fails, in accurately capturing meanings. There are many classification dictionaries which have been developed for particular domains of communications and each have varying degrees of reliability (González-Bailón and Paltoglou, 2015).

Combining heterogeneous kinds of data

Often individual communications and transaction records will appear quite noisy. Here, the combination of more than one data set in terms of its relational properties may be of use. For example, tweet data on political preferences and policy choices may become more interpretable when combined with geospatial data which can locate tweets as emerging from within particular localities with known socioeconomic statuses and other properties. Scholars of political communication and journalism have looked at intermedia, that is, interactions between different media sources (Chadwick, 2013; Conway et al., 2015; Rogstad, 2016). Examples of intermedia include agenda setting processes between social media platforms, such as blogs or Facebook, and coverage of news topics in newspapers and on television (Neuman et al., 2014; Guggenheim et al., 2015). Blogs can be scraped, tweets and Facebook posts can be harvested and many news sources from around the world are available to researchers through databases such as Lexis/Nexis and Factiva. These articles may be parsed (with varying degrees of errors) through programmes written in languages such as Python and R (Bouchet-Valat, 2014, 2016). These data may be combined and analysed relationally over time to identify the roles of each in agenda setting and framing processes.

Limitations to big data

Given the inextricable links between theories and methods (Kuhn, 1970), no methodological approach, including the wide range of methods that go under the heading of big data, can be leveraged to address every research question. There are three principal areas where big data approaches have limited or circumscribed capacities to address mainstream theoretical domains within the social sciences: representativeness of a population; theory development; and the development of metrics which operationalise concepts.

Many popular treatments of big data emphasise 'N=ALL' as a defining property. However, researchers working in the field are quick to point out that is highly misleading and such beliefs can lead one to draw errant inferences (O'Neil and Schutt, 2013). Normally, one needs to be attentive to the range of persons and processes involved in the production of the digital artefacts in question. Administrative data is collected for specific populations and for specific purposes. Consequently, a study of factors that predict success in the workplace may flag gaps in a résumé as a negative predictor of employee performance. Although one may have a complete record of all previous employees in a firm or a sector, it may produce a bias against women who take time off to have a family, erroneously treating them in the same way as someone who has endured long periods of unemployment for performance reasons. 'All' is a relative category and there is always a category of information and cases excluded as the criteria of inclusion always involves an exclusion of other data points. To the extent big data analyses are used to direct action, they make increase the focus on certain areas creating path dependencies which reinforce those exclusions based on previous data inputs (O'Neil, 2016).

Perhaps one of the most controversial big data applications has been efforts to mine Twitter posts in order to predict election results. A range of efforts have shown positive correlations between candidate mentions or sentiment voiced in relation to parties and politicians on Twitter and the final election results (Kravets, 2010; Tumasjan et al., 2011; Ceron et al., 2015; Cameron et al., 2016). At the same time, Twitter users constitute a very small portion of the likely voting population in most cases and Twitter users are not typical of the rest of the electorate (Bekafigo and McBride, 2013; Barberá and Rivero, 2014). More generally, social media-using populations are not representative of society as a whole, which would induce biases in analyses attempting to infer societal distributions of individual-level attributes from social media sources (Dalton, 2016; Hargittai, 2015). Indeed, recent research suggests that there is little analytical leverage behind very complex vote models that provide information beyond party identification and voting history (Hersh, 2015). Beyond the question of representativeness, big data often involve the properties of interactions directly rather than individuals. Although such data may in some cases be aggregated at the level of individuals, they only provide a limited picture of an individual identity performed, constructed, enacted or revealed under particular conditions.

Conclusion: big data and the future of social science

The big data revolution in social science goes beyond the development of a set of methods for data collection and analysis. It has more profound consequences for how we orient ourselves in disciplines of academic enquiry. The impact of most methodological innovations occurs within a wider movement within a discipline, such as the behaviouralist movement within the social sciences in the 1960s (Easton, 1965) or the Perestroika movement (Flyvbjerg, 2001; Monroe, 2015) in political science, which emerged at the start of the twenty-first century. Each of these movements in methods has come with claims of epistemic superiority and greater real-world relevance. Scholars in big data suggest likewise these data will be transformative, opening up wide spaces of social and political life to researchers who have struggled in the past, using imperfect proxies through surveys, experiments with questionable external validity and limited qualitative observations in the form of ethnographic research (boyd and Crawford, 2012; King, 2011, 2014). Each of these methods approach subject matters differently. Traditionally, methods and theories within the social sciences approach their subject in terms of either collectivities or individuals. Big data is better suited to systems analysis which sees communications and interactions, rather than actors in the form of individuals or collectivities, as constitutive of political and social life, as these are its unit of collected data (Easton, 1965; Luhmann, 1995).

Big data raises further issues for conventional thinking about methodologies. Social science methods have been traditionally separated into categories of qualitative and quantitative methods. Qualitative methods have traditionally concerned construing small sets of texts, notes, encounters, and so forth in terms of units of meaning which cannot be adequately represented as numerical symbols. However, to the extent those interpretations can be made explicit, and applied consistently thereby ensuring measurement reliability, they may be algorithmically operationalised. That is not to say a computer necessarily engages in the same process of interpretation as a computer renders outputs computationally. Nevertheless, to the extent computational means can classify data which has otherwise been approached only through qualitative means, at least some of the attributes of traditionally qualitative data analysis can scale to very large numbers of cases. This begins to bridge the gap between qualitative and quantitative social science which has been taken as a foundational divide within the social sciences.

Further reading

- For conceptual debates over the nature of big data, see boyd and Crawford (2012), Constantiou and Kallinikos (2014) and Ekbia and colleagues (2015).
- For a general overview of the opportunities presented by big data, see Savage and Burrows (2007). For a critical perspective from a political science perspective, see Dalton's (2016) critique of big data's limitations. For a data science perspective on the opportunities and limits of big data, see O'Neil (2016).
- For discussion of ethical concerns in conducting big data and ways to anonymise data, see Hewson (2016), Tene and Polonetsky (2012) and Willemsen (2016).
- For an introduction to natural language processing in the Python language which does not presume extensive programming knowledge, see Bird and colleagues (2009).

- For an overview of machine learning and how to build machine learning systems in Python, see Richert and Coelho (2013) and Grus (2015) which provide code snippets. For approaches to data science in R, see Wickham and Grolemund (2017).
- More generally, in building your own code, you will likely encounter bugs in the process of getting your code right; https://stackoverflow.com is an excellent resource to look for solutions or pose your questions to a community of experts.

Chapter 19

The Relevance of Political Science

GERRY STOKER, B. GUY PETERS AND JON PIERRE

In this chapter, we analyse the debate about relevance in political science. We think the debate has moved on quite a lot since we raised the issue in the third edition of *Theories and Methods* in 2010. Together with colleagues (Stoker et al., 2015) we published a book on the subject in 2015 which noted that while political science has constructed for itself a way of working that appears often to give little or no credence to the demands of relevance there was a sense of awakening to the issue that could be identified. We could find no 'in principle' objections to relevance that could plausibly be argued. Political science is engaged with the wider world whether its wants to be or not. It would be odd indeed if there was no connection between the agenda of political science and the concerns raised in 'real'-world politics. But that is the extent of the consensus. Some in political science are, reasonably enough, concerned about too narrow a focus on relevance as doing the bidding of policymakers. That is not the only type of relevance we are advocating; instead we want to celebrate the diverse ways in which political science is tackling the issue.

Our starting point – which we think is very widely shared – is that political science should be asking questions to which others, outside the profession, might want to know the answers. But, when getting to the detail of how relevance might be defined and delivered, some significant differences of opinion begin to emerge. The bulk of this chapter explores these emerging differences on relevance.

Before exploring these approaches, it can be noted that sometimes elites – political, media or technocratic – seem remarkably unwilling to listen to political science. Many citizens might also wonder about the relevance of political science. In part, because the insights and research produced by political science are so voluminous it is not surprising that non-academics argue that important issues are missed. There is just too much work to sift through and only certain types of work tend to achieve prominence. The 'surprise' expressed in some quarters over the Brexit vote in the UK or the Trump presidential election in the USA in 2016 reflected a narrow focus on the work of a few academics engaged in the vexed practice of spot predictions on elections. They might have been less shocked if the media and others had taken notice of the stream of more general academic writing about the democratic deficit in the European Union (EU), the rise of populism and the emerging cleavages created by powerful forces of economic globalisation, large-scale migration and increased inequality. More specifically in respect of political elites Ronald Rogowski (2013: 216) argues:

> Politicians simply do not like the policies that scholarly research supports, prefer policies (often put forward by charlatans) that better suit their interests, and seek to suppress or ignore evidence-based research that contradicts their own, or their 'base' voters', ideologies. When these same politicians assert piously that political science offers no policy-relevant research, what they really mean is that it offers no research that supports their own biases.

Rogowski goes on to identify diverse areas of policy over immigration, electoral rules and issues of redistribution where well-founded insights are simply not taken up. As Wildavsky (1989) argued decades ago speaking truth to power is a far from easy task. Nothing we argue in this chapter undermines the validity of these concerns. There is no easy tie-up between evidence and policy, indeed the two are quite regularly strangers (for some evidence on the non-use of evidence, see Stoker and Evans, 2016). Political science on its own cannot change the factors that drive policymakers to neglect evidence, but that does not absolve the profession from a need to focus on how to create the opportunity for its work to be relevant. To that end we need to understand the different takes on relevance within the profession. We can identify six positions, not all of which are mutually exclusive. But all are worthy of consideration.

Position 1: political science should do good science and if the science is good it will be relevant

This argument starts by recognising that what constitutes relevance is not fixed. It can vary according to time, circumstance and indeed the standpoint of the observer. Something that might appear irrelevant can, after a political crisis or turn of events, have a pressing relevance. Think of colleagues toiling away on some obscure part of a constitution or a country that is not a normal focus of attention and then something happens and all of a sudden that work is relevant. Peter John (2013) suggests that academics simply need to be more confident about their claims of relevance:

> Academics should stand their ground and have more confidence in their intellectual project. They can claim that the systemic study of politics adds value in a way that the methods of other knowledge professionals cannot. To be craven to the practitioner world makes academics too similar to other knowledge providers so they cannot

> claim comparative advantage. In this way, academics are bound to be less influential as politicians and policy makers can get that kind of expertise more easily elsewhere. If academics stick to the production of knowledge, which may involve the use of technical terms and complex models and methods, in the end the policy makers will come to them, rather than the other way round. (John, 2013: 172)

His point finds many echoes in the commentary of others (Lupia, 2000). Political science delivers robust knowledge and it is communicated in a way that those who take the time to consume it can do so.

There are several examples of this kind of relevance being demonstrated by political science and it can make its impact in different ways. It can be conceptualised as the *enlightenment* function where a level of conceptual and empirical work on political science has changed thinking in the world of practice. Here we take the case of work on governance which has captured a range of issues and concerns that are central to practice (see the claims made by Rhodes, 2007). The second type of impact could be referred to as *critical challenge* where the role of political science has been to point to the failings and consequences of current practice and outline alternatives. The work on the democratic deficit facing the EU would be a potential example, and given the Brexit vote in the UK it could be argued more attention should have been paid to it. The third type of impact could be described as *technical tweaking*, as it deals with those more focused and narrow interventions where detailed expert knowledge held by political science can help in the reform of established systems or institutions. Here the example of reforms to electoral systems might be relevant. All of these examples share in common a commitment to doing good political science, and then the arrival of a window of opportunity and a listening audience who find the work insightful and valuable.

Position 2: political science should be better at communicating its results; if it were it would be more relevant

The resources and commitment of the profession, comparatively speaking, go into the production of the research and not its delivery. Worse, there are times when political science articles appear to be deliberately sprinkled with jargon, complex language or non-intuitive formulae and diagrams. Sometimes it is difficult to realise you are doing this when, as an academic, you are embedded in a particular literature or debate. Sometimes it may be that there is a tendency to see the obscure or intricate as marks of academic excellence; they can also act in a gatekeeping role, letting only a few specialists enter the debate. Sometimes difficult writing styles evolve to mask commonplace insights with a cloak of profundity.

In the world where many actors and institutions face greater calls for accountability a failure to share and show the value of work funded by taxpayers puts political science in a vulnerable position. The focus for this challenge is on communication. Matt Flinders has led this line of attack arguing: 'it is not therefore that political science has become irrelevant, but that it has generally failed to promote and communicate the social value and benefit of the discipline in an accessible manner' (Flinders, 2013: 164). Resolving the situation requires more political imagination and for political scientists to become better in the arts of translation, that will require the acquisition of some new skills but a rebalancing of where effort is put within the profusion. What Flinders refers to as triple writing – a scholarly first piece, followed by a more popular summary and a journalistic short blog or media story to bring the study to life and attract attention – is the order of what is required to a much greater degree for the future.

Deborah Lupton (2014) conducted an international survey of the use of social media by academics that suggests that at least in terms of using social media many academics have incorporated communication at the heart of their professional practice. She shows that those academics that 'are using social media are doing so often in complex and sophisticated ways, creating a social media "ecosystem" in which they have learnt to work with and exploit the affordances of a variety of tools and platforms' (Lupton, 2014: 30). Using social media tools and platforms brings a direct benefit to academics in that it expands their networks and connections with others' research but it also fulfils the objective set by Flinders. Blogging, using Twitter and engaging through other social media platforms achieves 'the purpose of sharing information and providing advice as part of a gift economy of producing material to share freely with others. From this perspective scholarship and knowledge are not viewed as a marketable commodity but rather as a social good' (Lupton, 2014: 30).

Position 3: political science should be prepared to have its agenda set by problem-solving or puzzle-solving concerns that matter to policymakers and citizens; if it did it would be more relevant

This position rests on a call for political science to move to a problem-oriented focus to unify and share insights from various parts of the discipline, not least normative and empirical theorists. The argument is that there should be a relationship between the world of political analysis and the practice of politics in the world. Political science should, as part of its vocation, seek not to pursue an agenda driven by its own theories or methods as if it was in a separate world, sealed off from the concern of its fellow citizens. As Shapiro (2004: 40) puts it: the problems addressed by the profession need to be 'theoretically illuminating and convincingly intelligible to outsiders'. If the discipline was re-oriented in this manner it would enliven both normative and empirical theorising by bringing into focus new and challenging agendas and also provide a more powerful claim to relevance on the part of the discipline.

The idea of looking at problems and puzzles has an immediate appeal. A good example might be why did so many people in the USA vote against what would appear to be their self-interests in the 2016 US presidential election? Some of the areas supporting Donald Trump, and his proposals to repeal the Affordable Care Act, most strongly were those which had had the largest increase in health insurance coverage under the act. If rational choice theories are taken as our starting point, this is clearly a puzzle.

There are indeed many instances where political science does address problems or puzzles of concern to non-academic audiences. But there are also occasions when the main themes in debates in political science appear to have little in them that could command attention outside of that small world. Starting with puzzles that can be recognised by or shared with others offers a way forward that might bring greater relevance and impact in its slipstream.

Position 4: political science should be prepared to develop a capacity not just for analysing problems but also for developing solutions; that move would enhance its capacity for relevance

Stoker (2012, 2013a and 2013b) suggests that the way forward is not just to develop a problem-oriented political science; it is for a solution-seeking political science. Herbert Simon (1996) argues that in the sciences there are two great traditions: the science of nature and the science of the artificial. The former focuses on what is and the latter on things that are created by human beings. As Simon points out, the science of the artificial is not a simple derivative of pure science; it is a neglected pathway. It is a different, equally valid and demanding way of looking at the challenge of academic understanding. Engineering, the medical sciences and other disciplines embrace the challenge of the sciences of the artificial and in doing so have focused on the issue of design: how to achieve intentional change. Design thinking can be applied to all institutions, products and systems that are created by human beings. Political systems are not natural and so they could be viewed as artificial, with functions, goals and the capacity for adaptation. Political systems exist for a purpose and so are open to design thinking. As Simon (1996: 111) puts it: 'everyone designs who devises courses of action aimed at changing existing situations into the preferred ones'.

It is possible to identify some pioneering work in this style. Reynolds' (2010) work on *Designing Democracy in A Dangerous World* provides an example of this kind of design thinking in practice. Reynolds reviews a range of options for intervention but argues those interventions need to be understood in terms of the context, history and institutional environment in which they are being applied. He develops a complex diagnostic toolkit based on a careful synthesis of existing knowledge in order to judge what intervention might work and then applies that thinking in examples as diverse as Iraq, Burma, Sudan and Afghanistan. The intervention models that emerge have a mixed tracked record in application, reflecting the wider play of power and complexity of issues in real cases but, nevertheless, show the value of design thinking. Elinor Ostrom's work (1990) is worthy of celebration and is highly praised as her Nobel award indicates; she offers a rare example of explicit design focus. Ostrom identifies at least eight design principles. Her design principles include identifying who key stakeholders are and giving them rights to participate in the setting up of any system of management. She argues for graduated sanctions against rule-breakers and a nested capacity for governance in larger more complex settings. Underlying the overall approach is a focus on the importance of norm-building for successful collective action. Ostrom's work starts from value propositions about the nature of good governance which stresses the degree to which higher levels of government should not crowd out self-organisation at lower levels but equally it does not argue that allocation decisions should be left to the market, rather its focus is in designing the capacity for stakeholder-based collective action. The design and research work is on how to support collective action among stakeholders particularly in common pool resource settings where access to a valued good (water, fisheries) needs to be managed to sustain the resource.

The study of public policy is one area of political science that almost inherently has relevance for the public and for political leaders. If we accept Lasswell's dictum that politics is about 'who gets what' then to study politics is to study the distribution of goods and services within a society. We can discuss the relevance of designing institutions, but the design of public policy is perhaps even more important for shaping the life chances of citizens. And at least at one level the study of public policy is the study of designing. While much of the political science literature discusses policy in terms of processes (see Birkland, 2014), there should also be a focus on the content of the policy and its consequences.

The challenge for political science in dealing with public policy is to link our knowledge of policy processes with the substance. Detailing the way in which a piece of legislation is enacted and then implemented is important, but the process is largely the same whether the legislation is well designed or a disaster in the making. While we may never become true experts in public health or environmental science, we can (and many do) understand the content of policies. That knowledge of substance can enable political scientists to provide useful advice about the design of policies and their likelihood of success, and enable us to partner with other disciplines in the design of programmes that can be both effective and politically feasible.

Therefore, academics such as Ostrom and others have been concerned with the design of institutions, so too can political scientists be concerned with the design of policies (Howlett, 2010; Peters, 2017). Design involves at a minimum some knowledge of the causes of policy problems, and some knowledge of the instruments which the public sector uses for putting policies into effect. While this may appear a somewhat technocratic solution to a political problem, having a clear and integrated conception of what the policy should look like enables a better analysis of the substantive and political consequences of the policy.

Further, designing policies can be conceptualised in democratic terms (see Ingram, 2016). Just as we design institutions to promote democracy and/or effective decision-making, so too can we design policies for inclusiveness. In designing policies to promote political values, such as inclusiveness and participation, political scientists have a real advantage over other would-be designers who might focus just on technical detail. As argued above, if the duty of political science is to create better politics and democracy, then part of that duty is creating policies that fulfil those political goals.

In addition, however, political science in its pursuit of efficient policy design tends to forget the politics of policymaking. Politicians certainly want their policies to be designed in such a way that they can contribute to resolving the problems they are intended to address. But they also care deeply about strategic gains. Policies should not just be efficient but also pay off before the next election. If there is political capital to be harvested, policies should be managed closely by government, otherwise they could be decentralised or contracted out. Policies should be efficient but they should also speak to core constituencies and marginal voters and so on. Political science can make a contribution to the intellectual dimension of policy design, but is less equipped to speak to the strategic assessments of policy.

Position 5: political science needs to develop a more engaged co-production approach to research, working alongside actors outside academia to address their concerns and so advance the relevance of research

An initial carrier of this message became known as the Perestroika movement with its challenge to the American Political Science Association (Monroe, 2005; Schram and Caterino, 2006). The movement was mixed in its focus and depth of analysis, but one of the essential points to emerge was its criticism of mainstream political science for too great a reliance on highly sophisticated quantitative methods, rational choice modelling and game theory, and which neglects those qualitative traditions of study that might have a more direct engagement with those involved in politics as policymakers and citizens. A political science that is entirely dominated by esoteric presentations and technical disputes makes its work inaccessible and therefore unusable by ordinary citizens.

There are other streams in this approach that argue that research could be carried out with and through those that are the focus of its concerns. Richardson (2016b: 207) argues for a citizen social science:

> Citizen social science takes many forms, but, in essence, it is about greater hands-on involvement of lay people in scientific research: doing it, designing it, understanding it and debating it. Applied in the right way, citizen social science has untapped potential as a positive development in its own right, and as a tool for more direct policy use. Participatory approaches to both research and policy are designed to enhance research at the margins – whether this is with traditionally under-represented groups or sensitive, controversial and complex topics. An attraction of citizen social science is that it offers something that feels fresh and innovative and could grab the public interest.

The argument for engaging with those who are the focus of the research is that it means you can reach different groups, gain new insights, achieve a legitimacy and bring immediacy to your findings, giving them relevance.

A related argument is that co-production will help to drive the relevance of research by engaging potential users throughout. Armstrong and Alsop (2010: 209) argue:

> Engaging with potential users from the earliest stage of the research process is a key factor in helping to ensure that research findings are subsequently taken up and exploited. Our work has shown that sustained involvement of users is one of the most important determinants of policy impact. Namely, that users are involved throughout the research process, from agenda setting, through design, fieldwork and communication of outcomes. In co-production, the traditional distinction between research users and research producers becomes transcended and transparent.

There can be a great deal of value in working directly with users but there can be difficulties. Roles and relationships need to be carefully negotiated. Specialisation has its virtues so it is not unreasonable if users want the specialist researchers to make key technical decisions about how to collect data or how to analyse that data. Co-production does not mean the abandonment of expertise but rather a greater willingness to share its processes.

Position 6: political science needs to embrace a wider role in creating a civic culture essential to democracy; if it does that it will be relevant

There is a strong current in political science that has reacted against an over-emphasis on sophisticated methods. One of the first and most important proponents of this argument was Bernard Crick (2005). He was very concerned that the technical and methodological sophistication that was dominating American political science would encourage a way of studying politics that would see political science become disengaged from the practice of politics. That there are distinctive roles for those that study politics and those that engage in it is not in dispute. Political scientists are not politicians or activists and their core challenge involves seeking a version of truth rather than influence. Political science's job is not so much to provide daily commentary on politics or always to deal with current issues in politics but rather to focus on the fundamental features of how politics works. Crick (2005: 242) comments we 'argue only for relevance and an independent-minded critical engagement, not uncritical commitment or loyalty to party'. Political science, in Crick's opinion, needs to engage in creating the conditions for political citizenship to flourish. He led the way in debates about political education in the UK (Tonge et al., 2012) and there is evidence that citizenship education does impact effectively on some if not all groups. Around the world there is a well-established practice (Cogan and Derricott, 2014) that has shown some successes but also limitations.

For those political scientists concerned about political events – such as Brexit – which could be a product of a populism that will cause considerable damage the need to think about a wider civic engagement again comes into focus. Jennings and Lodge (2016) reacted to the events of 2106 in the UK and the USA with a sense of having witnessed a failed public debate or even the emergence of post-truth politics by arguing:

> For those believing in a pure version of 'science', the political science discipline is about 'knowledge' with little concern for the wider environment. This ignores a much more significant contribution that political science should play in promoting the normative foundations of liberal democracy. This is not to discourage critical analysis and commentary, but a renewed focus on the prerequisites for an open and tolerant society to conduct politics. This would require a much deeper engagement with society beyond one-off events such as open day events and school visits. This requires encouragement for universities to become part of the wider conversation about the importance of certain constitutional and democratic norms. In other words, political science, if it wants to live in a liberal democracy and be in a position to work openly and freely, needs to return to a concern with protecting the very foundations of liberal democracy.

The argument here is that political science has a wider duty to create the conditions for a better politics (on this argument, see also Stoker, 2017). If you study politics the argument goes that you cannot wash your hands of responsibility if the practice of politics appears to be falling into patterns that will undermine its very legitimacy as a means of decision-making. You cannot have democracy without politics; so, if you think democracy is worth protecting then so is politics.

Where next for relevance?

The final part of the chapter starts by restating the manifesto in our recent book on *The Relevance of Political Science* in order to provide guidelines for those within political science interested in taking relevance more seriously:

1. Have confidence in the value of rigorous scientific analysis and do not allow relevance to compromise high-quality investigation but embrace it as a critical friend, providing tough and different challenges for your evidence and argument.
2. Develop relevance not as an afterthought in the construction of your research but put it at the heart of what you select to investigate and how you present and share the outputs of your research. Set your agenda in dialogue with others outside the profession and improve your communication skills using traditional and new media.
3. Offer solutions as well as analyses of problems and take on board some of the arguments for a design orientation in your analysis so that evidence and argument can be applied as thoroughly to the construction of potential answers as well as to spelling out the challenges facing desired change.
4. Support methodological pluralism in the discipline as that variety of approaches is most likely to deliver a rich array of relevant work that can reach out to a diverse group of potential users.
5. Be committed to work in partnership with other disciplines to improve the relevance of your work. Good and innovative work often is cross-disciplinary. Many issues have a 'wicked' or multidimensional quality so again working across disciplinary boundaries enhances the chances of relevance.
6. Actively cultivate links with intermediaries as appropriate – think tanks, journalists, special advisers, political parties, citizens' organisations and social media networks – in order to boost the relevance of your work.
7. Celebrate the role of teaching as a means of delivering relevance by encouraging a cadre of critically aware citizens and policymakers.

The key shared factor in all of these recommendations is that they want to celebrate and promote a diversity of practice and a commitment to working across boundaries within the profession of political science. This theme is a key one for *Theories and Methods*. It seems worthwhile to return to it in the conclusion of both this chapter and the book.

Sometimes, political scientists express a certain envy of economics as a discipline (Wade, 2009). Economics has developed a near monoculture based around a narrow set of assumptions about human nature, a preference for formal models devoid of history or culture and a set of quantitative toolkit methods for undertaking research and judging evidence. This development was not natural but was the result of a movement. As

Wade (2009: 113) argues, 'convinced there was only one true approach, economists gave little value to the intellectual equivalent of biodiversity. In department after department, neoclassicals, once having reached a critical mass, tended to gang up on non-neoclassicals and force them out or block their appointment.' There were costs involved in this approach. Strangely the discipline lost its capacity to explain or investigate the structural workings of the economy. Hence the UK monarch asked academic economists at the London School of Economics why no one saw the 2007/08 financial crisis coming (www.telegraph.co.uk/news/uknews/theroyalfamily/3386353/The-Queen-asks-why-no-one-saw-the-credit-crunch-coming.html). But more than that when advice was offered by economists it propagated the constraining assumptions of self-interested behaviour and if anything helped to reinforce the influence of those behaviours and the assumption that they are normal and not significantly matched by value-based or moral commitments to do the right thing by others (Bowles, 2016). Moreover, the narrow focus on formal modelling appeared to encourage a neglect of the wider role of institutions in shaping outcomes or a concern with issues such as justice and fairness in market relations. The monoculture of economics has in the last decade come under counter-colonisation from psychology and history, and most notably through the rise of behavioural economics (Thaler, 2015) which has challenged assumptions about how people make decisions and what they value in making decisions. Yet economics has created a monocultural framework from which it may not be able to escape from very easily; indeed, it may decline to do so, given the path dependent nature of developments and sunk investments in a certain way of working.

Political science has avoided the path leading to a monoculture and our argument is that it should continue to do so. Diversity and cross boundary engagement should be the watchwords for the future of the discipline. Both understanding and relevance gain from not being too narrowly focused but equally appreciating and understanding the diverse threads of the discipline of political science becomes more pressing. Hence this book has made it to its fourth edition.

Bibliography

Abbott, A. (2001) *Chaos of Disciplines* (Chicago, IL: University of Chicago Press).

Abdelal, R. (2007) *Capital Rules: The Construction of Global Finance* (Cambridge, MA: Harvard University Press).

Abizadeh, A. (2007) 'Cooperation, Pervasive Impact and Coercion: On the Scope (Not Site) of Distributive Justice', *Philosophy and Public Affairs*, 35(4): 318–358.

Acker, J. (1990) 'Hierarchies, Jobs, Bodies: A Theory of Gendered Organisations', *Gender and Society*, 4(2): 139–158.

Ackerly, B., Stern, M. and True, J. (eds.) (2006) *Feminist Methodologies for International Relations* (Cambridge: Cambridge University Press).

Ackland, R. (2013) *Web Social Science: Concepts, Data and Tools for Social Scientists in the Digital Age* (Thousand Oaks, CA: Sage).

Adam, B. (1990) *Time and Social Theory* (Cambridge: Polity Press).

—— (1995) *Timewatch* (Cambridge: Polity Press).

—— (1998) *Timescapes of Modernity* (London: Routledge).

Adcock, R. and Collier, D. (2001) 'Measurement Validity: A Shared Standard for Qualitative and Quantitative Research', *American Political Science Review*, 95: 529–546.

Adler, E. (2002) 'Constructivism and International Relations', in W. Carlsnaes, Risse, T. and Simmons, B. (eds.) *Handbook of International Relations* (London: Sage): 95–118.

Adler, E. and Pouliot, V. (2011) *International Practices* (New York: Cambridge University Press).

Adorno, T.W. (1976) *The Positivist Dispute in German Sociology* (London: Heineman).

Adorno, T.W., Frenkel-Brunswik, E., Levinson, D.J. and Sanford, R.N. (1950) *The Authoritarian Personality* (New York: Harper & Row).

Ahmed, S., Jaidka, K. and Cho, J. (2016) 'Tweeting India's Nirbhaya Protest: A Study of Emotional Dynamics in an Online Social Movement', *Social Movement Studies*, 16(4): 1–19.

Akram, S. (2012) 'Fully Unconscious and Prone to Habit: The Characteristics of Agency in the Structure and Agency Dialectic', *Journal for the Theory of Social Behaviour*, 43(1): 45–65.

Allison, G.T. (1971) *Essence of Decision: Explaining The Cuban Missile Crisis* (Boston, MA: Little Brown).

Almond, G.A. (1990) *A Discipline Divided: Schools and Sects in Political Science* (Newbury Park, CA: Sage).

—— (1996) 'Political Science: The History of the Discipline', in Goodin, R. and Klingemann, H. (eds.) *A New Handbook of Political Science* (Oxford: Oxford University Press).

Almond, G.A. and Verba, S. (1963) *The Civic Culture: Political Attitudes and Democracy in Five Nations* (Princeton, NJ: Princeton University Press).

Altemeyer, R. (1981) *Right-Wing Authoritarianism* (Winnipeg: University of Manitoba Press).

Althusser, L. (2005) 'Marxism and Humanism', in Althusser, L. (ed.) *For Marx* (London: Verso).

Althusser, L. and Balibar, E. (2009) *Reading Capital* (London: Verso).
Alvarez, R.M. 2016. *Computational Social Science* (New York: Cambridge University Press).
Alvesson, M. and Kaj S. (2009) *Reflexive Methodology: New Vistas for Qualitative Research*, 2nd edition (London: Sage Publications).
Amin, S. (1974) *Accumulation on a World Scale* (New York: Monthly Review Press).
Anderson, C. and Mendes, S. (2006) 'Learning to Lose: Election Outcomes, Democratic Experience and Political Protest Potential', *British Journal of Political Science*, 36(1): 91–111.
Angrist, J., Bettinger, E., Bloom, E., King, E. and Kremer, M. (2002) 'Vouchers for Private Schooling in Colombia: Evidence from a Randomized Natural Experiment', *American Economic Review*, 92(5): 1535–1558.
Angrist, J., Bettinger, E. and Kremer, M. (2006) 'Long-Term Educational Consequences of Secondary School Vouchers: Evidence from Administrative Records in Colombia', *The American Economic Review*, 96(3): 847–862.
Anievas, A. (ed.) (2010) *Marxism and World Politics* (London: Routledge).
Annesley, C. and Gains, F. (2010) 'The Core Executive: Gender, Power and Change', *Political Studies*, 58(5): 909–929.
Antonsich, M. (2008) 'European Attachment and Meanings of Europe: A Qualitative Study in the EU-15', *Political Geography*, 27(6): 691–670.
Archer, M. (1995) *Realist Social Theory: The Morphogenetic Approach* (Cambridge: Cambridge University Press).
—— (2000) *Being Human: The Problems of Agency* (Cambridge: Cambridge University Press).
Arellano, M. (2003) *Panel Data Econometrics* (Oxford: Oxford University Press).
Arendt, H. (1961) *Eichmann in Jerusalem. A Report on the Banality of Evil* (New York: Viking Press).
Armstrong, F. and Alsop, A. (2010) 'Debate: Co-production Can Contribute to Research Impact in the Social Sciences', *Public Money & Management*, 30(4): 208–210.
Arnold, J.B., Leeper, T.J. and Linzer, D. (2016) pollstR: Client for the HuffPost Pollster API.
Avolio, B.J. and Gardner, W.L. (2005) 'Authentic Leadership Development: Getting to the Root of Positive Forms of Leadership', *The Leadership Quarterly*, 16(3): 315–338.
Axelsen, D. (2013) 'The State Made Me Do It: How Anti-cosmopolitanism is Created by the State', *Journal of Political Philosophy,* 21(4): 451–472.
Ayer, A.J. (1971) *Language, Truth and Logic*, 2nd edition (Harmondsworth: Penguin).
Baderin, A. (2016) 'Political Theory and Public Opinion: Against Democratic Restraint', *Politics, Philosophy and Economics*, 15(3): 209–233.
Badie, D. (2010) 'Groupthink, Iraq and the War on Terror: Explaining US Policy Shift Towards Iraq', *Foreign Policy Analysis*, 6(4): 277–296.
Baer, D.L. (1993) 'Political Parties: The Missing Variable in Women and Politics Research', *Political Research Quarterly*, 46(3): 547–576.
Baesens, B. (2014) *Analytics in a Big Data World: The Essential Guide to Data Science and its Applications* (New York: Wiley).
Bakker, R., de Vries, C., Edwards, E., Hooghe, L., Jolly, S., Marks, G., Polk, J., Rovny, J., Steenbergen, M. and Vachudova, M.A. (2012) 'Measuring

Party Positions in Europe: The Chapel Hill Expert Survey Trend File, 1999–2010', *Party Politics*, 21(1): 143–152.

Baldwin, D. (ed.) (1993) *Neorealism and Neoliberalism: The Contemporary Debate* (Princeton, NJ: Princeton University Press).

Banaszak, L.A., Beckwith, K. and Rucht, D. (eds.) (2003) *Women's Movements Facing the Reconfigured State* (Cambridge: Cambridge University Press).

Bandura, S. (2006) 'Toward a Psychology of Human Agency', *Perspectives on Psychological Science*, 1(2): 164–204.

Bankes, S., Lempert, R., Popper, S., 2002. 'Making Computational Social Science Effective Epistemology, Methodology, and Technology', *Social Science Computer Review*, 20: 377–388.

Barabas, J., Barrilleaux, C. and Scheller, D. (2007) 'Issue Turnout: Field Experiments with Ballot Initiatives in Florida', Paper presented at the annual meeting of the American Political Science Association, Chicago, IL, 16 August.

Barber, B.R. (2013) *If Mayors Ruled the World: Dysfunctional Nations, Rising Cities* (New Haven, CT: Yale University Press).

Barberá, P. (2015) 'Birds of the Same Feather Tweet Together: Bayesian Ideal Point Estimation Using Twitter Data', *Political Analysis*, 23(1): 76–91.

Barberá, P. and Rivero, G. (2014) 'Understanding the Political Representativeness of Twitter Users', *Social Science Computer Review*, 33(6): 712–729.

Barnes, S. and Kaase, M. (1979) *Political Action* (London: Sage).

Barry, B. (1970) *Sociologists, Economists and Democracy* (London: Collier-Macmillan).

—— (1990) *Political Argument: A Reissue with New Introduction* (Berkeley, CA: University of California Press).

Barthes, R. (1977) 'The Death of the Author', in Barthes, R. (ed.) *Image, Music, Text: Essays Selected and Translated by Stephen Heath* (London: Fontana Press).

Bartlett, M.S., Littlewort, G., Lainscsek, C., Fasel, I. and Movellan, J. (2004) 'Machine Learning Methods for Fully Automatic Recognition of Facial Expressions and Facial Actions', Presented at the 2004 IEEE International Conference on Systems, Man and Cybernetics: 592–597.

Bass, B.M., Avolio, B.J. and Goodheim, L. (1987) 'Biography and the Assessment of Transformational Leadership at the World-Class Level', *Journal of Management*, 13(1): 7–19.

Bates, D.W., Saria, S., Ohno-Machado, L., Shah, A. and Escobar, G. (2014) 'Big Data in Health Care: Using Analytics to Identify and Manage High-Risk and High-Cost Patients', *Health Affairs*, 33(7): 1123–1131.

Bates, S. (2006) 'Making Time for Change: On Temporal Conceptualizations within (Critical Realist) Approaches to the Relationship between Structure and Agency', *Sociology*, 40(1): 143–161.

Bates, S. and Jenkins, L. (2007) 'Teaching and Learning Ontology and Epistemology in Political Science', *Politics*, 27(1): 55–63.

Bates, S., Jenkins, L. and Pflaeger, Z. (2012) 'Women in the Profession: The Composition of UK Political Science Departments by Sex', *Politics*, 32(3): 139–152.

Bates, S. and Smith, N. (2008) 'Understanding Change in Political Science: On the Need to Bring Space into Theoretical Positions and Empirical Analyses', *Political Studies Review*, 6: 191–204.

Baubock, R. (2008) 'Normative Theory and Empirical Research', in Della Porta, D. and Keating, M. (eds.) *Approaches and Methodologies in the Social Sciences* (Cambridge: Cambridge University Press); 40–60.

Baumgartner, F. (2016) 'Creating an Infrastructure for Comparative Policy Analysis', *Governance*, 30(1): 59–65.

Baumgartner, F., Christian, B., Christoffer, G.-P., Bryan, D.J., Peter, B.M., Michiel, N. and Stefaan, W. (2009) 'Punctuated Equilibrium in Comparative Perspective', *American Journal of Political Science*, 53(3): 603–620.

Beckwith, K. (2005) 'A Common Language of Gender?', *Politics & Gender*, 1(1): 128–137.

—— (2010) 'A Comparative Politics of Gender Symposium', *Perspectives on Politics*, 8(1): 159–168.

Beitz, C. (1979) *Political Theory and International Relations* (Princeton, NJ: Princeton University Press).

Bekafigo, M.A. and McBride, A. (2013) 'Who Tweets About Politics? Political Participation of Twitter Users During the 2011 Gubernatorial Elections', *Social Science Computer Review*, 31(5): 625–643.

Bell, S. and Hindmoor A. (2014) 'Rethinking the Structural Power of Business: The Strange Case of the Australian Mining Tax', *New Political Economy*, 19(3): 470–486.

Bell, Stephen, and Andy Hindmoor. 2014a. "Rethinking the Structural Power of Business: The Strange Case of the Australian Mining Tax." *New Political Economy* 19 (3): 470–486.

Belsey, C. (2002) *Poststructuralism: A Very Short Introduction* (Oxford: Oxford University Press).

Bennett, A. (2015) 'Appendix: Disciplining Our Conjectures: Systematising Process Tracing with Bayesian Analysis', in Bennett, A. and Checkel, J.T. (eds.) (2015) *Process Tracing: From Metaphor to Analytic Tool* (Cambridge: Cambridge University Press).

Bennett, A., Barth, A. and Rutherford, K. (2003) 'Do We Preach What We Practice? A Survey of Methods in Political Science Journals and Curricula', *PS: Political Science*, July: 373–378.

Bennett, A. and J. Checkel (eds.) (2015) *Process Tracing. From Metaphor to Analytic Tool* (New York: Cambridge University Press).

Bennett, A. and Elman, C. (2006) 'Qualitative Research: Recent Developments in Case Study Methods', *Annual Review of Political Science*, 9: 455–476.

Bennett, W.L., Segerberg, A (2013) *The Logic of Connective Action: Digital Media and the Personalization of Contentious Politics* (New York: Cambridge University Press).

Bennister, M., 't Hart, P. and Worthy, B. (eds.) (2017) *The Leadership Capital Index: A New Perspective on Political Leadership* (Oxford: Oxford University Press).

Benoit, K., Conway, D., Lauderdale, B.E., Laver, M. and Mikhaylov, S. (2016) 'Crowd-Sourced Text Analysis: Reproducible and Agile Production of Political Data', *American Political Science Review*, 110(2): 278–295.

Berman, S. (1998) *The Social Democratic Moment: Ideas and Politics in the Making of Interwar Europe* (Cambridge, MA: Harvard University Press).

Bevir, M. and Ansari, N. (2012) 'Should Deliberative Democrats Eschew Modernist Social Science?', Paper presented at the Western Political Science Association Conference, 22–24 March, Portland, OR.

Bevir, M. and Kedar, A. (2008) 'Concept Formation in Political Science: An Anti-Naturalist Critique of Qualitative Methodology', *Perspectives on Politics*, 6(3): 503–517.

Bevir, M. and Rhodes, R. (2002) 'Interpretive Theory', in Marsh, D. and Stoker, G. (eds.) *Theory and Methods in Political Science*, 2nd edition (Basingstoke: Palgrave Macmillan): 131–152.

—— (2003) *Interpreting British Governance* (London: Routledge).
—— (2006) *Governance Narratives* (London: Routledge).
—— (2016) 'Interpretive Political Science. Mapping the Field', in Bevir, M. and Rhodes, R.A.W. (eds.) *The Routledge Handbook of Interpretive Political Science* (Abingdon and New York: Routledge): 3–27.
Bhagwati, J. (2004) *In Defence of Globalization* (Oxford: Oxford University Press).
Biernacki, R. (1995) *The Fabrication of Labor: Germany and Britain, 1640–1914* (Berkeley, CA: University of California Press).
Bird, S., Klein, E. and Loper, E. (2009) *Natural Language Processing with Python*, 1st edition (Sebastapol, CA: O'Reilly Media).
Birkland, T.A. (2014) *An Introduction to the Policy Process: Theories, Concepts and Models of Public Policy Making* (London: Routledge).
Bjarnegård, E. (2013) *Gender, Informal Institutions and Political Recruitment* (Basingstoke: Palgrave Macmillan).
Bjarnegård, E. and Kenny, M. (2015) 'Revealing the Secret Garden: The Informal Dimensions of Political Recruitment', *Politics & Gender*, 11(4): 748–753.
Blalock, H.M. (1964) *Causal Inferences in Non-Experimental Research* (Chapel Hill, NC: University of North Carolina Press).
—— (1969) *Theory Construction: From Verbal to Mathematical Formulations* (Englewood Cliffs, NJ: Prentice-Hall).
—— (1970) *An Introduction to Social Research* (Englewood Cliffs, NJ: Prentice-Hall).
—— (ed.) (1972) *Causal Models in the Social Sciences* (London: Palgrave Macmillan).
Blanchard, P., Benoît, R. and Priscilla, Á. (2016) 'Comprehensively Mapping Political Science Methods: An Instructors' Survey', *International Journal of Social Research Methodology*, 2: 209–224.
Blatter, J. and Haverland, M. (2012) *Designing Case Studies: Explanatory Approaches in Small-N Research* (Basingstoke: Palgrave Macmillan).
Bleiker, R. (2015) 'Pluralist Methods for Visual Global Politics', *Millennium: Journal of International Studies*, 43(3): 872–890.
Blom-Hansen, J., Morton, R. and Serritzlew, S. (2015) 'Experiments in Public Management Research', *International Public Management Journal*, 18(2): 151–170.
Blondel, J. (1999) 'Then and Now: Comparative Politics', *Political Studies*, 47(1): 152–160.
Blyth, M. (2002) *Great Transformations: Economic Ideas and Political Change in the Twentieth Century* (Cambridge: Cambridge University Press).
—— (2013) *Austerity: The History of a Dangerous Idea* (Oxford: OUP).
Bond, R., Fariss, C., Jones, J., Kramer, A., Marlow, C., Settle, J. and Fowler, J. (2012) 'A 61-million-Person Experiment in Social Influence and Political Mobilization', *Nature*, 489: 295–298.
Boswell, J. (2015) 'Toxic Narratives in the Deliberative System: How the Ghost of Nanny Stalks the Obesity Debate', *Policy Studies*, 36(3): 314–328.
Boswell, J. and Corbett, J. (2017) 'Why and How to Compare Deliberative Systems', *European Journal of Political Research*, Online Early View.
Bouchet-Valat, M. (2014) Import Articles from "Factiva" Using the "tm" Text Mining Framework [R package tm.plugin.factiva version 1.5].
—— (2016) tm.plugin.lexisnexis: Import Articles from "LexisNexis" Using the "tm" Text Mining Framework.

Bourdieu, P. (1977) *Outline of a Theory of Practice* (Cambridge: Cambridge University Press).

Bourque, S. and Grossholtz, J. (1974) 'Politics an Unnatural Practice: Political Science Looks at Female Participation', *Politics and Society*, 4(4): 225–266.

Bowles, S. (2016) *The Moral Economy* (New Haven, CT: Yale University Press).

Box-Steffensmeier, J., Brady, H. and Collier, D. (2008) 'Political Science Methodology', in Box-Steffensmeier, J., Brady, H. and Collier, D. (eds.) *The Oxford Handbook of Political Methodology* (Oxford: Oxford University Press).

boyd, D. and Crawford, K., (2012) 'Critical Questions for Big Data', *Information, Communication & Society*, 15: 662–679.

Bradley, M.T. and Gupta, R. (1997) 'Estimating the Effect of the File Drawer Problem in Meta-Analysis', *Perceptual and Motor Skills*, 85(2): 719–722.

Brady, H. and Collier, D. (2004) *Rethinking Social Inquiry: Diverse Tools and Shared Standards* (Lanham, MD: Rowman and Littlefield).

Bram, U. (2012) *Thinking Statistically* (Seattle, WA: Createspace).

Bray, T., Paoli, J. and Sperberg-McQueen, C.M. (1998) Extensible Markup Language (XML) 1.0 Available online. World Wide Web Consortium. URL www.w3.org/TR/1998/REC-xml-19980210 (accessed November 17, 2016).

Bray, Z. (2008) 'Ethnographic Approaches', in Della Porta, D. and Keating, M. (eds.) *Approaches and Methodologies in the Social Sciences: A Pluralist Perspective* (Cambridge: Cambridge University Press): 296–315.

Braumoeller, B.F. and Goertz, G. (2000) 'The Methodology of Necessary Conditions', *American Journal of Political Science*, 44(8): 844–858.

Brennan, G. and Hamlin, A. (2000) *Democratic Devices and Desires* (New York: Cambridge University Press).

Brook, R.H., Ware, J.E. Jr. and Rogers, W.H. (1983) 'Does Free Care Improve Adults' Health?', *New England Journal of Medicine* 309(23): 1426–1434.

Bryson, V. (1999) *Feminist Debates* (Basingstoke: Palgrave Macmillan).

Budge, I. and Fairlie, D. (1983) *Explaining and Predicting Elections: Issue Effects and Party Strategies in Twenty-Three Democracies* (London: Allen and Unwin).

Budge, I., Klingermann, H.-D., Volkens, A., Bara, J. and Tanenbaum, E. (2001) *Mapping Policy Preferences: Estimates for Parties, Electors, and Governments 1945–1998* (Oxford: Oxford University Press).

Budge, I. and Laver, M. (1992) *Party Policy and Government Coalitions* (London: Palgrave Macmillan).

Bukharin, N. (2003) *Imperialism and World Economy* (London: Bookmarks, first published c.1914).

Burke, K., 1974. *The Philosophy of Literary Form: Studies in Symbolic Action* (Berkeley, CA: University of California Press).

Burnham, P., Gilland Lutz, K., Grant, W. and Layton-Henry, Z. (2008) *Research Methods in Politics*, 2nd edition (Basingstoke: Palgrave Macmillan).

Burns, J. (2003) *Transforming Leadership: A New Pursuit of Happiness*, Vol. 213 (New York: Grove Press).

Burscher, B. et al. (2015) 'Using Supervised Machine Learning to Code Policy Issues. Can Classifiers Generalize across Contexts?', *The ANNALS of the American Academy of Political and Social Science*, 659(1): 122–131.

Burtless, G. (1995) 'The Case for Randomized Field Trials in Economic and Policy Research', *The Journal of Economic Perspectives*, 9(2): 63–84.

Butler, J. (1990) *Gender Trouble* (London and New York: Routledge).
—— (2006) *Precarious Life: The Powers of Mourning and Violence* (London: Verso).
Butler, S.H., (2011) 'Teaching Rhetoric Through Data Visualization', *Communication Teacher*, 25(1): 131–135.
Caglar, G., Prügl, E. and Zwingel, S. (2013) *Feminist Strategies in International Governance* (London: Routledge).
Calhoun, C. (2000) 'Social Theory and the Public Sphere', in Turner, B.S. (ed.) *The Blackwell Companion to Social Theory* (Oxford: Blackwell): 505–544.
Callinicos, A. (2009) *Imperialism and Global Political Economy* (Cambridge: Polity).
Cameron, M.P. et al. (2016) 'Can Social Media Predict Election Results? Evidence from New Zealand', *Journal of Political Marketing*, 15(4): 1–17.
Campbell, D.T. (1965) *Ethnocentric and Other Altruistic Motives* (Lincoln, NE: University of Nebraska Press).
Campbell, J. (2004) *Institutional Change and Globalization* (Princeton, NJ: Princeton University Press).
Campbell, R. (2006) *Gender and the Vote in Britain* (Colchester: ECPR Press).
Caney, S. (2005) *Justice Beyond Borders* (Oxford: Oxford University Press).
Caplan, B. (2007) *The Myth of the Rational Voter: Why Democracies Choose Bad Policies* (Princeton, NJ: Princeton University Press).
Carnap, R. (1936) 'Testability and Meaning', *Philosophy of Science,* 3(4): 419–471 and 4(1): 1–40.
—— (1950) 'Empiricism, Semantics and Ontology', *Revue Internationale de Philosophe*, 4: 20–40.
Caterino, B. and Schram, S. (2006) 'Introduction: Reframing the Debate', in Schram, S. and Caterino, B. (eds.) *Making Political Science Matter: Debating Knowledge, Research and Method* (New York: New York University Press): 1–16.
Catt, H. (1996) *Voting Behaviour: A Radical Critique* (London: Cassell).
Cederman, L., Gleditsch, K.S. and Buhaug, H. (2013) *Inequality, Grievances and Civil War* (Cambridge: Cambridge University Press).
Celis, K. and Childs, S. (eds.) (2014) *Gender, Conservatism and Political Representation* (Colchester: ECPR Press).
Celis, K., Childs, S. and Kantola, J. (2016) 'Regendering Party Politics', *Party Politics*, 22(5): 571–575.
Cerny, P (2010) *Rethinking World Politics: A Theory of Transnational Neopluralism* (Oxford: Oxford University Press).
Ceron, A., Curini, L., Iacus, S. (2015) 'Using Sentiment Analysis to Monitor Electoral Campaigns Method Matters – Evidence from the United States and Italy', *Social Science Computer Review,* 33(1): 3–20.
Cerulo, K. (1997) 'Identity Construction: New Issues, New Directions', *Annual Review of Sociology*, 23: 385–410.
Chadwick, A., (2013) *The Hybrid Media System: Politics and Power* (Oxford: Oxford University Press).
Chalmers, A.F. (1986) *What Is This Thing Called Science?* (Milton Keynes: Open University Press).
—— (1990) *Science and Its Fabrication* (Milton Keynes: Open University Press).
Chappell, L. (2002) *Gendering Government: Feminist Engagement with the State in Australia and Canada* (Vancouver, BC: UBC Press).

—— (2006) 'Comparing Political Institutions: Revealing the Gendered "Logic of Appropriateness"', *Politics & Gender*, 2(2): 223–234.

—— (2013) 'The State and Governance', in Waylen, G., Celis, K., Kantola, J. and Weldon, S.L. (eds.) *The Oxford Handbook of Gender and Politics* (Oxford: Oxford University Press): 603–626.

Checkel, J. (2005) 'International Institutions and Socialization in Europe: Introduction and Framework', *International Organization*, 59(4): 801–826.

Chhotray, V. and Stoker, G. (2009) *Governance Theory and Practice* (Basingstoke: Palgrave Macmillan).

Childs, S. (2008) *Women and British Party Politics* (London: Routledge).

Childs, S. and Krook, M.L. (2006) 'Gender and Politics: The State of the Art', *Politics*, 26(1): 18–26.

Chweiroth, J. (2007) 'Neoliberal Economists and Capital Account Liberalization in Emerging Markets', *International Organization*, 61(2): 443–463.

Clarke, H, Sanders, D., Stewart, M. and Whiteley, P. (2009) *Performance Politics and the British Voter* (Cambridge: Cambridge University Press).

Clarke, H.D., Kornberg, A., McIntyre, C., Bauer-Kaase, P. and Kaase, M. (1999) 'The Effect of Economic Priorities on the Measurement of Value Change', *American Political Science Review*, 93(3): 637–647.

Cockburn, C. (2010) 'Gender Relations as Causal in Militarization and War', *International Feminist Journal of Politics*, 12(2): 139–157.

Cogan, J. and Derricott, R. (2014) *Citizenship for the 21st Century: An International Perspective on Education* (London: Routledge).

Cohen, G.A. (2008) *Rescuing Justice and Equality* (Princeton, NJ: Princeton University Press).

——. (2011) 'How to Do Political Philosophy', in Michael, O. (ed.) *On the Currency of Egalitarian Justice and Other Essays* (Princeton, NJ: Princeton University Press): 225–235.

Cohn, C. (ed.) (2013) *Women and Wars* (Cambridge: Polity).

Collier, D. (2011) 'Understanding Process Tracing', *PS: Political Science & Politics*, 44, 823–830.

Collier, D. Brady, and Seawright, J. (2004) 'Sources of Leverage in Causal Inference: Toward an Alternative View of Methodology', in Brady, H.E. and Collier, D. (eds.) *Rethinking Social Inquiry. Diverse Tools, Shared Standards* (Lanham, MD: Rowman & Littlefield).

Collier, P. and Hoeffler, A. (2004) 'Greed and Grievance in Civil Wars', *Oxford Economic Papers*, 56(4): 563–595.

Comte, A. (1974) *Discourse on the Positive Spirit* (London: Heineman).

Connell, R. (1995) *Masculinities* (London: Polity).

Connell, R. and Pearse, R. (2015) *Gender: In World Perspective*, 3rd edition (Cambridge: Polity).

Connolly, W. (1991) *Identity/Difference: Democratic Negotiations of the Political Paradox* (Ithaca, NY: Cornell University Press).

Connolly, W.E. (1995) *The Ethos of Pluralization* (Minneapolis, MN: University of Minnesota Press).

Conte, R., Gilbert, N., Bonelli, G., Cioffi-Revilla, C., Deffuant, G., Kertesz, J., Loreto, V., Moat, S., Nadal, J.-P., Sanchez, A., Nowak, A., Flache, A., Miguel, M.S. and Helbing, D. (2012) 'Manifesto of Computational Social Science', *The European Physical Journal*, 214: 325–346.

Constantiou, I.D. and Kallinikos, J. (2014) 'New Games, New Rules: Big Data and the Changing Context of Strategy', *Journal of Information Technology*, 30(1): 44–57.

Conway, B.A., Kenski, K. and Wang, D. (2015) 'The Rise of Twitter in the Political Campaign: Searching for Intermedia Agenda-Setting Effects in the Presidential Primary', *Journal of Computer-Mediated Communication*, 20: 363–380.

Cottam, M.L., Mastors, E., Preston, T. and Dietz, B. (2015) *Introduction to Political Psychology* (New York, Routledge).

Cox, D.R. and Reid, N. (2000) *The Theory of the Design of Experiments* (New York: Chapman & Hall).

Cox, R.W. (1981) 'Social Forces, States and World Orders', *Millennium: Journal of International Studies*, 10(2): 126–155.

——. (1987) *Production, Power and World Orders: Social Forces in the Making of History* (New York: Columbia University Press).

Crenshaw, K. (1989) 'Demarginalizing the Intersection of Race and Sex: A Black Feminist Critique of Antidiscrimination Doctrine, Feminist Theory, and Antiracist Politics', *University of Chicago Legal Forum*, 140(1): 139–167.

_____ (2007) *Infinitely Demanding: Ethics of Commitment, Politics of Resistance* (London: Verso).

Crick, B. (2005) *In Defence of Politics* (London: A&C Black).

Critchley, S. (2007) *Infinitely Demanding: Ethics of Commitment, Politics of Resistance.* (London: Verso)

Crouch, C. (2005) *Capitalist Diversity and Change: Recombinant Governance and Institutional Entrepreneurs* (Oxford: Oxford University Press).

Crozier, M. (2010) 'Rethinking Systems', *Administration & Society*, 42(5): 504–525.

———. (2012) 'Governing Codes: Information Dynamics and Contemporary Coordination Challenges', *Administration & Society*, 47(2): 151–170.

Csada, R., James, P. and Espie, R. (1996) 'The "File Drawer Problem" of Non-Significant Results: Does It Apply to Biological Research?', *OIKOS*, 76(3): 591–593.

Culler, J. (1983) *On Deconstruction: Theory and Criticism after Structuralism* (London: Routledge).

Curtice, J. (2012) 'Closing the Gap', *Holyrood Magazine*, 5 November 2012.

Dahlerup, D. (ed.) (2006) *Women, Quotas and Politics* (London: Routledge).

Dale, A. and Strauss, A. (2007) 'Text Messaging as a Youth Mobilization Tool: An Experiment with a Post-Treatment Survey', Paper presented at the annual meeting of the American Political Science Association, Chicago, IL, 6 August.

Dalton, R. (2002) *Citizen Politics: Public Opinion and Political Parties in Advanced Industrial Democracies* (New York: Chatham House).

—— (2016) 'The Potential of Big Data for the Cross-National Study of Political Behavior', *International Journal of Sociology*, 46(1): 8–20.

Daniels, N. (2011) 'Reflective Equilibrium', in Zalta, E. (ed.) *Stanford Encyclopedia of Philosophy* (Stanford, CA: Stanford University Press).

Darden, K. and Grzymala-Busse, A. (2006) 'The Great Divide: Precommunist Schooling and Postcommunist Trajectories', *World Politics*, 59(1): 83–115.

Darmofal, D. (2009) 'Bayesian Spatial Survival Models for Political Event Processes', *American Journal of Political Science*, 53(1): 241–257.

Dawes, R.M., Orbell, J.M., Simmons, R.T. and Van De Kragt, A.J.C. (1986) 'Organizing Groups for Collective Action', *American Political Science Review*, 80(4): 1171–1185.

De Goede, M. (2005) *Virtue, Fortune, and Faith: A Genealogy of Finance* (Minneapolis, MN: University of Minnesota Press).

Della Porta, D. (2005) 'Deliberation in Movement: Why and How to Study Deliberative Democracy and Social Movements', *Acta Politica,* 40(3): 336–350.

Della Porta, D. and Keating, M. (2008) 'How Many Approaches in the Social Sciences? An Epistemological Introduction', in Della Porta, D. and Keating, M. (eds.) *Approaches and Methodologies in the Social Sciences: A Pluralist Perspective* (Cambridge: Cambridge University Press): 19–39.

Della Porta, D. and Keating, M. (eds.) (2008) *Approaches and Methodologies in the Social Sciences: A Pluralist Perspective* (Cambridge: Cambridge University Press).

Deleuze, G. (1983) *Nietzsche and Philosophy* (London: Althlone).

—— (1994) *Difference and Repetition* (New York: Columbia University Press).

De Meur, G. and Berg-Schlosser, D. (1994) 'Comparing political systems – establishing similarities and dissimilarities', *European Journal of Political Research,* 26: 193–219.

De Meur G. and Gottcheiner, A. (2009) 'The Logic and Assumption of MDSO-MSDO Designs', in Byrne, D. and Ragin, C.C. (eds.) *The SAGE Handbook of Case-Based Methods* (London: SAGE).

Der Derian, J. and Schapiro, M. (eds.) (1989) *International/Intertextual Relations: Postmodern Readings in World Politics* (New York: Lexington Books).

Derrida, J. (1976) *Of Grammatology* (Baltimore, MD: Johns Hopkins University Press).

—— (1978) 'Structure, Sign, and Play in the Discourses of the Human Sciences', in Derrida, J. (ed.) *Writing and Difference* (London: Routledge).

—— (2000) *Of Hospitality* (Stanford, CA: Stanford University Press).

Desai, M. (2002) *Marx's Revenge* (London: Verso).

De Souza, C.R.B., Redmiles, D., Cheng, L.-T., Millen, D. and Patterson, J. (2004) Sometimes You Need to See Through Walls: A Field Study of Application Programming Interfaces, in Proceedings of the 2004 ACM Conference on Computer Supported Cooperative Work, CSCW '04. ACM, New York, NY, USA: 63–71.

Dewan, T. and Dowding, K. (2005) 'The Corrective Effect of Ministerial Resignations on Government Popularity', *American Journal of Political Science,* 49(1): 46–56.

Dews, P. (1987) *Logics of Disintegration: Poststructuralist Thought and the Claims of Critical Theory* (London: Verso).

Diamond, L.J., Linz, J.L., Lipset, S.M. (eds.) (1990) *Politics in Developing Countries: Comparing Experiences with Democrac* (Boulder, CO: Lynne Rienner).

Dicken, P. (2015) *Global Shift,* 7th edition (London: Sage).

Diez, T. (1999) 'Speaking Europe: The Politics of Integration Discourse', *Journal of European Public Policy,* 6(4): 598–613.

Dillet, B., MacKenzie, I., Porter, R. (eds.) (2013) *The Edinburgh Companion to Poststructuralism* (Edinburgh: Edinburgh University Press).

DiMaggio, P. and Powell, W. (1991) 'Introduction', in Powell, W. and DiMaggio, P. (eds) *The New Institutionalism in Organizational Analysis* (Chicago, IL: Chicago University Press): 1–30.

Disch, L. and M. Hawkesworth (eds.) (2016) *The Oxford Handbook of Feminist Theory* (Oxford: Oxford University Press).

Dixon, D. and Jones III, J.P. (1998) 'My Dinner with Derrida, or Spatial Analysis and Poststructuralism do Lunch', *Environment and Planning A*, 30(2): 247–260.

Dobbin, F. (1994) *Forging Industrial Policy* (New York: Cambridge University Press).

Dodson, D.L. (2006) *The Impact of Women in Congress* (Oxford: Oxford University Press).

Donovan, C. and Larkin, P. (2006) 'The Problem of Political Science and Practical Politics', *Politics*, 26(1): 11–17.

Douglas, M. (1987) *How Institutions Think* (London: Routledge and Kegan Paul).

Dowding, K. (2015) *The Philosophy and Methods of Political Science* (Basingstoke: Palgrave Macmillan).

Driscoll, A. and Krook, M. (2012) 'Feminism and Rational Choice Theory', *European Political Science Review*, 4(2): 195–216.

Druckman, J.N., Green, D.P., Kuklinski J.H. and Lupia, A. (2006) 'The Growth and Development of Experimental Research in Political Science', *American Political Science Review*, 100(4): 627–636.

Druckman, J.N., Green, D., Kuklinski, J. and Lupia, A. (2011) *Cambridge Handbook of Experimental Political Science* (Cambridge: Cambridge University Press).

Dryzek, J. (2002) 'A Pox on Perestroika, a Hex on Hegemony: Towards a Critical Political Science', Paper presented at the annual meeting of the American Political Science Association, Boston, MA, 28 August.

—— (2010) *Foundations and Frontiers of Deliberative Governance* (Oxford: Oxford University Press).

Duckitt, J. and Sibley, C. (2010) 'Personality, Ideology, Prejudice, and Politics: A Dual-Process Motivational Model', *Journal of Personality*, 78(6): 1861–1894.

Duerst-Lahti, G. and R.M. Kelly (eds.) (1995) *Gender Power, Leadership and Governance* (Ann Arbor, MI: University of Michigan Press).

Duffield, M. (2006) 'International Security Institutions: Rules, Tools, Schools, or Fools?', in Rhodes, R.A.W., Binder, S. and Rockman, B. (eds.) *The Oxford Handbook of Political Institutions* (Oxford: Oxford University Press): 633–653.

Duflo, E., Glennerster, R. and Kremer, M. (2006) 'Using Randomization in Development Economics Research: A Toolkit', NBER Technical Working Paper Series.

Dumbill, E. (2012) "What Is Big Data? – O'Reilly Radar." http://radar.oreilly.com/2012/01/what-is-big-data.html (accessed May 10, 2012).

Duncanson, C. (2013) *Forces for Good? Military Masculinities and Peacebuilding in Afghanistan and Iraq* (Basingstoke: Palgrave Macmillan).

Dunleavy, P. (1991) *Democracy, Bureaucracy and Public Choice: Economic Explanations in Political Science* (Hemel Hempstead: Harvester-Wheatsheaf).

Dunleavy, P. and Jones, G. (1993) 'Leaders, Politics and Institutional Change: The Decline of Prime Ministerial Accountability to the House of Commons, 1968–1990', *British Journal of Political Science*, 23(3): 267–298.

Dunning, T. (2012) *Natural Experiments in the Social Sciences. A Design-Based Approach*, (New York: Cambridge University Press).

Durkheim, E. (1984 [1893]) *The Division of Labor in Society* (New York: Free Press, tr. W. Halls).

Easton, D. (1965) *A Framework for Political Analysis* (Englewood Cliffs, NJ: Prentice-Hall).

Eavey, C. and Miller, G. (1984a) 'Bureaucratic Agenda Control: Imposition or Bargaining', *American Political Science Review*, 78(3): 719–733.

—— (1984b) 'Fairness in Majority Rule Games with a Core', *American Journal of Political Science*, 28(3): 570–586.

Eckstein, H. (1992) *Regarding Politics: Essays on Political Theory, Stability, and Change* (Berkeley, CA: University of California Press).

Edward, P. and Sumner, A. (2013) 'The Geography of Inequality: Where and by How Much Has Income Distribution Changed since 1990', Washington, DC: Center for Global Development Working Paper no.341: 1–42.

Ekbia, H. et al. (2015) "Big Data, Bigger Dilemmas: A Critical Review." *Journal of the Association for Information Science and Technology*, 66(8): 1523–1545.

Ekman, J. and Amnå, J. (2012) 'Political Participation and Civic Engagement: Towards a New Typology', *Human Affairs*, 22(3): 283–300.

Elder Vass, D. (2007) 'For Emergence: Refining Archer's Account of Social Structure', *Journal for the Theory of Social Behaviour*, 37(1): 25–44.

Eliasoph, N. (2000) *Avoiding Politics* (Cambridge: Cambridge University Press).

Elman, C. and Lupia, A. (2015) Data Access and Research Transparency (DA-RT): A Joint Statement by Political Science Journal Editors. *The Political Methodologist*, 22(2): 1–24.

Elman, C. and Kapiszewski, D. (2014) 'Data Access and Research Transparency in the Qualitative Tradition', *PS – Political Science and Politics*, 47(1): 43–47.

Elshtain, J.B. (1987) *Women and War* (New York: Basic Books).

Elster, J. (1985) *Making Sense of Marx* (Cambridge: Cambridge University Press).

—— (2007) *Explaining Social Behavior. More Nuts and Bolts for the Social Sciences* (Cambridge: Cambridge University Press).

Emirbayer, M. and Mische, A. (1998) 'What Is Agency?', *American Journal of Sociology*, 103(4): 962–1023.

Engels, F. (1890) 'Letter to Bloch', available at www.marxists.org/archive/marx/works/1890/letters/90_09_21.htm (accessed October 6, 2016).

Epstein, C. (2008) *The Power of Words in International Relations: Birth of an Anti-Whaling Discourse* (Cambridge: Cambridge University Press).

Ercan, S.A. (2014) 'Deliberative Democracy', in Phillips, D. (ed.) *Encyclopedia of Educational Theory and Philosophy* (Los Angeles, CA: Sage): 214–218.

—— (2015) 'Democratizing Identity Politics: A Deliberative Approach to the Politics of Recognition', in Gozdecka, D. and Kmak, M. (eds.) *Europe at the Edge of Pluralism* (Benelux: Intersentia): 11–26.

Ercan, S.A., Hendriks, C.M. and Boswell, J. (2015) 'Studying Public Deliberation After the Systemic Turn. The Crucial Role for Interpretive Research', *Policy and Politics*, 45, 1–16.

Ercan, S.A. and Marsh, D. (2016) 'Qualitative Methods in Political Science', in Keman, H. and Woldendorp, J. (eds.) *Handbook of Research Methods and Applications in Political Science* (Cheltenham: Edward Elgar Publishing).

Eriksson, L. (2011) *Rational Choice Theory: Potential and Limits* (London: Palgrave Macmillan).

Erikson, R. and Stoker, L.G. (2011) 'Caught in the Draft: The Effects of Vietnam Draft Lottery Status on Political Attitudes', *American Political Science Review*, 105(2): 221–237.

Escher, T., Margetts, H., Petricek, V. and Cox, I. (2006) 'Governing from the Centre? Comparing the Nodality of Digital Governments', Paper presented at the annual meeting of the American Political Science Association, Philadelphia, PA, 31 August.

Enloe, C. (1989) *Bananas, Beaches and Bases* (Berkeley, CA: University of California Press).

—— (1993) *The Morning After: Sexual Politics at the End of the Cold War* (Berkeley, CA: University of California Press).

Epstein, C. (2008) *The Power of Words in International Relations: Birth of an Anti-Whaling Discourse* (Cambridge, MA: MIT Press).

Estlund, D. (2014) 'Utopophobia', *Philosophy & Public Affairs*, 42(2): 113–134.

Evans, E. (2015) *The Politics of Third Wave Feminisms* (Basingstoke: Palgrave Macmillan).

Evans, E. and Amery, F. (2016) 'Gender and Politics in the UK: Banished to the Sidelines', *European Political Science*, 15(3): 314–321.

Ezrow, L. (2008) 'Parties', Policy Programmes and the Dog that Didn't Bark: No Evidence that Proportional Systems Promote Extreme Party Positioning', *British Journal of Political Science*, 38(3): 479–497.

Ezzy, D. (2002) *Qualitative Analysis: Practice and Innovation* (Sydney: Allen & Unwin).

Fairclough, I. and Fairclough, N. (2012) *Political Discourse: A Method for Advanced Students* (London: Routledge).

Falleti, T. (2010) 'Infiltrating the State: The Evolution of Health Care Reforms in Brazil', in Mahoney, J. and Thelen, K. (eds.) *Explaining Institutional Change: Ambiguity, Agency, and Power* (Cambridge: Cambridge University Press): 38–62.

Farnen, R., German, D., Dekker, H., Landtsheer, C., de Sünker, H. (eds.) (2008) *Political Culture, Socialization, Democracy, and Education: Interdisciplinary and Cross-National Perspectives for a New Century.* (Frankfurt am Main: Peter Lang).

Fearon, J. and Laitin, D. (2003) 'Ethnicity, Insurgency and Civil War', *American Political Science Review,* 97(1): 75–90.

Fehr, E. and Fischbacher, U. (2004) 'Third-Party Punishment and Social Norms', *Evolution and Human Behaviour,* 25(2): 63–87.

Fehr, E. and Gächter, S. (2002) 'Altruistic Punishment in Humans', *Nature,* 415(6868): 137–140.

Feinerer, I., Hornik, K. (2015) tm: Text Mining Package. R Cran.

Feyerabend, P. (2010) *Against Method*, 4th edition (London: Verso).

Findley, M., Jensen, N., Malesky, E. and Pepinsky, T. (2016) 'Can Results-Free Review Reduce Publication Bias? The Results and Implications of a Pilot Study', *Comparative Political Studies*, 49(3): 1667–1703.

Finer, H. (1932) *The Theory and Practice of Modern Government* (London: Methuen).

Finlayson, A. (2014) 'Proving, Pleasing and Persuading? Rhetoric in Contemporary British Politics', *The Political Quarterly*, 85(4): 428–436.

Finlayson, A. and Valentine, J. (2002) 'Introduction', in Finlayson, A. and Valentine, J. (eds.) *Politics and Poststructuralism: An Introduction* (Edinburgh: Edinburgh University Press).

Finnemore, M. (1996) 'Norms, Culture, and World Politics: Insights from Sociology's Institutionalism', *International Organization*, 50(2): 325–347.

Finnemore, M. and Sikkink, K. (1998)'International Norm Dynamics and Political Change', *International Organization*, 52(4): 887–917.

Fioretos, O., Falleti, T. and Sheingate, A. (eds.) (2016) *The Oxford Handbook of Historical Institutionalism* (Oxford: Oxford University Press).

Fiorina, M. and Plott, C.R. (1978) 'Committee Decisions Under Majority Rule: An Experimental Study', *American Political Science Review*, 72(2): 575–598.

Flinders, M. (2013) 'The Tyranny of Relevance and the Art of Translation', *Political Studies Review*, 11(2): 149–167.

Flyvbjerg, B. (2001) *Making Social Science Matter* (Cambridge: Cambridge University Press).

—— (2006) 'A Perestroikan Straw Man Answers Back', in Schram, S. and Caterino, B. (eds.) *Making Political Science Matter: Debating Knowledge, Research and Method* (New York: New York University Press): 56–85.

Foster, E., Kerr, P., Hopkins, A., Byrne, C. and Ahall, L. (2012) 'The Personal Is Not Political: At Least in the UK's Top Politics and IR Departments', *British Journal of Politics & International Relations* 15(4): 566–585.

Foucault, M. (1975) *Discipline and Punish: The Birth of the Prison* (New York: Random House).

—— (1991) *Discipline and Punish: The Birth of the Prison* (London: Penguin).

—— (2001a) *Power* (London: Allen Lane, ed. J. Faubion).

—— (2001b) *Madness and Civilisation* (London: Routledge).

—— (2002) 'The Subject and Power', in Faubion, J. (ed.) *Michel Foucault: Power Essential Works of Foucault 1954–1984*, Vol. 3 (London: Penguin).

—— (2007) *Madness and Civilisation* (London: Routledge).

—— (2008) *The Order of Things* (London: Routledge).

Fox, C. and Miller, H. (1995) *Postmodern Public Administration* (Thousand Oaks, CA: Sage).

Franceschet, S., Krook, M.L. and Piscopo, J. (eds.) (2012) *The Impact of Gender Quotas* (New York: Oxford University Press).

Franzosi, R. (1994) 'Outside and Inside the Regression "Black Box" from Exploratory to Interior Data Analysis', *Quality and Quantity*, 28(1): 21–53.

Freelon, D., Lynch, M. and Aday, S. (2015) 'Online Fragmentation in Wartime: A Longitudinal Analysis of Tweets about Syria, 2011–2013', *The ANNALS of the American Academy of Political and Social Science*, 659: 166–179.

Freidenvall, L. and Krook, M.L. (2011) 'Discursive Strategies for Institutional Reform: Gender Quotas in Sweden and France', in Krook, M.L. and Mackay, F. (eds.) *Gender, Politics and Institutions: Towards a Feminist Institutionalism* (London: Palgrave Macmillan).

Frey, B.S. and Meier, S. (2004) 'Social Comparisons and Pro-social Behaviour: Testing "Conditional Cooperation" in a Field Experiment', *American Economic Review*, 94(5): 1717–1722.

Friedman, T. (2005) *The World is Flat* (New York: Allen Lane).

Friedrich, R. (1982) 'In Defense of Multiplicative Terms in Multiple Regression Equations', *American Journal of Political Science*, 26(4): 797–833.

Fuss, D. (1989) *Essentially Speaking. Feminism, Nature and Difference* (London: Routledge).

Gamble, A. (1990) 'Theories of British Politics', *Political Studies*, 38(3): 404–420.

Gates, S., Hegre, H., Jones, M., Strand, H. (2006) 'Institutional Inconsistency and Political Instability: Polity Duration 1800–2000', *American Journal of Political Science*, 50: 893–908.
Geddes, B. (2003) *Paradigms and Sandcastles: Theory Building and Research Design in Comparative Politics* (Ann Arbor, MI: The University of Michigan Press).
—— (2009) 'What Causes Democratisation?', in Boix, C. and Stokes, S. (eds.) *The Oxford Handbook of Comparative Politics* (Oxford: Oxford University Press).
Geertz, C. (1973) *The Interpretation of Cultures* (New York: Basic Books).
Gelman, A. (2011) 'Causality and Statistical Learning', *American Journal of Sociology*, 117(3): 955–966.
George, A. and Bennett, A. (2005) *Case Studies and Theory Development in the Social Sciences* (Cambridge, MA: MIT Press).
Gerber, A., Arceneaux, K., Boudreau, C., Dowling, C., Hillygus, S., Palfrey, T., Biggers, D.R. and Hendry, D.J. (2014) 'Reporting Guidelines for Experimental Research: A Report from the Experimental Research Section Standards Committee', *Journal of Experimental Political Science*, 1(1): 81–98.
Gerber, A.S. and Green, D.P. (2000) 'The Effects of Canvassing, Telephone Calls, and Direct Mail on Voter Turnout: A Field Experiment', *American Political Science Review*, 94(3): 653–663.
—— (2001a) 'Do Phone Calls Increase Voter Turnout? An Experiment', *Public Opinion Quarterly*, 65(1): 75–85.
—— (2001b) 'Getting Out the Youth Vote: Results from Randomized Field Experiments', Unpublished manuscript, Yale University, 29 December.
—— (2003) 'Partisan Mail and Voter Turnout: Results from Randomized Field Experiments', *Electoral Studies*, 22(4): 563–579.
—— (2005) 'Correction to Gerber and Green (2000) Replication of Disputed Findings, and Reply to Imai (2005)', *The American Political Science Review*, 99(2): 301–313.
—— (2012) *Field Experiments: Analysis, Design and Interpretation* (New York: W.W. Norton).
Gerber, A.S., Green, D.P. and Shachar, R. (2003) 'Voting May be Habit-Forming: Evidence from a Randomized Field Experiment', *American Journal of Political Science*, 47(3): 540–550.
Gerber, A.S., Huber, G.A., Doherty, D. and Dowling, C.M. (2011) 'The Big Five Personality Traits in the Political Arena', *Annual Review of Political Science*, 14(3): 265–287.
Gerber, A. and Malhotra, N. (2006) 'Can Political Science Literatures be Believed? A Study of Publication Bias in the APSR and the AJPS', unpublished paper.
Gerring, J. (2007) 'Is There a (Viable) Crucial-Case Method?', *Comparative Political Studies*, 40(3): 231–253.
—— (2012a) *Social Science Methodology: A Unified Framework*, 2nd edition (Cambridge Universtiy Press).
—— (2012b) 'Mere Description', *British Journal of Political Science*, 42(4): 721–746.
Gheaus, A. (2013) 'The Feasibility Constraint on the Concept of Justice', *The Philosophical Quarterly*, 63(252): 445–464.
Gilabert, P. (2012) 'Comparative Assessments of Justice, Political Feasibility, and Ideal Theory', *Ethical Theory and Moral Practice*, 15(1): 39–56.

Gilabert, P. and Lawford-Smith, H. (2012) 'Political Feasibility: A Conceptual Exploration', *Political Studies*, 60(4): 809–825.

Giddens, A. (1984) *The Constitution of Society: Outline of the Structuration Theory* (Cambridge: Polity Press).

—— (1987) *Social Theory and Modern Sociology* (Cambridge: Polity Press).

Gill, J. (1999) 'The Insignificance of Null Hypothesis Significance Testing', *Political Research Quarterly*, 52(3): 647–674.

—— (2007) *Bayesian Methods: A Social and Behavioral Sciences Approach*, 2nd edition (London: Chapman & Hall).

Gill, S. (ed.) (1993) *Gramsci, Historical Materialism and International Relations* (Cambridge: Cambridge University Press).

—— (2003) *Power and Resistance in the New World Order* (Basingstoke: Palgrave Macmillan).

Gilpin, R. (2001) *Global Political Economy: Understanding the International Economic Order* (Princeton, NJ: Princeton University Press).

Gladwell, M. (2007) *Blink: The Power of Thinking Without Thinking* (New York: Back Bay Books).

Glennerster, R. and Takavarasha, K.. (2013) *Running Randomized Evaluations: A Practical Guide* (Princeton, NJ: Princeton University Press).

Glymour, B. (1998) 'Contrastive, Non-Probabilistic Statistical Explanations', *Philosophy of Science*, 65(3): 448–471.

Glymour, M.M. (2006) 'Using Causal Diagrams to Understand Common Problems in Social Epidemiology', in Oakes, J.M. and Kaufman, J.S. (eds.) *Methods in Social Epidemiology* (San Francisco, CA: Jossey Bass).

Glynos, J. and Howarth, D. (2007) *Logics of Critical Explanation in Social and Political Theory* (London: Routledge).

Goertz, G. (2006) *Social Science Concepts. A User's Guide* (Princeton, NJ: Princeton University Press).

Goertz, G. and Mahoney, J. (2012) A Tale of Two Cultures: Qualitative and Quantitative Research in the Social Sciences, (Princeton, NJ: Princeton University Press).

Goertz, G. and Mazur, A.G. (eds.) (2008) *Politics, Gender and Concepts* (Cambridge: Cambridge University Press).

Goetz, A.M. (2007) 'Gender Justice, Citizenships and Entitlements: Core Concepts, Central Debates and New Directions for Research', in Mukhopadhyay, M. and Singh, N. (eds.) *Gender Justice, Citizenship and Developmen* (New Delhi: Zubaan): 15–57.

González-Bailón, S. and Paltoglou, G. (2015) 'Signals of Public Opinion in Online Communication: A Comparison of Methods and Data Sources', *The ANNALS of the American Academy of Political and Social Science*, 659, 95–107.

González-Bailón, S., Wang, N., (2016) 'Networked Discontent: The Anatomy of Protest Campaigns in Social Media', *Social Networks*, 44(1): 95–104.

Goodin, R. (1995) 'Political Ideals and Political Practice', *British Journal of Political Science*, 25(1): 37–56.

—— (ed.) (1996) *The Theory of Institutional Design* (Cambridge: Cambridge University Press).

Goodin, R. and Klingemann, H.-D. (eds.) (1996) *A New Handbook of Political Science* (Oxford: Oxford University Press).

Gordon, C. (ed.) (1980) *Power/Knowledge: Selected Interviews and Other Writings by Michel Foucault 1972–1977* (Brighton: Harvester).

Gould, C.C. (2000) 'Racism and Democracy Reconsidered', *Social Identities*, 6(4): 425–439.

Grafstein, R. (1988) 'The Problem of Institutional Constraint', *Journal of Politics*, 50(3): 577–599.

Gramsci, A. (2005) *Selections from the Prison Notebooks* (London: Lawrence and Wishart).

Grant, W. and Marsh, D. (1977) *The Confederation of British Industry* (Sevenoaks: Hodder and Stoughton).

Gray, V. and Lowery, D. (2000) *The Population Ecology of Interest Representation* (Ann Arbor, MI: Michigan University Press).

Grbich, C. (2007) *Qualitative Data Analysis* (London: Sage).

Green, D.P. and Gerber, A.S. (2003) 'The Underprovision of Experiments in Political Science', *Annals of the American Academy of Political and Social Science*, 589: 94–112.

Green, D.P. and Shapiro, I. (1994) *Pathologies of Rational Choice Theory: A Critique of Applications in Political Science* (New Haven, CT: Yale University Press).

Greenberg, D., Linkz, D. and Mandell, M. (2003) *Social Experimentation and Public Policy Making* (Washington, DC: The Urban Institute Press).

Greene, W. (2007) *Econometric Analysis*, 6th edition (Upper Saddle River, NJ: Prentice Hall).

Grimmer, J. (2015) 'We Are All Social Scientists Now: How Big Data, Machine Learning, and Causal Inference Work Together', *PS: Political Science & Politics*, 48: 80–83.

Grimmelikhuijsen, S. and Meijer, A. (2012) 'The Effects of Transparency on the Perceived Trustworthiness of a Government Organization: Evidence from an Online Experiment', *Journal of Public Administration Research and Theory*, 24(1): 137–157.

Grofman, B. (2001) 'Introduction: The Joy of Puzzle Solving', in Grofman, B. (ed.) *Political Science as Puzzle Solving* (Ann Arbor, MI: University of Michigan Press): 1–12.

Grus, J., (2015) *Data Science from Scratch: First Principles with Python,* 1st edition (Sebastopol, CA: O'Reilly Media).

Gschwend, T. and Schimmelfennig F. (eds.) (2007) *Research Design in Political Science: How to Practice What They Preach* (Basingstoke and New York: Palgrave Macmillan).

Guba, E. and Lincoln, Y. (1994) 'Competing Paradigms in Qualitative Research', in Denzin, N. and Lincoln, Y. (eds.) *Handbook of Qualitative Research* (Thousand Oaks, CA: Sage): 105–117.

Guggenheim, L., Jang, S.M., Bae, S.Y. and Neuman, W.R. (2015) 'The Dynamics of Issue Frame Competition in Traditional and Social Media', *The ANNALS of the American Academy of Political and Social Science*, 659: 207–224.

Gujarati, D.N. (2003) *Basic Econometrics* (New York: McGraw-Hill Education).

Gulalp, H. (1986) 'Debate on Capitalism and Development: The Theories of Samir Amin and Bill Warren', *Capital and Class,* 28(1): 39–59.

Gunnell, J. (2015) 'Pluralism and the Fate of Perestroika', *Perspectives on Politics*, 13(2): 408–415.

Guth, W. and Weck-Hannemann, H. (1997) 'Do People Care about Democracy? An Experiment Exploring the Value of Voting Rights', *Public Choice*, 91(1): 27–47.

Habermas, J. (1976) *Legitimation Crisis* (London: Heineman).
—— (1994) *The Philosophical Discourse of Modernity* (Cambridge: Polity).
Hainmueller, J., Dominik H. and Teppei Y. (2015) 'Validating Vignette and Conjoint Survey Experiments against Real-world Behavior', *Proceedings of the National Academy of Sciences*, 112(8): 2395–2400.
Halfpenny, P. (1982) *Positivism and Sociology: Explaining Social Life*, 1st edition (London: Allen and Unwin).
Hall, M., Marsh, D. and Vines, E. (2017) 'Does BREXIT Mark the End of the British Political Tradition?' available from david.marsh@canberra.edu.au.
Hall, P.A. (1986) *Governing the Economy: The Politics of State Intervention in Britain and France* (Oxford: Oxford University Press).
—— (ed.) (1989) *The Political Power of Economic Ideas: Keynesianism Across Nations* (Princeton, NJ: Princeton University Press).
—— (1992) 'The Movement from Keynesianism to Monetarism: Institutional Analysis and British Economic Policy in the 1970s', in Steinmo, S., Thelen, K. and Longstreth, F. (eds.) *Structuring Politics: Historical Institutionalism in Comparative Analysis* (Cambridge: Cambridge University Press).
—— (1993) 'Policy Paradigms, Social Learning and the State: The Case of Economic Policy-Making in Britain', *Comparative Politics*, 25: 175–196.
—— (2011) *Political Traditions and UK Politics* (Basingstoke: Palgrave Macmillan).
—— (2013) 'Tracing the Progress of Process Tracing', *European Political Science*, 12(1): 20–30.
Hall, P.A. and Soskice, D. (eds.) (2001) *Varieties of Capitalism: The Institutional Foundations of Competitiveness* (Oxford: Oxford University Press).
Hall, P.A. and Taylor, R. (1996) 'Political Science and the Three New Institutionalisms', *Political Studies*, 44(4): 936–957.
—— (1998) 'The Potential of Historical Institutionalism: A Response to Hay and Wincott', *Political Studies*, 46(5): 958–962.
Hall, P.A. and Thelen, K. (2008) 'Institutional Change in Varieties of Capitalism', *Socio-Economic Review*, 7(1): 7–34.
Hanisch, C. (1969) 'The Personal is Political', in Firestone, S. and Koedt, A. (eds.) *Notes from the Second Year: Women's Liberation* (New York: New York Radical Feminists).
Hanson, R. (1958) *Patterns of Discovery* (Cambridge: Cambridge University Press).
Hardin, G. (1968) 'The Tragedy of the Commons, *Science*, 162: 1243–1248.
Harding, S. (1986) *The Science Question in Feminism* (Ithaca, NY: Cornell University Press).
Harford, T. (2006) *The Undercover Economist* (Oxford: Oxford University Press).
Hargittai, Eszter. (2015) 'Is Bigger Always Better? Potential Biases of Big Data Derived from Social Network Sites', *The ANNALS of the American Academy of Political and Social Science*, 659(1): 63–76.
Harlow, L. and Mulaik, S. (1997) *What If There Were No Significance Tests?* (London: Lawrence Erlbaum Associates).
Hartsock, N. (1983) 'The Feminist Standpoint: Developing the Ground for a Specifically Feminist Historical Materialism', in Harding, S. and Hintikka, M.B. (eds.) *Discovering Reality* (Boulder, CO: Westview Press): 283–210.

—— (ed.) (1998) *The Feminist Standpoint Revisited and Other Essays* (Boulder, CO: Westview Press).

Haslam, S. and Reicher, S. (2007) 'Beyond the Banality of Evil: Three Dynamics of an Interactionist Social Psychology of Tyranny', *Personality and Social Psychology Bulletin*, 33(5): 615–622.

—— (2012) 'Contesting the 'Nature' of Conformity: What Milgram and Zimbardo's Studies Really Show', *PLoS Biology*, 10(11), e1001426.

Haslam, S.A., Reicher, S.D. and Platow, M.J. (2011) *The New Psychology of Leadership: Identity, Influence and Power* (London and New York: Psychology Press).

Haste, H., Monroe, K. and Jones, J. (2015) 'Political Psychology' in Bevir, M. and Rhodes, R.A.W. (eds.) *The Routledge Handbook of Interpretive Political Science* (London: Routeledge).

Hausman, D.M. and Welch, B. (2010) 'To Nudge or Not to Nudge', *Journal of Political Philosophy*, 18(1): 123–136.

Hawkesworth, M. (2003) 'Congressional Enactments of Race-Gender: Toward a Theory of Raced-Gendered Institutions', *American Political Science Review*, 97(4): 529–550.

—— (2005) 'Engendering Political Science: An Immodest Proposal', *Politics & Gender*, 1(1): 141–156.

Hay, C. (1995) 'Structure and Agency', in Stoker, G. and Marsh, D. (eds.) *Theory and Methods in Political Science* (London: Palgrave Macmillan): 189–207.

—— (1996) *Re-Stating Social and Political Change* (Buckingham: Open University Press).

—— (2002) *Political Analysis* (Basingstoke: Palgrave Macmillan).

—— (2006a) 'Constructivist Institutionalism', in Rhodes, R.A.W., Binder, S. and Rockman, B. (eds.) *The Oxford Handbook of Political Institutions* (Oxford: Oxford University Press): 56–74.

—— (2006b) 'Constructive Institutionalism ... Or, Why Ideas into Interests Don't Go', in Beland, D. and Cox, R. (eds.) *Ideas and Politics in Social Science Research* (Oxford: Oxford University Press).

—— 2007. 'Does Ontology Trump Epistemology? Notes on the Directional Dependence of Ontology and Epistemology in Political Analysis', *Politics*, 27(2): 115–118.

Hay, C. and Marsh, D. (eds.) (2000) *Demystifying Globalisation* (Basingstoke: Palgrave Macmillan).

Hay, C. and Wincott, D. (1998) 'Structure, Agency and Historical Institutionalism', *Political Studies*, 46(5): 951–957.

Heath, A.F. (ed.) (1991) *Understanding Political Change* (Oxford: Pergamon Press).

Heath, A.F., Jowell, R. and Curtice, J. (1985) *How Britain Votes* (Oxford: Pergamon Press).

Heath, A.F., Jowell, R., Curtice, J. and Taylor, B. (eds.) (1994) *Labour's Last Chance? The 1992 General Election and Beyond* (Aldershot: Dartmouth).

Heckman, J.J. (1979) 'Sample Selection Bias as a Specification Error', *Econometrica*, 47(1): 153–161.

Held, D. and McGrew, A. (2007) *Globalization in Question* (Cambridge: Polity).

Held, D. et al. (1999) *Global Transformations: Politics, Economics and Culture* (Cambridge: Polity Press).

Helmke, G. and Levitsky, S. (2006) 'Introduction', in Helmke, G. and Levitsky, S. (eds.) *Informal Institutions and Democracy: Lessons from Latin America* (Baltimore, MD: Johns Hopkins University Press).

Helms, L. (ed.) (2012) *Poor Leadership and Bad Governance* (Cheltenham: Elgar).

Hempel, C. (1965) *Aspects of Scientific Explanation and Other Essays in the Philosophy of Science* (New York: Free Press).

—— (1966) *Philosophy of Natural Science* (Englewood Cliffs, NJ: Prentice Hall).

Hendriks, C.M. (2011) *The Politics of Public Deliberation: Citizen Engagement and Interest Advocacy* (London: Palgrave Macmillan).

Hermann, M.G. (2002) 'Political Psychology as a Perspective in the Study of Politics', in Monroe, K.R. (ed.) *Political Psychology* (Mahwah, NJ: Erlbaum): 43–60.

Hersh, E.D., 2015. *Hacking the Electorate: How Campaigns Perceive Voters* (New York: Cambridge University Press).

Hewson, C. (2016) 'Ethics Issues in Digital Methods Research', in Roberts, S., Snee, H., Hine, C., Moery, Y. and Watson, H. (eds.) *Digital Methods for Social Science* (Basingstoke: Palgrave Macmillan): 206–221.

Hilferding, R. (1981) *Finance Capital* (London: Routledge, first published 1910).

Hindman, M. (2015) 'Building Better Models Prediction, Replication, and Machine Learning in the Social Sciences', *The ANNALS of the American Academy of Political and Social Science*, 659(1): 48–62.

Hindmoor, A. (2011) 'Major Combat Operations Have Ended? Arguing About Rational Choice', *British Journal of Political Science*, 41(1): 191–210.

Hindmoor, A. and Taylor, B. (2015) *Rational Choice*, 2nd edition (London: Palgrave Macmillan).

Hinojosa, M. (2012) *Selecting Women, Electing Women* (Philadelphia, PA: Temple University Press).

Hirst, P. and Thompson, G. (1999) *Globalisation in Question* (Cambridge: Polity).

Hobson, J. and Seabrooke, L. (2007) *Everyday Politics of the World Economy* (New York: Cambridge University Press).

Hochschild, J. (2005) 'Inventing Perspectives on Politics', in Monroe, K. (ed.) *Perestroika! The Raucous Rebellion in Political Science* (New Haven, CT: Yale University Press): 330–341.

Hoekstra, V., Kittilson, M.C. and Bond, E.A. (2014) 'Gender, High Courts and Ideas about Representation in Western Europe', in Escobar-Lemmon, M.C. and Taylor-Robinson, M.M. (eds.) *Representation: The Case of Women* (Oxford: Oxford University Press): 103–117.

Höjer, M. and Åse, C. (1999) *The Paradoxes of Politics: An Introduction to Feminist Political Theory* (Lund: Academia Adacta).

Holland, P. (1986) 'Statistics and Causal Inference', *Journal of the American Statistical Association*, 81(396): 945–960.

Hollis, M. and Smith, S. (1991) *Explaining and Understanding in International Relations* (Oxford: Clarendon Press).

Hooghe, M. (2014) 'Defining Political Participation: How To Pinpoint an Elusive Target?, *Acta Politica*, 49(3): 338–341.

Hopf, T. (1998) 'The Promise of Constructivism in International Relations', *International Security*, 23(1): 171–200.

Horiuchi, Y., Imai, K. and Taniguchi, N. (2007) 'Designing and Analyzing Randomized Experiments: Application to a Japanese Election Survey Experiment', *American Journal of Political Science,* 51(3): 669–687.

Horkheimer, M. and Adorno, T.W. (1979) *Dialectic of Enlightenment* (London: Verso).

Houghton, D. (2008) *Political Psychology: Situations, Individuals and Cases* (London: Routledge).

—— (2014) *Political Psychology: Situations, Individuals, and Cases,* 2nd edition (London: Routledge).

Howarth, D. (1995) 'Discourse Theory', in Marsh, D. and Stoker, G. (eds.) *Theory and Methods in Political Science,* 1st edition (Basingstoke: Palgrave Macmillan): 115–133.

—— (2000) *Discourse* (Buckingham: Open University Press).

—— (2013) *Poststructuralism and After: Structure, Subjectivity and Power* (Basingstoke: Palgrave Macmillan).

Howarth, D., Norval, A. and Stavrakakis, Y. (2000) *Discourse Theory and Political Analysis: Identities, Hegemonies, and Social Change* (Manchester: Manchester University Press).

Hovland, C.J. and Sears, R.R. (1940) 'Minor Studies in Aggression: VI. Correlation of Lynchings with Economic Indices', *The Journal of Psychology: Interdisciplinary and Applied,* 9(2): 301–310.

Howlett, M. (2010) *Designing Public Policies: Principles and Instruments* (London: Routledge).

Htun, M. and Weldon, S.L. (2011) 'State Power, Religion and Women's Rights: A Comparative Analysis of Family Law, *Indiana Journal of Global Legal Studies,* 18(1): 145–165.

Huddy, L., Sears, D.O. and Levy, J.S. (eds.) (2013) *The Oxford Handbook of Political Psychology* (Oxford: Oxford University Press).

Huff, D. (1991) *How to Lie with Statistics* (London: Penguin).

Hug, S. (2013) 'Qualitative Comparative Analysis: How Inductive Use and Measurement Error Lead to Problematic Inference', *Political Analysis,* 21(2): 252–265.

Hume, D. (1975 [1748]) *An Enquiry Concerning Human Understanding,* 3rd edition (Oxford: Clarendon).

Humphreys, M., Sanchez de la Sierra, R. and van der Windt, P. (2013) 'Fishing, Commitment, and Communication: A Proposal for Comprehensive Nonbinding Research Registration', *Political Analysis,* 21(1): 1–20.

Huntington, S.P. (1968) *Political Order in Changing Societies* (New Haven, CT: Yale University Press).

—— (1991) *The Third Wave: Democratization in the Late 20th Century* (Norman, OK: University of Oklahoma Press).

Imbens, G. (2011) 'Experimental Design for Unit and Cluster Randomid Trials', *International Initiative for Impact Evaluation Paper.*

Imbens, G. and Rubin, D. (2015) *Causal Inference for Statistics, Social, and Biomedical Sciences. An Introduction* (New York: Cambridge University Press).

Immergut, E. (1992) 'The Rules of the Game: The Logic of Health Policy-Making in France, Switzerland and Sweden', in Steinmo, S., Thelen, K. and Longstreth, F. (eds.) *Structuring Politics: Historical Institutionalism in Comparative Analysis* (Cambridge: Cambridge University Press): 57–89.

Indridason, I. and Kam, C. (2008) 'Cabinet Reshuffles and Ministerial Drift', *British Journal of Political Science*, 38(4): 621–656.

Ingram, H. (2016) 'Public Policy Theory and Democracy: The Elephant in the Room', in Peters, B.G. and Zittoun, P. (eds.) *Contemporary Approaches to Public Policy: Theories, Controversies and Perspectives* (London: Palgrave Macmillan).

Inter-Parliamentary Union (2017) 'Women in National Parliaments' http://www.ipu.org/wmn-e/classif.htm.

Isaac, J. (2010) 'Perestroika and the Journals: A Brief Reply to My Friend Greg Kasza', *PS: Political Science*, 43, 735–737 (October).

—— (2015) 'Further thoughts on DA-RT' The PLOT blog, November 2, www.the-plot.org/2015/11/02/further-thoughts-on-da-rt/ (accessed April 21, 2017).

Jabko, N. (1999) 'In the Name of the Market: How the European Commission Paved the Way for Monetary Union', *Journal of European Public Policy*, 6(3): 475–495.

Jachtenfuchs, M. (1995) 'Theoretical Perspectives on European Governance', *European Law Journal*, 1(2): 115–133.

Jacobs, K. (2006) 'Discourse Analysis', in M. Walter (ed.) *Social Research Methods: An Australian Perspective* (Melbourne: Oxford University Press): 135–158.

Jacobsen, J.K. (2003) 'Dueling Constructivisms: A Postmortem on the Ideas Debate in IR/IPE', *Review of International Studies*, 29(1): 39–60.

Jaggar, A. and Rothenberg, P. (eds.) (1993) *Feminist Frameworks* (New York: McGraw-Hill).

James, C.L.R. (2001) *The Black Jacobins* (London: Penguin).

Janis, I.L. (1972) *Victims of Groupthink* (Boston: Houghton Mifflin).

Janos, A. (1986) *Politics and Paradigms: Changing Theories of Change in the Social Sciences* (Stanford, CA: Stanford University Press).

Jennings, W. and Lodge, M. (2016) 'The Failures of Political Science: Trump, Brexit and Beyond…' https://sotonpolitics.org/2016/11/11/the-failures-of-political-science-trump-brexit-and-beyond/ (accessed March 23, 2017).

Jensen, M.J. (2016) 'Social Media and Political Campaigning: Changing Terms of Engagement?', *The International Journal of Press/Politics*, 22(1): 23–42.

Jensen, P.B., Jensen, L.J. and Brunak, S. (2012) 'Mining Electronic Health Records: Towards Better Research Applications and Clinical Care', *Nature Review Genetics*, 13(6): 395–405.

Jessop, B. (1990) *State Theory: Putting the Capitalist State in its Place* (Cambridge: Polity Press).

Jockers, M.L. (2013) *Macroanalysis: Digital Methods and Literary History* (Champaign, IL: University of Illinois Press).

Johal, S., Moran, M. and Williams, K. (2014) 'Power, Politics and the City of London: Before and After the Great Crisis', *Government and Opposition*, 49(3): 400–425.

John, P. (1999) *Analysing Public Policy* (London: Pinter).

—— (2013) 'Political Science, Impact and Evidence', *Political Studies Review*, 11(2): 168–173.

—— 2017. *Field Experiments in Political Science and Public Policy: Practical Lessons in Design and Delivery* (New York: Taylor and Francis).

John, P., Smith, G. and Stoker, G. (2009) 'Nudge Nudge, Think Think: Two Strategies for Changing Civic Behaviour', *The Political Quarterly*, 80(3): 361–370.

Johnson, N. (1975) 'The Place of Institutions in the Study of Politics', *Political Studies*, 23(2–3): 271–283.

Jørgensen, K.E. (2000) 'Continental IR Theory: The Best Kept Secret', *European Journal of International Relations*, 6(9): 9–42.

Jost, J.T. (2011) 'System Justification Theory as Compliment, Complement, and Corrective to Theories of Social Identification and Social Dominance', in Dunning, D. (ed.) *Social Motivation* (New York: Psychology Press): 223–263.

Jost, J.T., Nam, H., Adodio, D., and Van Bavel, J.J. (2014) 'Political Neuroscience: The Beginning of a Beautiful Friendship', *Advances in Political Psychology*, 35(1): 3–42.

Jost, J.T. and Sidanius, J. (2004) *Political Psychology* (New York: Psychology Press).

Jowell, R. (2003) *Trying it Out: The Role of 'Pilots' in Policy-Making* (London: Cabinet Office).

Jung, C. (2000) *Then I Was Black: South African Political Identities in Transition* (New Haven, CT: Yale University Press).

—— (2006) 'Race, Ethnicity and Culture', in Goodin, R.E. and Tilly, C. (eds.) *The Oxford Handbook of Contextual Policy Analysis* (Oxford: Oxford University Press): 360–376.

Jungherr, A. (2015) *Analyzing Political Communication with Digital Trace Data: The Role of Twitter Messages in Social Science Research* (Springer, New York).

Kahan, D.M., Peters, E., Dawson, E. and Slovic, P. (2013) 'Motivated Numeracy and Enlightened Self-Government', *Yale Law School, Public Law Working Paper*: 1–35.

Kahneman, D. (2011) *Thinking, Fast and Slow* (London: Allen Lane).

Kahneman, D. and Tversky, A. (1979) 'Prospect Theory: An Analysis of Decision Under Risk', *Econometrica: Journal of the Econometric Society*, 47(2): 263–291.

—— (2000) *Choices, Values and Frames* (New York: Cambridge University Press).

Kallinikos, J., Aaltonen, A. and Marton, A. (2010) 'A Theory of Digital Objects', *First Monday*, 15(6–7).

Kantola, J. (2006) *Feminists Theorize the State* (Basingstoke: Palgrave Macmillan).

—— (2007) 'The Gendered Reproduction of the State', *British Journal of Politics & International Relations*, 9(2): 270–283.

Kasza, G. (2010) 'Perestroika and the Journals', *PS: Political Science*, October: 733–734.

Katz, B. and Bradley, J. (2013) *The Metropolitan Revolution: How Cities and Metros Are Fixing Our Broken Politics and Fragile Economy* (Washington, DC: Brookings Institution Press).

Katzenstein, P. (1985) *Small States in World Markets. Industrial Policy in Europe* (Ithaca, NY: Cornell University Press).

—— (ed.) (1996) *The Culture of National Security* (New York: Columbia University Press).

Kautsky, K. (1970) 'Ultra-Imperialism', *New Left Review*, I/5: 41–46 (first published 1914).

Kellerman, B. (2004) *Bad Leadership* (Boston, MA: Harvard Business).

Kelman, H., Hamilton, V.L. (1989) *Crimes of Obedience* (New Haven, CT: Yale University Press).

Kenney, S. (1996) 'New Research on Gendered Political Institutions', *Political Research Quarterly*, 49(2): 445–466.

Kenny, M. (2007) 'Gender, Institutions and Power: A Critical Review', *Politics*, 27(2) 445–466.

—— (2013) *Gender and Political Recruitment* (Basingstoke: Palgrave Macmillan).

Kenny, M. and Verge, T. (eds.) (2016) 'Candidate Selection: Parties and Legislatures in a New Era', *Special Issue of Government & Opposition*, 51(3).

Kenworthy, L. (2007) 'Toward Improved Use of Regression in Macro-Comparative Analysis', *Comparative Social Research*, 24: 343–350.

Keohane, N. (2010) *Thinking about Leadership* (Princeton, NJ: Princeton University Press).

Keohane, R.O. (1984) *After Hegemony: Cooperation and Discord in the International Political Economy* (Princeton, NJ: Princeton University Press).

Keynes, J.M. (1964) *The General Theory of Employment, Interest and Money* (New York: Harcourt Brace and World).

Khan, G. (2017) 'Beyond the Ontological Turn: affirming the relative autonomy of politics' in *Political Studies Review* (15)4, forthcoming.

Khan, G. and Wenman, M. (eds.) (2017) 'The Politics of Poststructuralism Today', *Political Studies Review* (15)4 (Symposium): in press.

Kiely, R. (2010) *Rethinking Imperialism* (Basingstoke: Palgrave Macmillan).

Kinder, D.R. and Palfrey, T.R. (eds.) (1993) *Experimental Foundations of Political Science* (Ann Arbor, MI: University of Michigan Press).

King, A. (ed.) (1985) *The British Prime Minister* (London: Palgrave Macmillan).

—— (2002) 'The Outsider as Political Leader: The Case of Margaret Thatcher', *British Journal of Political Science*, 32(3): 435–454.

King, D. (1995) *Actively Seeking Work: The Politics of Welfare and Unemployment and Welfare Policy in the United States* (Chicago, IL: University of Chicago Press).

King, G. (1986) 'How Not to Lie with Statistics: Avoiding Common Mistakes in Quantitative Political Science', *American Journal of Political Science*, 30(3): 666–687.

—— (1989) *Unifying Political Methodology* (Cambridge: Cambridge University Press).

—— (1995) 'Replication, Replication', *Political Science and Politics*, 28(3): 444–452.

—— (2011) 'Ensuring the Data-Rich Future of the Social Sciences', *Science*, 331: 719–721.

—— (2014) 'Restructuring the Social Sciences: Reflections from Harvard's Institute for Quantitative Social Science', *PS: Political Science & Politics*, 47: 165–172.

King, G., Gakidou, E., Ravishankar, N., Moore, R., Lakin, J., Vargas, M., Téllez-Rojo, M., Hernández Avila, J.E., Hernández, Á. and Hernández, L. (2005) 'A "Politically Robust" Experimental Design for Public Policy Evaluation, with Application to the Mexican Universal Health Insurance Program', *Journal of Policy Analysis and Management*, 26(3): 479–506.

King, G., Keohane, R.O. and Verba, S. (1994) *Designing Social Enquiry: Scientific Inference in Qualitative Research* (Princeton, NJ: Princeton University Press).

King, G., Pan, J. and Roberts, M.E. (2013) 'How Censorship in China Allows Government Criticism but Silences Collective Expression', *American Political Science Review*, 107(2): 326–343.

King, G., Tomz, M. and Lee, J. (2000) "Making the Most of Statistical Analysis: Improving Interpretation and Presentation', *American Journal of Political Science*, 44(2): 347–361.

King, L. (2007) 'Central European Capitalism in Comparative Perspective', in Hancké, B., Rhodes, M. and Thatcher, M. (eds.) *Beyond Varieties of Capitalism: Conflict, Contradiction and Complementarities in the European Economy* (Oxford: Oxford University Press).

Kirk, C., (2012) 'Obama 2012 Campaign Stops: A Map of the Candidate's Travels in Red States, Blue States, and Campaign Battlegrounds'. Available online: www.slate.com/articles/news_and_politics/map_of_the_week/2012/08/obama_2012_campaign_stops_a_map_of_the_candidate_s_travels_in_red_states_blue_states_and_campaign_battlegrounds_.html (accessed November 17, 2016).

Kirk, J. and Miller, M. (1986) *Reliability and Validity in Qualitative Research* (London: Sage).

Kiser, L. and Ostrom, E. (1982) 'Three Worlds of Actions: A Metatheoretical Synthesis of Institutional Approaches', in Ostrom, E. (ed.) *Strategies of Political Enquiry* (Beverley Hills, CA: Sage) 179–222.

Kitchin, R. (2014) *The Data Revolution: Big Data, Open Data, Data Infrastructures and Their Consequences* (Thousand Oaks, CA: Sage).

Kittel, B., Luhan, W. and Morton, R.B. (2012) *Experimental Political Science. Principles and Practices* (Basingstoke: Palgrave Macmillan).

Kittilson, M.C. (2006) *Challenging Parties, Changing Parliaments: Women and Elected Office in Contemporary Western Europe* (Columbus, OH: Ohio State University Press).

Klare, M. (2008) 'Past Its Peak', *London Review of Books*, 14 August.

Klein, G. (1997) 'The Recognition-Primed Decision (RPD) Model: Looking Back, Looking Forward', in Zsambok, C. and Klein, G. (eds.) *Naturalistic Decision Making* (Mahwah, N.J.: Lawrence Erlbaum Associates): 285–292.

Knight, J. (1992) *Institutions and Social Conflict* (Cambridge: Cambridge University Press).

Koning, E.(2015) 'The Three Institutionalisms and Institutional Dynamics: Understanding Endogenous and Exogenous Change', *Journal of Public Policy*, 36(4): 639–664.

Koopmans, R. (1996) 'Explaining the Rise of Racist and Extreme Right Violence in Western Europe: Grievances or Opportunities?', *European Journal of Political Research*, 30(2): 185–216.

Kramer, A., Guillory, J. and Hancock, J. (2014) 'Experimental Evidence of Massive-Scale Emotional Contagion Through Social Networks', *Proceedings of the National Academy of Sciences*, 111(24): 8788–8790.

Krasner, S. (1984) 'Approaches to the State: Alternative Conceptions and Historical Dynamics', *Comparative Politics* 16(2): 223–246.

Krasno, J. and LaPides, S. (eds.) (2015) *Personality, Political Leadership, and Decision Making: A Global Perspective* (Santa Barbara, CA: Praeger).

Kravets, D. (2010) 'Analysis: Bigger Twitter, Facebook Flock Boosts Election Odds' *Wired.com*. www.wired.com/threatlevel/2010/11/election-odds-twitter/ (accessed April 23, 2017).

Krippendorff, K. (1980) *Content Analysis* (London: Sage).

Kristeva, J. (1986) 'Revolution in Poetic Language', in Moi, T. (ed.) *The Kristeva Reader* (Oxford: Blackwell).
Krogslund, C., Choi D.D. and Poertner, M. (2015) 'Fuzzy Sets on Shaky Ground: Parameter Sensitivity and Confirmation Bias in FSQCA," *Political Analysis*, 23(1): 21–41.
Krook, M.L. (2009) *Quotas for Women in Politics* (Oxford: Oxford University Press).
Krook, M.L. and Mackay, F. (eds.) (2011) *Gender, Politics and Institutions: Towards a feminist institutionalism* (London: Palgrave Macmillan).
Krook, M.L. and True, J. (2012) 'Rethinking the Life Cycles of International Norms: The United Nations and the Global Promotion of Gender Equality', *European Journal of International Relations,* 18(1): 103–127.
Krueger, A.B. (1999) 'Experimental Estimates of Education Production Functions', *Quarterly Journal of Economics*, 114(2): 497–532.
Kuhn, T. (1970) *The Structure of Scientific Revolutions* (Chicago, IL: University of Chicago Press).
Kurki, M. (2008) *Causation in International Relations: Reclaiming Causal Analysis* (Cambridge: Cambridge University Press).
Lacan, J. (1977) *Écrits: A Selection* (New York: W.W. Norton, tr. A. Sheridan).
——— (1998) *Ecrits: A Selection* (London: Routledge).
Lacey A. (1976) *A Dictionary of Philosophy* (London: Routledge and Keegan Paul).
Laclau, E. (1990) *New Reflections on the Revolutions of Our Time* (London: Verso).
——— (2000) 'Identity and Hegemony: The Role of Universality in the Constitution of Political Logics', in Butler, J., Laclau, E. and Žižek, S. (eds.) *Contingency, Hegemony, Universality* (London: Verso).
Laclau, E. and Mouffe, C. (1985) *Hegemony and Socialist Strategy* (London: Verso).
Lakatos, I. (1971) 'Falsification and the Methodology of Scientific Research Programmes', in Lakatos, I. and Musgrave, A. (eds.) *Criticism and the Growth of Knowledge* (Cambridge: Cambridge University Press).
Lakoff, G. and Johnson, M. (1980) *Metaphors We Live By* (Chicago, IL: University of Chicago Press).
Landman, T. (2000) *Issues and Methods in Comparative Politics* (London: Routledge).
Lane, R.E. (1959) *Political Life* (Glencoe, IL: Free Press).
Laney, D. (2001) '3D Data Management: Controling Data Volume, Velocity, and Variety' http://blogs.gartner.com/doug-laney/files/2012/01/ad949-3D-Data-Management-Controlling-Data-Volume-Velocity-and-Variety.pdf (accessed January 8, 2015).
——— (2012) 'Deja VVVu: Others Claiming Gartner's Construct for Big Data' http://blogs.gartner.com/doug-laney/deja-vvvue-others-claiming-gartners-volume-velocity-variety-construct-for-big-data/ (accessed January 8, 2015).
Lanzara, G. (1998) 'Self-Destructive Processes in Institution Building and Some Modest Countervailing Mechanisms', *European Journal of Political Research*, 33(1): 1–39.
Larrain, J. (1989) *Theories of Development* (Cambridge: Polity).
Lasswell, H.D. (1986 [1930]) *Psychopathology and Politics* (Chicago, IL: University of Chicago Press).

Lavine, H. (ed.) (2010) *Political Psychology: Four Volumes* (London: Sage).

Lebovic, J. (2004) 'Uniting for Peace? Democracies and United Nations Peace Operations after the Cold War', *Journal of Conflict Resolution*, 48(6): 910–936.

LeCun, Y., Bengio, Y. and Hinton, G. (2015) 'Deep Learning', *Nature*, 521: 436–444.

Leftwich, A. (1984a) 'On the Politics of Politics', in Leftwich, A. (ed.) *What Is Politics?* (Oxford: Blackwell).

—— (1984b) *What Is Politics?: The Activity and Its Study* (Oxford: Polity Press).

Lehnert, M., Miller, B. and Wonka, A. (2007) 'Increasing the Relevance of Research Questions. Considerations on Theoretical and Social Relevance', in Gschwend, T. and Schimmelfennig, F. (eds.) *Research Design in Political Science. How to Practice What They Preach* (Basingstoke: Palgrave Macmillan): 21–40.

Lenin, V. (1977) 'Imperialism: The Highest Stage of Capitalism', in Lenin, V. (ed.) *Selected Works* (Moscow: Progress, first published 1916).

Lévi-Strauss, C. (1966 [1962]). *The Savage Mind* (Chicago, IL: University of Chicago Press).

—— (1971) *The Elementary Structures of Kinship* (Boston: Beacon Press).

Levitt, S. and Dubner, S. (2005) *Freakonomics: A Rogue Economist Explores the Hidden Side of Everything* (New York: William Morrow).

Lewis, D. (1973) 'Causation', *Journal of Philosophy*, 70(17): 556–567.

—— (1986) *Causal Explanation* (Oxford: Oxford University Press).

Lewis, J. (2005) 'The Janus Face of Brussels: Socialization and Everyday Decision-Making in the European Union', *International Organization*, 59(4): 937–971.

Lewis, S.C. (2015) 'Journalism in an Era of Big Data', *Digital Journalism*, 3(3): 321–330.

Lichbach, M. (1989) 'An Evaluation of "Does Economic Inequality Breed Political Conflict?" Studies', *World Politics*, 41(4): 431–470.

—— (1997) 'Social Theory and Comparative Politics', in Lichbach, M.I. and Zuckerman, A.S. (eds.) *Comparative Politics: Rationality, Culture, and Structure* (Cambridge: Cambridge University Press): 239–276.

Lieberman, E.S. (2005) 'Nested Analysis as a Mixed-Method Strategy for Comparative Research', *American Political Science Review*, 99(3): 435–452.

Lieberman, R. (2002) 'Ideas, Institutions, and Political Order: Explaining Political Change', *American Political Science Review*, 96(4): 697–712.

Lieberson, S. (1994) 'More on the Uneasy Case for Using Mill-Type Methods in Small-N Comparative Studies', *Social Forces*, 72(4): 1225–1237.

Lijphart, A. (1968) *The Politics of Accommodation. Pluralism and Democracy in the Netherlands* (Berkeley, CA: University of California Press).

—— (1971) 'Comparative Politics and the Comparative Method', *American Political Science Review*, 65(3): 682–693.

Lin, J. (2015) "On Building Better Mousetraps and Understanding the Human Condition. Reflections on Big Data in the Social Sciences." *The ANNALS of the American Academy of Political and Social Science*, 659(1): 33–47.

Lindblom, C. (1977) *Politics and Markets* (New York: Basic Books).

Linde, J. and Vis, B. (2016) 'Do Politicians Take Risky Decisions Like the Rest of Us? An Experimental Test of Prospect Theory Under MPs', *Political Psychology*, 37(1): 101–117.

Linden, G., Kraemer, K., and Dedrick, J. (2007) *Who Captures Value in a Global Innovation System?: The Case of Apple's Ipod* (Irvine: Personal Computing Industry Centre): 1–10

Lipman-Blumen, J. (2006) *The Allure of Toxic Leaders* (New York: Oxford University Press).

Lipset, M.S. (1963) *Political Man: The Social Bases of Politics* (London: Mercury Books).

List, C. and Valentini, L. (2016) 'The Methodology of Political Theory', in Cappelen, H., Gendler, T. and Hawthorne, J. (eds.) *The Oxford Handbook of Philosophical Methodology* (Oxford: Oxford University Press): 525–553.

List, F. (1966) *The National System of Political Economy* (New York: Augustus Kelley, first published in English 1885).

Little, D. (1991) *Varieties of Social Explanation: An Introduction to the Philosophy of Social Science* (Boulder, CO: Westview Press).

Little, G. (1985) *Political Ensembles: A Psychosocial Approach to Politics and Leadership* (Oxford: Oxford University Press).

Locke, J. (1980) *Second Treatise of Government* (Indianapolis, IN: Hackett, first published 1690).

Lohr, S. (2009) *Sampling: Design and Analysis*, 2nd edition (Boston, MA: Brooks-Cole).

Long, M. (2005) *Introduction to Xml*, 1st edition (Stephens City, VA: Virtual Training Company, Inc.).

Loukides, M. (2011) *What Is Data Science?*, 1st edition (Sebastapol, CA: O'Reilly Media).

Lovenduski, J. (1981) 'Toward the Emasculation of Political Science: The Impact of Feminism', in Spender, D. (ed.) *Men's Studies Modified* (Oxford: Pergamon): 83–98.

—— (1998) 'Gendering Research in Political Science', *Annual Review of Political Science,* 1: 333–356.

—— (2005) *Feminizing Politics* (Cambridge: Polity).

—— (2011) 'Foreword', in Krook, M.L. and Mackay, F. (eds.) *Gender, Politics and Institutions* (Basingstoke: Palgrave Macmillan): vii–xi.

—— (2015) 'Conclusion: Does Feminism Need Political Science?', in *Gendering Politics, Feminising Political Science* (Colchester: ECPR Press): 337–347.

Lovenduski, J. and Norris, P. (eds.) (1993) *Gender and Party Politics* (London: Sage).

Lowell, A.L. (1910) 'The Physiology of Politics', *American Political Science Review*, 4(1): 1–15.

Lowndes, V. (1996) 'Varieties of New Institutionalism: A Critical Appraisal', *Public Administration*, 74(2): 181–197.

—— (2005) 'Something Old, Something New, Something Borrowed… How Institutions Change (and Stay the Same) in Local Governance', *Policy Studies,* 26(3): 291–309.

Lowndes, V., Pratchett, L. and Stoker, G. (2006) 'Local Political Participation: The Impact of Rules-in-Use', *Public Administration*, 84(3): 539–561.

Lowndes, V. and Roberts, M. (2013) *Why Institutions Matter: The New Institutionalism in Political Science* (Basingstoke: Palgrave Macmillan).

Lucas, S.R. and Szatrowski, A. (2014) 'Qualitative Comparative Analysis in Critical Perspective', *Sociological Methodology*, 44(1): 1–79.

Luhmann, N. (1995) *Social Systems* (Stanford, CA: Stanford University Press).

Lupia, A. (2000) 'Evaluating Political Science Research: Information for Buyers and Sellers', *PS: Political Science & Politics*, 33(1): 7–14.

Lupton, D. (2014) *"Feeling Better Connected': Academics' Use of Social Media'* (Canberra: News & Media Research Centre, University of Canberra).

Lyotard, J.-F. (1986) *The Postmodern Condition: A Report on Knowledge* (Manchester: Manchester University Press).

Lynch, C. (1999) *Beyond Appeasement: Interpreting Interwar Peace Movements in World Politics* (Ithaca, NY: Cornell University Press).

Mackay, F. (2004) 'Gender and Political Representation in the UK: The State of the Discipline', *British Journal of Politics & International Relations*, 6(1): 99–120.

—— (2008) '"Thick" Conceptions of Substantive Representation: Women, Gender and Political Institutions', *Representation*, 44(2): 125–139.

—— (2011) 'Conclusion: Towards a Feminist Institutionalism?', in Krook, M.L. and Mackay, F. (eds.) *Gender, Politics and Institutions* (Basingstoke: Palgrave Macmillan): 181–196.

Mackay, F., Kenny, M. and Chappell, L. (2010) 'New Institutionalism Through a Gender Lens: Towards a Feminist Institutionalism?', *International Political Science Review*, 31(5): 573–588.

Mackenzie, I (2010) 'Unravelling the Knots: Poststructuralism and Other 'Post-isms'', *Journal of Political Ideologies*, 6(3): 331–345.

Mahoney, J. (2012) 'The Logic of Process Tracing Tests in the Social Sciences', *Sociological Methods & Research*, 41(4): 570–597.

Mahoney, J. and Goertz, G. (2006) 'A Tale of Two Cultures: Contrasting Quantitative and Qualitative Research', *Political Analysis*, 14(3): 227–249.

Mahoney, J. and Thelen, K. (eds.) (2010) *Explaining Institutional Change: Ambiguity, Agency, and Power* (Cambridge: Cambridge University Press).

Manning, W.G., Newhouse, J.P., Duan, N., Keeler, E.B. and Leibowitz, A. (1987) 'Health Insurance and the Demand for Medical Care: Evidence from a Randomized Experiment', *American Economic Review*, 77(3): 251–277.

Mansbridge, J. (1999) 'Should Blacks Represent Blacks and Women Represent Women? A Contingent Yes', *Journal of Politics*, 61(3): 628–657.

March, J.G. and Olsen, J.P. (1984) 'The New Institutionalism: Organizational Factors in Political Life', *American Political Science Review*, 78(3): 734–749.

—— (1989) *Rediscovering Institutions* (New York: Free Press).

—— (2006) 'Elaborating the "New Institutionalism"', in Rhodes, R.A.W., Binder, S. and Rockman, B. (eds.) *The Oxford Handbook of Political Institutions* (Oxford: Oxford University Press): 3–21.

Marchart, O. (2007) *Post-Foundational Political Thought: Political Difference in Nancy, Lefort, Badiou and Laclau* (Edinburgh: Edinburgh University Press).

Margetts, H., John, P., Escher, T. and Reissfelder, S. (2011) 'Social Information and Political Participation on the Internet: An Experiment', *European Political Science Review*, 3(3): 321–344.

Marsh, D. (2017) 'Brexit and the Politics of Truth, British Politics', Forthcoming.

Marsh, D. and Furlong, P. (2007) 'On Ontological and Epistemological Gatekeeping: A Response to Bates and Jenkins', *Politics*, 27(3): 204–207.

Marsh, D. and Hall, M. (2007) 'The British Political Tradition: Explaining the Fate of New Labour's Constitutional Reform Agenda', *Journal of British Politics*, 2(2): 215–238.

Marsh, D., Lewis, C. and Chesters, J. (2014) 'The Political Power of Big Business: The Big Miners and the Mining Tax', *Australian Journal of Political Science*, 49(4): 711–725.

Marsh, D. and Read, M. (2002) 'Combining Quantitative and Qualitative Methods', in Marsh, D. and Stoker, G. (eds.) *Theory and Methods in Political Science*, 2nd edition (Basingstoke: Palgrave Macmillan): 231–248.

Marsh, D. and Rhodes, R.A.W. (eds.) (1992) *Policy Networks in British Government* (Oxford: Oxford University Press).

Marsh, D. and Savigny, H. (2004) 'Political Science as a Broad Church: The Search for a Pluralist Discipline', *Politics*, 24(3): 155–168.

Marsh, D., Smith, N. and Holti, N. (2006) 'Globalisation and the State', in Hay, C., Lister, M. and Marsh, D. (eds.) *The State* (Basingstoke: Palgrave Macmillan).

Marsh, D. and Tant, T. (1989) 'There is No Alternative: Mrs Thatcher and the British Political Tradition', *Essex Papers in Politics and Government*, Number 69.

Maruyama, G. (1998) *Basics of Structural Equation Modelling* (London: Sage).

Marx, K. (1976) *Capital*, Vol.1 (Harmondsworth: Penguin, first published 1867).

—— (1982) 'Pathways of Social Development: A Brief against Suprahistorical Theory', in Alavi, H. and Shanin, T. (eds.) (1982) *Introduction to the Sociology of Developing Societies* (Basingstoke: Palgrave Macmillan): 109–111.

—— (1984) 'The Reply to Zauslich', in Shanin, T. (ed.) (1984) *Late Marx and the Russian Road* (London: Routledge): 123–126.

—— (2000a) 'Speech on Free Trade, 1848', in McLellan, D. (ed.) *Selected Writings* (Oxford: Oxford University Press): 295–296.

—— (2000b) 'Preface to a Critique of Political Economy', in McLellan, D. (ed.) *Selected Writings* (Oxford: Oxford University Press): 424–428.

Marx, K. and Engels, F. (1974) *On Colonialism* (Moscow: Progress).

—— (2000) 'Manifesto of the Communist Party', in McLellan, D. (ed.) *Selected Writings* (Oxford: Oxford University Press): 245–272.

Mateo Diaz, M. (2005) *Representing Women: Female Legislators in West European Parliaments* (Colchester: ECPR Press).

Mauss, M. (1954 [1923]) *The Gift* (London: Cohen & West, tr. I. Cunnison).

Mayer, F. (2014) *Narrative Politics: Stories and Collective Action* (Oxford: Oxford University Press).

McAnulla, S. (2002) 'Structure and Agency', in Marsh, D. and Stoker, G. (eds.) *Theory and Methods in Political Science*, 2nd edition (Basingstoke: Palgrave Macmillan): 65–89.

—— (2006) 'Challenging the New Interpretivist Approach: Towards a Critical Realist Alternative', *Journal of British Politics*, 1(1): 113–138.

McBride, D. and Mazur, A.G. (2010) *The Politics of State Feminism* (Philadelphia, PA: Temple University Press).

McDermott, D. (2002) 'Experimental Methods in Political Science', *Annual Review of Political Science*, 5(1): 31–61.

—— (2008) 'Analytic Political Philosophy', in Leopold, D. and Stears, M. (eds.) *Political Theory: Methods and Approaches* (Oxford:Oxford University Press): 11–28.

—— (2013) 'The Ten Commandments of Experiments', PS: *Political Science and Politics*, 46(3): 605–611.

McDermott, R. and Hatemi, P.K. (2014) 'The Study of International Politics in the Neurobiological Revolution: A Review of Leadership and Political Violence', *Millennium: Journal of International Studies*, 43(1): 92–123.

McGraw, K., Morton, R. B. and Williams, K. (2001) 'Introduction: The Advent of an Experimental Political Science, in *Experimental Methods in Political Science* (Preliminary Draft Version – June 28).

McGuire, D. and Hutchings, K. (2007) 'Portrait of a Transformational Leader: The Legacy of Dr Martin Luther King Jr.', *Leadership & Organization Development Journal*, 28(2): 154–166.

McLellan, D. (1977) *Karl Marx: Selected Writings* (Oxford: Oxford University Press).

Mearsheimer, J. and Walt, S. (2013) 'Leaving Theory Behind: Why Simplistic Hypothesis Testing Is Bad for International Relations', *European Journal of International Relations*, 19(3): 427–457.

Meyer, J. and Rowan, B. (1991) 'Institutionalised Organisations: Formal Structure as Myth and Ceremony', in Powell, W. and DiMaggio, P. (eds.) *The New Institutionalism in Organisational Analysis* (Chicago, IL: University of Chicago Press).

Meyer, J, Boli, J., Thomas, G. and Ramirez, F. (1997) 'World Society and the Nation-State', *American Journal of Sociology*, 103(1): 144–181.

Michelson, M.R. (2006) 'Mobilizing the Latino Youth Vote: Some Experimental Results', *Social Science Quarterly*, 87(5): 1188–1206.

Milgram, S. (1963) 'Behavioral Study of Obedience', *Journal of Abnormal and Social Psychology*, 67(4): 371–378.

—— (1974) *Obedience to Authority* (New York: Harper and Row).

Mill, J.S. (1843 [1950]) 'Philosophy of Scientific Method', reprinted in Nagel, E. (ed.) *John Stuart Mill's Philosophy of Scientific Method* (New York: Hafner).

—— (1984) 'A Few Words on Non-Intervention', in Robson, J. (ed.) *Collected Works*, vol.18 (Toronto: University of Toronto Press, first published 1859): 109–124.

—— (2002 [1843]) *A System of Logic: Ratiocinative and Inductive*, vol. 3 (Honolulu, HI: University of The Pacific Press).

Miller, D. (2000) *Citizenship and National Identity* (Cambridge: Polity).

—— (2013) *Justice for Earthlings* (Oxford: Oxford University Press).

Miller, W.L. (1995) `Quantitative Methods', in Marsh, D. and Stoker, G. (eds.) *Theory and Methods in Political Science* (Basingstoke: Palgrave Macmillan): 154–172.

Miller, W.L., Dickson, M. and Stoker, G. (2000) *Models of Local Governance: Public Opinion and Political Theory* (Basingstoke: Palgrave Macmillan).

Mintz, A., Redd, S. and Vedlitz, A. (2006) 'Can We Generalize from Student Experiments to the Real World in Political Science, Military Affairs and International Relations?', *Journal of Conflict Resolution*, 50(5): 757–776.

Mitchell, T. (1991) *Colonising Egypt* (Berkeley, CA: University of California Press).

Mols, F., Haslam, S.A., Jetten, J. and Steffens, N.K. (2015) 'Why a Nudge Is Not Enough: A Social Identity Critique of Governance by Stealth', *European Journal of Political Research*, 54(1): 81–98.

Mols, F. and Jetten, J. (2014) 'No Guts, No Glory: How Framing the Collective Past Paves the Way for Anti-immigrant Sentiments', *International Journal of Intercultural Relations*, 43(1): 74–86.

—— (2016) 'Explaining the Appeal of Populist Right-Wing Parties in Times of Economic Prosperity', *Political Psychology*, 37(2): 275–292.

—— (2017) *The Wealth Paradox: Economic Prosperity and the Hardening of Attitudes* (Cambridge: Cambridge University Press).

Mols, F. and Weber, M. (2013) 'Laying Sound Foundations for SIT Inspired EU Attitude Research: Beyond Attachment and Deeply Rooted Identities', *Journal of Common Market Studies*, 51(3): 505–521.

Monroe, K.R. (ed.) (2005) Perestroika! *The Raucous Rebellion in Political Science* (New Haven, CT: Yale University Press).

—— (2015) 'What Did Perestroika Accomplish?', *Perspectives on Politics*, 13(2): 423–424.

Moon, D. (2013) 'Tissue on the Bones': Towards the Development of a Post-structuralist Institutionalism', *Politics*, 33(2): 112–123.

Mooney, C. (1996) 'Bootstrap Statistical Inference: Examples and Evaluations for Political Science', *American Journal of Political Science*, 40(2): 570–602.

Mooney, C. and Duval, R. (1993) *Bootstrapping: A Non-Parametric to Statistical Inference* (Newbury Park, CA: Sage).

Mooney, C. and Krause, G. (1997) 'Review Article: Of Silicon and Political Science – Computationally Intensive Techniques of Statistical Estimation and Inference', *British Journal of Political Science*, 27(1): 83–110.

Moran, Michael, and Anthony Payne. 2014. "Introduction: Neglecting, Rediscovering and Thinking Again about Power in Finance." *Government and Opposition* 49 (3): 331–341.

Morgan, S. and Winship, C. (2015) *Counterfactuals and Causal Inference. Methods and Principles for Social Research*, 2nd edition (Cambridge: Cambridge University Press).

Morton, A. (2005) 'A Double Reading of Gramsci: Beyond the Logic of Contingency', *CRISP*, 8(4): 439–453.

Morton, R.B. and Williams, K.C. (2008) 'Experimentation in Political Science', in Box-Steffensmeier, J., Collier, D. and Brady, H. (eds.) *The Oxford Handbook of Political Methodology* (Oxford: Oxford University Press): 339–356.

—— 2010. *Experimental Political Science and the Study of Causality: From Nature to the Lab* (Cambridge: Cambridge University Press).

Mosley, L. (2013) *Interview Research in Political Science* (Ithaca, NY: Cornell University Press).

Mousazadeha, M. and Izadkhah, M. (2015) 'The Ultimatum Game: A Comprehensive Literature Review', *Applied Mathematics in Engineering, Management and Technology*, 3(1) 2015: 158–165.

Mudde, C. (2004) 'The Populist Zeitgeist', *Government & Opposition*, 39(4): 541–563.

Mueller, D.C. (1993) 'The Future of Public Choice', *Public Choice*, 77(1): 145–150.

Mukhopadhyay, M. (2007) 'Situating Gender and Citizenship in Development Debates: Towards a Strategy", in Mukhopadhyay, M. and Singh, N. (eds.) *Gender Justice, Citizenship and Development* (New Delhi: Zubaan): 263–314.

Muller, E. (1988) 'Democracy, Economic Development and Income Inequality', *American Sociological Review*, 53 (February): 50–68.

Munzert, S., Rubba, C., Meißner, P. and Nyhuis, D. (2014) *Automated Data Collection with R: A Practical Guide to Web Scraping and Text Mining* (London: John Wiley & Sons).

Murray, R. (2008) 'Is Deliberative Democracy a Falsifiable Theory?', *Annual Review of Political Science*, 11: 521–538.

—— (2014) 'Quotas for Men: Reframing Gender Quotas as a Means of Improving Representation for All', *American Political Science Review*, 108(3): 520–532.

Mutz, D.C. (2008) 'Is Deliberative Democracy a Falsifiable Theory', *Annual Review of Political Science* 11: 521–538.

NAO (2007) *Government on the Internet: Progress in Delivering Information and Services On-Line.* Report by the Comptroller and Auditor General, HC 529 Session 2006–7, 13 July (National Audit Office/The Stationary Office).

Nelson, B.J. (1989) 'Women and Knowledge in Political Science: Texts, Histories and Epistemologies', *Women and Politics*, 9(2): 1–25.

Neuman, W.R., Guggenheim, L., Jang, S.M., Bae, S.Y. (2014) 'The Dynamics of Public Attention: Agenda-Setting Theory Meets Big Data', *Journal of Communication*, 64(1): 193–214.

Nietzsche, F. (1976) 'On Truth and Lie in an Extra-Moral Sense', in Kaufmann, W. (ed.) *The Portable Nietzsche* (Harmondsworth: Penguin).

Norris, P. and Lovenduski, J. (1995) *Political Recruitment: Gender, Race and Class in the British Parliament* (Cambridge: Cambridge University Press).

North, D. (1990) *Institutions, Institutional Change and Economic Performance* (Cambridge: Cambridge University Press).

North, D., Wallis, J. and Weingast, B. (2009) *Violence and Social Orders. A Conceptual Framework for Interpreting Recorded Human History* (New York: Cambridge University Press).

Norval, A. (2007) *Aversive Democracy Inheritance and Originality in the Democratic Tradition* (Cambridge: Cambridge University Press).

Nownes, A.J. and Lipinski, D. (2005) 'The Population Ecology of Interest Group Death: Gay and Lesbian Rights Interest Groups in the United States', *British Journal of Political Science*, 35(2): 303–319.

Nussbaum, M. (2000) 'The Professor of Parody', in *The New Republic*, November 28.

Nye, J. (2004) *Soft Power* (New York: Public Affairs).

Nyhan, B. and Reifler, J. (2010) 'When Corrections Fail: The Persistence of Political Misperceptions', *Political Behavior*, 32(2): 303–330.

Offe, C. (1996) 'Political Economy: Sociological Perspectives', in R. Goodin and H.-D. Klingemann (eds.) *A New Handbook of Political Science* (Oxford: Oxford University Press): 675–690.

Ohmae, K (1996) *The End of the Nation State: The Rise of Regional Economies* (London: Harper Collins).

Olson, M. (1965) *The Logic of Collective Action: Public Goods and the Theory of Groups* (Cambridge, MA: Harvard University Press).

O'Neil, C. (2016) *Weapons of Math Destruction: How Big Data Increases Inequality and Threatens Democracy* (New York: Crown).

O'Neil, C. and Schutt, R. (2013) *Doing Data Science: Straight Talk from the Frontline*, 1st edition (Beijing : Sebastopol: O'Reilly Media).

O'Neill, J. (2013) *The Growth Map* (London: Portfolio Penguin).

Onuf, N. (1989) *World of Our Making: Rules and Rule in Social Theory and International Relations* (Columbia, SC: University of South Carolina Press).

Open Government Data Platform India (n.d.) Nirmal Bharat Abhiyan – District-wise Financial Progress.

Ormston, R. (2014) *Minding the Gap: Women's Views of Independence in 2014* (Edinburgh: ScotCen Social Research).

Ostrom, E (1986) 'An Agenda for the Study of Institutions', *Public Choice*, 48(1): 3–25.

—— (1990) *Governing the Commons: The Evolution of Institutions for Collective Action* (Cambridge: Cambridge University Press).

—— (2005) *Understanding Institutional Diversity* (Princeton, NJ: Princeton University Press).

—— (2007) 'Why Do We Need Laboratory Experiments in Political Science?', Paper presented at the annual meeting of the American Political Science Association, Chicago, IL, 30 August–2 September.

—— (2012) 'Nested Externalities and Polycentric Institutions: Must We Wait for Global Solutions to Climate Change Before Taking Actions at Other Scales?', *Economic Theory*, 49(2): 353–369.

Ostrom, E., Gardner, R. and Walker, J. (1994) *Rules, Games, and Common-Pool Resources* (Ann Arbor, MI: University of Michigan Press).

Ostrom, E. and Walker, J. (eds.) (2003) *Trust and Reciprocity: Interdiscip linary Lessons from Experimental Research* (New York: Russell Sage Foundation).

Outhwaite, W. (1994) *Habermas: A Critical Introduction* (Cambridge: Polity).

Pachirat, T. (2013) *Every Twelve Seconds: Industrialized Slaughter and the Politics of Sight* (New Haven, CT: Yale University Press).

Padilla, A., Hogan, R., Kaiser, R.B. (2007) 'The Toxic Triangle: Destructive Leaders, Susceptible Followers, and Conducive Environments', *The Leadership Quarterly*, 18(2): 176–194.

Palfrey, T.R. (2005) 'Laboratory Experiments in Political Economy', CEPS Working Paper, 111 (July). www.princeton.edu/ceps/workingpapers/111palfrey.pdf (accessed April 19, 2017).

Panitch, L. and Gindin, S. (2012) *The Making of Global Capitalism* (London: Verso).

Panizza, F. (2005) (ed.) *Populism and the Mirror of Democracy* (London: Verso).

Parkinson, J. (2006) *Deliberating in the Real World: Problems of Legitimacy in Deliberative Democracy* (Oxford: Oxford University Press).

Parry, G., Moyser, G. and Day, N. (1992) *Political Participation and Democracy in Britain* (Cambridge: Cambridge University Press).

Parsons, C. (2002) 'Showing Ideas as Causes: The Origins of the European Union', *International Organization*, 56(1): 47–84.

—— (2007) *How to Map Arguments in Political Science* (New York: Oxford University Press).

—— (2015) 'Before Eclecticism: Competing Alternatives in Constructivist Research', *International Theory*, 7(3): 501–538.

Paxton, P. (2000) 'Women's Suffrage in the Measurement of Democracy: Problems of Operationalization', *Studies in Comparative International Development*, 35(3): 92–111.

—— (2008) 'Gendering Democracy', in Goertz, G. and Mazur, A.G. (eds.) *Politics, Gender and Concepts* (Cambridge: Cambridge University Press): 47–70.

Paxton, P. and Hughes, M.M. (2017) *Women, Politics and Power*, 3rd edition (London: Sage).

Pearl, J. (2009) *Causality*, 2nd edition (New York: Cambridge University Press).

Peirce, C.S. (1955) *Philosophical Writings of Peirce* (New York: Dover).

Peters, B.G. (1996) 'Political Institutions, Old and New', in R. Goodin and H.-D. Klingemann (eds.) *A New Handbook of Political Science* (Oxford: Oxford University Press): 205–221.

—— (1999) *Institutional Theory in Political Science: The 'New Institutionalism'* (London: Pinter).

—— (2005) *Institutional Theory in Political Science: The 'New Institutionalism'*, 2nd edition (London: Continuum).

—— (2013) *Strategies for Comparative Research in Political Science* (Basingstoke: Palgrave).

—— (2017) *The Design of Public Policy* (Cheltenham: Edward Elgar).

Phillips, A. (1995) *The Politics of Presence* (Oxford: Clarendon).

Phillips, J.A. (2001) 'Using E-mail to Mobilize Voters: A Field Experiment', Unpublished Manuscript, *Yale University*, 27 March. www.yale.edu/ccr/phillips.doc .

Pierce, R. (2008) *Research Methods in Politics: A Practical Guide* (London: Sage Publications).

Pierre, J. (1999) 'Models of Urban Governance: The Institutional Dimension of Urban Politics', *Urban Affairs Review*, 34(3): 372–396.

Pierson, P. (2004) *Politics in Time: History, Institutions and Social Analysis* (Princeton, NJ: Princeton University Press).

—— (2007) 'The Costs of Marginalisation: Qualitative Methods in the Study of American Politics', *Comparative Political Studies*, 40(2): 145–169.

Plümper, T., Troeger, V.E. and Manow, P. (2005) 'Panel Data Analysis in Comparative Politics. Linking Method to Theory', *European Journal of Political Research*, 44(2): 327–354.

Polanyi, K. (1944) *The Great Transformation* (Boston, MA: Beacon).

Polsby, N. (1975) 'Legislatures', in Greenstein, F. and Polsby, F. (eds.) *A Handbook of Political Science* (Reading, MA: Addison-Wesley).

Poletta, F. (2002) *Freedom Is an Endless Meeting: Democracy in American Social Movements* (Chicago, IL: University of Chicago Press).

Popper, K. (1959) *The Logic of Scientific Discovery* (London: Hutchinson).

Post, J.M. (2014) 'Personality Profiling Analysis', in Rhodes, R.A.W. and 't Hart, P. (eds.) *Oxford Handbook of Political Leadership* (Oxford: Oxford University Press): 328–344.

Poster, M. (1990) *The Mode of Information: Poststructuralism and Social Context* (Chicago, IL: University Of Chicago Press).

Pouliot, V. (2010) *International Security in Practice* (New York: Cambridge University Press).

Powell, W. and DiMaggio, P. (eds.) (1991) *The New Institutionalism in Organizational Analysis* (Chicago, IL: University of Chicago Press).

Pressman, J. and Wildavsky, A. (1973) *Implementation* (Berkeley, CA: University of California Press).

Preston, T. (2001) *The President and His Inner Circle* (Princeton, NJ: Princeton University Press).

Pringle, R. and Watson, S. (1992) '"Women's Interests" and the Post-Structuralist State', in M. Barrett and A. Phillips (eds.) *Destabilizing Theory* (Cambridge: Polity): 53–73.

Proffitt, B. (2013) 'What APIs Are and Why They're Important – ReadWrite' Available online. ReadWrite. URL http://readwrite.com/2013/09/19/api-defined/ (accessed November 16, 2016).

Przeworski, A. and Teune, H. (1970) *The Logic of Comparative Social Inquiry* (New York: Wiley-Interscience).

Quattrone, G.A. and Tversky, A. (1988) 'Contrasting Rational and Psychological Analyses of Political Choice', *American Political Science Review*, 82(3): 719–736.

Quine, W. (1961) *From a Logical Point of View* (New York: Harper and Row).

R Development Core Team (2014) *R: A Language and Environment for Statistical Computing. R Foundation for Statistical Computing* (Vienna: R Foundation for Statistical Computing) www.R-project.org/ (accessed April 04, 2017).

Ragin, C. and Becker, H. (eds.) (1992) *What Is a Case? Exploring the Foundations of Social Inquiry* (Cambridge: Cambridge University Press).

Ragin, C.C. (1987) *The Comparative Method: Moving Beyond Qualitative and Quantitative Strategies* (Berkeley, CA: University of California Press).

—— (2000) *Fuzzy-Set Social Science* (Chicago, IL: Chicago University Press).

Ragin, C.C., Berg-Schlosser, D. and de Meur, G. (1996) 'Political Methodology: Qualitative Methods', in Goodin, R. and Klingeman, H.-D. (eds.) *A New Handbook of Political Science* (Oxford: Oxford University Press): 749–768.

Rai, S. and Waylen, G. (eds.) (2008) *Global Governance: Feminist Perspectives* (Basingstoke: Palgrave Macmillan).

Ramsay, S. (2011) *Reading Machines: Toward an Algorithmic Criticism* (Champlain: University of Illinois Press).

Randall, V. (2010) 'Feminism', in Marsh, D. and Stoker, G. (eds.) *Theory and Methods in Political Science,* 3rd edition (Basingstoke: Palgrave Macmillan): 114–135.

Randall, V. and Waylen, G. (eds.) (1998) *Gender, Politics and the State* (London: Routledge).

Rawls, J. (1971) *A Theory of Justice* (Oxford: Oxford University Press).

—— (1993) *Political Liberalism* (Columbia University Press).

—— (1996) *Political Liberalism* (New York: Columbia University Press).

—— (1999) *The Law of Peoples* (Cambridge, MA: Harvard University Press).

Reed, M. (1993) 'Organisations and Modernity', in Hassard, J. and Parker, M. (eds.) *Postmodernism and Organizations* (London: Sage): 163–182.

Rehurek, R. (2016) 'GitHub – 'RaRe-Technologies/gensim: Topic Modelling for Humans' Available online. URL https://github.com/RaRe-Technologies/gensim (accessed November 18, 2016).

Reich, R.B. (1991) *The Work of Nations: Preparing Ourselves for 21st-Century Capitalism* (New York: A.A. Knopf).

Reicher, S. and Haslam, S.A. (2006) 'Rethinking the Psychology of Tyranny: The BBC Prison Study', *The British Journal of Social Psychology*, 45(1): 47–53.

—— (2011) 'After Shock? Towards a Social Identity Explanation of the Milgram "Obedience" Studies', *British Journal of Social Psychology*, 50(1): 163–169.

Reicher, S.D. and Hopkins, N. (2001) *Self and Nation: Categorization, Contestation and Mobilisation* (London: Sage).

Reinharz, S. (1992) *Feminist Methods in Social Research* (New York: Oxford University Press).

Renshon, S. (2014) Psychoanalytical Theories. In Rhodes, R.A.W. and 't Hart, P. (eds.) *Oxford Handbook of Political Leadership* (Oxford: Oxford University Press): 132–148.

Reynolds, A. (2010) *Designing Democracy in a Dangerous World* (Oxford: Oxford University Press).

Rhodes, R.A.W. (1988) *Beyond Westminster and Whitehall* (London: Unwin-Hyman).

—— (1995) 'The Institutional Approach', in D. Marsh and G. Stoker (eds.) *Theory and Methods in Political Science* (London: Palgrave Macmillan): 42–57.

—— (1997) *Understanding Governance* (Buckingham: Open University Press).

—— (2002) 'Putting People Back into Networks', *Australian Journal of Political Science,* 37(3): 399–416.

—— (2007) 'Understanding Governance: Ten Years On', *Organization Studies*, *28*(8): 1243–1264.

—— (2009) 'In Search of Australian Political Science', in Rhodes, R. (ed.) *The Australian Study of Politics* (Basingstoke: Palgrave Macmillan): 1–15.

Rhodes, R.A.W., Binder, S.A. and Rockman, B.A. (2006) *The Oxford Handbook of Political Institutions* (Oxford: Oxford University Press).

Rhodes, R.A.W. and 't Hart, P. (eds.) (2014) *Oxford Handbook of Political Leadership* (Oxford: Oxford University Press).

Richardson, L. (2016a). 'beautifulsoup4 4.5.1 : Python Package Index' Available online. URL https://pypi.python.org/pypi/beautifulsoup4 (accessed November 17, 2016).

—— (2016b) 'Citizen Social Science and Policymaking', in Stoker, G. and Evans, M. (eds.) *Evidence-based Policymaking in the Social Sciences* (Bristol: Policy Press): 207–228.

Richert, W. and Coelho, L. (2013) *Building Machine Learning Systems with Python* (Birmingham: Packt Publishing).

Riek, B.M., Mania, E.W., Gaertner, S.L., McDonald, S.A. and Lamoreaux, M.J. (2010) 'Does a Common Ingroup Identity Reduce Intergroup Threat?', *Group Processes & Intergroup Relations*, 13(4): 403–423.

Rittberger, V. (1993) *Regime Theory and International Relations* (Oxford: Clarendon Press).

Roberts, M.E., Tingley, B.M.S. and Tingley, D. (2016) 'stm: R Package for Structural Topic Modules', *Journal of Statistical Software*, 10(2): 1–40.

Robinson, A. and Tormey, S. (2007) 'Beyond Representation? A Rejoinder', *Parliamentary Affairs*, 60(1): 127–137.

Robinson, B. (2004) *A Theory of Transnational Capitalism* (Baltimore: Johns Hopkins University Press).

—— (2015) 'The Transnational State and the BRICS: A Global Capitalism Perspective', *Third World Quarterly*, 36(1): 1–21.

Robson, W.A. (1960) *Nationalised Industry and Public Ownership* (London: Allen & Unwin).

Rodney, W. (1972) *How Europe Underdeveloped Africa* (London: Bogle L'Ouverture).

Rogers, R. (2009) *The End of the Virtual: Digital Methods* (Amsterdam: Amsterdam University Press).

Rogowski, R. (2013) 'Shooting (or Ignoring) the Messenger', *Political Studies Review*, *11*(2): 216–221.

Rogstad, I. (2016) 'Is Twitter Just Rehashing? Intermedia Agenda Setting between Twitter and Mainstream Media', *Journal of Information Technology & Politics*, 13(1): 142–158.

Rohlfing, I. (2008) 'What You See and What You Get: Pitfalls and Principles of Nested Analysis in Comparative Research', *Comparative Political Studies*, 41(11): 1492–1514.

—— (2012) *Case Studies and Causal Inference an Integrative Framework* (Basingstoke: Palgrave Macmillan).

—— (2014) 'Comparative Hypothesis Testing via Process Tracing', *Sociological Methods & Research*, 43(4): 606–642.

—— (2015) 'Mind the Gap: A Review of Simulation Designs for Qualitative Comparative Analysis', *Research and Politics*, October–December: 1–4.

Rorty, R (1989) *Contingency, Irony and Solidarity* (Cambridge: Cambridge University Press).

Rosamond, B. (1999) 'Discourses of Globalization and the Social Construction of European Identities', *Journal of European Public Policy*, 6(4): 652–668.

Rose, J.D. (2011) 'Diverse Perspectives on Groupthink Theory: A Literature Review', *Emerging Leadership Journeys*, 4(1): 37–57.

Rosenbaum, P.R. (2005) 'Heterogeneity and Causality', *The American Statistician*, 59(1): 147–152.

Rosenau, J. (1969) *International Politics and Foreign Policy: A Reader in Research and Theory* (New York: Free Press).

Rosenthal, R. (1979) 'The File Drawer Problem and Tolerance for Null Results', *Psychological Bulletin*, 86(3): 638–641.

Rothstein, B. (1996) 'Political Institutions: An Overview', in Goodin, R. and Klingemann, H.-D. (eds.) *A New Handbook of Political Science* (Oxford: Oxford University Press): 133–166.

—— (1998) *Just Institutions Matter: The Moral and Political Logic of the Universal Welfare State* (Cambridge: Cambridge University Press).

Rotton, J., Foos, P., Vanmeek, L. and Levitt, M. (1995) 'Publication Practices and the File Drawer Problem – A Survey of Published Authors', *Journal of Social Behaviour and Personality*, 10(1): 1–13.

Rowe, P., Ercan, S., Halupka, M. and Marsh D. (2017) 'Understanding Political Participation: Beyond Arena and Process Definitions of Politics', available from david.marsh@canberra.edu.au.

Rubinstein, A. (2012) *Economic Fables* (Cambridge: Open Book Publishers).

Rudner, R. (1966) *Philosophy of Social Science* (Englewood Cliffs, NJ: Prentice-Hall).

Ruggie, J.G. (1998) *Constructing the World Polity* (New York: Routledge).

Ryan, M., Haslam, K., Alexander, S. and Kulich, C. (2010) 'Politics and the Glass Cliff: Evidence that Women are Preferentially Selected to Contest Hard-to-Win Seats', *Psychology of Women Quarterly*, 34(1): 56–64.

Rydgren, J. (2005) 'Is Extreme-Right Populism Contagious? Explaining the Emergence of a New Party Family', *European Journal of Political Research*, 44(3): 413–437.

—— (2007) 'The Sociology of the Radical Right', *Annual Review of Sociology*, 33: 241–262.

Salganik, M., Dodds, P. and Watts, D. (2006) 'Experimental Study of Inequality and Unpredictability in an Artificial Cultural Market', *Science*, 311(5762): 854–856.

Salmon, W. (1998) *Causality and Explanation* (New York: Oxford University Press).

Sanders, D. (1990) *Losing an Empire, Finding a Role: British Foreign Policy Since 1945* (London: Palgrave Macmillan).

—— (2002) 'Behaviouralism', in Marsh D. and Stoker, G. (eds.) *Theory and Methods in Political Science*, 2nd edition (Basingstoke: Palgrave Macmillan): 45–64.

Sandler, T. (2004) *Global Collective Action* (Cambridge: Cambridge University Press).

Sangiovanni, A. (2007) 'Global Justice, Reciprocity and the State', *Philosophy and Public Affairs*, 35(1): 3–39.

Sapiro, V. (1998) 'Feminist Studies and Political Science – and Vice Versa', in Phillips, A. (ed.) *Feminism and Politics* (Oxford: Oxford University Press): 67–91.

Sarlvik, B. and Crewe, I. (1983) *Decade of Dealignment* (Cambridge: Cambridge University Press).

Sartori, G., Riggs, F. and Teune, H. (1975) *The Tower of Babel* (Storrs, CT: International Studies Association).

Sarup, M. (1993) *An Introductory Guide to Poststructuralism and Postmodernism* (Brighton: Harvester Wheatsheaf).

Saussure, F. de (1998) *Course in General Linguistics* (London: Gerald Duckworth).

Savage, M. and Burrows, R. (2007) 'The Coming Crisis of Empirical Sociology', *Sociology*, 41(5): 885–899.

Savage, M. and Witz, A. (eds.) (1992) *Gender and Bureaucracy* (Oxford: Blackwell).

Savolainen, J. (1994) 'The Rationality of Drawing Big Conclusions Based on Small Samples: In Defense of Mill's Methods', *Social Forces*, 72(4): 1217–1224.

Sawer, M. and Curtin, J. (2016) 'Organising for a More Diverse Political Science: Australia and New Zealand', *European Political Science*, 15(4): 441–456.

Sayer, A. (2000) *Realism and Social Science* (London: Sage).

—— (2005) *The Moral Significance of Class* (Cambridge: Cambridge University Press).

Sayer, D. (1989) *Readings from Karl Marx* (London: Routledge).

Schafer, M. and Crichlow, S. (2010) *Groupthink vs High Quality Decision Making in International Relations* (New York: Columbia University Press).

Schlick, M. (1974) *General Theory of Knowledge* (New York: Springer Verlag).

Schmidt, V. (2002) *The Futures of European Capitalism* (Oxford: Oxford University Press).

—— (2006) 'Institutionalism', in Hay, C., Lister, M. and Marsh, D. (eds.) *The State: Theories and Issues* (Basingstoke: Palgrave Macmillan): 98–117.

—— (2009) 'Putting Political Back into the Political Economy by Bringing the State Back in Yet Again', *World Politics*, 61(3): 516–546.

Schneider, C.Q. and Rohlfing, I. (2013) 'Combining QCA and Process Tracing in Set-Theoretic Multi-Method Research', *Sociological Methods & Research*, 42(4): 559–597.

Schneider, C.Q. and Wagemann, C. (2012) *Set-Theoretic Methods for the Social Sciences: A Guide to Qualitative Comparative Analysis* (Cambridge: Cambridge University Press).

Schram, S.F. (2006) 'Return to Politics: Perestroika, Phronesis and Post-Paradigmatic Political Science', in Schram, S.F. and Caterino, B. (eds.) *Making Political Science Matter: Debating Knowledge, Research and Method* (New York: New York University Press): 17–32.

Schram, S.F. and Caterino, B. (eds.) (2006) *Making Political Science Matter: Debating Knowledge, Research and Method* (New York: New York University Press).

Schumacker, R. and Lomax, R. (1996) *A Beginner's Guide to Structural Equation Modeling* (Mahwah, NJ: IEA).

Schwartz-Shea, P. and Yanow, D. (2002) '"Reading" "Methods" "Texts": How Research Methods Texts Construct Political Science', *Political Research Quarterly*, 55(2): 457–486.

—— (2012) *Interpretive Research Design. Concepts and Processes* (New York: Routledge).

Schwindt-Bayer, L. (2010) 'Comparison and Integration: A Comparative Politics of Gender', *Perspectives on Politics,* 8(1): 177–182.

Scott, J.W. (1986) 'Gender: A Useful Category of Historical Analysis', *American Historical Review*, 91(5): 1053–1075.

—— (2008) *Institutions and Organizations: Ideas and Interests*, 3rd edition (Thousand Oaks, CA: Sage).

Sears, D.O., Huddy, L. and Jervis, R. (2013) 'The Psychologies Underlying Political Psychology', in Sears, D.O., Huddy, L. and Jervis, R. (eds.) *Oxford Handbook of Political Psychology* (New York: Oxford University Press).

Searle, J. (1995) *Construction of Social Reality* (New York: Free Press).

Sekhon, J.S. (2008) 'The Neyman-Rubin Model of Causal Inference and Estimation via Matching Methods', in Box-Steffensmeier, J., Brady, H. and Collier, D. (eds.) *The Oxford Handbook of Political Methodology* (Oxford: Oxford University Press): 271–299.

Sen, A. (2009) *The Idea of Justice* (London: Allen Lane).

Shah, D., Cappella, J. and Neuman, W. (2015) 'Big Data, Digital Media, and Computational Social Science Possibilities and Perils', *The ANNALS of the American Academy of Political and Social Science*, 659(1): 6–13.

Shapiro, I. (2004) 'Problems, Methods, and Theories, or: What's Wrong with Political Science and What to Do about It', in Shapiro, I., Smith, R.M. and Masoud, T.E. (eds.) *Problems and Methods in the Study of Politics* (Cambridge: Cambridge University Press): 19–42.

Shapiro, I., Smith, R.M. and Masoud, T.E. (2004) *Problems and Methods in the Study of Politics* (Cambridge: Cambridge University Press).

Shapiro, M. (2016) *Politics and Time* (Cambridge: Polity Press).

Shepsle, K. (1989) 'Studying Institutions: Some Lessons from the Rational Choice Approach', *Journal of Theoretical Politics*, 1(2): 131–147.

Sheridan, C.L. and King, R.G. (1972) 'Obedience to Authority with an Authentic Victim', Proceedings of the eightieth annual convention of the American Psychological Association (Washington, DC: American Psychological Association): 165–166.

Sherif, M., Harvey, O.J., White, B.J., Hood, W.R. and Sherif, C.W. (1961) *Intergroup Cooperation and Competition: The Robbers' Cave Experiment* (Norman, OK: University Book Exchange).

Siegler, M.G. (2010) 'Eric Schmidt: Every 2 Days We Create as Much Information as We Did Up to 2003', *TechCrunch*. http://techcrunch.com/2010/08/04/schmidt-data/ (accessed January 8, 2015).

Sikkink, K. (1991) *Ideas and Institutions: Developmentalism in Argentina and Brazil* (Ithaca, NY: Cornell University Press).

Simmons, A.J. (2010) 'Ideal and Nonideal Theory', *Philosophy and Public Affairs*, 38(1): 5–36.

Simon, H.A. (1992) Egidi, M., Marris, R., 'Colloquium with H.A. Simon' *Economics, Bounded Rationality and the Cognitive Revolution* (Aldershot: Edward Elgar).

—— (1996) *The Sciences of the Artificial* (Boston: MIT press).

Simonton, D.K. (1993) Putting the Best Leaders in the White House: Personality, Policy, and Performance, *Political Psychology*, 14(3): 537–548.

Skinner, C., Holt, D. and Smith, T. (eds.) (1989) *Analysis of Complex Surveys* (New York: John Wiley).

Skocpol, T. (1979) *States and Social Revolutions* (Cambridge: Cambridge University Press).

Sloman, S. (2005) *Causal Models: How People Think About the World and Its Alternatives* (New York: Oxford University Press).

Small, M.L. (2011) 'How to Conduct a Mixed Methods Study: Recent Trends in a Rapidly Growing Literature', *Sociology*, 37, 57.

Smirnov, O., Dawes, C.T., Fowler, J.H., Johnson, T. and McElreath, R. (2007) 'The Behavioral Logic of Collective Action: Partisans Cooperate and Punish More than Non-Partisans', 25 September. http://papers.ssrn.com/sol3/papers.cfm?abstract_id=1017065 (accessed June 18, 2009).

Smith, A.M. (1998) *Laclau and Mouffe: The Radical Democratic Imaginary* (London and New York: Routledge).

Smith, S. (1996) 'Positivism and Beyond', in Smith, S. et al. (eds.) *International Theory: Positivism and Beyond* (Cambridge: Cambridge University Press): 11–46.

Smooth, W. (2011) 'Standing for Women? Which Women? The Substantive Representation of Women's Interests and the Research Imperative of Intersectionality', *Politics and Gender*, 7(3): 436–441.

Sniderman, P.M. and Grob, D.B. (1996) 'Innovations in Experimental Design in Attitude Surveys', *Annual Review of Sociology*, 22: 377–399.

Sørenson, E. and Torfing, J. (2008) 'Theoretical Approaches to Governance Network Dynamics', in Sørenson, E. and Torfing, J. (eds.) *Theories of Democratic Network Governance* (London: Palgrave Macmillan).

Southwood, N. (2016) 'Does "Ought" Imply "Feasible"?', *Philosophy and Public Affairs*, 44(1): 7–45.

Spencer, N (2000) 'On the Significance of Distinguishing Ontology and Epistemology', Paper presented at the Hegel Summer School. www.ethicalpolitics.org/seminars/neville.htm (accessed November 30, 2016).

Squires, J. (2007) *The New Politics of Gender Equality* (Basingstoke: Palgrave Macmillan).

Starrs, S. (2013) 'American Economic Power Hasn't Declined – It Globalized! Summoning the Data and Taking Globalization Seriously', *International Studies Quarterly*, 57(4): 817–830.

StataCorp. (2015) *Stata Statistical Software: Release 14* (College Station, TX: StataCorp LP).

Steffens, N.K., Haslam, S.A., Reicher, S.D., Platow, M.J., Fransen, K., Yang, J., Jetten, J., Ryan, M.K., Peters, K.O. and Boen, F. (2014) 'Leadership as Social Identity Management: Introducing the Identity Leadership

Inventory (ILI) to Assess and Validate a Four-dimensional Model', *The Leadership Quarterly*, 25(1): 1001–1024.

Steffens, N.K., Mols. F, Haslam, S.A. and Okimoto, T. (2016) 'True to What We Stand For: Championing Collective Interests as a Path to Authentic Leadership', *The Leadership Quarterly*, 27(5): 726–744.

Steinmo, S., Thelen, K. and Longstreth, F. (1992) (eds.) *Structuring Politics: Historical Institutionalism in Comparative Analysis* (Cambridge: Cambridge University Press).

—— (1993) *Taxation and Democracy: Swedish, British and American Approaches to Financing the Welfare State* (New Haven, CT: Yale University Press).

—— (2008) 'Historical Institutionalism', in Della Porta, D. and Keating, M. (eds.) *Approaches and Methodologies in the Social Sciences: A Pluralist Perspective* (Cambridge: Cambridge University Press): 118–138.

Steinmo, S. (2008) Historical Institutionalism in Donatella della Porta, and Michael Keating (eds) *Approaches and Methodologies in the Social Sciences: a pluralist perspective*, Cambridge University Press, Cambridge, pp. 118–138.

—— (2016) 'Historical Institutionalism and Experimental Methods', in Fioretos, O., Falleti, T. and Sheingate, A. (eds.) *The Oxford Handbook of Historical Institutionalism*, (Oxford: Oxford University Press).

Stemplowska, Z. (2008) 'What's Ideal about Ideal Theory?', *Social Theory and Practice*, 34(3): 319–340.

Stemplowska, Z. and Swift, A. (2012) 'Ideal and Nonideal Theory', in Estlund, D. (ed.) *The Oxford Handbook of Political Philosophy* (Oxford: Oxford University Press): 373–389.

Stoker, G. (2010) 'Translating Experiments into Policy', *Annals of the American Academy of Political and Social Science*, 628(1): 47–58.

—— (2012) 'In Defence of Political Science', *The Political Quarterly*, Special Crick Issue, November, 83(4): 677–684.

—— (2013a) 'Designing Politics: A Neglected Justification for Political Science', *Political Studies Review*, 11(1): 174–181.

—— (2013b) 'How Social Science Can Contribute to Public Policy: The Case for a 'Design Arm', in Taylor-Gooby, P. (ed.) *New Paradigms in Public Policy* (Oxford: The British Academy/Oxford University Press).

—— (2017) *Why Politics Matters*, 2nd edition (London: Palgrave Macmillan).

Stoker, G. and Evans, M. (eds.) (2016) *Evidence-based Policymaking in the Social Sciences: Methods that Matter* (Bristol: Policy Press).

Stoker, G. and John, P. (2009) 'Design Experiments: Engaging Policy Makers in the Search for Evidence about What Works', *Political Studies*, 57(2): 356–373.

Stoker, G., Peters, B.G. and Jon Pierre, J. (eds.) (2015) *The Relevance of Political Science* (London: Palgrave Macmillan).

Streeck, W. and Thelen, K. (eds.) (2005) *Beyond Continuity: Institutional Change in Advanced Political Economies* (Oxford: Oxford University Press).

Sturrock, J. (ed.) (1979) *Structuralism and Since: From Levi-Strauss to Derrida* (Oxford: Oxford University Press).

Suarez, S.L. (2005) 'Mobile Democracy: Text Messages, Voter Turnout, and the 2004 Spanish General Election', Paper presented at the annual meeting of the American Political Science Association.

Sunstein, C. and Thaler, R. (2008) *Nudge: Improving Decisions About Health, Wealth and Happiness* (London: Penguin).

Swedberg, R. and Granovetter, M. (eds.) (2001) *The Sociology of Economic Life,* 2nd edition (Boulder, CO: Westview).

Swers, M.L. (2002) *The Difference Women Make: The Policy Impact of Women in Congress* (Chicago, IL: University of Chicago Press).

Swidler, A. (1986) 'Culture in Action: Symbols and Strategies', *American Sociological Review,* 51(2): 273–286.

Swift, A. and White, S. (2008) 'Political Theory, Social Science and Real Politics', in Leopold, D. and Stears, M. (eds.) *Political Theory: Methods and Approaches* (Oxford: Oxford University Press): 49–69.

Tajfel, H. and Billig, M. (1974) 'Familiarity and Categorization in Intergroup Behaviour', *Journal of Experimental Social Psychology*, 10(1): 159–170.

Talpin, J. (2012) 'What Can Ethnography Bring to the Study of Deliberative Democracy?', *Revista Internacional de Sociolgia*, 70(2): 143–163.

Tanenbaum, E. and Scarbrough, E. (1998) 'Research Strategies in the New Environment', in Scarbrough, E. and Tanenbaum, E. (eds.) *Research Strategies in the Social Sciences* (Oxford: Oxford University Press): 11–27.

—— (2008) 'Polarization and Convergence in Academic Controversies', *Theory and Society*, 37(6): 513–536.

Tarrow, S. (2008) 'Polarization and Convergence in Academic Controversies', *Theory and Society*, 37(6): 513–536.

Taylor, C. (2008) 'Interpretation and the Science of Man', in *Philosophy and the Human Sciences, (vol. 2 of) Philosophical Papers* (Cambridge: Cambridge University Press): 15–57.

Taylor, Charles. 1971. "Interpretation and the Sciences of Man," Review of Metaphysics 25, no. 1: 3–51.

Tene, O. and Polonetsky, J. (2012) 'Big Data for All: Privacy and User Control in the Age of Analytics', *Northwestern Journal of Technology and Intellectual Property,* 11(5): 239–273.

Tetlock, P.E. and Belkin, A. (eds.) (1996) *Counterfactual Thought Experiments in World Politics* (Princeton, NJ: Princeton University Press).

Thaler, R. (2015) *Misbehaving. The Making of Behavioural Economics* (London: Penguin).

Thaler, R.H. and Sunstein, C.R. (2008) *Nudge: Improving Decisions about Human Health, Wealth and Happiness* (New Haven, CT: Yale University Press).

't Hart, P. (1994) *Groupthink in Government: A Study of Small Groups and Policy Failure* (Baltimore, MD: Johns Hopkins University Press).

't Hart, P., Stern, E. Sundelius, B. (eds.) (1998) *Beyond Groupthink: Political Group Dynamics and Foreign Policymaking* (Ann Arbor, MI: University of Michigan Press).

Thelen, K. (1999) 'Historical Institutionalism in Comparative Politics', *Annual Review of Political Science*, 2: 369–404.

—— (2003) 'How Institutions Evolve', in Mahoney, J. and Rueschemeyer, D. (eds.) *Comparative Historical Analysis in the Social Sciences* (Cambridge: Cambridge University Press): 208–240.

Thiem, A., Baumgartner, M. and Bol, D. (2016) 'Still Lost in Translation! A Correction of Three Misunderstandings between Configurational Comparativisits and Regression Analysts', *Comparative Political Studies*, 49(6): 742–774.

Thiem, A., Spöhel, R. and Dusa, A. (2016) 'Enhancing Sensitivity Diagnostics for Qualitative Comparative Analysis: A Combinatorial Approach', *Political Analysis*, 24(1): 104–120.

Thies, C. (2002) 'A Pragmatic Guide to Qualitative Historical Analysis in the Study of International Relations', *International Studies Perspectives*, 3(4): 351–372.

Theuwissen, M. (2015) 'R vs Python for Data Science: The Winner is ...' Available online. KD Nuggets. URL www.kdnuggets.com/2015/05/r-vs-python-data-science.html (accessed November 16, 2016).

Thomas, D. (1979) *Naturalism and Social Science: A Post-Empiricist Philosophy of Social Science* (Cambridge: Cambridge University Press).

Thomassen, L. (2007) 'Beyond Representation?', *Parliamentary Affairs*, 60(1): 111–126.

Tickner, J.A. (1992) *Gender in International Relations* (New York: Columbia University Press).

Tilly, C. (2006) 'Why and How History Matters', in Goodin, R. and Tilly, C. (eds.) *The Oxford Handbook of Contextual Political Analysis* (Oxford: Oxford University Press): 417–437.

Tonge, J., Mycock, A. and Jeffery, B. (2012) 'Does Citizenship Education Make Young People Better-Engaged Citizens?', *Political Studies*, 60(3): 578–602.

Tonkiss, F. (1998) 'Continuity/Change', in Jenks, C. (ed.) *Core Sociological Dichotomies* (London: Sage): 34–48.

Torfing, J. (1999) *New Theories of Discourse: Laclau, Mouffe, Žižek* (Oxford: Blackwell).

Torgerson, D. and Torgerson, C. (2008) *Designing Randomised Trials in Health, Education and the Social Sciences: An Introduction* (Basingstoke: Palgrave Macmillan).

Tormey, S. (2006) 'Not in My Name: Deleuze, Zapatismo and the Critique of Representation', *Parliamentary Affairs*, 59(1): 138–154.

Toshkov, D. (2016) *Research Design in Political Science* (Basingstoke: Palgrave Macmillan).

Trotsky, L. (1970) *The Third International after Lenin* (New York: Pathfinder, first published 1936).

Tripp, A.M. (2015) *Women and Power in Postconflict Africa* (Cambridge: Cambridge University Press).

Tufte, E. (1974) *Data Analysis for Politics and Policy* (Englewood Clifts, NJ: Prentice Hall).

Tumasjan, A., Sprenger, T., Sandner, P. and Welpe, I. (2011) 'Election Forecasts with Twitter: How 140 Characters Reflect the Political Landscape', *Social Science Computer Review*, 29(4): 402–418.

Uçar, A., Demir, Y. and Güzeliş, C. (2016) 'A New Facial Expression Recognition Based on Curvelet Transform and Online Sequential Extreme Learning Machine Initialized with Spherical Clustering', *Neural Comput & Applic*, 27(1): 131–142.

Valentini, L. (2009) 'On the Apparent Paradox of Ideal Theory', *Journal of Political Philosophy*, 17(3): 332–355.

Valliant, R., Dever, J. and Kreuter, F. (2013) *Practical Tools for Designing and Weighting Survey Samples* (New York: Springer).

Van Death, J.(2014) 'A Conceptual Map of Political Participation', *Acta Politica*, 49(3): 349-367.

Van Evera, S. (1997) *Guide to Methods for Students of Political Science* (Ithaca, NY: Cornell University Press).

Van Willigen, J. (2002) *Applied Anthropology: An Introduction*, 3rd edition (Westport, CT: Greenwood Publishing Group).

Verba, S., Schlozman, K. and Brady, H. (1995) *Voice and Equality: Civic Volunteerism in American Politics* (Cambridge, MA: Harvard University Press).

Verge, T., Guinjoan, M. and Rodon, T. (2015) 'Risk Aversion, Gender, and Constitutional Change', *Politics & Gender*, 11(3): 499–521.

Victoroff, J.E. and Kruglanski, A.W. (2009) *Psychology of Terrorism: Classic and Contemporary Insights* (Abingdon: Psychology Press).

Vis, B. (2010) *Politics of Risk-Taking: Welfare State Reform in Advanced Democracies* (Amsterdam: Amsterdam University Press).

Vromen, A. and Gauja, A. (2009) 'Protesters, Parliamentarians, Policymakers: The Experiences of Australian Green MPs', *Journal of Legislative Studies*, 15(1): 87–110.

Wade, R. (2009) 'Beware What You Wish For: Lessons for International Political Economy from the Transformation of Economics', *Review of International Political Economy*, 16(1): 106–121.

Waever, O. (1995) 'Identity, Integration and Security: Solving the Sovereignty Puzzle in EU Studies', *Journal of International Affairs*, 48(2): 389–426.

Wagenaar, H. (2011) *Meaning in Action. Interpretation and Dialogue in Policy Analysis* (New York: M.E. Sharpe).

Wagener, H. (2011), *Meaning in Action – Interpretation and Dialogue in Policy Analysis*. (New York: M.E. Sharpe).

Walker, H.A. and Cohen, B.P. (1985) 'Scope Statements: Imperatives for Evaluating Theory', *American Sociological Review*, 50(3): 288–301.

Walker, R.B.J. (1993) *Inside/Outside: International Relations as Political Theory* (Cambridge: Cambridge University Press).

Waller, V., Farquharson, K. and Dempsey, D. (2016) *Qualitative Social Research: Contemporary Methods for the Digital Age* (Los Angeles, CA: Sage).

Wängnerud, L. (2000) 'Testing the Politics of Presence: Women's Representation in the Swedish Riksdag', *Scandinavian Political Studies*, 23(1): 67–91.

Ward, H. and John, P. (1999) 'Targeting Benefits for Electoral Gain: Constituency Marginality and Central Grants to Local Government', *Political Studies*, 47(1): 32–52.

Ward, M.D. and Gleditsch, K.S. (2008) *Spatial Regression Models*, Vol. 155 (Los Angeles, CA: Sage).

Warren, B. (1980) *Imperialism: Pioneer of Capitalism* (London: Verso).

Waylen, G. (1994) 'Women and Democratisation: Conceptualising Gender Relations in Transition Politics', *World Politics*, 46(3): 327–354.

—— (2011) 'Gendered Institutionalist Analysis: Understanding Democratic Transitions', in Krook, M.L. and Mackay, F. (eds.) *Gender, Politics and Institutions: Towards a Feminist Institutionalism* (London: Palgrave Macmillan).

—— (2017) (eds.) *Gender and Informal Institutions* (London: Rowman and Littlefield).

Waylen, G., Celis, K., Kantola, J. and Weldon, S.L. (2013) *The Oxford Handbook of Gender and Politics* (Oxford: Oxford University Press).

Weaver, R. and Rockman, B. (1993) *Do Institutions Matter?* (Washington, DC: Brookings Institution).

Weaver, V. (2003) 'The Colour of the Campaign: A Quasi-Experimental Study of the Influence of Skin Color on Candidate Evaluation', Paper presented at the annual meeting of the American Political Science Association, Philadelphia, PA, 27 August.

—— (2005) 'Race, Skin Color, and Candidate Preference', Paper presented at the annual meeting of the American Political Science Association, Chicago, IL, 7 April.

Weber, M. (1958 [1922]) 'Social Psychology of the World's Religions', in Gerth, H.H. and Wright Mills, C. (eds.) *From Max Weber: Essays in Sociology* (New York: Cambridge University Press).

—— (1978 [1922]) *Economy and Society* (Berkeley, CA: University of California Press).

—— 1992 [1930] *The Protestant Ethic and the Spirit of Capitalism* (New York: Routledge).

Wedeen, L. (1999) *Ambiguities of Domination: Politics, Rhetoric and Symbols in Contemporary Syria* (Chicago, IL: University of Chicago Press).

—— (2008) *Peripheral Visions: Publics, Power and Performance in Yemen* (Chicago, IL: University of Chicago Press).

Weingast, B.R. (1996) 'Political Institutions: Rational Choice Perspectives', in Goodin, R. and Klingemann, H.D. (eds.) *A New Handbook of Political Science* (Oxford: Oxford University Press): 167–190.

Weisberg, H. (ed.) (1986) *Political Science: The Science of Politics* (New York: Agathon Press).

Weldon, S.L. (2002) 'Beyond Bodies: Institutional Sources of Representation for Women in Democratic Policymaking', *The Journal of Politics*, 64(4): 1153–1174.

——. (2006) 'The Structure of Intersectionality: A Comparative Politics of Gender', *Politics & Gender*, 2(2): 235–248.

—— (2014) 'Using Statistical Methods to Study Institutions', *Politics & Gender*, 10(4): 661–672.

Weller, N. and Barnes, J. (2014) *Finding Pathways. Mixed-Method Research for Studying Causal Mechanisms* (Cambridge: Cambridge University Press).

Wendt, A. (1992) 'Anarchy Is What States Make of It: The Social Construction of Power Politics', *International Organization*, 46(2): 391–425.

—— (1998) 'On Constitution and Causation in International Relations', *Review of International Studies*, 24(5): 101–118.

—— (1999) *Social Theory of International Politics* (New York: Cambridge University Press).

Wenman, M. (2013) *Agonistic Democracy: Constituent Power in the Era of Globalization* (Cambridge: Cambridge University Press).

—— (2000) *Sustaining Affirmation: The Strengths of Weak Ontology in Political Theory* (Princeton, NJ: Princeton University Press).

White, S. (2000) *Sustaining Affirmation: The Strengths of Weak Ontology in Political theory* (Princeton: Printceton University Press).

Wickham, H. (2016) 'rvest: Easily Harvest (Scrape)' Web Pages. Available online. RStudio Blog: URL https://blog.rstudio.org/2014/11/24/rvest-easy-web-scraping-with-r/ (accessed April 25, 2017).

Wickham, H. and Grolemund, G. (2017) *R for Data Science: Import, Tidy, Transform, Visualize, and Model Data* (Sebastopol, CA: O'Reilley Media).

Wight, C. (2006) *Agents, Structures and International Relations: Politics as Ontology* (Cambridge: Cambridge University Press).

Wildavsky, A. (1989) *Speaking Truth to Power* (Somerset, NJ: Transaction Publishers, 1989).

Willemsen, M. (2016) 'Anonymizing Unstructured Data to Prevent Privacy Leaks During Data Mining', Paper presented at the Twente Student Conference on IT, Enschede, the Netherlands.

Williams, E. (1964) *Capitalism and Slavery* (London: Andre Deutsch).

Williams, J. (2005) *Understanding Poststructuralism* (London: Routledge).

—— (2007) 'The Power of Local Political Debates to Influence Prospective Voters: An Experiment at the Congressional Level', Paper presented at the annual meeting of the American Political Science Association, Chicago, IL.

Wilson, G. (1990) *Interest Groups* (London: Blackwell).

—— G. (2015) 'Why Did Nobody Warn Us? Political Science and the Crisis', in Stoker, G., Peters, G. and Pierre, J. (eds.) *The Relevance of Political Science* (Basingstoke: Palgrave Macmillan): 104–117.

Wilson, R. (1992) *Compliance Ideologies: Rethinking Political Culture* (New York: Cambridge University Press).

Wilson, W. (1956) *Congressional Government: A Study in American Politics* (Cleveland, OH: World Publishing).

Winch, P. (1958) *The Idea of a Social Science and Its Relation to Philosophy* (London: Routledge and Keegan Paul).

Winter, D.G. (1973) *The Power Motive* (New York: Free Press).

—— (2013) 'Personality Profiles of Political Elites', in Huddy, L., Sears, D.O. and Levy, J.S. (eds.) *The Oxford Handbook of Political Psychology* (New York: Oxford University Press): 423–458.

Wittman, D (2013) 'Personality Profiles of Political Elites', in Huddy, L., Sears, D.O. and Levy, J.S. (eds.) *The Oxford Handbook of Political Psychology* (New York: Oxford University Press).

Wolff, J. (2013) 'Analytic Political Philosophy.', in Beaney, M. (ed.) *The Oxford Handbook of the History of Analytic Philosophy* (Oxford: Oxford University Press): 795–822.

Wood, D. (2000) 'Weak Theories and Parameter Instability: Using Flexible Least Squares to Take Time Varying Relationships Seriously', *American Journal of Political Science*, 44(3): 603-618.

Wong, J. (2005) 'Mobilizing Asian American Voters: A Field Experiment', *Annals of the American Academy of Political and Social Science*, 601: 102–114.

Wonnacott, T. and Wonnacott, R. (1990) *Introductory Statistics* (New York: Wiley).

Woodward, J. (2003) *Making Things Happen: A Theory of Causal Explanation* (New York: Oxford University Press).

World Bank (1996) *World Development Report* (Washington, DC: World Bank).

World Bank (2002) *Globalisation, Growth and Poverty* (Washington, DC: World Bank).

Xing, Y. and Detert, N. (2010) 'How the iPhone Widens the Trade Deficit with the PRC', ADBI Working Paper Series, no.257.

Yanow, D. and Schwartz-Shea, P. (eds.) (2006) *Interpretation and Method: Empirical Research Methods and the Interpretive Turn* (Armonck, NY: M.E. Sharpe).

—— (2010) 'Perestroika Ten Years After: Reflections on Methodological Diversity', *PS: Political Science*, October: 741–745.

Yanow, D,, Schwartz-Shea, P. and Freitas, M. (2010) 'Case Study Research in Political Science', in Mills, A., Durepos, G. and Wiebe, E. (eds.) *Encyclopedia of Case Study Research* (London: Sage Publications).

Yoo, Y. (2015) 'It is Not about Size: A Further Thought on Big Data', *Journal of Information Technology*, 30(1): 63–65.

Young, L. (2000) *Feminists and Party Politics* (Vancouver: UBC Press).

Ypi, L. (2012) *Global Justice and Avant-Garde Political Agency* (Oxford: Oxford University Press).

Zehfuss, M. (2002) *Constructivism in International Relations: The Politics of Reality* (Cambridge: Cambridge University Press).

Zimbardo, P.G. (2007) *Lucifer Effect* (Oxford: Blackwell).

DATASET WEBSITE REFERENCES

From chapter one

G-Econ: gecon.yale.edu

Geo-EPR: www.icr.ethz.ch/data/geoepr

GRUMP: http://sedac.ciesin.columbia.edu/data/collection/grump-v1

Uppsala Conflict Data Program/Peace Research Institute Oslo Armed Conflict dataset: www.pcr.uu.se/research/ucdp/datasets/

Index